**WordPerfect** ®
For D...

## Creating a Web-formatted WordPerfect document

Web publishing in WordPerfect requires a specially-formatted WordPerfect document. To create a Web-formatted document, simply switch to Web view in any of three ways:

- Click this button:
- Choose File⇨Internet publisher⇨Format as web document
- Choose View⇨Web page

Always save your work as a WordPerfect document to make editing easier. You can edit an HTML file, but editing a WordPerfect document is better.

## Publishing to HTML

To create the HTML file you need for the Web, plus the special graphics files you need for illustrations, you "publish to HTML" in WordPerfect terminology. Choose either of these ways to publish to HTML:

- Choose File⇨Internet publisher⇨Publish to HTML
- Click this button:

The Publish to HTML dialog box requires you to enter three items: the HTML file name, the name of the folder for graphics files, and the folder the graphics will be in on the Web server. To make your life easier when you test your files, enter those three items in the following way, leaving off the `.htm` extension:

Publish to: `C:\myfiles\website\yourfile`

Save new images and sound clips in: `C:\myfiles\website\yourfile`

Location of graphics on Web server: `./yourfile`

Publishing to HTML does the following:

- Creates an HTML file containing your text and links to your graphics
- Converts document graphics to individual graphics files in the GIF or JPG format the Web requires

Copyright © 1997 IDG Books Worldwide, Inc. All rights reserved.
Cheat Sheet $2.95 value. Item 0155-0
For more information about IDG Books, call 1-800-762-2974.

*...For Dummies: #1 Computer Book Series for Beginners*

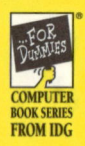

# WordPerfect® 8 Web Publishing For Dummies®

### Cheat Sheet

## Web text styles

Text on the Web is always in some style. Click anywhere in the paragraph to which you want to apply a style, then press F9 or click the Text Styles button to choose a style.

Choose the style by referring to the following table:

| Your Text | What Style to Choose |
| --- | --- |
| Regular old paragraphs | Normal |
| **Headings** | Heading 1 through Heading 6 |
| Lines in italics with no spacing between the lines | Address |
| Paragraphs indented from left and right | Indented Quotation |
| Text that uses   multiple spaces     or tabs | Preformatted Text |
| 1. Numbered lines | Numbered List |
| • Bulleted lines | Bullet List |
| Indented lines | Definition List |

## Hyperlinks

**Quick hyperlinking:** Simply type the document's URL (its Web address, as in: `http://www.gurus.com`), followed by a space.

**Regular hyperlinking:** Select (highlight) the text or graphic; choose Tools⇨Hyperlink, or (for text only) click the Hyperlink button, and then choose Create Link from the drop-down menu that appears.

In the Hyperlink Properties dialog box that appears, enter the URL (Web address) of the document you want the link to jump to.

## Graphics

To insert graphics, choose Insert⇨Graphics, and then from the submenu that appears, choose what kind of graphic to insert. If you insert GIF or JPG files, be sure to copy those files to the folder you specify for the document's graphics when you publish to HTML.

WordPerfect initially attaches graphics in line with the text: "Character attachment." To make text that precedes the graphic wrap around the graphic, choose Graphics⇨Position. In the Box Position dialog box that appears, choose Paragraph for the text box labeled "Attach box to".

*...For Dummies: #1 Computer Book Series for Beginners*

# ...For Dummies®: References for the Rest of Us!®

## COMPUTER BOOK SERIES FROM IDG

Are you intimidated and confused by computers? Do you find that traditional manuals are overloaded with technical details you'll never use? Do your friends and family always call you to fix simple problems on their PCs? Then the ...*For Dummies*® computer book series from IDG Books Worldwide is for you.

...*For Dummies* books are written for those frustrated computer users who know they aren't really dumb but find that PC hardware, software, and indeed the unique vocabulary of computing make them feel helpless. ...*For Dummies* books use a lighthearted approach, a down-to-earth style, and even cartoons and humorous icons to diffuse computer novices' fears and build their confidence. Lighthearted but not lightweight, these books are a perfect survival guide for anyone forced to use a computer.

> "I like my copy so much I told friends; now they bought copies."
> — Irene C., Orwell, Ohio

> "Quick, concise, nontechnical, and humorous."
> — Jay A., Elburn, Illinois

> "Thanks, I needed this book. Now I can sleep at night."
> — Robin F., British Columbia, Canada

Already, millions of satisfied readers agree. They have made ...*For Dummies* books the #1 introductory level computer book series and have written asking for more. So, if you're looking for the most fun and easy way to learn about computers, look to ...*For Dummies* books to give you a helping hand.

**IDG BOOKS WORLDWIDE**™

5/97

# WORDPERFECT® 8 WEB PUBLISHING FOR DUMMIES®

**By David Kay**

**IDG BOOKS WORLDWIDE**

IDG Books Worldwide, Inc.
An International Data Group Company

Foster City, CA ♦ Chicago, IL ♦ Indianapolis, IN ♦ Southlake, TX

## WordPerfect® 8 Web Publishing For Dummies®

Published by
**IDG Books Worldwide, Inc.**
An International Data Group Company
919 E. Hillsdale Blvd.
Suite 400
Foster City, CA 94404
`www.idgbooks.com` (IDG Books Worldwide Web site)
`www.dummies.com` (Dummies Press Web site)

Copyright © 1997 IDG Books Worldwide, Inc. All rights reserved. No part of this book, including interior design, cover design, and icons, may be reproduced or transmitted in any form, by any means (electronic, photocopying, recording, or otherwise) without the prior written permission of the publisher.

Library of Congress Catalog Card No.: 97-80120

ISBN: 0-7645–0155-0

Printed in the United States of America

10 9 8 7 6 5 4 3 2 1

1M/ST/QX/ZX/IN

Distributed in the United States by IDG Books Worldwide, Inc.

Distributed by Macmillan Canada for Canada; by Transworld Publishers Limited in the United Kingdom; by IDG Norge Books for Norway; by IDG Sweden Books for Sweden; by Woodslane Pty. Ltd. for Australia; by Woodslane Enterprises Ltd. for New Zealand; by Longman Singapore Publishers Ltd. for Singapore, Malaysia, Thailand, and Indonesia; by Simron Pty. Ltd. for South Africa; by Toppan Company Ltd. for Japan; by Distribuidora Cuspide for Argentina; by Livraria Cultura for Brazil; by Ediciencia S.A. for Ecuador; by Addison-Wesley Publishing Company for Korea; by Ediciones ZETA S.C.R. Ltda. for Peru; by WS Computer Publishing Corporation, Inc., for the Philippines; by Unalis Corporation for Taiwan; by Contemporanea de Ediciones for Venezuela; by Computer Book & Magazine Store for Puerto Rico; by Express Computer Distributors for the Caribbean and West Indies. Authorized Sales Agent: Anthony Rudkin Associates for the Middle East and North Africa.

For general information on IDG Books Worldwide's books in the U.S., please call our Consumer Customer Service department at 800-762-2974. For reseller information, including discounts and premium sales, please call our Reseller Customer Service department at 800-434-3422.

For information on where to purchase IDG Books Worldwide's books outside the U.S., please contact our International Sales department at 415-655-3200 or fax 415-655-3295.

For information on foreign language translations, please contact our Foreign & Subsidiary Rights department at 415-655-3021 or fax 415-655-3281.

For sales inquiries and special prices for bulk quantities, please contact our Sales department at 415-655-3200 or write to the address above.

For information on using IDG Books Worldwide's books in the classroom or for ordering examination copies, please contact our Educational Sales department at 800-434-2086 or fax 817-251-8174.

For press review copies, author interviews, or other publicity information, please contact our Public Relations department at 415-655-3000 or fax 415-655-3299.

For authorization to photocopy items for corporate, personal, or educational use, please contact Copyright Clearance Center, 222 Rosewood Drive, Danvers, MA 01923, or fax 508-750-4470.

**LIMIT OF LIABILITY/DISCLAIMER OF WARRANTY: AUTHOR AND PUBLISHER HAVE USED THEIR BEST EFFORTS IN PREPARING THIS BOOK. IDG BOOKS WORLDWIDE, INC., AND AUTHOR MAKE NO REPRESENTATIONS OR WARRANTIES WITH RESPECT TO THE ACCURACY OR COMPLETENESS OF THE CONTENTS OF THIS BOOK AND SPECIFICALLY DISCLAIM ANY IMPLIED WARRANTIES OF MERCHANTABILITY OR FITNESS FOR A PARTICULAR PURPOSE. THERE ARE NO WARRANTIES WHICH EXTEND BEYOND THE DESCRIPTIONS CONTAINED IN THIS PARAGRAPH. NO WARRANTY MAY BE CREATED OR EXTENDED BY SALES REPRESENTATIVES OR WRITTEN SALES MATERIALS. THE ACCURACY AND COMPLETENESS OF THE INFORMATION PROVIDED HEREIN AND THE OPINIONS STATED HEREIN ARE NOT GUARANTEED OR WARRANTED TO PRODUCE ANY PARTICULAR RESULTS, AND THE ADVICE AND STRATEGIES CONTAINED HEREIN MAY NOT BE SUITABLE FOR EVERY INDIVIDUAL. NEITHER IDG BOOKS WORLDWIDE, INC., NOR AUTHOR SHALL BE LIABLE FOR ANY LOSS OF PROFIT OR ANY OTHER COMMERCIAL DAMAGES, INCLUDING BUT NOT LIMITED TO SPECIAL, INCIDENTAL, CONSEQUENTIAL, OR OTHER DAMAGES.**

**Trademarks:** All brand names and product names used in this book are trade names, service marks, trademarks, or registered trademarks of their respective owners. IDG Books Worldwide is not associated with any product or vendor mentioned in this book.

IDG BOOKS WORLDWIDE™ is a trademark under exclusive license to IDG Books Worldwide, Inc., from International Data Group, Inc.

## About the Author

**David Kay** is a writer, engineer, and aspiring artist, combining professions in the same way as his favorite business establishment, Acton Muffler, Brake, and Ice Cream (now defunct). Dave has written more than ten computer books with Margy, Jordan, and other friends, including *Web Publishing with WordPerfect 8 For Dummies, VRML and 3D on the Web For Dummies,* and various editions of *Works For Windows For Dummies, WordPerfect For Windows For Dummies, MORE WordPerfect For Windows For Dummies,* and *Graphics File Formats.*

In his other life, as the Poo-bah of Bright Leaf Communications, Dave creates promotional copy, graphics, and Web sites for high-tech firms. In his spare time, he studies human and animal tracking, munches edible wild plants, makes strange blobs from molten glass, sings Gilbert and Sullivan tunes, hikes in whatever mountains he can get to, and longs to return to New Zealand and track kiwis and hedgehogs in Wanaka. He hates writing about himself in the third person like this and will stop now.

# ABOUT IDG BOOKS WORLDWIDE

Welcome to the world of IDG Books Worldwide.

IDG Books Worldwide, Inc., is a subsidiary of International Data Group, the world's largest publisher of computer-related information and the leading global provider of information services on information technology. IDG was founded more than 25 years ago and now employs more than 8,500 people worldwide. IDG publishes more than 275 computer publications in over 75 countries (see listing below). More than 60 million people read one or more IDG publications each month.

Launched in 1990, IDG Books Worldwide is today the #1 publisher of best-selling computer books in the United States. We are proud to have received eight awards from the Computer Press Association in recognition of editorial excellence and three from *Computer Currents'* First Annual Readers' Choice Awards. Our best-selling ...*For Dummies*® series has more than 30 million copies in print with translations in 30 languages. IDG Books Worldwide, through a joint venture with IDG's Hi-Tech Beijing, became the first U.S. publisher to publish a computer book in the People's Republic of China. In record time, IDG Books Worldwide has become the first choice for millions of readers around the world who want to learn how to better manage their businesses.

Our mission is simple: Every one of our books is designed to bring extra value and skill-building instructions to the reader. Our books are written by experts who understand and care about our readers. The knowledge base of our editorial staff comes from years of experience in publishing, education, and journalism — experience we use to produce books for the '90s. In short, we care about books, so we attract the best people. We devote special attention to details such as audience, interior design, use of icons, and illustrations. And because we use an efficient process of authoring, editing, and desktop publishing our books electronically, we can spend more time ensuring superior content and spend less time on the technicalities of making books.

You can count on our commitment to deliver high-quality books at competitive prices on topics you want to read about. At IDG Books Worldwide, we continue in the IDG tradition of delivering quality for more than 25 years. You'll find no better book on a subject than one from IDG Books Worldwide.

John Kilcullen
CEO
IDG Books Worldwide, Inc.

Steven Berkowitz
President and Publisher
IDG Books Worldwide, Inc.

*Eighth Annual Computer Press Awards ≥1992*

*Ninth Annual Computer Press Awards ≥1993*

*Tenth Annual Computer Press Awards ≥1994*

*Eleventh Annual Computer Press Awards ≥1995*

IDG Books Worldwide, Inc., is a subsidiary of International Data Group, the world's largest publisher of computer-related information and the leading global provider of information services on information technology. International Data Group publishes over 275 computer publications in over 75 countries. Sixty million people read one or more International Data Group publications each month. International Data Group's publications include: **ARGENTINA:** Buyer's Guide, Computerworld Argentina, PC World Argentina; **AUSTRALIA:** Australian Macworld, Australian PC World, Australian Reseller News, Computerworld, IT Casebook, Network World, Publish, Webmaster; **AUSTRIA:** Computerwelt Osterreich, Networks Austria, PC Tip Austria; **BANGLADESH:** PC World Bangladesh; **BELARUS:** PC World Belarus; **BELGIUM:** Data News; **BRAZIL:** Annuário de Informática, Computerworld, Connections, Macworld, PC Player, PC World, Publish, Reseller News, Supergamepower; **BULGARIA:** Computerworld Bulgaria, Network World Bulgaria, PC & MacWorld Bulgaria; **CANADA:** CIO Canada, Client/Server World, ComputerWorld Canada, InfoWorld Canada, NetworkWorld Canada, WebWorld; **CHILE:** Computerworld Chile, PC World Chile; **COLOMBIA:** Computerworld Colombia, PC World Colombia; **COSTA RICA:** PC World Centro America; **THE CZECH AND SLOVAK REPUBLICS:** Computerworld Czechoslovakia, Macworld Czech Republic, PC World Czechoslovakia; **DENMARK:** Communications World Danmark, Computerworld Danmark, Macworld Danmark, PC World Danmark, Techworld Denmark; **DOMINICAN REPUBLIC:** PC World Republica Dominicana; **ECUADOR:** PC World Ecuador; **EGYPT:** Computerworld Middle East, PC World Middle East; **EL SALVADOR:** PC World Centro America; **FINLAND:** MikroPC, Tietoverkko, Tietoviikko; **FRANCE:** Distributique, Hebdo, Info PC, Le Monde Informatique, Macworld, Reseaux & Telecoms, WebMaster France; **GERMANY:** Computer Partner, Computerwoche, Computerwoche Extra, Computerwoche FOCUS, Global Online, Macwelt, PC Welt; **GREECE:** Amiga Computing, GamePro Greece, Multimedia World; **GUATEMALA:** PC World Centro America; **HONDURAS:** PC World Centro America; **HONG KONG:** Computerworld Hong Kong, PC World Hong Kong, Publish in Asia; **HUNGARY:** ABCD CD-ROM, Computerworld Szamitastechnika, Internetto online Magazine, PC World Hungary, PC-X Magazin Hungary; **ICELAND:** Tolvuheimur PC World Island; **INDIA:** Information Communications World, Information Systems Computerworld, PC World India, Publish in Asia; **INDONESIA:** InfoKomputer PC World, Komputek Computerworld, Publish in Asia; **IRELAND:** ComputerScope, PC Live!; **ISRAEL:** Macworld Israel, People & Computers/Computerworld; **ITALY:** Computerworld Italia, Macworld Italia, Networking Italia, PC World Italia; **JAPAN:** DTP World, Macworld Japan, Nikkei Personal Computing, OS/2 World Japan, SunWorld Japan, Windows NT World, Windows World Japan; **KENYA:** PC World East African; **KOREA:** Hi-Tech Information, Macworld Korea, PC World Korea; **MACEDONIA:** PC World Macedonia; **MALAYSIA:** Computerworld Malaysia, PC World Malaysia, Publish in Asia; **MALTA:** PC World Malta; **MEXICO:** Computerworld Mexico, PC World Mexico; **MYANMAR:** PC World Myanmar; **NETHERLANDS:** Computer! Totaal, LAN Internetwerking Magazine, LAN World Buyers Guide, Macworld Netherlands, Net, WebWereld; **NEW ZEALAND:** Absolute Beginners Guide and Plain & Simple Series, Computer Buyer, Computer Industry Directory, Computerworld New Zealand, MTB, Network World, PC World New Zealand; **NICARAGUA:** PC World Centro America; **NORWAY:** Computerworld Norge, CW Rapport, Datamagasinet, Financial Rapport, Kursguide Norge, Macworld Norge, Multimediaworld Norge, PC World Ekspress Norge, PC World Nettverk, PC World Norge, PC World ProduktGuide Norge; **PAKISTAN:** Computerworld Pakistan; **PANAMA:** PC World Panama; **PEOPLE'S REPUBLIC OF CHINA:** China Computer Users, China Computerworld, China InfoWorld, China Telecom World Weekly, Computer & Communication, Electronic Design China, Electronics Today, Electronics Weekly, Game Software, PC World China, Popular Computer Week, Software Weekly, Software World, Telecom World; **PERU:** Computerworld Peru, PC World Profesional Peru, PC World SoHo Peru; **PHILIPPINES:** Click!, Computerworld Philippines, PC World Philippines, Publish in Asia; **POLAND:** Computerworld Poland, Computerworld Special Report Poland, Cyber, Macworld Poland, Networld Poland, PC World Poland, PCaktiv, Windows World Sweden; **PORTUGAL:** Cerebro/PC World, Computerworld/Correio Informático, Dealer World Portugal, Mac*In/PC*In Portugal, Multimedia World; **PUERTO RICO:** PC World Puerto Rico; **ROMANIA:** Computerworld Romania, PC World Romania, Telecom Romania; **RUSSIA:** Computerworld Russia, Mir PK, Publish, Seti; **SINGAPORE:** Computerworld Singapore, PC World Singapore, Publish in Asia; **SLOVENIA:** Monitor; **SOUTH AFRICA:** Computing SA, Network World SA, Software World SA; **SPAIN:** Communicaciones world España, Computerworld España, Dealer World España, Macworld España, PC World España; **SRI LANKA:** Infolink PC World; **SWEDEN:** CAP&Design, Computer Sweden, Corporate Computing Sweden, Internetworld Sweden, it.branschen, Macworld Sweden, MaxiData Sweden, MikroDatorn, Natverk & Kommunikation, PC World Sweden, PCaktiv, Windows World Sweden; **SWITZERLAND:** Computerworld Schweiz, Macworld Schweiz, PCtip; **TAIWAN:** Computerworld Taiwan, Macworld Taiwan, NEW ViSiON/Publish, PC World Taiwan, Windows World Taiwan; **THAILAND:** Publish in Asia, Thai Computerworld; **TURKEY:** Computerworld Turkiye, Macworld Turkiye, Network World Turkiye, PC World Turkiye; **UKRAINE:** Computerworld Kiev, Multimedia World Ukraine, PC World Ukraine; **UNITED KINGDOM:** Acorn User UK, Amiga Action UK, Amiga Computing UK, Apple Talk UK, Computing, Macworld, Parents and Computers UK, PC Advisor, PC Home, PSX Pro, The WEB; **UNITED STATES:** Cable in the Classroom, CIO Magazine, Computerworld, DOS World, Federal Computer Week, GamePro Magazine, InfoWorld, I-Way, Macworld, Network World, PC Games, PC World, Publish, Video Event, THE WEB Magazine, and WebMaster; online webzines: JavaWorld, NetscapeWorld, and SunWorld Online; **URUGUAY:** InfoWorld Uruguay; **VENEZUELA:** Computerworld Venezuela, PC World Venezuela; and **VIETNAM:** PC World Vietnam.

3/24/97

## Dedication

To my fabulous friends, especially Jordan, Margy, Deb, and Doug; to my marvelous spousal support unit, Katy; and to our exceedingly fabulous goddaughter Meg, unquestionably our favorite little girl in the entire world.

(And, with with a hey, nonny-nonny and a hot cha-cha to my guiding light, P.G. Wodehouse, despite his lamentable failure to write anything new recently.)

## Author's Acknowledgments

I would like to acknowledge my friends and family, of whose company I am sadly deprived with every one of these books I write. Thanks also to Matt Wagner and the rest of the folks at Waterside, and the congenial editors at IDG, including:

- Project Editor Bill Helling, who not only wields his awesome power to choose his own lunch hour responsibly, but also tolerates author foibles admirably;
- Copy Editor Kathy Simpson for untangling my tormented sentence structure;
- Technical Editor Jim McCarter for keeping me as honest as I can stand;
- Permissions Editor Joyce Pepple and support wizard Mark Kory for help getting goodies on the CD.

## Publisher's Acknowledgments

We're proud of this book; please send us your comments about it by using the IDG Books Worldwide, Inc. Registration Card at the back of the book or by e-mailing us at feedback/dummies@idgbooks.com. Some of the people who helped bring this book to market include the following:

### Acquisitions, Development, and Editorial

**Project Editor:** Bill Helling

**Acquisitions Editor:** Gareth Hancock

**Product Development Director:** Mary Bednarek

**Media Development Manager:** Joyce Pepple

**Associate Permissions Editor:** Heather H. Dismore

**Copy Editor:** Kathy Simpson

**Technical Editor:** Jim McCarter

**Editorial Manager:** Mary C. Corder

**Editorial Assistant:** Darren Meiss

### Production

**Project Coordinator:** Sherry Gomoll

**Layout and Graphics:** Elizabeth Cárdenas-Nelson, J. Tyler Connor, Pamela Emanoil, Lou Boudreau, Mark Owens

**Proofreaders:** Laura L. Bowman, Christine Sabooni, Christine Berman, Joel Draper, Nancy Price

**Indexer:** Lynnzee Elze Spense

### Special Help

Gwenette Gaddis, Mark Kory, Media Development Intern, Publication Services

---

### General and Administrative

**IDG Books Worldwide, Inc.:** John Kilcullen, CEO; Steven Berkowitz, President and Publisher

**IDG Books Technology Publishing:** Brenda McLaughlin, Senior Vice President and Group Publisher

**Dummies Technology Press and Dummies Editorial:** Diane Graves Steele, Vice President and Associate Publisher; Judith A. Taylor, Product Marketing Manager; Kristin A. Cocks, Editorial Director; Mary Bednarek, Aquisitions and Product Development Director

**Dummies Trade Press:** Kathleen A. Welton, Vice President and Publisher

**IDG Books Production for Dummies Press:** Beth Jenkins, Production Director; Cindy L. Phipps, Manager of Project Coordination, Production Proofreading, and Indexing; Kathie S. Schutte, Supervisor of Page Layout; Shelley Lea, Supervisor of Graphics and Design; Debbie J. Gates, Production Systems Specialist; Robert Springer, Supervisor of Proofreading; Tony Augsburger, Supervisor of Reprints and Bluelines; Leslie Popplewell, Media Archive Coordinator

**Dummies Packaging and Book Design:** Patti Sandez, Packaging Specialist; Lance Kayser, Packaging Assistant; Kavish + Kavish, Cover Design

♦

The publisher would like to give special thanks to Patrick J. McGovern, without whom this book would not have been possible.

♦

# Contents at a Glance

Introduction ................................................................................................ 1

## Part I: Web Weaving 101 with WordPerfect ........................................ 7
Chapter 1: Behind the Scenes: How the Web Works ............................................. 9
Chapter 2: Weaving Web-Site Plans .................................................................... 19
Chapter 3: Creating, Editing, and Checking Your Web Files ................................ 33
Chapter 4: Weaving a Simple Site from Scratch .................................................. 49
Chapter 5: Brewing Web Documents with Java .................................................. 63
Chapter 6: Serving Up Your Files to the Web ..................................................... 71

## Part II: Text Tricks ............................................................................... 87
Chapter 7: Helpful Hyperlinks ............................................................................. 89
Chapter 8: Standard Styles and Alignment ........................................................ 109
Chapter 9: Frisky Fonts and Crazy Colors .......................................................... 119
Chapter 10: Tantalizing Tables ........................................................................... 133

## Part III: Getting Graphical ................................................................ 147
Chapter 11: General Graphics ............................................................................. 149
Chapter 12: Building Blocks: Banners, Backgrounds, Bullets . . . ....................... 171
Chapter 13: Better, Fancier Graphics .................................................................. 187
Chapter 14: Speedier, Smaller Graphics .............................................................. 205

## Part IV: Wayout Layouts and Dazzling Designs ............................ 215
Chapter 15: Quick Tricks for Layout and White Space ....................................... 217
Chapter 16: Initial Layout and Design ................................................................. 225
Chapter 17: Doing Layouts by Using Tables ....................................................... 237
Chapter 18: Layout with Browser Tricks: Frames and Columns ......................... 251
Chapter 19: Lazy Layouts and Indolent Authoring ............................................. 257

## Part V: Beyond WordPerfect: Web Site Sizzle .............................. 263
Chapter 20: Graphics That Really Click ............................................................... 265
Chapter 21: Documents That Sing and Dance .................................................... 273
Chapter 22: Forms and Feedback ........................................................................ 295
Chapter 23: Stupid Browser Tricks for Special Effects ....................................... 311

## Part VI: The Part of Tens .................................................................... 315
Chapter 24: Ten Design Do's ............................................................................... 317
Chapter 25: Ten Design Don'ts ............................................................................ 323
Chapter 26: Ten Common Problems ................................................................... 327
Chapter 27: Ten WordPerfect Tricks ................................................................... 333
Appendix: About the CD ...................................................................................... 339
Index ..................................................................................................................... 347
License Agreement .............................................................................................. 362
Installation Instructions ..................................................................................... 364
IDG Books Worlwide Registration ............................................................ Back of Book

# Cartoons at a Glance

*By Rich Tennant*

page 7

"Hold your horses. It takes time to build a home page for someone your size."
page 87

page 147

page 315

page 263

page 215

Fax: 508-546-7747 • E-mail: the5wave@tiac.net

# Table of Contents

## *Introduction* .................................................................... 1

What Goes On in This Book ........................................................ 1
Who Are You? ........................................................................... 2
How to Use This Book and CD ..................................................... 2
How This Book Is Organized ........................................................ 3
    Part I: Web Weaving 101 with WordPerfect ............................. 3
    Part II: Text Tricks ................................................................. 4
    Part III: Getting Graphical ....................................................... 4
    Part IV: Wayout Layouts and Dazzling Designs ......................... 4
    Part V: Beyond WordPerfect: Web Site Sizzle ............................ 4
    Part VI: The Part of Tens ......................................................... 5
    The CD and Appendix ............................................................. 5
Icons Used in This Book ............................................................. 5
Where to Go from Here .............................................................. 6

## *Part I: Web Weaving 101 with WordPerfect* ...................... 7

### Chapter 1: Behind the Scenes: How the Web Works ............................. 9

How Documents Get on the Web: Web Servers .............................. 10
Pointing to Documents on the Web (URLs) ................................... 12
What Are Those Documents on the Web? ..................................... 13
Web Graphics ........................................................................... 15
Other Types of Web Documents .................................................. 16
    Java ..................................................................................... 16
    Extended HTML .................................................................... 17

### Chapter 2: Weaving Web-Site Plans ............................................. 19

Objectives: Why Weave Your Web and for Whom? ......................... 20
    Objectives ............................................................................ 20
    Audiences ............................................................................ 22
Tactics: Weaving Your Web Site ................................................... 23
    Content: The strands of your Web site .................................... 23
    Structure: Arranging your strands .......................................... 25
Resources: Weaving Wisely ......................................................... 28
    Money ................................................................................. 28
    Time .................................................................................... 29
    Fancy site features that you'll need additional help for ............ 30
Planning and Design Do's and Don'ts ........................................... 31

## Chapter 3: Creating, Editing, and Checking Your Web Files ........... 33

The Big Picture ............................................................................................. 34
Using the Internet Publisher Dialog Box ................................................... 35
Switching to Web View ................................................................................ 36
    Click the button! .................................................................................. 36
    Converting WordPerfect documents ................................................ 37
Using WordPerfect in Web View ................................................................. 38
Previewing from WordPerfect ..................................................................... 39
Saving Your Web Document ........................................................................ 40
Publishing to HTML ...................................................................................... 40
    Create a folder for your HTML files .................................................. 41
    Publish to HTML .................................................................................. 41
    Understanding what results from publishing to HTML ................. 43
Viewing Your Web Files in Browsers .......................................................... 44
Editing Your Web File ................................................................................... 45
    Editing by using the Web-formatted WordPerfect file ................... 45
    Editing an HTML file ........................................................................... 46

## Chapter 4: Weaving a Simple Site from Scratch ..................................... 49

Creating a New Web File .............................................................................. 49
Getting Your Heading Together ................................................................... 50
Typing Normal Text ...................................................................................... 51
Adding Second-Level Headings ................................................................... 52
Changing Background and Overall Text Color ......................................... 52
Changing the Color of Your Headings ........................................................ 53
Aligning (Justifying) Text ............................................................................. 53
Adding a Line and a Bulleted Table of Contents ...................................... 54
Adding the Date and Your Signature .......................................................... 55
Previewing Your Work .................................................................................. 56
Saving Your Work .......................................................................................... 57
Publishing to HTML ...................................................................................... 57
Creating Another Page ................................................................................. 58
Linking the New Page Back to Home .......................................................... 59
Publishing Your New Page to HTML ........................................................... 59
Linking the Home Page's Table of Contents to the New Page ................. 60
Testing Your Results .................................................................................... 61
Editing Your Pages ........................................................................................ 62

## Chapter 5: Brewing Web Documents with Java ..................................... 63

Deciding to "Do the Barista" ....................................................................... 64
Sending to Barista ......................................................................................... 66
Printing to Barista ......................................................................................... 68
Putting Barista Documents on Your Web Site .......................................... 70

## Chapter 6: Serving Up Your Files to the Web ......................................... 71

Getting a Web Server .................................................................................... 71
How a Document Gets on the Web ............................................................. 72

Copying Files to Your Server ............................................................. 73
    Cloning: The key to success ..................................................... 73
    The copying procedure ............................................................. 74
Managing Files on Your Server ........................................................... 79
Using index.htm for Home Pages and Folder Indexes ..................... 80
Getting Visitors ..................................................................................... 81
    Getting visitors through search engines ................................... 81
    Links to your site and other publicity ....................................... 84
    Becoming www.me.com .............................................................. 85

# Part II: Text Tricks .................................................................. 87

## Chapter 7: Helpful Hyperlinks .................................................................. 89

How Hyperlinks Help ........................................................................... 89
Using Automatic Hyperlinking ............................................................ 90
Creating Hyperlinks from Text or Graphics ....................................... 91
    Hyperlinking from graphics a different way ............................. 93
    Linking to other documents ....................................................... 93
    Hyperlinks for jumping to places within a document ............. 97
Using QuickLinks ................................................................................ 100
Clicking and Testing Your Hyperlinks .............................................. 101
    Clicking and testing links in WordPerfect .............................. 101
    Deactivating and Activating links in WordPerfect ................. 101
    Clicking and testing links in your Web browser .................... 102
Doing Things Besides Jumping .......................................................... 102
    Viewing graphics, playing sounds ........................................... 102
    Downloading a file .................................................................... 103
    Sending an e-mail message to you .......................................... 104
Editing and Removing Hyperlinks ..................................................... 104
Different Hyperlink Appearances ...................................................... 105
    Colors: beating the blues ......................................................... 105
    Graphics: beating the frame .................................................... 106
    Buttons ....................................................................................... 106
When Hyperlinks Go Bad ................................................................... 107

## Chapter 8: Standard Styles and Alignment .................................................. 109

Choosing Style .................................................................................... 110
    Giving text some style .............................................................. 110
    Things that won't work ............................................................ 112
Normal Text ........................................................................................ 112
Headings .............................................................................................. 113
Address Style ...................................................................................... 113
Indented Quotations ........................................................................... 113
Preformatted Text ............................................................................... 113
Numbered Lists ................................................................................... 114
Bulleted Lists ...................................................................................... 115

Definition Lists ........................................................................................... 115
Line and Paragraph Spacing ..................................................................... 116
Achieving Alternative Alignments ............................................................ 116

## Chapter 9: Frisky Fonts and Crazy Colors ................................................. 119

Choosing Fonts ........................................................................................... 119
Being Bold, Italic, Underlined, or Monospace ......................................... 120
  Bold and italic buttons ................................................................... 120
  Font box freaks ................................................................................ 121
Accessing All Attributes ............................................................................ 121
  Bold and italic again, and friends ................................................. 122
  Text of all sizes ................................................................................ 123
Text of All Tints ........................................................................................... 123
  Central color control ....................................................................... 124
  Color schemes and dreams ............................................................ 125
  Regular text color ............................................................................ 126
  Hypertext color ................................................................................ 127
  Background color and wallpaper .................................................. 127
  Coloring selected text .................................................................... 128
  More colors: palettes for the picky .............................................. 129
Using Characters of All Kinds ................................................................... 130
When Fancy Fonts and Formats Go Bad .................................................. 131

## Chapter 10: Tantalizing Tables .................................................................. 133

What's Weird about Web Tables ............................................................... 134
The Table Property Bar .............................................................................. 135
Making a Table ............................................................................................ 135
  The fast way ..................................................................................... 135
  The careful way ............................................................................... 136
Entering Stuff in the Table ......................................................................... 136
Formatting the Entire Table ...................................................................... 137
  Adding or deleting rows or columns ............................................ 138
  Sizing the table ................................................................................ 138
  Controlling borders and space ..................................................... 140
  Positioning the table left or right ................................................. 141
Selecting Rows, Columns, and Cells ........................................................ 141
Aligning Contents in Their Cells ............................................................... 142
Sizing Columns, Rows, and Cells — Not! ................................................. 142
  So what are those width and height controls for? ..................... 143
  So how can I control width and height? ...................................... 143
Using Borders and Fills — Not! ................................................................. 143
Splitting Cells .............................................................................................. 144
Attractive Tablecloths: Background Color ............................................. 145
Cheating at the Table ................................................................................. 146

## Part III: Getting Graphical ............................................................. 147

### Chapter 11: General Graphics ............................................................. 149

Putting Graphics in Documents .............................................................. 150
    Deciding where to insert a graphic ............................................... 150
    Types of graphics that you can insert ............................................ 150
Inserting Graphics from WordPerfect's Scrapbook ........................................... 151
Inserting All Kinds of Other Graphics ..................................................... 153
    Bitmap graphics (images) ........................................................ 154
    The usual drawings and charts ................................................... 154
Creating Cool Graphical Text .............................................................. 155
    Terrific TextArt ................................................................ 155
    Tasteful Text Boxes ............................................................. 158
Sizing up Graphics and Other Boxes ....................................................... 160
Vying for Position ....................................................................... 161
    Left or right, with text alongside .............................................. 161
    Left, right, or center, but standing alone ...................................... 162
    In line with the text ........................................................... 163
Adding "Alternate" Text for Graphics-Free Browsing ....................................... 164
    When to use alternate text ...................................................... 165
    How to apply and test alternate text ............................................ 165
Publishing to HTML with Graphics ......................................................... 166
    Walking the straight and narrow path ............................................ 166
    If you have used GIF or JPG graphic files ....................................... 168
    Understanding what's going on ................................................... 168

### Chapter 12: Building Blocks: Banners, Backgrounds, Bullets ........ 171

Downloading Building Blocks from the Web ................................................. 172
Lines .................................................................................... 173
    The same old line ............................................................... 173
    Party lines ..................................................................... 174
    Vertical lines .................................................................. 176
Banners .................................................................................. 177
Interesting Backgrounds (Wallpaper) ...................................................... 178
Boffo Bullets ............................................................................ 181
Basic and Beautified Buttons ............................................................. 183
    Basic buttons and icons ......................................................... 183
    Beautified buttons .............................................................. 183
Keeping Your Buttons Together ............................................................ 185
    A right-handed control panel .................................................... 185
    A left- or right- handed control panel .......................................... 186

### Chapter 13: Better, Fancier Graphics ............................................... 187

Creating Captions ........................................................................ 187
Using WordPerfect's Graphical Borders and Fills .......................................... 189
Using HTML Borders and Spaces ............................................................ 191

**WordPerfect 8 Web Publishing For Dummies**

Making Graphics Fade in During Downloading ........................................... 192
Flipping, Rotating, Brightening, and Contrasting ....................................... 193
Using and Creating See-Through Graphics ................................................. 194
    Transparency using ClipArt and other WordPerfect artwork ........... 195
    Transparency using BMP and scanned-in images ............................. 196
Using Photo House for Transparency and Other Effects ........................... 198
    Opening and importing files .................................................................. 198
    Saving files .............................................................................................. 199
    Creating a uniformly colored area for transparency ........................ 201
    Photo catalog ......................................................................................... 203
    Special effects ........................................................................................ 203

## Chapter 14: Speedier, Smaller Graphics ........................................... 205

Reuse and Rejoice! ........................................................................................ 206
    Getting a GIF or JPG graphic ................................................................ 206
    Inserting the GIF or JPG graphic .......................................................... 207
    Using ClipArt bullets ............................................................................. 207
Publish to JPG or GIF .................................................................................... 207
    Give me GIF ............................................................................................. 208
    Make mine JPG ....................................................................................... 208
    Choosing JPG ......................................................................................... 209
Convert File Types by Using Graphics Tools ............................................. 209
Reduce Image Size or Resolution ................................................................ 210
Reduce Color Depth ...................................................................................... 211
Adjust JPG Compression Quality ................................................................ 213
Use a Stupid Browser Trick ......................................................................... 213

# Part IV: Wayout Layouts and Dazzling Designs ............ 215

## Chapter 15: Quick Tricks for Layout and White Space ........................ 217

Positioning Graphics: An Overview ............................................................ 217
Using Text Boxes: An Overview .................................................................. 218
Breaking Text to Resume After a Graphic .................................................. 218
Using Text Tricks for White Space .............................................................. 220
    Text tricks for horizontal spacing ....................................................... 220
    Text tricks for vertical spacing ............................................................ 222
Stupid Browser Tricks for White Space ..................................................... 222
    Netscape spacers ................................................................................... 222
    Microsoft margins .................................................................................. 223

## Chapter 16: Initial Layout and Design ............................................. 225

Thinking about Design .................................................................................. 225
    Contemplating your content ................................................................ 225
    Deliberating about identity .................................................................. 226
    Considering your controls ................................................................... 227
    Pondering readability ........................................................................... 228
    Developing a consistent style .............................................................. 228

## Table of Contents   *xvii*

Sketching a Layout .................................................................... 229
Analyzing Your Sketch ............................................................... 230
    Identify browser wrap problems .......................................... 231
    Anticipate table troubles ...................................................... 231
    Try your ideas ....................................................................... 232
Creating Some Simple Layouts ................................................. 232
    Pages that go with the flow ................................................. 232
    Basic left- or center-aligned pages ...................................... 232
    Simple, text-based navigation controls .............................. 233
    Simple multiple-part banners .............................................. 234

### Chapter 17: Doing Layouts by Using Tables .................................... 237

Creating a Table for Layout ....................................................... 238
Removing Table Borders for Layout .......................................... 240
Setting Table Width ..................................................................... 240
Walking Through an Example .................................................... 240
    The sketch ............................................................................. 241
    The table ................................................................................ 241
    The logo ................................................................................. 242
    The site name ....................................................................... 242
    Navigation controls .............................................................. 243
    Document name ................................................................... 244
    Aligning banner elements .................................................... 245
    Left- and right-column text .................................................. 246
    Arrow symbols ...................................................................... 246
    Removing the border ............................................................ 247
    Illustrations ........................................................................... 247
    Bottom stuff ........................................................................... 248
    Cleanup and troubleshooting .............................................. 248

### Chapter 18: Layout with Browser Tricks: Frames and Columns ........ 251

Using Frame-Based Home Pages from the CD-ROM ................ 252
Hyperlinking: The Frame Name Game ...................................... 254
Netscape Multiple Columns ....................................................... 255

### Chapter 19: Lazy Layouts and Indolent Authoring ............................ 257

Perfect Indolence ........................................................................ 257
Lazy Layouts ................................................................................. 259
    Gazing languorously upon two examples .......................... 260
    Opening the starter files ...................................................... 260
    Changing text, graphics, and hyperlinks in web documents ........ 261

## *Part V: Beyond WordPerfect: Web Site Sizzle* ................ 263

### Chapter 20: Graphics That Really Click ............................................ 265

Understanding Clickable Graphics ........................................... 265
Using Tools for Clickable Graphics ........................................... 266

Using Live Image .................................................................................. 267
Using Corel Presentations ................................................................. 270
    Creating the image-map file ...................................................... 270
    Inserting the image map into your document ........................ 272
    Linking the image map to the graphic ..................................... 272

## Chapter 21: Documents That Sing and Dance .................................. 273

Singing Documents ............................................................................. 273
    Click-to-play sound .................................................................... 274
    Background sound ...................................................................... 275
    Inserted sounds .......................................................................... 275
    Controlled sounds in Netscape Navigator ............................... 276
Dancing Documents ............................................................................ 276
    Animated GIFs ............................................................................. 276
    Animation with Ulead GIF Animator .......................................... 279
    Animation with GIF Construction Set ....................................... 280
    Video (movies) ............................................................................. 281
    Converting AVI to GIF in Ulead's GIF Animator ....................... 282
    Converting AVI to GIF in GIF Construction Set ....................... 283
Documents with 3-D Stuff in Them .................................................... 284
Singing, Dancing, Java-Stimulated Documents ............................... 285
    Java applets ................................................................................. 285
    JavaScript .................................................................................... 291

## Chapter 22: Forms and Feedback ....................................................... 295

The Sad Truth about Forms ............................................................... 295
Copying or Borrowing an Existing CGI Script ................................. 297
Why You Still May Care about Forms ............................................... 297
If CGI Scripts Are Not for You ........................................................... 299
How Forms and Scripts Communicate: Names and Values .......... 299
Creating a Form ................................................................................... 300
    Using gizmos: their names and values .................................... 300
    Connecting your form to your CGI script ................................ 306
A Cheesy JavaScript Compromise .................................................... 307
Forms and Tables ................................................................................ 307
Using Standardized Forms at ISPs .................................................... 308

## Chapter 23: Stupid Browser Tricks for Special Effects .................... 311

Automated Slide Shows in Navigator and Internet Explorer ......... 311
Embedded Multimedia ........................................................................ 312
Internet Explorer Scrolling Marquees .............................................. 313

# Part VI: The Part of Tens .................................................. 315

## Chapter 24: Ten Design Do's ............................................................... 317

Do Sketch Your Design First .............................................................. 317
Do Use a Consistent Design Throughout ......................................... 318

Do Provide a Document Title ................................................................. 318
Do Pay Attention to Navigation Controls ............................................. 319
Do Test Your Pages on Multiple Browsers ........................................... 319
Do Design Your Site for Information Gathering ................................. 320
Do Use Color ............................................................................................ 320
Do Provide Alternate Text for Graphics .............................................. 320
Do Provide Tables of Contents for Long Documents ....................... 321
Do Keep Your Pages Up to Date ............................................................ 321

## Chapter 25: Ten Design Don'ts ................................................................. 323

Don't Make a Long or Wide Home Page .............................................. 323
Don't Make Complex Layouts ................................................................ 324
Don't Design for Only One Browser ..................................................... 324
Don't Use Enormous Graphics .............................................................. 324
Don't Use Headings for Body Text ........................................................ 325
Don't Rely Exclusively on Graphics ...................................................... 325
Don't Rely Heavily on Fonts ................................................................... 325
Don't Trust the WYSIWYG Display ........................................................ 326
Don't Use Endlessly Looping Anythings ............................................... 326
Don't Use "Under Construction" Signs ................................................. 326

## Chapter 26: Ten Common Problems ........................................................ 327

WordPerfect Displays Error Messages ................................................. 327
Regular Documents Lose Formatting in Web View ............................ 328
Can't Find Features That This Book Describes .................................. 328
Hyperlinks Don't Work ........................................................................... 328
Graphics Don't Display ........................................................................... 329
Graphics Look Speckly ........................................................................... 330
Text Formats Incorrectly ....................................................................... 330
Extra Space Appears in Browsers ......................................................... 331
Barista Doesn't Work .............................................................................. 331
Tables Don't Come Out Right ................................................................ 331

## Chapter 27: Ten WordPerfect Tricks ........................................................ 333

Automatic Links ....................................................................................... 333
QuickLinks ................................................................................................ 334
Browse to Link ......................................................................................... 334
Automatic Date ........................................................................................ 335
Title from Heading .................................................................................. 335
Automatically Hyperlinked Endnotes ................................................... 335
Text Boxes as Sidebars ........................................................................... 336
Comments ................................................................................................ 336
Inserting Spreadsheets as Tables ......................................................... 336
Inserting Charts from Quattro Pro ....................................................... 337

## Appendix: About the CD ........................................................ 339
Introducing the CD .................................................................. 339
System Requirements ............................................................. 339
Using the CD: Installation Instructions .................................. 340
Starter and Example Documents ............................................ 340
    Home pages ....................................................................... 340
    Frames-based Home pages ............................................... 341
    GIF Animation Files ........................................................... 341
    Internet Explorer Marquees ............................................. 342
    Navigator timed slides ..................................................... 342
    JavaScript examples ......................................................... 342
Software You'll Find on the CD .............................................. 343
If You've Got Problems (Of the CD Kind) .............................. 345

## Index ........................................................................ 347

## License Agreement ................................................... 362

## Installation Instructions .......................................... 364

## IDG Books Worlwide Registration ................. Back of Book

# Introduction

*I*f you use WordPerfect and wonder if, perhaps, you could get a document of your own "on the Web" . . .

If you, your business, or your organization (say, the Parents' Soccer Haters' League of which you are a founding member) could really use a Web site . . .

If you think the WordPerfect Web Publishing feature looks promising, but you are not so sure it's for you . . .

Congratulations! You have come to the right place! The Web isn't just for hackers anymore; it's for "the rest of us" — a giant public bulletin board just waiting for you to tack something up. And if you're a WordPerfect user, you have a great — if sometimes perplexing — tool for the job.

Anyone who can write a document in WordPerfect can turn it into a simple Web page with a few keystrokes and mouse clicks. With a little more effort, and this book, you can get a Web site and put documents online yourself. With a few more tricks, tips, and tools (on the CD), you can create an entire Web site anyone would be proud of.

This book is a reference book for any WordPerfect 8 user. Whether you simply want to put a document on the Web, or create a jazzy, attractive Web site with graphics, animation, and sounds, this book has information you need.

The basic idea in this book is to thumb through it whenever you have a question. It's also a book where you can start at the beginning, get the basic ideas, and then move on to more detailed or advanced topics.

## *What Goes On in This Book*

Just what goes on here? Like all *...For Dummies* books, this book is a light-hearted software guide that tries to avoid "geekspeak" wherever possible — and helps you get results as quickly as possible. Using plain English and detailed step-by-step instructions, it helps you

- Start from the beginning, even if you've only browsed the Web
- Convert a WordPerfect document to a Web document

- Create a new Web document from scratch
- Understand the weird world of Web formatting
- Link your new documents to others you've created and others on the Web
- Add graphics and other media to your Web pages
- Keep you away from pitfalls that make Web documents "break"
- Plan, get, and manage a Web site of your own
- Deal with WordPerfect's peculiarities
- Add as many features as you can without actually being a programmer

Publishing Web documents is easy when done in the right way. This book makes suggestions that will help keep you "on the straight and narrow." Starting your own Web site takes more than just WordPerfect, however, and this book (together with its CD) provides the tool and the instructions to get you going. It also steers you around common problems that cause documents to "break" between your PC and the Web, helps you correct common mistakes that make Web pages unattractive or slow, and guides you in the judicious use of "stupid browser tricks" — features that (while not really stupid) will only work in certain browsers.

## Who Are You?

This book, having been granted three assumptions by the patron spirit of mathematicians (on sabbatical), assumes the following about you, its esteemed reader:

- You are a WordPerfect 8 user.
- You have basic Windows 95 survival skills, like using the Start button and finding the My Computer icon.
- You have a Web browser and have browsed the Web a few times.

Other than that, this book hasn't the foggiest idea who you are. (It is, after all, only a book.) It is proud and happy to have you read its Introduction.

## How to Use This Book and CD

No one wants to sit down and read a book before sitting down with the software, so this book isn't designed to be read that way. If you have figured out how to do some Webbish things, go for it. Refer to the Index or the Table of Contents when you run into a problem.

If you are new to the Web and Web documents, thumb through Part I first and get the big picture. Part I deals with planning issues, steps you through creating your first simple Web documents, and tells you how to "publish" files and put them on the Web.

If all you need are a few hints and tips, see the Part of Tens at the back. See the rest of the book for nitty-gritty details on doing text, hyperlinks, graphics, layout, design, and special effects.

You don't have to "install" the CD, but you may want to install some of the software on it. The CD has programs for putting your files on the Web and for doing things with graphics. It also has some sample, "starter" documents for you to try, plus Web documents for more advanced tricks. See the Appendix for more details.

# How This Book Is Organized

Computer manuals are compelled to document every bell, whistle, and gizmo, so they're often organized by feature. What's more, as a result, they often don't have room for the fundamentals — fundamentals that would tell you why you should even care about a given bell or whistle.

Instead of giving you a section on, say, the "HTML Properties dialog box," this book gives you sections on the task you're trying to do. (If you want an in-depth discussion of a particular piece of gizmology, you always have the Corel manual!) If you're trying to make a link from one document to another, and that happens to involve part of the HTML Properties dialog box, this book will step you through the process of using it.

So, what this book does is break things down into the following six useful categories:

## Part I: Web Weaving 101 with WordPerfect

Part I is Web publishing in a nutshell. This part takes you from understanding how the Web works; through the basics of planning, designing, and getting a site on the Web; through the basics of creating Web documents in WordPerfect; and ends with your documents nestling happily in their very own Web site.

## Part II: Text Tricks

Text is different on the Web. It contains interesting things like "hyperlinks" for people to click on. It uses weird Web "styles." It does peculiar things with fonts, cute things with colors, and enigmatic things with tables. Part II shows you the ins and outs of dealing with text on the Web the WordPerfect way.

## Part III: Getting Graphical

The Web is famous (and notorious) for its graphics. As in any other media, graphics on the Web can inform, entertain, or just make documents easier on the eyes. Part III shows you how to insert graphics, position and size them, use them for jazzier text, and use them for banners, backgrounds, bullets, buttons, and other conventional "building blocks" of Web documents. Graphics can, however, become troublesome, so Part III shows you how to make sure they stay properly plugged in to your document, keep them attractive, and keep them from turning your Web page into a "slow boat" instead of a show boat.

## Part IV: Wayout Layouts and Dazzling Designs

Even if you'd settle for a likable layout and a decent design, Part IV has tips you need for controlling where things go and how they look. Part IV starts with help for problems like adding white space and placing items in a table, moves on to a popular "frames" feature that WordPerfect doesn't support (but that you can use), and ends with help for folks who would really rather not do any more layout or design than they have to!

## Part V: Beyond WordPerfect: Web Site Sizzle

The Web is slowly turning into a singing, dancing, multimedia circus that entertains you, informs you, and offers to hold your wallet for a while. If you've always wanted to join the circus, now is your chance! Or, you may simply want to keep up with the competition. Whatever your motivation, Part V can help you create some of the more advanced features you find on the Web: audio, animation, video, forms, and — for the bold — even use the current darling of Web developers, Java. Part V even shows you how to create your own animations using WordPerfect artwork and a tool from the CD.

## Part VI: The Part of Tens

The Part of Tens is the place to turn for quick inspiration, guidance, and troubleshooting. Here you find "Do's" and "Don'ts" for design, solutions to common problems, and special tricks that WordPerfect can do for Web documents.

## The CD and Appendix

The Appendix gives you a quick rundown on the contents of the CD. The CD includes WordPerfect examples, starter files, and building blocks, plus some of the best programs available for doing the Web work that WordPerfect doesn't do. (The programs come with "evaluation" licenses that let you try before you buy.)

# Icons Used in This Book

We are living in the Age of Icons, where everything from appliances to elevators is equipped with a cryptic symbol instead of words. While this book does not intend to buck the trend, it certainly intends to co-opt it by using actual legible icons, with words, to point out important stuff:

This icon flags related information or other, easier ways of doing things.

This icon cheerfully denotes things that are likely to blow up in your face (figuratively speaking).

This intelligent-looking fellow marks stuff that is probably only interesting to the more technically-inclined reader.

This icon notes an important subject that was brought up earlier, which you may have never read or have forgotten by now.

This icon points out something that is on the CD.

## Where to Go from Here

If you're interested in Web stuff, you've probably already tried out a few WordPerfect features — and run into a few problems. Check the Index or Table of Contents and see if you can straighten things out.

Otherwise, Part I is a good place to start. If you are not really sure you understand what Web publishing is all about and how the Web works, check into Chapter 1. If you're planning to create your own Web site, see Chapter 2. To see how WordPerfect does Web publishing, or to simply convert a WordPerfect document to a Web document, see Chapter 3.

If you're a hands-on, "show me" kind of person, try Chapter 4 first. It steps you through creating a simple set of linked Web pages. If you just want to crank out a Web page fast, jump all the way to Chapter 19.

But first, this book suggests that you walk it over to the checkout counter, buy it, and take it home, where it will faithfully serve you until obsolescence do you part. If you find the book useful, amusing, or problematic, I'd love to hear from you. Let me know if you create a fabulous Web site with WordPerfect! Drop an e-mail note to `winwpweb@dummies.net`. A robot will cheerfully acknowledge its receipt, and — while I can't promise an answer — I will promise to read it.

(See? Here's one of those icons already!) If you're struggling with WordPerfect 8, pick up a copy of *WordPerfect 8 For Windows For Dummies* while you're standing in the bookstore.

# Part I
# Web Weaving 101 with WordPerfect

The 5th Wave By Rich Tennant

"Would you like Web or non-Web?"

## In this part . . .

"Oh, what a tangled Web we weave . . ." says the poet — and boy! Poets don't know the half of it. Today, everyone of every generation from my 7-year-old goddaughter to her 70-something grandfather has a Web site. Many Web sites are plenty tangled, too, simply for lack of a good ...*For Dummies* book to guide their creators through some of the peculiarities and pitfalls of the Web.

WordPerfect 8 is a fabulous tool for WordPerfect users who want or need to make Web documents. However, for most folks, a lot of important questions remain unanswered, such as how to plan, design, and "get" a site on the Web; how to handle the multiple files and Web features that simply don't arise with paper documents; and what the fastest way is to get a Web document. Hence this part, Web Weaving 101 with WordPerfect.

# Chapter 1
# Behind the Scenes: How the Web Works

## In This Chapter
- How documents get on the Web
- Pointing to documents on the Web (URLs)
- Understanding what Web documents are
- HTML, the language
- Special features that work only in certain browsers
- What's different about Web graphics
- Java and other types of Web features

This whole World Wide Web thing seems to be pretty mysterious, technoid, and maybe even creepy when you start looking at it closely. Just what's going on here, anyway? Are people peering into one another's computers around the world and looking at other people's files? What's inside Web documents, anyway? And what is that weird code you enter, which looks like `http://www.blah.com/stuff`, really saying?

If you have surfed the Web (and in this book, I assume that you have at least gotten your feet wet by browsing the Web), you probably have some rough idea how the Web works. Among the things you probably know are

- Electronic documents are available for public viewing on computers all over the world.
- To get to those documents, you must connect your PC to the Internet.
- To display the documents, you need to use Netscape Navigator or another Web browser.
- To view the documents, you must enter the addresses (URLs) of those documents — or click links in other Web documents.

*URL* is pronounced "earl," and — just so you know — it stands for Uniform Resource Locator. Now *there's* a term that doesn't explain much! (And believe me, learning what it does mean isn't worth your while.) But if you're wondering why the term looks so weird, see "Pointing to Documents on the Web (URLs)" in this chapter.

The basic facts above are what you probably know from viewing web documents. If you are going to put documents on the Web, however, you probably ought to know a few more details about how these basics actually work. You don't have to understand it all in order to create Web documents, but if you do understand it, life will make more sense. (And couldn't we all use more of that?)

## How Documents Get on the Web: Web Servers

As you've probably figured out from the amount of time it takes for documents to appear in your browser (the World Wide Wait), viewing distant documents isn't exactly like viewing distant objects through a telescope. The documents on a distant computer have to be transmitted to your browser, one tiny chunk of data at a time, across the Internet.

Viewing files on a distant computer is not exactly like viewing files on your PC, either. Instead of simply opening the files, as you do on the PC, a special program on the distant computer *serves* (transmits) the document that you request. In a remarkable spasm of clarity, software engineers call that program the *server*. To put your documents on the Web, you need access to a Web server.

### The client (not Grisham's)

Your browser is considered to be a client of the server. The client sends requests for information to the server's address, along with your own return address (a long number that you rarely see). The server interprets the request and sends the data that you requested to your return address. The client (your browser) then interprets the data and displays it in your browser window. This arrangement is known as a *client/server system*. (I suppose that your browser should be called a waiter because of the long time it has to wait for documents, but then you might confuse "waiter" with "server"!) All Internet programs that you may have heard of — including Archie, e-mail, telnet, and FTP — use this client/server approach.

## Chapter 1: Behind the Scenes: How the Web Works

Web servers nearly always run on some computer other than a PC. Servers run on more powerful computers, ones that are permanently connected to the Internet over high-speed data lines. Such a computer may belong to your company and be located somewhere on the company premises, or it may belong to your *Internet service provider* — the company that you pay money to each month to get on the Net. (If the latter is true, you may be required to pay still more money to use the provider's Web server.)

For a document to be on the Web, it only has to be in one of the folders (directories) that the server is set up to use. When the document is in such a folder, the server delivers it to anyone on the Web who correctly enters the folder and document name (the document's address or URL) in a browser. As shown in Figure 1-1, the process is a bit like ordering a meal; you can get only items that are on the menu (in the folder).

For security's sake, the server can deliver only files that are in specific folders. That way, Web surfers can't see any files that they shouldn't. (They can't see into the kitchen, to continue the analogy.) Also, for security's sake, only certain people (the chefs, if you will) are allowed to put Web documents into those folders. The person who controls how the server works and what folders it uses is called the Webmaster.

Most small companies and individuals don't have their own Web servers; instead, they rent a folder on a server operated by their Internet service provider. Only the renter is allowed to add or remove files from the folder. When you use an arrangement like this one, you are said to be *co-hosted* by your Internet service provider.

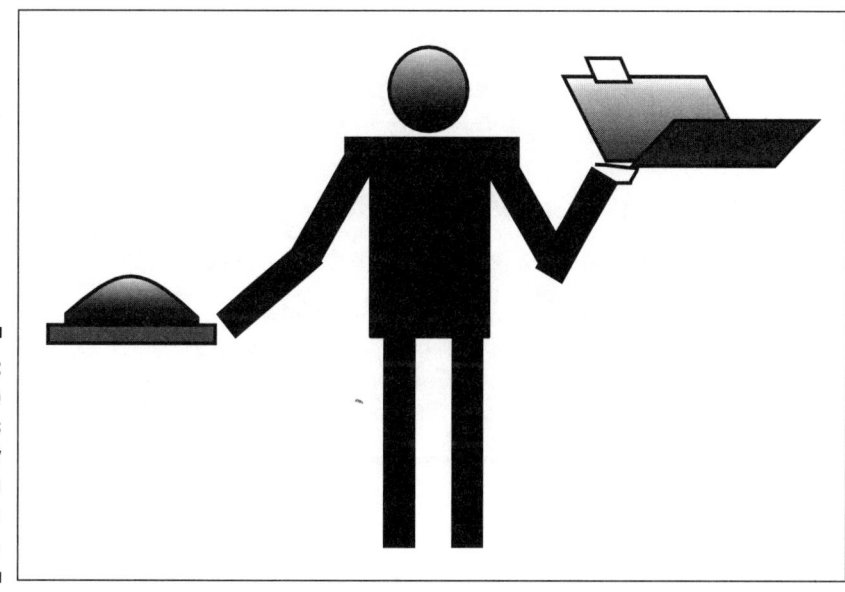

**Figure 1-1:** Web servers deliver tasty files from specific folders.

Some companies' Web servers have special, private folders for documents that the company wants only its employees to see. In such cases, the server is programmed to deliver the documents only to people within the company's address, or *domain*. This sort of private Web site is part of a network called an *intranet*.

## Pointing to Documents on the Web (URLs)

Anyone who has surfed the Web has wondered why the heck, when you want to point your browser at a particular document, you use a rather cryptic-looking location, address, or URL that looks like this:

```
http://www.blah.com/goodies/cookies.html
```

Believe it or not, behind this mess is logic. More to the point, by understanding the logic of URLs, you'll be a finer, more moral person. No, just kidding about the moral part, but you will be a better Web weaver because URLs are what you use to link the pieces of your Web site.

The first part of the URL tells the browser what sort of program it will be talking to on the remote computer. In particular, `http://` says to the browser, "You will be talking to a Web server, which will be transmitting a Web document. So follow the rules for Web servers." If you leave this part off, most modern browsers assume that you'll be talking to a Web server anyway.

### HTTP: Not just a hiccup

HTTP stands for *Hypertext Transfer Protocol*, which is the set of rules that the Internet uses for transmitting Web documents (called "Hypertext Markup Language" or "HTML" documents) for viewing. Web browsers can also use other *protocols*, which are sets of rules for transmitting files. If you've ever downloaded programs over the Web, you may have noticed that in many cases, clicking the link that starts the downloading process makes the browser display a location that begins with `ftp://` instead of `http://`. Using `ftp://` tells the browser that you expect to receive a file from an *FTP server*, which uses *File Transfer Protocol*.

The `www.blah.com` part is actually a two-part address, like an apartment number and street address. The `www` part is like an apartment number, referring to a particular computer — in this case, the Web server — located behind a particular door (a *port* in geekspeak) at the address `blah.com`. The `blah.com` part is like the street address where the server lives, and it is called the *domain name*.

*TECHNICAL STUFF*

The domain name is a name that — for the sake of humans — substitutes for a really long number. Everybody who uses the Internet is identified by a really long number, which is what Internet computers actually use to send messages. If you're creating a Web site for a business, university, or other organization, you may want to pay the necessary fee to get a domain name, to make it easier for people to find you on the Internet. When someone uses a domain name on the Internet, a program called a Domain Name Server (DNS) looks up the number automatically. If you know the IP address for `blah.com`, for example, you can substitute that number for the name in your browser.

The rest of the URL, which looks something like `/goodies/cookies.html`, lists the folder (`goodies`) and filename of the document (`cookies.html`) that you want to view. The slashes are used just to separate the folder and filenames. This arrangement is much like the shorthand that PCs use for folders and filenames, except that the slashes go the other way — forward slashes, not backslashes, as on PCs.

*TECHNICAL STUFF*

If no filename adorns the end of the URL (if, in the preceding example, `cookies.html` is missing), the server automatically looks for a file named `index.html` or `index.htm` (or any other name specified as a default on the server) in the folder (`goodies/`). This process happens when you give the address for the main page, or so-called *home* page, which typically does not include a filename (`http://www.blah.com`, for example). What the server actually gives you is an `index.html` file in the main folder for the Blah company.

# What Are Those Documents on the Web?

All electronic documents, including Web documents, are written in some sort of code, language, or format that communicates all the fancy appearance features, such as italics and paragraph spacing. (Electronic mail is a notable exception; it's written in plain text, which is why it usually doesn't look very fancy.) Every program — Microsoft Word, Microsoft Works, WordPerfect, AmiPro, and so on — has its own document language. You normally never see these languages; you see only their effects, which make text bold, create bullets, indent paragraphs, and so on.

## Part I: Web Weaving 101 with WordPerfect

When the Web was created, a more universal language clearly was needed — one that was not owned by anyone. That language is *Hypertext Markup Language* (HTML). HTML was not created by a software vendor but by official Web-standards people (today known as the World Wide Web Consortium). As a result, HTML is the universal language that all browsers can handle and that is most commonly used on the Web.

Unlike the languages used for WordPerfect and Word documents, you can see and edit HTML, if you like. (WordPerfect and Word documents are in code that only computers can read, whereas HTML files are plain-text files.) Anytime you view a document in Netscape Navigator, for example, just choose View⇨Document Source to see the HTML that created that document. Figure 1-2 shows an example of HTML code.

**Figure 1-2:**
Why you should be glad that you don't have to write the HTML language.

```
<HTML>
<HEAD>
<META NAME="Generator" CONTENT="Corel WordPerfect 8">
<TITLE>Cornwall Chicken Palace Egg Farm</TITLE>
</HEAD>
<BODY TEXT="#000000" LINK="#0000ff" VLINK="#551a8b"
ALINK="#ff0000" BGCOLOR="#ffe6cc">
<H1 ALIGN="CENTER"><FONT COLOR="#b30000">Cornwall Chicken
Palace Egg Farm</FONT></H1>

<P>Eggs can fly! The very freshest of organic eggs are
available by express delivery from the
<A HREF="#On Our Site">Chicken Palace Egg Farm in Cornwall,
Vermont</A>. Yup, every morning we gently sneak the
eggs out from under our sleeping, pampered hens, stuff the
eggs and the kids into the truck,
drive like maniacs for Burlington International Airport,
and have them sent all over the world
(the eggs, that is, not the kids).
<H2 ALIGN="CENTER"><FONT COLOR="#b30000">What Makes Our
```

In the Stone Age, until word processors such as WordPerfect offered automatic conversion to and from HTML, people had to write HTML themselves by using programs such as Windows' Notepad and WordPad (or by carving in rock). Some good reasons still exist to use this seemingly Neanderthal approach. You can do advanced tricks and refinements by writing HTML that you can't do by using WordPerfect commands and features. If, at some point, you want to do tricks that WordPerfect doesn't provide a command for, you need to edit the HTML directly, and I suggest that you pick up a copy of *HTML For Dummies*, 2nd edition (IDG Books Worldwide, Inc.)!

> **TIP:** WordPerfect allows you to enter HTML directly. If you decide to experiment with HTML, type the HTML code, select (highlight) it, then format it with the command Format⇨Custom HTML. (You must be in Web view for this menu item to appear.)

When it comes to making fancy-looking text, HTML isn't as powerful as, say, WordPerfect's document language. HTML can describe only a limited variety of formats. The capability to create tables, for example, was added to HTML only recently. Features such as precise graphic positioning and multiple columns are still not standard even in the most recent version — HTML 3.2.

**TECHNICAL STUFF:** This lack of formatting power in HTML actually was intentional on the part of the Web-standards people, whose idea was that details of formatting — such as what font is used and what color is used for hyperlinks — should be under the control of the Web surfer. The document creator should just specify that certain text is, say, a top-level heading, body text, or a hyperlink to another document, and let the Web surfer decide how to display it. That idea was fine for the simple academic stuff that the Web founders envisioned, but when the Web went commercial, companies wanted to show you fancier documents.

# Web Graphics

The Web wouldn't be nearly as exciting or entertaining if it didn't deliver graphics (but it would be faster). Only a few browsers, such as Lynx, do not display graphics, so nearly everyone expects some sort of entree for the eyeballs. Fortunately, WordPerfect has some nice features for adding Web graphics.

You need to be a bit more careful about putting graphics in Web documents than you do about putting graphics in paper documents, however. This book gives you step-by-step guidelines that make the job easier, but if you also understand what's going on, you can sound extremely knowledgeable at cocktail parties. Oh, yes — your Web site will work better, too.

One point to understand is that, whereas graphics are part of an HTML Web *document*, they are not part of the Web document *file*. "Huh?" you ask — and rightly so. Okay. The Web document (HTML) file has your text in it. But instead of actually containing a graphic image, that HTML file contains a link (an URL) that points to a separate graphics file. The Web browser downloads the text and graphics files separately and puts them together in a document.

So if you have an HTML document with, say, two graphics, you have a total of three files: the HTML file and one file for each of the two graphics. This scheme means that you have to be careful in creating those links, and in copying and moving files, because otherwise, the link may point to the wrong place. The result is a symbol on the Web page in place of the graphic that you wanted, like this one:

The second great understanding that will make you a better Web weaver and valued party guest is that only two types of images are used in HTML Web documents. The two types are GIF (which stands for Graphics Interchange Format, a format created by CompuServe) and JPG (or JPEG, which stands for Joint Photographic Experts Group — the international standards committee that created the format). GIF is the most commonly used graphics type on the Web; it even provides a way to create animated graphics and movies. JPEG is a newer standard; its strength is that for photograph-quality images, the files are smaller and take less time to download. For any other graphic image that you want to use, you must convert to GIF or JPEG format.

GIF and JPEG are *bitmap* graphics, in which a picture is made up of dots. Bitmap graphics are harder to edit than the so-called *vector* graphics that WordPerfect uses for its draw and chart functions and in its clip-art (WPD) files. WordPerfect solves this problem by using special Web-formatted documents; you can use WordPerfect's vector graphics and have WordPerfect take care of converting these graphics.

# Other Types of Web Documents

Some software vendors decided that HTML wasn't powerful enough. (Some folks can never get enough power.) So these vendors marketed, for Web use, special languages that can be interpreted only by certain browsers — or by browsers equipped with special viewers or plug-ins. Adobe, for example, created the Acrobat language, and if your browser is equipped with an Acrobat viewer, you can view Acrobat documents. WordPerfect has a similar language, called Envoy. You can create a document in Envoy format and put it on the Web. Then anyone whose browser is equipped with an Envoy viewer can read that document.

The catch with Acrobat or Envoy, of course, is that not everyone has the necessary viewer. Adobe and Corel suggest that you provide links from your Web pages to their company sites so that people can download the necessary viewers. Downloading a viewer is not particularly hard to do, but it is time-consuming, so you must have a very interesting document to motivate people to spend that much time.

## Java

Java is the most recent of the languages used on the Web. Java is not an official Web standard, but most popular browser vendors either support it now or plan to do so in the future — without installing an additional viewer.

Java is a general-purpose language that can perform all kinds of tricks, such as opening additional windows on-screen and animating objects. One of the language's many capabilities allows you to control a document's appearance as precisely as you do in WordPerfect. If a browser can read Java (as Netscape for Windows 95 can), it can display very fancy formatting. WordPerfect 8 allows you to create Java documents.

*Technical Stuff:* A Java document actually has to be sort of sugar-coated (encapsulated) with HTML for a Web browser to read it. The Java document contains just enough HTML to say, "Hey, here comes some Java." Technically, this makes Java documents HTML documents, so like HTML files, Java files still end in .htm or .html.

## Extended HTML

Some of the fancy features that you see on the Web in a Netscape browser, you can't see when you use other browsers. Features such as frames (scrollable areas), typefaces other than Roman (such as Helvetica and Garamond), multiple columns, and in-document multimedia in Netscape aren't created in standard HTML. Such features use custom Netscape extensions to HTML.

You can create some of these special Netscape features because Corel and Netscape work together fairly closely; Corel has built Netscape features into WordPerfect (see Figure 1-3, for example). You can choose exactly what font to use — a Netscape-invented feature that Microsoft now supports, too. The trouble is that people who don't use the latest Netscape or Microsoft browsers can't see these features. These people can read your documents and see the images, but the documents won't appear as they did when you created them in WordPerfect.

**Figure 1-3:** Columns are one of the Netscape features that WordPerfect allows.

This book refers to Netscape and Microsoft extensions as "stupid browser tricks." The description is apt not because the tricks are particularly stupid, but, as with the "stupid pet tricks" on *Late Show with David Lettermen,* because the tricks are often not particularly useful.

How did this nonstandard stuff happen? The creators of Web browsers — in particular, Netscape — decided that the HTML standards just weren't moving fast enough for them. They wanted to be able to offer you more bells and whistles than the next guy, so they designed their browsers to interpret cool, special commands that weren't in the HTML standard, such as commands to control text size and color. These commands are called *extensions* to HTML. Then they told Web-page designers all about those extensions; the designers started using them to create cooler Web pages; and the next thing we Web surfers knew, everyone was using them.

This series of events left other browser vendors (including Mosaic and Microsoft) in a tough spot. These vendors had to follow along and allow Netscape to dictate the language, stick to their guns and stay with the standard HTML, or introduce their own extensions to the HTML language. Microsoft and Mosaic decided to introduce a few of their own extensions, but mostly stay with standard HTML.

Extended HTML may become less important if Java eventually becomes a standard on the Web. Java can perform many of the tricks that HTML extensions do.

# Chapter 2
# Weaving Web-Site Plans

### In This Chapter
▶ Deciding on your objectives
▶ Considering your audience
▶ Deciding what to put on the site
▶ Choosing a structure for linking
▶ Pondering the home page
▶ Estimating costs
▶ Thinking about time requirements
▶ Contemplating fancy site features
▶ Planning and design do's and don'ts

*I*f all you want to do is knock out some cool Web pages and have some fun, give this chapter a miss. This chapter is for the businesslike folks who are creating a Web site for more objective results, such as making money, boosting church attendance, or saving the world.

If you're the chief honcho of your Web site — the Big Kahuna, the main dude, the Web weaver — you've got your hands full. In fact, you've got the whole World Wide Web in your hands. You also have a real challenge on your hands. On one hand, you have the (sinister-sounding) intention of snaring the attention of your Internet audience. On the other hand, you need to dexterously decide just who this audience is; what you want to say to those people; and just what those decisions imply for making Web documents, anyway.

Well, this chapter can't exactly provide handy answers; it realizes that you must provide your own answers. But the chapter would be happy for you to sit down among its leaves and ponder its convenient lists of handy questions. The chapter also has a few humble suggestions to make. Some of those humble suggestions refer to subjects in following chapters, so just look up any unfamiliar subjects in the index and read about them elsewhere in this book, or return to this chapter after you've read some of the others.

*Note:* This book uses the term *Web weaver* to mean someone who creates and links the Web pages — a content person. *Webmaster* is a more general term used on the Internet to mean someone who might also be a content person but who probably also manages the technical operation of the Web server. (Thanks to Jordan Young for introducing me to the term, *Web weaver!*)

# Objectives: Why Weave Your Web and for Whom?

Unless you simply have an unrestrainable urge to express yourself on the Web, at some point, you've gotta ask yourself, "Why, exactly, am I doing this?", "What do I hope to get out of it?", and "Who am I writing this stuff for?" To help you through this existential crisis, the following sections provide a couple of helpful checklists. (If the checklists don't do the job, try a hot fudge sundae and a nap. That combination works for me.)

## Objectives

Lots of people throw a Web site together just to have fun. That's fine, but if you stop to think for a minute, you'll probably find that you want some specific results from your Web site. If you design your site for those results, you'll waste much less time and money — and you'll probably have a Web site that people like better as well. See whether any of the following objectives match yours:

- **Coordinating activities for a group.** News (events) and information on whom to contact are important categories to pay attention to. Provide background details on the group if you want to encourage prospective members. Keep news to one page to facilitate updating. Provide an e-mail link to yourself so that people can send you updates. Consider having multiple Web weavers besides yourself, in case you're absent. Privacy may be an issue; if so, use a hidden directory (one that no other home page links to). If your company owns its own Web server, your Webmaster can provide a special private directory that is visible only within your company network.

- **Getting people to attend an event.** Put an event link on your home page, including event dates. Create a list of people who are interested in your events and who will permit you to e-mail them a notice announcing new information on your site. Encourage registration by providing an e-mail link from the site. Provide contact information, maps, and links to additional information on speakers or sponsors. Keep the event page up to date; people expect Web information to be absolutely current.

- **Publishing a library of useful documents.** Pay attention to providing good tables of contents (TOCs). Put TOCs at the beginning of long documents, with links to subject sections. Spend time organizing your information and structuring your Web site well. Link frequently between documents and other, related sites.

- **Showing off.** Include portfolio samples if you work in text, graphics, audio, or other media (scan graphics in or insert graphics files into a WordPerfect Web document). Use graphics, audio, and multimedia, but don't force long downloads on the site visitor by embedding big files in the document. Allow the visitor to click links to view big files. Consider using a professional Web developer.

- **Educating.** Use appropriate graphics, but optimize them for shorter downloading; full-time students rarely have the fastest modems. For lessons that use sequential organization, add multiple-choice quizzes at the end of a lesson; link from each choice to another Web document, with an explanation of why the answer is right or wrong. Link to the next lesson only from the correct answer's page. Also use links as they are used in Windows Help, to provide documents that contain additional background information.

- **Promoting products or services.** Link directly to descriptions of the product or service from eye-catching type or graphics on the home page. Don't assume that the reader is an insider in your industry. Reserve some information; don't give full information on the site if a salesperson should be involved. Contact information (such as sales offices) is important; tell visitors what action to take.

- **Generating sales leads.** Provide a prominent, easy-to-use response mechanism — a form or e-mail link — that enables people to give you their names, addresses, and phone numbers. Ask site visitors to provide information on their interests, and ask for permission to e-mail them. Provide links to the response mechanism from nearly every page on your Web site. Offer literature or a sample as an incentive. Feature your Web site or special promotional pages in direct-mail ads. For selling software, consider providing a link to a compressed (zipped) downloadable sample.

- **Taking orders.** Ask for the order! Provide a prominent, convenient way to order, such as a form to be e-mailed or printed and faxed. Be aware, however, that ordering over the Web without e-mailing or faxing requires complex work that is best done by Web professionals and run on a secure server. If you are a distributor or reseller, check into cooperative ordering by using your source's Web-based ordering system, rather than rolling out your own.

## *Audiences*

How you weave your Web site depends a great deal on whom you expect your visitors to be. Are they businesspeople who are being very businesslike? If so, don't try to be too entertaining. Are they Web newbies? America Online subscribers? Mac users? Who they are may affect the sort of Web browser that your visitors use and what they can see. Go down the following list and underline anything that you think may describe the visitors you expect to have. Read about the precautions that you may have to take to make your site attractive to them:

- **Unmotivated visitors.** Consider how most visitors will reach your site — by following a link? by using a search engine? through advertisements? by word of mouth? If you're taking the simple *Field of Dreams* approach that relies on the Web to bring you visitors ("if you build it, they will come"), don't expect those visitors to be highly motivated. The less motivated your visitors are, the more clear, exciting, and easy to use your site must be to get the result that you want. What information and what sort of presentation will visitors find to be exciting? To motivate, consider using a simple, flat structure and a minimal set of navigation links to click. (See "Structure: Arranging your strands" in this chapter.) Avoid creating documents with large graphics or excessive download times, but also avoid putting up a big wall of boring text. Use lots of white space.

- **Business prospects.** For business visitors, make sure that a link to your e-mail address or response form is never far away. Consider using a professional Web designer. For high-level managers, keep the site design simple and fast to use. Use a flat structure, organizing material in a way that visitors will find to be most familiar, logical, or convenient. Provide short, clear directions. For engineers, provide full details as well as summaries, and use a drill-down (hierarchical) structure. Avoid using graphics or frills that distract attention or take a long time to download. Provide "alternate" text (described in Chapter 11) for all graphics. Provide FAQs (lists of frequently asked questions and their answers).

- **Visitor's Internet connection.** You may be using a fast modem and a great Internet service provider, but your visitors may not be. Home users generally have the slowest connections; business users, the fastest. Just in case your visitor has a slow connection, optimize your graphics for fastest downloading. Don't rely entirely on graphics — use "alternate" text for every graphic, and provide backup navigation controls that use just text, in case users have image-loading capability turned off. Make sure that of all your pages, your home page downloads fastest.

✓ **Visitor's browser.** People use an amazing variety of browsers. Although most Web surfers (about 80 percent) currently use Netscape Navigator, many use Microsoft Internet Explorer, Mosaic, the America Online (AOL) and CompuServe interfaces, the no-graphics LYNX browser, or some browsers that you've never heard of. Often, people don't install the latest release of their browsers, either, so standard but new features (such as backgrounds and tables) may not show up properly for them. If, however, you stick to the standard HTML document features that WordPerfect provides, you'll be okay with most of your audience. Enlist a bunch of friends and relations who have different browsers to test your site. If you do add fancy browser-specific features, don't rely on those features for presenting essential information.

✓ **Visitor's computer.** Visitors to your Web site could be using anything from a laptop with no audio and a low-resolution screen to a UNIX workstation with a wide screen, high resolution, and no color to a Macintosh with all the bells and whistles. Some color images look terrible on a laptop; use standard 256-color or 16-color palettes for your images if laptop users are important to you. Design your document to look okay if it's wrapped to a small window size. Don't force the visitor to use an unreasonably large window size for his or her computer by using overly large graphics or a table of fixed width. Don't rely on audio for presenting critical information. If AOL, Macintosh, or UNIX users are important to you, have a few of them test your site. Macintosh versions of Web browsers typically lag behind Windows versions and may not have the latest features that your version does.

# Tactics: Weaving Your Web Site

When it comes to putting together your Web site, take a clue from the original Web weaver, the spider. Link your site together in an elegant, organized pattern designed for easy navigation. Like the spider, you must ponder two important ponderables:

✓ Content: what you have to say

✓ Structure: how best to arrange your content

(At least, I presume spiders spend a lot of time pondering. They sit around a lot, in any event.)

## Content: The strands of your Web site

Here are some common categories of "content" you might want on your Web site. You don't necessarily have to make a separate page or set of pages for each category. If you are creating a Web site that deals mostly in seminars, for example, contact information could be part of each seminar page rather than on a separate page.

- **Background:** your organization's history, goals, product or service, form of organization, location, and principal honchos
- **Contacts:** fax numbers, phone numbers, office locations, names of people to contact, phone numbers, and links to e-mail addresses (including yours)
- **Events:** trade shows, seminars, and meetings
- **Directions:** to your place of business or to the event, perhaps including a map
- **Products:** things you sell, make, or give away
- **Services:** consulting services or product support, expertise, policies, hours of operation, and phone and e-mail contacts
- **Literature:** notes, papers, research documents, or popular documents you may have converted from paper publications to Web documents
- **Employment:** jobs or volunteer positions available and contact person
- **Links:** to parent organizations, partners, distributors, or other related organizations
- **Content guides:** indexes, help pages, and tables of contents
- **Help:** answers to frequently asked questions about your organization or Web site
- **News:** press releases or articles in magazines about you or your organization
- **Kudos:** a page listing nice things people have said about you (and which you have permission to quote)

If a particular category, such as *Literature,* is important to your site and you have many documents to put in that category, create a folder for that category on your Web site and place the documents there. Then create a table-of-contents page for that category (a document that provides links to all the documents in *Literature*) and put it in that folder. Finally, put a link to the page from text such as `Browse Our Literature` on your home page. Any visitor who clicks `Browse Our Literature` then sees the table-of-contents page. Chapter 7 gives you the details about creating such folders and putting files on your Web site.

## Structure: Arranging your strands

A Web site is not just a bunch of stuff. No, indeed. A Web site is a bunch of stuff tied together by gee-whiz, high-tech, clickable hyperlinks! One of the high arts of Web weaving is linking your material in a way that makes visiting your site a pleasure — or at least doesn't drive your visitors (or you) nuts.

First, a quick review: *Hyperlinks* (or links, for short) are those things that you click to move to another document. Links are either underlined and colored text or certain clickable graphics. Without links, your visitors would have to know the URL (the `http://www.whatever.com/whimsy.html` stuff) of any document that they want to visit, so that they could enter the URL in their browsers.

Entering URLs would be way too boring, so links were invented. You, the Web weaver, have to create these links. (Chapter 7 tells you how.) You could, of course, provide a link from every document to every other document. With four documents, you have to create 4 × 3 (lessee, that's 12) links. With 10 documents, you have 10 × 9, or 90 links! You would also have to add a new link to every page every time you added a document! Pretty soon, you'd be spending your life on the links rather than, say, playing golf. You need to create a more efficient structure (or give up golf).

The structure that you create with links is what your visitor sees. You create another kind of structure — the folder (or directory) structure of your Web site — for your own sake, to help you stay organized. For more information about directory structure, see Chapter 6.

You can come up with any number of ways to structure your Web site with links. Following are three ways:

- String-in-the-junk-drawer structure (which is not recommended)
- Drill-down, or deep, structure (which is traditional but tedious)
- Flat structure (which is way-cool and turn-of-the-millennium)

The one piece that all these structures have in common is the home page: the official front-door entrance of your Web site. I begin with that.

### The home page

Metaphorically speaking, the *home page* is the front cover of a book made up of your Web documents. This page provides the top-level information about your Web site: what your site is about and what the visitor will find to be new or exciting about your site, your products, or your organization. In short, the home page answers every visitor's subconscious question about your Web site (such as "Why should I give a hoot?").

Technically speaking, the home page is a file that you should name `index.html` or `index.htm` (or `default.html` depending on your Web server) and place in the master folder of your Web site. If you give your home page that name and put it in that folder, visitors don't have to type as much when they enter your location or address (the URL) in their Web browsers. Visitors can enter `www.coolsite.com` instead of `www.coolsite.com/index.html`, for example. Different Web servers (the programs that run Web sites) have different requirements about the exact extension (the `.htm` or `.html` part of the filename) that you need to use, so check with your Webmaster.

### What to put on your home page

A home page usually has two jobs. Job one is to lure visitors to your Web site; job two is to get them the information that they want ASAP. If you already have highly motivated visitors, such as members of your chocolate-tasting club, you don't have to worry so much about luring them with exciting stuff on the home page. Even then, however, you still want to announce new and exciting information (*"Lindt now offers downloadable chocolate samples!"*) on your home page, because your visitors really want that information ASAP!

You can't put everything on your home page, however. (Well, you could, but you probably shouldn't.) A home page should be short and quick to download, so instead of putting entire paragraphs of information on that page, just put phrases or graphics on the home page and wire them up as links to other documents.

With these links on it, your home page serves as a sort of high-level table of contents for your Web site. The home page doesn't have to list every single document on your site, however. That job — if it's done at all — usually is reserved for a site map or contents page, and you provide just a link to that page on your home page.

Generally, a home page displays

- A banner at the top that identifies the Web site.
- A welcome message.
- Links to the latest and greatest stuff on your site.
- A set of links to every major category of information on your site (such as Events, Products, or Customer Support) or to things that a visitor may want to do (such as Order Products).
- A set of links that is repeated on every major page of your Web site, grouped to form what are called *navigation controls*.

A home page sets the layout and style for the Web site. Users should expect to find similar type styles and positioning on each page of the site. The navigation controls on other pages should appear in the same location as they do on the home page. Every document should have a link back to the home page.

Home pages are special because they are your visitors' springboard to the rest of your site. A home page that works with a broad variety of browsers, computers, and Internet connections is especially important unless you know exactly what technology most of your visitors use. For tips, see "Planning and Design Do's and Don'ts" later in this chapter.

### *String-in-the-junk-drawer structure*

Have you ever tossed a handful of string into the household junk drawer? Eventually, everything in the drawer gets tied together. If you just keep putting documents on your site and haphazardly tying them together with links, the result is just about as useful and easy to untangle when you eventually have to add a new page.

### *Drilling deep*

When Web sites first appeared, they usually were structured like an outline. Each subcategory of information had its own page, like this:

All About Cooking Home Page
    Baking
        About Cookies
            About Chocolate-Chip Cookies
                Chocolate-Chip/Macadamia Nuts Cookie Recipe

Starting from the All About Cooking home page, you would have to follow a link to Baking, and from there to About Cookies, and so on. This process is called *drilling down*. By the time you found the actual recipe, you would be drooling on your keyboard. (The example is a bit of an exaggeration, but you get the idea.)

Today, this structure generally is considered to be boring; it usually wastes visitors' time, and it's really not true to the freewheeling linking idea of the Web.

The attraction of this structure for Web weavers, however, is that it's orderly and easy to maintain, so it's still a valid structure if you have many documents. Links exist only between the page about a given category and the documents in that category (plus, perhaps, a "return to home page" link in each document). So if a document becomes obsolete (if, say, macadamia nuts are eaten into extinction), the Web weaver has to remove only the document and a single link from the About Chocolate-Chip Cookies page. In a more complex structure, he or she might have to remove links to the recipe from all over the site.

### Going flat

In a flat structure, visitors get to the document quickly without having to go through many different pages. A flat structure goes sort of like this:

```
All About Cooking Home Page
    Index of Cookie Recipes
        Chocolate-Chip/Banana Cookies
        Chocolate-Chip/Macadamia Nuts Cookies
    Index of Fish Recipes
        Broiled Sturgeon
        Fish and Chips
    About Baking
    About Broiling
```

In a flat structure, links don't just go down the hierarchy, from home page to cookie index to cookie recipe. A link might go from About Baking to Index of Cookie Recipes, for example. A new or really outstanding recipe might have a link directly from the home page.

The advantage of a flat structure is that visitors get their cookies faster. The disadvantage is that the structure contains more links, and you need to be more careful to add or remove links as you add or remove documents.

## Resources: Weaving Wisely

If you had infinite time, skill, and money, you probably would be at the beach right now. And if you were at the beach, you would have better things to do than read this book. So if you're reading this book, you should consider what resources a Web site requires.

## Money

If you put your site on an Internet service provider's Web server, you may be charged in any of several conventional ways. If you're already buying access services, a pretty good chance exists that you can put your site on the Web server for free. If the provider charges a fee, that fee may run from about $5 to $30 per month. If you put up a large site, the more data you put on the Web, the more the site costs you. Following are two ways in which you might be billed:

✔ **By storage space.** If you are already buying Internet access from a provider, you may be given a free Web site on your provider's Web server, with up to 5MB of storage for your Web documents. You may be billed for additional storage space.

✔ **By data downloaded to visitors.** You probably won't be charged on this basis unless the downloading from your site exceeds some vast amount each month, such as 1GB (1,000MB). Above that amount, a charge per additional gigabyte or 100MB may be applied.

Most individuals and small organizations do not exceed the limits for a free or flat fee Web site because their entire set of Web documents may not require more than 0.1 to 0.2MB and may not be downloaded all that often. On such a site, visitors could visit 5,000 to 10,000 times, reading all the information on the site, before hitting a limit of 1GB! To estimate your monthly downloading rate, add up the file sizes of all your Web files in kilobytes (KB), divide by 1,000 to get megabytes or by 1,000,000 to get gigabytes, then multiply that figure by the number of visitors you expect to have each month.

Other fees for Web-related services may include

✔ Registering a domain name (such as `rutabagas.com`) with InterNIC. You can register the name yourself on the Web at `http://www.internic.net`. At present, the organization that registers domain names (InterNIC) charges $100 for two years.

✔ Applying your registered domain name to your Web site (a process called *creating a virtual domain* or *performing virtual Web addressing*). This service is necessary before you can tell people to go to `www.rutabagas.com` instead of `www.cheapskates.net/users/rutabagas`.

✔ Reviewing any computer programs (scripts) that you give your provider to run on its Web server. Scripts are necessary only for handling Web forms, which are relatively advanced features.

✔ Use of a secure server and order forms for financial transactions.

✔ Creating your Web site for you!

## Time

If you don't get too fancy, sticking mostly to standard text and Web formats, you can create the materials for a decent Web site in very little time. A day or less usually is enough time to create, install, and test a simple Web site, like the ones that religious and volunteer organizations have. If you must have a clever home page full of advanced features such as clickable graphical controls and Netscape frames, you can easily spend a week on the job. The best approach usually is to start simple and add fancy features later.

Maintaining a Web site — not creating it — often takes a surprisingly large amount of time. A Web site is most useful when visitors can rely on it to be absolutely up to date, especially if you intend your site to be a bulletin board for your organization's activities or to publicize special events. To make your job easier, try to put material that changes most rapidly (such as weekly or monthly events) on a single page. Another good idea is to train at least one other person to manage your organization's Web site so that you can take a vacation!

## Fancy site features that you'll need additional help for

Some fancy Web features take some special expertise and special tools. Following are a few features that you shouldn't plan on creating yourself by using just WordPerfect (except for the predesigned files on the CD-ROM that comes with this book). Some of the other programs in WordPerfect Suite 8 can help you create some of these features. For customized versions of these features, your best bet is to find some experienced technical help. Your Internet service provider usually can suggest Web professionals or may offer help itself. Following are the features that you might want to seek additional help for.

If you can't find a computer professional to handle these features, find a 10-year-old Nintendo player. They often work for food.

- **Frames.** Frames are a way to divide a Netscape Navigator or Internet Explorer screen so that one part remains intact while another part changes. See Chapter 18 for more discussion of frames, and for instructions on using the "frames-based" starter files on this book's CD.

- **Forms for collecting information from visitors.** Forms are easy enough to create, but to use forms to collect data in the way that you usually see on the Web, you need a special program, called a *CGI script,* that runs on the Web server. The CGI script reads the form and stores the data. Some Internet service providers can provide forms and CGI scripts for you to use (for a fee). See Chapter 22 for ways of gathering information.

- **Searches.** Many sites allow visitors to search the site for key words or phrases. This feature also requires a CGI script running on the Web site.

- **Interactive pages.** Some Web pages interact with visitors, which means that the pages do different things, depending on information that the visitors provide. The page may ask for a login and password, calculate mortgage payments, retrieve information from a database, or put an item in a shopping basket. These features require either a CGI script on the Web server or some fancy Java programming in the Web page.

## Planning and Design Do's and Don'ts

By now, you probably have started to form a mental image of your Web site. Before you run off to create your site, however, here are a few suggestions to keep in mind. If you don't understand some of the concepts mentioned in this list right now, just look 'em up in the index and read all about them.

- Shop carefully for your Web service so that you don't have to change providers — a process may change your URL and confuse your audience.
- Keep your objectives and your audience in mind.
- Keep the Web site's structure as flat as possible.
- Design for the lowest common denominator: smallest screen, lowest screen resolution, slowest Internet connection, and most limited browser that you expect most of your visitors to use.
- Avoid creating a home page that is more than two screens long or that takes more than a few seconds to start providing meaningful content, given the connection that you expect your visitors to have. Total download time should not exceed 15 seconds, under normal conditions.
- Don't use enormous graphics.
- Keep things simple; certain special effects may not work with all browsers. This book tells you when a certain feature may not work well in all browsers.
- Make layout and navigation controls consistent throughout the Web site, and include a link to the home page from every page.
- Avoid using unlabeled arrows for navigation between documents. People have different ideas about what up, down, left, and right mean in this context.
- Provide TOCs for long documents.
- Don't use `Under Construction` signs in place of a page you haven't written yet. You will annoy people who take the time to follow the link.
- Don't use `Click Here` for links. (See Chapter 7.)
- Provide clear, reliable navigation controls.
- Use white or light backgrounds with contrasting type.
- Avoid using distracting or high-contrast background images.
- Don't use enormous graphics.
- Don't rely exclusively on graphics.
- Use "alternate" text with graphics.
- Build for the widest possible range of browsers.

- Don't rely on browser-specific capabilities for critical features.
- Limit the variety of type sizes, styles, and colors.
- Avoid using perpetual motion (continuously animated images, continuous music, or blinking text).
- Don't use enormous graphics.
- Work with, not against, browsers' word-wrap features.
- Date and sign the pages.
- Provide a contact link to allow people to send corrections to you.
- Test every link after putting a document online.
- Use titles and keywords.
- Construct headers and initial text with "search engines" (Web sites that help people find stuff) in mind. See Chapter 6 for information on search engines.
- Don't use enormous graphics.

Don't use enormous graphics.

# Chapter 3
# Creating, Editing, and Checking Your Web Files

● ● ● ● ● ● ● ● ● ● ● ● ● ● ● ● ● ● ● ● ● ● ● ● ● ● ● ● ● ● ● ● ● ● ● ● ● ● ● ● ● ● ● ● ●

## In This Chapter
▶ Getting the big picture
▶ Introducing the WordPerfect Internet Publisher
▶ Converting existing documents
▶ Preparing documents for the Web
▶ Publishing to HTML
▶ Understanding your HTML file and its folders
▶ Viewing and previewing your Web files in browsers
▶ Editing your Web document

● ● ● ● ● ● ● ● ● ● ● ● ● ● ● ● ● ● ● ● ● ● ● ● ● ● ● ● ● ● ● ● ● ● ● ● ● ● ● ● ● ● ● ● ●

If you're ready to boogie (start creating Web documents) you're in the right place. Here are the basics of creating, editing, and testing Web documents in a single chapter. Although these subjects sound pretty simple, they take an entire chapter because they involve juggling many different files and folders, as well as converting files from one form to another.

If you're in a rush, and all you want to do is to put a copy of an ordinary document on the Web, jump to "Converting WordPerfect documents." More likely, you want a brand-new document that uses Web features such as links to other Web documents. In that case, start with "Click the button!"

If you have installed WordPerfect's "publishing to Java" feature (which Corel calls *Barista* technology), you may want to try that feature instead of using the steps described in this chapter. Publishing to Java avoids having to deal with Web styles and Web formatting at all. You simply publish to Java and you get a document that looks very much like your regular WordPerfect document. Although the result is generally good, publishing to Java has certain substantial drawbacks; see Chapter 5 for details. If Barista works for you, you can ignore the rest of the book! Otherwise, read on.

## *The Big Picture*

Before you get up to your abdomen in alligators, take a flyover view of the swamp (Where the Webbed Things Are). Following is an aerial view of the stepping stones that you need to cross the swamp:

**Step 1. Switch to WordPerfect's Web view.**

When you switch to Web view, WordPerfect creates a Web-formatted document. You can start with a blank screen to create a fresh Web-formatted document from scratch, or you can start with an existing WordPerfect document open and convert it to a Web document.

**Step 2. Create the Web document that you want.**

With WordPerfect in Web view, you have all kinds of tools to create a document that uses Web features and formatting. Using those tools is what the rest of this book is about. As you create the document, you can periodically preview the document in a Web browser to check its appearance.

**Step 3. Save your document.**

The document that you save is a Web-formatted WordPerfect file, not the file that ultimately goes on the Web.

**Step 4. Publish to HTML.**

What WordPerfect calls *publishing to HTML* creates an HTML (Hypertext Markup Language) file. Your objective is the HTML file — the file that gets copied to your Web server (which is the computer that puts your files on the Web). Publishing also creates separate files for graphics, which also must go on the Web. But before you put any files on the Web. . . .

**Step 5. Check your HTML file in an actual Web browser, such as Netscape Navigator.**

Checking the actual files that will go on the Web, including testing all the links, is important.

**Step 6. Copy your HTML file (and its graphics or audio files) to the Web server.**

WordPerfect itself doesn't help you much with this task, but certain other programs can; see Chapter 6 for details. Putting files on the server may be the job of someone else in your organization: the so-called Webmaster.

The entire process takes about 10 minutes when you get used to it. The process just looks complicated when you write it all down.

# Using the Internet Publisher Dialog Box

If you like to have all your Web controls in one location, you'll like the Internet Publisher dialog box. This dialog box contains the main controls for creating and converting Web files, as Figure 3-1 shows. Check out the dialog box yourself by choosing File⇨Internet Publisher. (When you finish peeking, click the Close button.)

**Figure 3-1:** The central control panel for creating HTML Web documents.

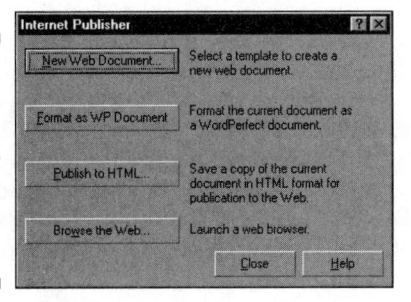

Frankly, WordPerfect gives you other, more convenient buttons that do exactly the same things as the buttons in the Internet Publisher dialog box. In Web view, WordPerfect provides buttons in the various bars at the top of the window. In this book, I favor using the bar buttons. See "Using WordPerfect in Web View" later in this chapter for more details on bars.

If Internet Publisher is grayed out in the File menu, some image or other object probably is selected in your document. Click anywhere in the text of the document and try again.

The buttons in the Internet Publisher dialog box work like this:

- **New Web Document:** Click this button if you want to create a new WordPerfect document in Web view from scratch.

- **Format as Web Document**: Click this button if you have created or opened a regular document file in WordPerfect and want to transform it, Cinderella-like, into a Web document.

    When you edit a Web-formatted document, this button becomes Format as WP Document, which turns your Web-formatted silver coach into a normally formatted pumpkin.

- **Publish to HTML:** Click this button to create files to be put on the Web (an HTML file and associated graphics files).

- **Browse the Web:** If you have a properly installed browser (such as Netscape Navigator or Microsoft Internet Explorer), this button launches that browser.

## Switching to Web View

To create files for the Web, you must work in a special Web view. Web view is more than a view; it actually creates a specially formatted document. Web view also changes many of the buttons and the menus in WordPerfect.

### Click the button!

WordPerfect makes starting a fresh new Web document easy. Click a button or two, and you're off to the races.

The absolute simplest way to switch to Web view is to click the Web view button at the far right end of the Toolbar, shown to the left of this paragraph. If you prefer using menus, choose View⇨Web Page from the WordPerfect Menu bar. If you like the Internet Publisher dialog box, you can click the New Web Document button there instead. (Refer to the preceding section, "Using the Internet Publisher Dialog Box.")

If you want to create a fresh, blank Web document, click the New Blank Document button at the left end of the Toolbar before you switch to Web view. Otherwise, WordPerfect thinks that you want to convert the currently open document to Web format, and the scary warning box shown in Figure 3-2 may appear. If the box appears, fear not; click the OK button. (The warning applies only when you are converting ordinary WordPerfect documents to Web documents.)

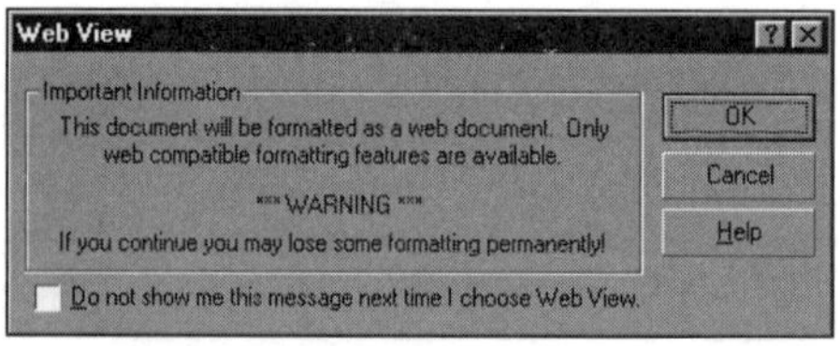

Figure 3-2: WordPerfect's scary warning box may appear. Click OK.

Now you have a Web-formatted WordPerfect document. You can type and format away to your heart's content, and be reasonably certain that whatever you see on WordPerfect's screen will be what your Web document looks like.

WordPerfect, however, is now in Web view, which means that it looks and works differently. The rest of this book is all about working on your Web-formatted document in Web view. For a brief discussion of what's different, see "Using WordPerfect in Web View" later in this chapter.

**Chapter 3: Creating, Editing, and Checking Your Web Files** 37

## *Converting WordPerfect documents*

Often, the fastest way to create a Web document is to convert an existing WordPerfect document. The more simply formatted the file is, the easier it is to convert. If the file has many indented paragraphs, or tabs and spaces that create white space, you may, however, lose all that formatting.

Here are the precise steps to follow to convert a humble WordPerfect document into a glorious, turn-of-the-millennium Web document:

1. **Create or load a regular WordPerfect file.**

   If possible, use WordPerfect heading styles for the headings in the regular WordPerfect file. (Select the heading, press Alt+F8, and double-click a heading style in the Style List dialog box that appears.) Feel free to use illustrations, bullets, or numbered lists in your document.

2. **Switch to Web view.**

   Click the Web view button (shown in "Click the button!" earlier in this chapter) or choose View➪Web Page from WordPerfect's Menu bar. If the button is grayed out, some image or other object probably is selected in your document. Click anywhere in the text of the document and try again.

3. **When the little warning box appears (refer to Figure 3-2 earlier in this chapter), click the OK button.**

4. **Choose File➪Save As (or press the F3 key) and save your file with a new name.**

   The Save As dialog box appears. In the File name box, type a new name for the file.

In Step 4, you don't save this file by choosing File➪Save, pressing Ctrl+S, or clicking the floppy-disk button in the Toolbar because, by doing so, you would replace the original file (which you probably want to use for other, non-Web purposes) with your new file, which has special Web features.

> **TIP**
> 
> If you must convert a WordPerfect document in which some uninformed person (someone who hasn't read *WordPerfect 8 For Windows for Dummies*) has used lots of spaces to position text or graphics, there is a way to salvage that positioning. After you convert the file to a Web-formatted WordPerfect document, format all text in the "Preformatted" style, as Chapter 8 describes, and then apply the original font(s) to that text using any of the WordPerfect customary font controls. This trick will work only for certain people in your audience: those who are using fairly new Netscape or Microsoft browsers and whose computers are equipped with your chosen font(s).

## Using WordPerfect in Web View

Whoa! What's going on here? You've switched to Web view, and now your WordPerfect screen is all gray and funky? Well, don't panic. (After all, you will probably be gray and funky someday, too.)

First, the gray part. Your document background is gray because gray is the exciting official standard background color for Web pages. (The color was chosen by a committee of engineers; what did you expect?) Most of the popular Web browsers today allow other backgrounds, and you certainly can change the background color of your document if you like (choose Format⇨Text/Background Colors).

Not only is your document a boring gray, but its formatting is more boring, too. The Web allows far less fancy formatting than the printed page does, so WordPerfect can't use all the formatting that it's normally capable of using. If you create your Web document by converting an existing WordPerfect document, WordPerfect finds the closest Web formatting that is available. Some stuff just doesn't translate.

Now comes the "funky" part: namely, the changes in the Toolbar (the bar on the screen that is full of buttons), the Property Bar (the bottom bar on the screen, which also is full of buttons), and the Menu bar. When you use a Web-formatted document, WordPerfect changes its menus and buttons so that you can do Web things — and *only* Web things — by using formats and features that are used on the Web. This change gives you quick access to tools that you may need, such as a Web browser, and ensures that you won't waste your time by making document edits that won't show up on the Web.

Figure 3-3 gives you a rundown of important buttons that are new or work differently in Web view.

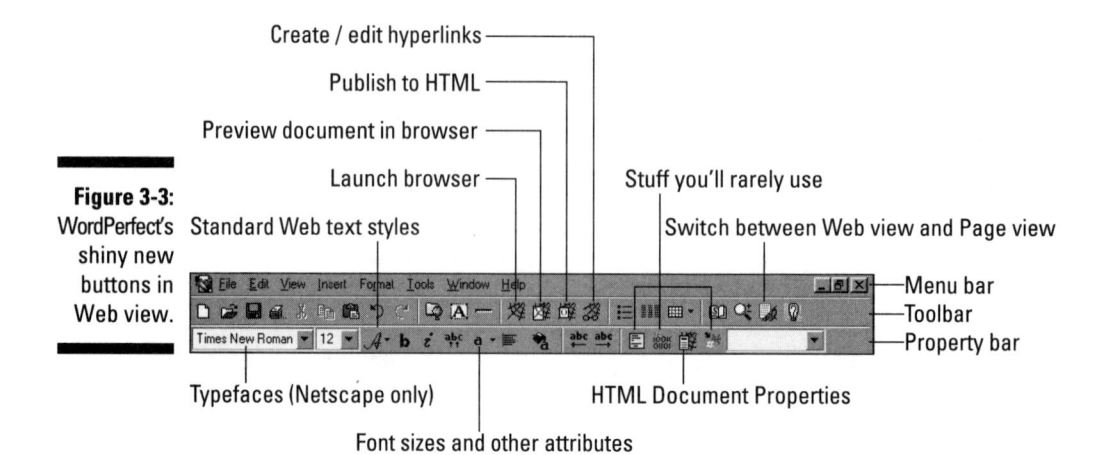

**Figure 3-3:** WordPerfect's shiny new buttons in Web view.

In WordPerfect 8, the bar right above your document window (the Property Bar) changes according to whatever you're working on at the time. If you have a graphic image selected, for example, the bar shows graphics-type buttons.

The chefs at Corel made a few changes in the standard menu items. Some of the most important changes are in the Format menu. Following are some of the changes:

- **Fonts:** Web documents don't have fonts in quite the same way that other documents have fonts. See Chapters 8 and 9 for the gory details on fonts.
- **Formatting for paragraphs, pages, lines, margins:** These formats are utterly gone. Web documents rely on standard styles to control formats, and things like pages have no real meaning. See Chapter 8 for details on standard styles.
- **Justification:** The Web offers fewer choices for justifying or "aligning" text: left, right, and center are your only choices.
- **Formatting text as HTML:** This new formatting option allows you to enter actual HTML codes, in case you want to do something special on the Web that WordPerfect can't do for you. Text formatted as HTML doesn't appear in your document, but instead acts as a command in the HTML language.
- **Text and background colors:** Color is important on the Web, so in Web view the Format menu provides a selection that sets the colors for normal text, hypertext, and the background of your Web document. (You may also set colors through a Property Bar button called HTML Document Properties.)

WordPerfect in Web view has many other peculiarities. Some are obvious (like the changes in the Format menu) and some are subtle. This book deals with all these peculiarities as they crop up.

# *Previewing from WordPerfect*

In Web view, WordPerfect gives you a pretty good idea how your document looks, but not . . . um . . . a word perfect one. You should still view your document in a real Web browser.

WordPerfect gives you a nice, shortcut preview approach: Click the View in Web Browser button in the Toolbar, shown in Figure 3-4. (If the button is grayed out, you probably have a graphic or some other nontext object selected in your document; click elsewhere.) If you prefer, you can choose View➪View in Web Browser instead.

**Figure 3-4:**
The View in Web Browser button.

———Really important button. Use it a lot.

Clicking the View in Web Browser button makes temporary HTML and graphics files from the Web-formatted document that you're looking at, launches your Web browser (if it's not already running), and loads the temporary HTML file into the browser so that you can preview the file before you publish to HTML.

*TIP*

When you preview your document this way, the links that you see in your Web browser do not work. The only way to test your links is to view the actual HTML file; see "Viewing Your Web Files in Browsers" later in this chapter.

## Saving Your Web Document

After you create your fabulous new Web document, be sure to save it for posterity by pressing Ctrl+S or choosing File⇨Save, just as you would for any other WordPerfect document. If you created your Web document by converting an existing WordPerfect file, press F3 to save the Web-formatted file under a new name so that you don't accidentally smoosh the original file.

You can name your document file anything you like. (Don't bother adding a three-letter extension to the end; allow WordPerfect to give it the usual .WPD ending.) You'll usually find life easier, however, if you use the same name that you intend to use for your HTML file. If you are creating your home page, I suggest that you call it `index`. In general, I suggest that the name be lowercase; have no punctuation, spaces, or characters other than letters or numbers; and be fewer than eight characters long.

## Publishing to HTML

WordPerfect calls creating an HTML file (together with its associated graphics and audio files) publishing to HTML. When you publish to HTML, WordPerfect spits a complete set of Web-ready files onto your disk, leaving your original WordPerfect document on-screen.

## Create a folder for your HTML files

Publishing to HTML in WordPerfect can create many files, and not getting them all mixed up is important. I suggest that you create a separate folder — called, say, website — for all your Web files. A good place for this folder is within WordPerfect's default folder — the one where it wants to put everything unless you tell it otherwise. The usual name for the default folder is MyFiles, which is on the hard disk where WordPerfect is installed.

You can create a folder for your HTML files by double-clicking the My Computer icon, double-clicking disks and folders until you open MyFiles, and then choosing File➪New➪Folder. Windows will create a new folder temporarily named "New Folder." The name will be highlighted, which means Windows wants you to type the folder name that you want to use (such as website) and press the Enter key. Do so.

TIP

If you publish to HTML repeatedly, consider setting up WordPerfect so that your website folder opens automatically whenever you save a file or publish to HTML. Choose Tools➪Settings; double-click Files; and in the Files Settings dialog box that appears, enter **c:\MyFiles\website** or whatever folder you intend to use in the Default document folder box.

## Publish to HTML

Publishing to HTML is easy, but doing it without complicating your life involves a little care. The following steps help keep the publishing task easy:

1. **Click the Publish to HTML button in the Toolbar.**

   If you prefer to use the Internet Publisher dialog box, choose File➪Internet Publisher and then click the Publish to HTML button there.

   The tiny Publish to HTML dialog box appears (see Figure 3-5).

2. **In the Publish to box, enter a filename and folder for your HTML file.**

   I suggest that you put your HTML files in the separate folder that you created in the preceding section. You might begin your entry in the Publish to box with C:\MyFiles\website and finish with the name of the HTML file, as shown in Figure 3-5.

   About that filename, I also suggest that to eliminate the risk of certain problems, you make your HTML filename lowercase; use no punctuation, spaces, or characters other than letters or numbers; and give it fewer than eight characters (yes, that's right — boring old DOS rules).

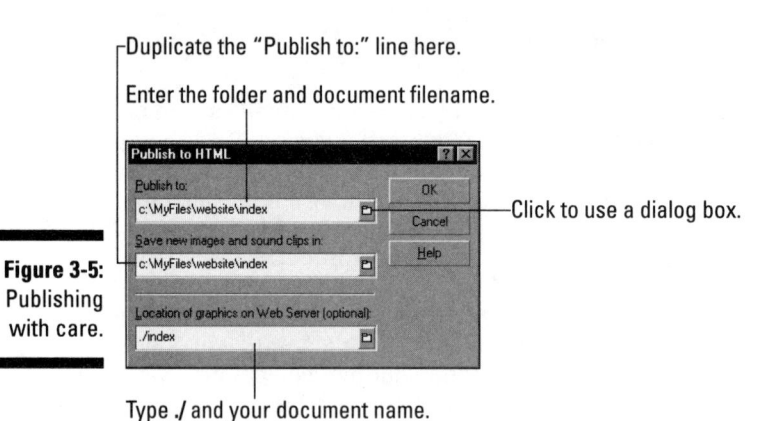

**Figure 3-5:** Publishing with care.

- Duplicate the "Publish to:" line here.
- Enter the folder and document filename.
- Click to use a dialog box.
- Type ./ and your document name.

After those eight characters, you could add .htm yourself, but I suggest that you leave it off; WordPerfect adds it for you automatically.

On some Web servers, you must use files with four-letter extensions (.html), not three-letter extensions (.htm). Your Web server provider can tell you whether this situation is true for you. If so, use the extension .html.

*WARNING!*

If you prefer choosing filenames and folders from a dialog box (as you do in the Save As dialog box) instead of typing them, you can click the file-folder icons shown in Figure 3-5. If you click one of these icons, WordPerfect displays a big dialog box (also named "Publish to HTML"), which looks and works exactly like the WordPerfect Save As dialog box that you already know and love.

 3. **If you have graphics or sound clips in your document, enter a folder name in the box called Save new images and sound clips in.**

(If you have no graphics, you can leave this box blank.)

*TIP*

As shown in Figure 3-5, I suggest that you simply duplicate the first line, which ends in the first name of your document, such as index. This approach creates a folder within the same folder as the .htm file, with the same name. If you publish a file named animals (animals.htm), for example, you create a folder called animals. This approach prevents you from accidentally overwriting the image and sound-clip files of another document.

The quickest way to name your folder is to copy text from the Publish to box. Select (highlight) the text in the Publish to box; double-clicking does the job if no spaces are present. Press Ctrl+C to copy the text. Press the Tab key to advance to the Save new images and sound clips in box and press Ctrl+V to paste the copied text. Press the Backspace key four times to delete the .htm characters, if they are present.

4. **If you have graphics, sound, or other media files in your document, enter their location in the Location of graphics on Web Server box.**

   (If you have no graphics, sound, or other media files, you can leave this box blank.)

   You need to write this location in a special way. I suggest you begin with the symbols ./ and end with the name that you use for your graphics folder. Figure 3-5, earlier in this chapter, shows an example. (This way of describing the location of your files is a form of "URL" called a "relative" URL — a form I recommend because it works on your PC as well as on the Web. For more on URLs, see Chapters 1 and 7.)

5. **Click the OK button in the Publish to HTML dialog box.**

   WordPerfect may tell you that your folder for images and sound clips does not exist and ask whether you want to create it. Click Yes if you are asked.

You now have an HTML file and a folder, both with the same first names, ready to be copied to your Web site. For more information on publishing to HTML when you have graphics in your document, see Chapter 11.

## Understanding what results from publishing to HTML

When you publish to HTML, WordPerfect usually creates more than one file. HTML documents that have graphics, audio, or other nontext stuff keep that stuff in separate files. Knowing where these files are is important, so that you can move them all to the Web server when you're ready to make them public. Here's what you get when you publish to HTML:

- Your HTML (.HTM or .HTML) file.
- A folder that conveniently holds associated graphics, audio, or other media files. If you followed the instructions in the preceding section of this chapter, the folder is in the same location as, and has the same name as, your HTML file.

When copying or moving files to your Web server, you must be careful to use exactly the same *tree* (hierarchy) of folders and files, and exactly the same file and folder names. Chapter 6 gives you instructions that help make the process easy.

## Part I: Web Weaving 101 with WordPerfect

# Viewing Your Web Files in Browsers

One of the funky things about all Web documents is that they look different depending on what browser or other program you're viewing them with. That behavior is not a flaw, it's intentionally designed into the rules of the Web to give Web surfers, not Web weavers, the ultimate control. The engineers at Corel understand that document appearances will vary, so even though they do a pretty good job of showing you what your Web document will look like, they also intend for you to check your work in actual Web browsers.

WordPerfect gives you two ways to check your work. The fast way to check appearances is to preview your document by clicking the View in Web Browser button. To test all the links or see how your files look in several browsers, you need to actually publish to HTML and load the Web files into a browser.

Before you expose your actual HTML file to the rest of the world by putting it on the Web, you really should see how it looks in at least one — and preferably several — actual Web browsers. People on the Web use a wide variety of browsers, and each browser displays your HTML file slightly differently. Also, the only way to check links from your document is to load the actual HTML file into a browser.

If you don't have another browser on your PC, consider obtaining and installing one. If that's not an option, see whether you can find someone who has a different browser, and take your Web files to that person's PC. I say "Web files" because you should test both your HTML file (the one that ends in .HTM) and the associated folder (the one with the graphics and audio files). Copy both the file and the folder to a floppy disk.

You probably are used to viewing Web documents by going online. When you're simply checking a file on your disk (called a *local file*), you don't need to go online. If your PC begins to go online automatically when you launch the browser (that is, if the PC begins dialing to your Internet service provider), you may want to cancel that action to save connect charges. Look for a Cancel button and click it. If your PC uses Windows 95 Dial-Up Networking software, for example, click the Cancel button in the Connect To dialog box that appears as the browser tries to go online.

You can open an HTML file in a browser in various ways. Not all methods work with all browsers, so if one doesn't work, try another. Here are some of the ways you can open an HTML file:

- ✓ **Double-click the HTML file.** If you have a properly installed browser, double-clicking the file should both launch your usual browser and load the file.

- ✓ **Enter the filename and location in the place where you would enter any URL in your browser.** In the Netscape Navigator Location box (right below the big buttons), for example, you might enter **D:\COOKING\SPINACH.HTM** and then press the Enter key.

- ✓ **Press Ctrl+O or choose File⇨Open; then enter the file location and name in the dialog box that appears.**

- ✓ **Drag the HTML file to the browser if the browser is already running.**

- ✓ **If the browser is not already running, and if you have a shortcut icon to the browser on your screen, drag the file to the icon.** The browser launches itself and loads the HTML file.

Now you can see your file exactly as it would look on the Web. If you find any problems, see the next section, "Editing Your Web File."

## Editing Your Web File

When you need to edit your Web file, you may wonder, "Just which file should I open?" After all, you have two possibilities to consider:

- ✓ You can edit the Web-formatted WordPerfect file, from which you published to HTML.
- ✓ You can edit the HTML file itself.

For most purposes, the better choice is to use the Web-formatted WordPerfect file, if you have one. For details, read on.

### Editing by using the Web-formatted WordPerfect file

If you have a Web-formatted WordPerfect file, use that file for editing. Open the file by choosing File⇨Open, make your changes, and save the file as you would any other WordPerfect file. Then publish the file to HTML, overwriting the original HTML file (and its folder). Figure 3-6 shows how the process goes.

*Note:* To replace your old files, make sure that you use the original HTML filename and folder name. WordPerfect asks whether you want to overwrite the existing file and/or folder; choose Yes.

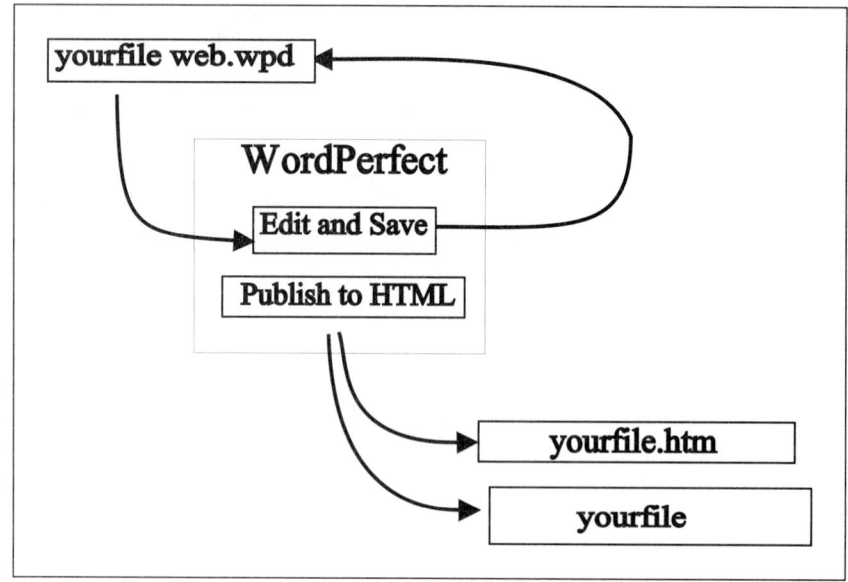

**Figure 3-6:** Edit your WordPerfect file and republish it.

Editing by using the Web-formatted file may seem to be a roundabout way to go, but it's usually a better choice than using the HTML file itself. In particular, if the Web-formatted file contains WordPerfect graphics, those graphics are easier to edit in that form than in the GIF form to which WordPerfect converts them when you publish to HTML.

## Editing an HTML file

After you create an HTML file, your natural inclination probably is to make your edits in the HTML file. You can do that, but first, read the last paragraph of the preceding section.

Besides your own natural inclination, another motivation for editing an HTML file directly is that someone might hand you an HTML file to update or to use as a model. If so, here's how to start from that existing HTML file (a file with a name that ends in .HTM or .HTML):

1. **Choose File⇔Open.**
2. **In the Open File-Suite 8 dialog box, select the HTML file that you want to load.**

   (HTML files end in .HTM.)

   WordPerfect displays the Convert File Format dialog box, which tells you that it's about to convert an HTML file.

3. **Click the OK button.**

*Note:* If someone copied the document that you're using from another PC or from your Web site, but forgot to copy the document's associated image files, the document's graphics may not appear. In their places, you'll probably see big, red `IMAGE NOT AVAILABLE` boxes. If so, you can still move, resize, and reposition those boxes; you just can't see the images. As long as your modified HTML file goes back in the folder where the original HTML file was, the graphics will work.

When you finish editing the Web-formatted document, simply publish to HTML again. Publishing to HTML replaces the HTML file that you originally opened.

In addition to publishing to HTML, choose File⇨Save (or press Ctrl+S). WordPerfect then displays several choices in the dialog box shown in Figure 3-7.

**Figure 3-7:** Choose wisely; choose WordPerfect format.

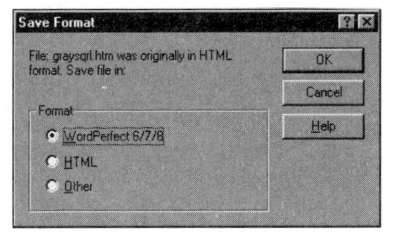

Following is what each of those various choices does:

- **WordPerfect format:** This option creates a Web-formatted document file, which is a good file to have for doing future edits. Be especially sure to choose this option if you have added any WordPerfect graphics (clip art, TextArt, WPG files, or drawings) to the document during editing.

- **HTML format:** This option is the same as publishing to HTML, except that WordPerfect does not, with this choice, create new graphics files for the Web. It only updates the HTML file to include edits to text and repositioning or resizing of graphic boxes. Any changes you might have made to the images themselves won't appear in the HTML document. Choose this option if you have simply edited the text and don't want to bother with all the gobbledygook in the Publish to HTML dialog box.

- **Other:** This option makes a copy of the Web file in some other format besides WordPerfect or HTML. Choose this option if, for instance, someone in your organization wants to use your Web document but uses another word processor.

# Chapter 4
# Weaving a Simple Site from Scratch

*In This Chapter*
- Creating a simple home page
- Creating and linking other pages
- Setting colors and background
- Creating and editing headings and normal text
- Creating an e-mail link for return mail
- Saving your Web documents
- Publishing to HTML
- Testing your results
- Saving and editing files

*E*ngage your warp drive and tune up your woofers! No, it's not time to do audio, it's time to start weaving an engaging warp and a fine-tuned woof on the Web. This chapter shows you how to build a simple homestead in hyperspace: a basic Web site, complete with links.

## Creating a New Web File

The first step in creating your Web site is creating a home page, which is the starting point for people who visit your Web site. The following two-step procedure gives you a blank Web document that you can use for your home page (or any other page, for that matter):

1. **Clear the decks for action.**

    Click the New Blank Document button (the white-paper-with-folded-corner icon) at the left end of the Toolbar.

2. **Switch to Web view, if you're not in Web view already.**

    In Web view, a new document's background is gray and the Toolbar sports a bunch of buttons with spiders' webs on them.

    If the background isn't gray, you're not in Web view. Click the Change View button near the right end of the Toolbar.

    Bingo! You have a fresh, untrammeled Web document in tasteful gray. Chapter 3 describes other ways to create a Web document (such as using the Internet Publisher dialog box), if you don't care for using a Toolbar button.

## Getting Your Heading Together

Respectable documents of any sort never go out in public without wearing a heading, and Web pages are no exception. A heading is not required but is a good idea. The Web allows for many levels of headings — more than you'll ever use. You can choose to head your document with any level of heading you want to use; you don't have to start with Heading 1 if you think the type is too big. Here's how to get your heading together:

1. **Type a line of text for your heading.**

    This heading is important, so make it as short and yet as descriptive as possible for your visitors. Don't use a heading like My Web Site, which both states the obvious (it's a Web site) and fails to provide any real information (who the heck are you?).

2. **Select (highlight) the text that you just typed.**

    Selecting the text before formatting is a good habit to get into. It prevents mistakes when applying fonts, colors, and other text attributes. For applying Web styles, however (which is what you're about to do) you don't really need to select the text, as long as your "insertion point" (blinking cursor) still is somewhere in the line that you just typed.

3. **Click the Font/Size button (the big script *A* near the left of the WordPerfect Property Bar).**

    A drop-down menu appears. Figure 4-1 shows both the button and the menu.

    Alternatively, you can press F9 or choose Format⇨Font to use the Font dialog box.

4. **Click Heading 1.**

    If you are using the Font dialog box, you'll find Heading 1 in the Styles (HTML elements) section; click the OK button after you click Heading 1.

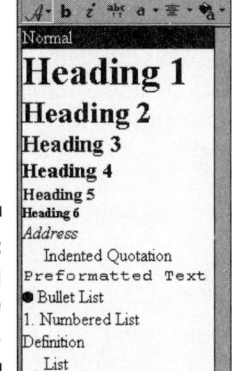

**Figure 4-1:**
Click the big
*A* to choose
a text style.

You now have a top-level heading for your document in exciting black. WordPerfect also uses this heading as your Web document's title — the text that appears in the top bar of your visitor's browser.

- See Chapter 6 for more information on the importance of headings and titles.
- See Chapter 8 for more information on headings and other standard text styles for Web documents.

# Typing Normal Text

Click at the end of your heading and press the Enter key. This action switches you to regular (nonheading) text called Normal. Normal also is a style that you can apply (just as you apply a heading) by selecting text, clicking the Font/Size button, and choosing Normal from the drop-down list. (Refer to Figure 4-1, earlier in this chapter.)

The first text below your top heading is your big chance to tell the visitor what your Web site or organization is about. (As the saying goes, try to "say it in 25 words or less!") That text should get the most important points across in as few words as possible, without repeating your top heading. At this point, if you have a top heading and introductory text, your document should look a bit like Figure 4-2.

**Figure 4-2:**
Get your
main point
across
quickly.

See Chapter 6 for more information about introductory text.

*TIP:* You can use different typefaces (fonts), just as you do in regular WordPerfect documents, but probably only Netscape and Microsoft browser users will be able to see them. Likewise, you can choose type sizes, but the sizes that result aren't exactly the point sizes you specify.

## Adding Second-Level Headings

If you find it easy to think in outline form, and especially if you have a great deal to say on a page, feel free to add second-level or even third-level headings to break your text into different topics. Lower-level headings use progressively smaller type.

Just as you did to create your top heading, simply type the text for your heading, select it, click the Font/Size button in the WordPerfect Property Bar, and then choose Heading 2 or any other heading level from the drop-down list.

A home page shouldn't be as long and full of headings as a research paper, though. If you are doing a home page for your religious organization, for example, having second-level headings for brief paragraphs on "What We Believe" and "You Are Welcome to Attend" is okay, but plan to put the histories of martyrs and philosophers on separate pages, with links from the home page.

## Changing Background and Overall Text Color

If you're unimpressed by that battleship-gray background and basic-black text, WordPerfect allows you to choose nicer colors. Follow these steps to choose colors for your background and text:

1. **Choose Format➪Text/Background Colors.**

    A charming HTML Document Properties dialog box appears, displaying the lovely Text/Background Colors page.

    WordPerfect's Department of Redundancy Department, as usual, provides several other ways to get to this dialog box. See Chapter 9 for the other ways.

2. **Click the button to the right of the label** Regular text.
3. **In the lovely multicolor box that appears, click a dark color.**

Chapter 4: Weaving a Simple Site from Scratch  **53**

Basic black is always fashionable and still one of the best choices for readability.

4. **At the bottom of the dialog box, click the button to the right of the label** Background color.

5. **In the multicolor box that appears, click a light color for your document background.**

   White is always in good taste. Choose the white square at the far right end of the top row for a white background.

6. **Click the OK button.**

*TIP*

Light background colors with dark type tend to be easier on the eye than the other way around.

For more information on background colors and on using background images, see Chapter 9.

## Changing the Color of Your Headings

Uniformly colored type certainly is classic, elegant, and easy to read, but for a little excitement or fun, some selected color is called for. Use the following steps to apply a different color to your headings. You can use the same procedure to color any selected text (except hyperlink text), whether the text is a heading or not.

1. **Select the heading (or whatever text you want to color).**

2. **Click the Font Color button (a paint bucket spilling on an *a*) in the WordPerfect Property Bar.**

3. **In the multicolor box that appears, click a color.**

   Colors that you have used recently are in the top row.

You probably shouldn't choose bright blue. That color is often used for hyperlinks, and people may mistakenly think that they are supposed to click the blue text.

## Aligning (Justifying) Text

Why stick with left-justified text? You can make text on your Web page justify left, right, or center. The entire document can have a single justification, or you can have different justifications for each heading or paragraph. For a home page, try center justification of your headings.

**Part I: Web Weaving 101 with WordPerfect**

To justify the entire page the same way, follow these steps:

1. **Press Ctrl+Home to move your cursor to the top of your document.**
2. **Click the Justification button in the WordPerfect Property Bar to choose an alignment.**

   To identify the button, look for one of the symbols shown in Figure 4-3.
3. **Click Left, Right, or Center in the drop-down list that appears, shown in Figure 4-3.**

Figure 4-3:
Justifying your work.

To justify a heading or paragraph by itself, select that heading or paragraph and then follow Steps 2 and 3.

Figure 4-4 shows a down-home example that you might have created by following the steps this far. The figure shows a home page with centered first- and second-level headings, black body text, and barn-red headings on a brown-egg background. (Trust me on the colors!)

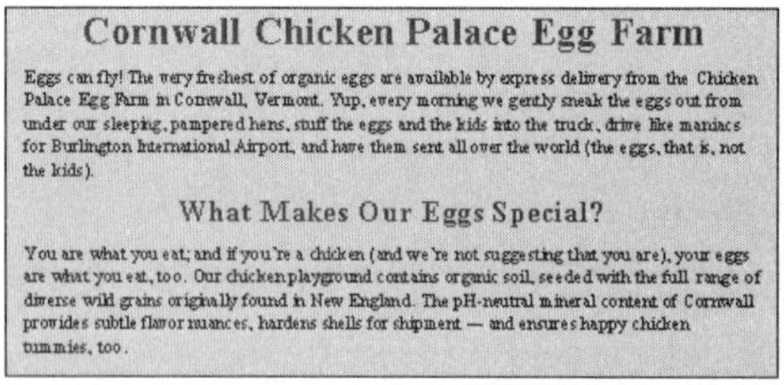

Figure 4-4:
The egg-farm home page.

# Adding a Line and a Bulleted Table of Contents

One job of a home page is to provide clickable links (hyperlinks) to the rest of the Web site. You can use ordinary text in the middle of a sentence for links — an approach that the founders of the World Wide Web would approve of. In the egg-farm example in the preceding section (refer to Figure 4-4), the words *express delivery* in the first sentence could be a link to a page on how to order via express delivery. You can also provide links to other documents in the form of a table of contents. Most home pages use the table-of-contents approach.

The following steps give you a table of contents separated from the body text by a horizontal line. You could create the actual clickable links right now, but waiting until you actually create the pages to which you'll be linking makes more sense.

1. **Click at the bottom of the page (or press Ctrl+End); then press Ctrl+F11 to create a horizontal line.**
2. **Press the Enter key to start a new line.**
3. **Create a heading for your table of contents.**

   Type **Contents** or **On This Site**, for example. Then, with your cursor still in the line that you just typed, click the big *A* button at the far left end of WordPerfect's Property Bar and choose Heading 2 from the list that drops down.
4. **On separate lines below the heading, type one-line descriptions of the other pages.**

   See Figure 4-5 for examples. Press Enter at the end of each line, including the last one.

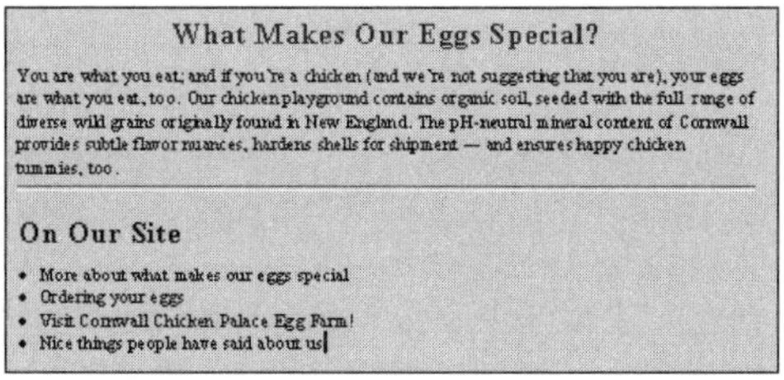

**Figure 4-5:** Adding a table of contents, but no links yet.

> **What Makes Our Eggs Special?**
>
> You are what you eat; and if you're a chicken (and we're not suggesting that you are), your eggs are what you eat, too. Our chicken playground contains organic soil, seeded with the full range of diverse wild grains originally found in New England. The pH-neutral mineral content of Cornwall provides subtle flavor nuances, hardens shells for shipment — and ensures happy chicken tummies, too.
>
> **On Our Site**
>
> - More about what makes our eggs special
> - Ordering your eggs
> - Visit Cornwall Chicken Palace Egg Farm!
> - Nice things people have said about us

5. **Format the descriptions as a bulleted list.**

   Select all the descriptions, click the Font/Size button (the big *A*) at the far left end of the WordPerfect Property Bar, and choose Bullet List from the list that drops down.

# *Adding the Date and Your Signature*

To be a responsible Internet citizen, you should give your Web pages the date on which the page was last updated and a way to contact you. Usually, this information goes at the bottom of the page. In WordPerfect, being responsible is actually fun! Read on for details:

1. **Click at the bottom of the page (or press Ctrl+End); then press Ctrl+F11 to create a horizontal line.**
2. **Press the Enter key to start a new line.**
3. **Type** Created by, **your name, and your electronic-mail address.**

    Now here's the fun part: Press the spacebar after the electronic-mail address. Suddenly, your e-mail address turns into a hyperlink! WordPerfect automatically turns e-mail addresses into *mailto* hyperlinks. A mailto link is a link that, when it is clicked upon by your Web visitor, launches an e-mail program with your address already filled in so that the visitor can send you a message.

4. **Type the words** Last updated on **and the date.**
5. **Format the line in the Address style.**

    Click the Font/Size button (the big *A*) at the far left end of the WordPerfect Property Bar and choose Address from the list that drops down.

(Okay, so adding this obligatory address was only moderately amusing, not exactly fun.) You don't have to use address style just because the line contains an address; you could use Normal style instead. Address style is simply conventional for this purpose and is actually useful when an address has several lines, because it eliminates space between lines.

## Previewing Your Work

WordPerfect makes it easy to check your work in Netscape (or whatever browser is installed as your usual browser in Windows 95). Simply click the cobwebby-looking View in Web Browser button near the center of the WordPerfect Toolbar. As shown in Figure 4-6, the picture on the button looks like a document caught behind a web. Alternatively, you can choose View➪View in Web Browser. Either way, WordPerfect launches your browser (if it's properly installed), which displays a temporary version of what your final Web HTML document will look like.

**Figure 4-6:** Click this button to see what your document will look like when it grows up.

The cobwebby-looking View in Web Browser button is supposed to look like a document caught behind a web.

## Saving Your Work

Choose File➪Save (or press Ctrl+S) and save your file. To make publishing to HTML easier later, I recommend using the short, simple name `index` for your home page. (WordPerfect adds the extension of `.wpd` for you, so leave the extension off.) For other pages, I suggest using names that have eight or fewer characters (letters or numbers) and no spaces or punctuation.

What you are saving is a Web-formatted WordPerfect document that you can use for editing, not the HTML document that you need for the Web. WordPerfect doesn't create the HTML file until you publish to HTML.

## Publishing to HTML

*Publishing to HTML* is WordPerfectese for "creating the files that actually go on the Web." When a document looks good and you have saved it, perform the following steps to create the HTML file (and possibly other files) to be copied to your Web server's computer:

1. **If you haven't already done so, create a special directory for your Web files.**

   Here's one way: Double-click the My Computer icon in Windows, double-click disks and folders until you open the Corel MyFiles folder, and then choose File➪New➪Folder. Type the folder name that you want to use (such as `website`) and press the Enter key.

2. **Click the Publish to HTML button in the Toolbar.**

   The Publish to HTML dialog box appears (see Figure 4-7).

3. **In the Publish to text box, enter a filename and folder for your HTML file.**

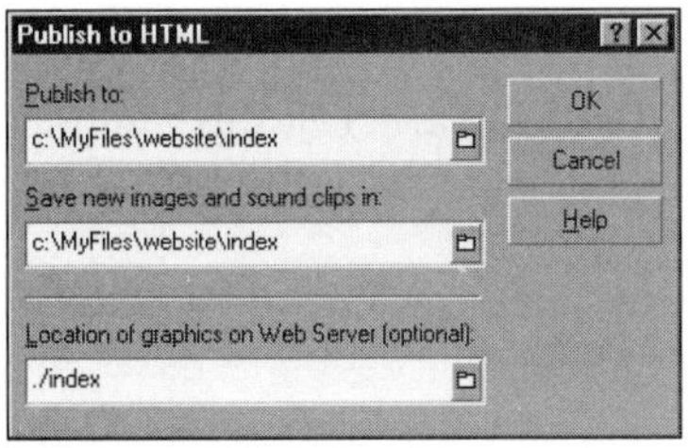

**Figure 4-7:** The name `index` often is useful for home pages.

For a home page, I suggest that you use `index` as the filename. WordPerfect automatically applies the extension .HTM to the file when you click the OK button.

> **TIP:** On some Web servers, you must use files that have four-letter extensions (`.html`), not three-letter extensions (`.htm`). Your Web server provider can tell you whether this situation is true for you. If so, add your own extension of `.html`.

You can click in the white areas of the Publish to HTML dialog box to type the names and folders, or you can click the file-folder icons to use dialog boxes that look and work much like the familiar WordPerfect Save As dialog box.

This chapter hasn't suggested that you use any graphics, so you need not worry about the Save new images and sound clips in box. But if you've gone wild and added graphics on your own, use Figure 4-7 as a guide. See Chapter 11 for details.

**4. Click the OK button in the Publish to HTML dialog box.**

WordPerfect may squawk that folders do not exist and ask whether you want to create them. Click Yes.

## Creating Another Page

If you are reasonably happy with your simple home page, the time has come to create one or more additional pages for your Web site. Choose one of your topics from your table of contents for this new page, and follow the same procedure that you did to create a home page. (You don't have to close your home-page document first; just start a second document.)

Start with "Creating a New Web File," earlier in this chapter. Then add headings, normal text, and a signature, as you did for the home page. Unlike the home page, this page's initial text doesn't need to be as short and to the point, and it doesn't need a table of contents.

When you finish editing, save your file with a name of eight characters or fewer (as described in "Saving Your Work," earlier in this chapter), but don't bother publishing to HTML yet.

Now that you have two documents to link, why not take a minute to add a link to the home page, as described in the next section?

## Linking the New Page Back to Home

Clicking your heels three times and saying, "There's no place like home" may work in Oz but is not a particularly effective way for your visitor to return to your home page. Give your visitor a return-to-home link at the top or bottom of the page. (Unlike heels, a hyperlink needs to be clicked only once.) If you put this link at the bottom of the page, put it above the signature line.

Here's how to create the link:

1. **Type a line that says** Return to Home Page **or something similar, using the Normal text style.**

    Actually, any text style works for hyperlinks. Normal just looks better for this purpose.

2. **Select the text that you typed.**

3. **Click the Hypertext button in the Toolbar and select Create Link from the drop-down menu that appears.**

    The Web Link Properties dialog box appears.

4. **Type** index.htm **in the Document text box.**

    Make sure that you include the .htm part; you're linking to an HTML document.

5. **Click the OK button.**

*Warning!* Do not click the file-folder icon at the right end of the Document text box. Clicking the icon will display a dialog box for choosing what file to link to. If you use that dialog box, you end up with local-file links that work on your PC but not on the Web!

*Note:* If, when you published your home page to HTML, you gave the file the four-letter extension .html, substitute .html for .htm in Step 4.

## Publishing Your New Page to HTML

Publish your new page to HTML just as you published your home page: by clicking the Publish to HTML button. (Refer to "Publishing to HTML," earlier in this chapter.) The Publish to HTML dialog box appears. In the Publish to

## Part I: Web Weaving 101 with WordPerfect

box, I suggest that you enter the same folder that you used for your home page (such as `C:\MyFile\website\`), but not the same filename. Figure 4-8 shows an example for a document named "resume."

**Figure 4-8:** Putting a second document in the same website folder as the home page.

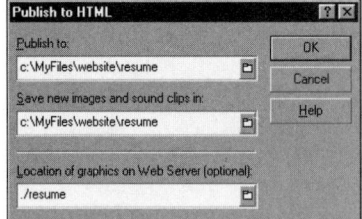

If you have already saved your new page as a WordPerfect document — say, `resume` — WordPerfect suggests the filename `resume.htm` for your HTML document. Go ahead and use that name. As always, I suggest that you make sure that the filename is lowercase, with eight characters or fewer, and with no punctuation. In this case, you've already used `index.htm` for your home page, so don't use that name or the name of any other existing file in your folder.

## Linking the Home Page's Table of Contents to the New Page

Now that you have at least one other document besides your home page, you're ready to start wiring up that table of contents on your home page. Here's how to turn your plain-vanilla table of contents into a spiffy clickable table of contents:

1. **Open the WordPerfect home page file (`index.wpd`, not `index.htm`), if it's not already open.**

    If the home-page document is still open in WordPerfect, just switch to it. (Click Window in the Menu bar; then choose `index.wpd` from the bottom of the menu.)

2. **In the table of contents (the bulleted list), select the line of text that you want to link to your new page.**

3. **Click the Hyperlink button (web-with-links icon) in the Toolbar and choose Create Link from the drop-down list.**

    The Web Link Properties dialog box appears.

Chapter 4: Weaving a Simple Site from Scratch    **61**

4. **In the Document text box, type the name of the new HTML file that you're linking to (such as** `resume.htm`**) — nothing more.**

   Because the HTML file that you're linking to is in the same folder as the home page, don't specify the folder. The Document text box in Figure 4-9 shows how you would link to a file named `order.htm`.

5. **Publish to HTML and replace your original HTML home-page file.**

   You're an expert in publishing to HTML by now, so I won't repeat the instructions. (No? You're not? Okay — refer to "Publishing to HTML" earlier in the chapter.) Just make sure that you publish to the original folder and filename (`index`, for a home page) so that the new HTML file replaces the old one.

As you create additional documents for your site, link them from the home page's table of contents, too. Now you have a simple but working set of Web documents for your site.

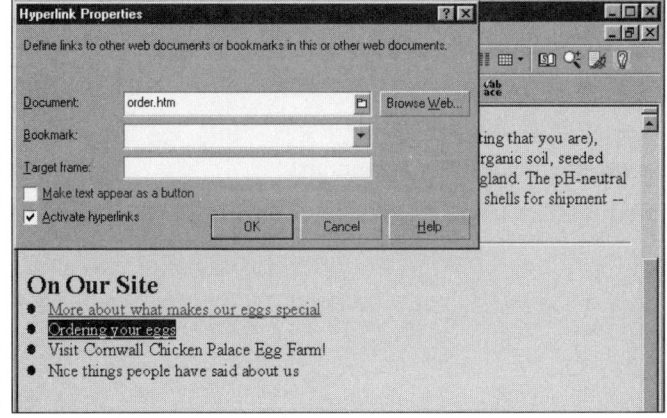

**Figure 4-9:** Linking "Ordering your eggs" to the order page, `order.htm`.

## Testing Your Results

To test your links and see how the document set works together, open your home page (`index.htm`) in your browser. Here's how to open a home page or any other HTML document in your browser:

1. **Launch your browser, if it's not already open.**

   Click the convenient Browse the Web button in the Toolbar, which is available in Web view in WordPerfect. The button's icon is a simple spider's web (with nothing stuck in it).

   If your PC starts to dial out, click the Cancel button in the dial-up software's dialog box; you don't need to go online yet.

2. **Press Ctrl+O.**

      Typically, a dialog box of some sort will appear.

   3. **Enter the location of the** `index.htm` **file that you created.**

      You might enter **D:\MyFiles\website\index.htm**, for example.

   4. **Review your work, and try clicking your links to make sure that they work.**

      If the links don't work properly, see the detailed discussion of hyperlinks in Chapter 7.

## Editing Your Pages

To edit your pages, you can open either the Web-formatted WordPerfect document (the WPD file) or the HTML file. See Chapter 3 for a discussion of the pros, cons, hows, and whys, but the short story is this:

   1. **Open your Web-formatted WordPerfect document (WPD file) or HTM file.**
   2. **Edit the file.**
   3. **Save the file (as a WPD document).**
   4. **Publish to HTML and replace your earlier files.**

# Chapter 5
# Brewing Web Documents with Java

*In This Chapter*
▶ Choosing whether to use Barista
▶ Sending to Barista
▶ Printing slide-show presentations
▶ Putting Barista documents on your Web site

Now for something completely different: a word processor with not one, but two completely different ways to create Web documents. WordPerfect gives you these options for creating Web documents:

✔ Publishing to HTML
✔ Publishing to Barista (which uses Java)

The rest of this book is about publishing to HTML, which is what you do to create conventional Web documents. That leaves the question, "Who is this Barista person, anyway; why does he drink java; and why should we publish to him?" If I recall correctly, Barista is either Spanish for *lawyer* or part of a staircase. Neither interpretation appears to shed much light on the problem of publishing Web pages, however, so I am forced to drop the fascinating question of name origin and get to the point.

*Barista* is Corel's technology for creating Web pages that look almost exactly like your original WordPerfect document. One motivation for using Barista is that you don't have to fret (much) about special formatting for the Web — just make a WordPerfect document and publish it.

Figure 5-1 shows a document published to Barista. Notice the neat margins on all sides and the use of varying width columns for layout.

**Part I: Web Weaving 101 with WordPerfect**

> **TECHNICAL STUFF**
>
> ### Barista and Java: Lawyers on coffee?
>
> Barista uses Java. As you have undoubtedly read, Java is the latest thing on the Web; it promises (if I recall correctly) to end world hunger, balance the U.S. national budget, and make really fab Web pages. Java is a programming language. People who write Java are, in effect, creating little programs that do stuff in people's Web browsers.
>
> When you publish to Barista, you make Web pages that, when downloaded to a browser, tell the browser to download Corel's special Java programs from your Web site. These programs then interpret all the words and the formatting data in your Web document and more-or-less exactly reconstruct the original appearance of your WordPerfect document. For this scheme to work (as of this writing) not only must your document (along with any graphics files) be on your Web site, but also, the entire collection of Corel Java programs must be there.

**Figure 5-1:** One Barista advantage: using columns of varying width for layout.

Barista documents do not word-wrap (or anything-wrap). Barista documents, can, however, boogie! See the following section for ways to make them boogie.

## Deciding to "Do the Barista"

Barista is fine for creating precisely laid-out Web documents that look pretty much like regular WordPerfect documents. Barista can reproduce WordPerfect formatting like nothing else can (without involving special non-standard viewers and other gizmos). See "Sending to Barista" later in this chapter for instructions on creating normal Barista documents.

The better excuse for using Barista, however, is to create slide-show style presentations. Frankly, Barista makes much more sense for publishing Corel presentations than for publishing WordPerfect documents. Nonetheless, all you need to do is create a multiple-page WordPerfect document with text and/or graphics and then use Barista to create a boffo slide show of one slide per page. See "Printing to Barista" later in this chapter for more information.

If the Macarena — I mean, Barista — is so great, why publish Web documents any other way? Following are some of the current drawbacks of publishing to Barista:

- Barista documents can be seen only by people who use Java-capable Web browsers, including recent releases of Netscape Navigator and Microsoft Internet Explorer.
- Fonts are limited in Barista to Times Roman, Helvetica, and Courier New. Anything else is translated into one of these fonts.
- The first time your visitor downloads from your site, the browser takes eons to download and display the result, even for a small document. The browser must download a whole bucket of Java to get rolling (a failing that I can sympathize with).
- If your document contains WordPerfect graphics (WPG files, or WordPerfect drawings, TextArt, or ClipArt), it is large and, therefore, slower than snail sweat to download.
- You must upload a whole bucketload of Corel Java files and folders to your Web site (more than 800KB), and put them in the same folder as your document. If you aren't allowed much Web-site space, this requirement could be a problem.
- In early releases of WordPerfect 8, at least, I have encountered flakiness in various forms: mistranslation of ordinary symbols, such as bullets and dashes; strange PC behavior if things go wrong while I'm browsing the document; peculiar handling of graphics; and failure to display in some copies of Internet Explorer.

Barista is young, and Corel is working to improve it, particularly in the key area of eliminating the long initial downloading time. Until Corel succeeds, you probably should use Barista only if

- The Web document must have exactly the same formatting as an existing WordPerfect document.
- You get poor results from converting a regular WordPerfect document to a Web document by switching to Web view.
- You want a timed, sequential presentation of pages, as in a slide show, with groovy fades between slides and sound effects.

Otherwise, give Barista a miss until it's a little more ready for prime time.

> ## Setting page size
>
> Page size is not normally something you would have to think about for Web pages, because text in normal Web pages wraps to fit the browser window. When you use Barista, however, text doesn't wrap. To create a new page size, do the following:
>
> 1. Choose Format⇨Page⇨Page Setup to display the Page Setup dialog box.
> 2. In the Size tab, click the New button to display the New Page Size dialog box.
> 3. In the Name text box, enter a name (such as Web page).
> 4. Set Width to about 6 inches, Height to about 7 inches, and click OK.
>
> You are returned to the Page Setup dialog box.
>
> 5. Click Apply to see the result in the document window of WordPerfect.
> 6. If you like the result, click OK in the Page Setup dialog box.
>
> Once you have followed these instructions and created a named page size that's suitable for the Web, you can use the page size again and again. To reuse the page size, do the following:
>
> 1. Choose Format⇨Page⇨Page Setup to display the Page Setup dialog box.
> 2. In the Size tab, click the named size in the Page information list, then click OK.

# Sending to Barista

To publish to Barista, you normally send your document to Barista. If you want to create a sequential, timed slide-show presentation, see "Printing to Barista" later in this chapter. Otherwise, follow these steps:

1. **Use a regular document in the normal view.**

    Do not use a Web-formatted document (a document in Web view).

2. **For best results, press Ctrl+Home and then set page size to something appropriate for a Web page.**

    If you're not already familiar with the page size controls, see the sidebar, "Setting page size."

3. **Choose Format⇨Margins.**

    The Page Setup dialog box appears, displaying the Page Margins tab.

4. **Set Left to 0.25 inches.**

    You can use any margins you like, but small margins are best for the Web.

5. **Click the Make all margins equal check box.**
6. **Click OK.**

7. **Save your file with File⇨Save (or Ctrl+S).**
8. **Choose File⇨Send to⇨Corel Barista.**

   The Send to Corel Barista dialog box appears, as Figure 5-2 shows. You could change the settings in this dialog box, but using the settings that WordPerfect suggests really is the best choice. Change the filename, if you like.

**Figure 5-2:** Accept WordPerfect's suggestions when sending to Barista.

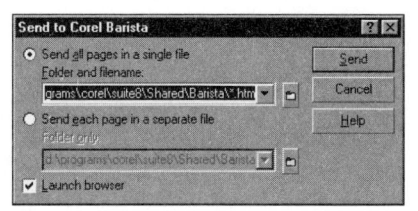

   If you change the settings, you must publish to a folder that contains all the Barista class files and all the folders. If you want to publish to another folder, you must copy all files and folders from `c:\programs\corel\suite8\Shared\Barista\` to that other folder before you can test your document on your PC.

9. **Click Send.**

   WordPerfect busies itself preparing your document and puts up a temporary dialog box proudly telling you so. After much head-scratching, it launches your browser so you can view the result.

10. **Examine the result in a Java-enabled Web browser.**

    Assuming you have left the Launch Browser checkmark enabled, as Figure 5-2 shows, WordPerfect launches your browser and attempts to load the document (see the tips later in this section).

Recent releases of both Netscape Navigator and Microsoft Internet Explorer for Windows 95 are Java-capable. (To enable or disable Java in Netscape Navigator 3.01, choose Options⇨Network Preferences to display the Preferences dialog box. In the Languages tab, click the Enable Java and Enable JavaScript check boxes. In later versions, choose Edit⇨Preferences and look in the Advanced category of settings.)

If you publish a multiple-page document, Barista creates a navigation bar, as Figure 5-3 shows. The bar appears at the top and bottom of each page. (A single Web file can have multiple pages when you use Barista.)

**Figure 5-3:** Barista's navigation bar appears in multi-page documents.

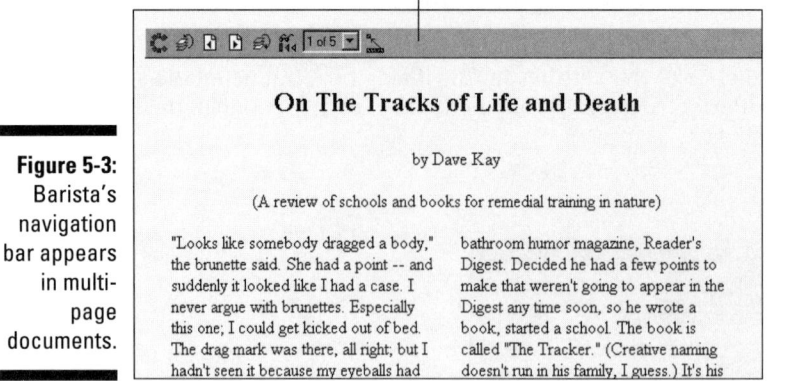

- ✓ Sending to Barista can be like waiting for Godot. After Navigator launches, unless you allow it to connect to the Internet (which it wants to do, for no particularly good reason), it may sit there and pout for many minutes before suddenly cheering up and deciding to display your document. Perhaps *Barista* is Flemish for *brief tantrum* or something.

- ✓ If, after editing your document and republishing it, the document doesn't seem to reload, try clearing your cache (if you know how) or closing Navigator and then reopening it.

## Printing to Barista

Barista, like any good coffee-drinking lawyer, can also get down and boogie. Barista can create a slide show with wild and crazy fades, automatic sequencing, and even sound effects.

To give yourself a complete fit of the giggles, add music. I like adding the `dance.au` file on the Corel WordPerfect Suite 8 CD-ROM. (The file is `d:\corel\suite8\sounds\dance.au`, assuming your CD drive is `d:`.)

Instead of merely sending to Barista, follow these steps to print to Barista:

1. **Choose File⇨Print.**

   The Print dialog box sashays into view.

## Chapter 5: Brewing Web Documents with Java    69

2. **Click the selection box labeled Current Printer and choose Corel Barista from the list that appears.**

3. **Click the Properties button.**

   The Corel Barista Driver Properties dialog box appears on the scene.

4. **In the Destination tab, chose Save to Disk.**

5. **In the Special Effects tab, click the Slide Show check box.**

6. **Specify what kind of show you want using the following controls:**

   *Transition on.* Choose Time for automatic, timed sequencing; choose User Input to allow the person who views the show to advance the slides.

   *Type.* Choose any interesting-looking special effect for the transition (fade) between slides.

   *Direction.* Some special effects, such as Beam In, have directions; choose one.

   *Speed.* Choose Slow, Medium, or Fast.

   *Time.* If you're using a timed show, enter **1000** for each second that you want to display the slide (page).

   *Sound.* To amuse your visitor between slides, choose an AU audio file. (Don't forget to copy the file to the Web site later.)

   *Document sound.* To accompany your presentation with sound, choose an AU file.

7. **Click OK.**

   You return to the Print to Corel Barista dialog box.

8. **Click Print.**

   After a while, the Save As dialog box appears.

9. **Save your document, with the extension .htm, in the Corel Barista folder (**c:\programs\corel\suite8\Shared\Barista\**).**

Go make a cup of coffee; then come back and launch your browser. Open the HTM file in the browser and — unless you allow the browser to go online, as it wants to — take a nap by the keyboard. When the music starts, wake up and enjoy the show.

## Putting Barista Documents on Your Web Site

Chapter 6 goes into the details of putting documents on your Web site. When you publish Barista documents, the process is a little different.

For conventional HTML documents, this book tells you to put on your Web site (a) the HTM file itself and (b) a bunch of graphics files. The same is true for Barista documents, except that you must copy from `c:\programs\corel\suite8\Shared\Barista\` all the following files and folders:

- The HTM file that WordPerfect creates (ending in .htm)
- Any folder that has the same name as the HTM file (which contains the graphics and audio files that WordPerfect creates)
- Any JPG or GIF files that are in the Barista folder along with the HTM file (the most recent ones, if you've been doing much publishing)
- All the Barista files and folders (files that end in .class and all folders in `c:\programs\corel\suite8\Shared\Barista\`)

The Barista stuff takes a while to upload. Take a nap by the keyboard and wake up when you hear the train whistle. (No kidding. The program on the book's CD-ROM for copying to your Web site, WS_FTP, plays a train sound when it's done.)

# Chapter 6
# Serving Up Your Files to the Web

*In This Chapter*
▶ Getting a Web server
▶ Getting a document on the Web
▶ Copying files to the server
▶ Managing files and folders
▶ Getting visitors to your Web site

*I*f you're like me, the term *Web server* conjures up an image of a specialist in a Beijing duck restaurant. (I'm being treated for my problem, however.) In fact, a Web server is a program that lives on a computer that has a permanent connection to the Internet. Like a 24-hour pizzeria, a server's job is to deliver Web files, steaming-hot and fresh, to anyone who requests them, day or night. You need one. (A Web server, that is. And if you're going to manage a Web site, you may need a 24-hour pizzeria, too. And a box of fudge brownies.)

## Getting a Web Server

How do you get a Web server? Shout "*Garçon!*" in Chinese? No, actually, the answer is: Don't get one at all! Or, more precisely, if your organization doesn't already have its own Web server, the best way for you to get one is to share space on a server. The easiest server on which to get space probably is the one that is run by your Internet Service Provider — the nice organization that you pay money to each month to listen to busy signals when you try to get on the Net.

Most Internet service providers (ISPs) have Web servers that they share with all their users — often, for free or a modest monthly charge. Call your provider, send e-mail to the provider, or look at the provider's home page on the Web to find out what servers are available. If your Internet Service provider doesn't offer a Web server, take your Web business elsewhere! Rent space from any of hundreds of other providers anywhere in the world. You don't have to change your Internet Service Provider to do so.

You can buy Web-server software for your PC, but it won't do you much good. Web servers nearly always need a computer that is permanently running and connected to the Internet, has enough power to spend time serving data to the Internet, and has a higher-speed connection to the Internet than the dial-up connection that most PC users use. Web-server software also can be complicated to set up and maintain. Only if your organization has a technical staff and a budget for the necessary computer, software, labor, and Internet service should you consider having your own Web server on the premises.

If you need an ISP for your Web site, the publisher of this book (IDG Books Worldwide — soon to be galaxy-wide) has arranged a special deal for you with a growing ISP called Mindspring Enterprises, Inc. Mindspring has waived certain fees for readers of this book. This book's CD-ROM contains software for registering with these folks, plus electronic documentation on their services. Mindspring offers a variety of pricing schemes, and on their Web site they provide special goodies for doing "forms" — a vital Web site feature this book discusses in Chapter 22. You can read more about them at `http://www.mindspring.com`.

## How a Document Gets on the Web

Web servers put files on the Web only when those files are in specific locations: specific folders or directories on a specific disk drive connected to the server's computer. To put documents on the Web, you copy the documents to one of the folders.

If you're using a shared Web server, you have your own folder. A password system makes sure that only you can add files to or remove files from your folder. You also can create and use folders within that folder (create a directory structure).

You need the help of your Webmaster to put documents on the Web. Wherever a Web server exists, you'll find a Webmaster to . . . well, master that unruly Web server. After you make the requisite obeisance (involving money, cookies, or Hostess-brand cream-filled cupcake-like food products), your Webmaster gives you the information that you need to connect to the server. The Webmaster also must set up your folder on the server. (If your Web server is on your organization's premises, you may be able to just give the Webmaster a diskette that contains your files, rather than put them on the server yourself.)

## Copying Files to Your Server

Whenever you create a Web document that uses graphics or sound, you have several files to copy to the Web server, not just one. You have an HTML file (which ends in .HTM or .HTML), and you have graphics or audio files. You must carefully copy all these files to the Web server if the document is to work properly.

### Cloning: the key to success

The key trick to copying your Web files is cloning. (Don't be sheepish about cloning; this book makes it as easy as possible.) If you clone your Web site — that is, create on your Web site exactly the same files and folders that you have on your PC — everything works well.

The recommendations in this book for filenames, folders, and hyperlinks make adding a document to your Web site easy. If you create a document called `yourdoc`, for example, and if you follow this book's suggestions, you only have to copy the following HTML file and folder:

- `yourdoc.htm` (the HTML file)
- `yourdoc` (the folder that contains graphics and audio files for `yourdoc.htm`; it exists only if you used graphics or audio in your file)

See Figure 6-1 for an example of the sort of simple directory and file structure that you will have on your PC and on your Web site if you follow this book's recommendations.

If you don't clone — if you change filenames or folders, or change the organization of folders between your PC and the Web server — things get tricky fast. The next thing you know, your hyperlinks or graphics don't work. If, for example, `contacts.htm` on the PC is renamed `contact.htm` or `contacts.html` on the server, links to that file fizzle. Also, if the `.htm` files are put inside the graphics folders instead of outside, their links to their graphics files do not work.

**Figure 6-1:**
Clone your Web folders and files.

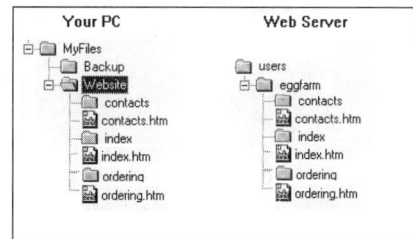

You can use a different name for your main folder on the server (`eggfarm`, as opposed to `Website` in Figure 6-1) than you do on the PC. Names matter only within that main folder. The name of your main folder — your account name, for example — probably is assigned by the Webmaster.

If you have a site that has many documents (and you feel that you understand all this stuff), you may want to change to a folder-within-folder tree structure, which allows you to create files without having to worry about unique names for each file. As long as the server uses the same structure that you use on the PC, everything should work fine.

## *The copying procedure*

The actual procedure for copying your files and folders depends on your situation. Following are the most common situations:

- If your organization owns its own Web server, ask your Webmaster how to copy files and folders to the server.
- If you use America Online, CompuServe, or some other commercial network service, you have to go online and look up the procedure for putting files on that service's Web server.
- If you connect to your Web server by dialing up an Internet Service Provider (ISP), you need a program called FTP. Because you were clever enough to buy this book, you have such a program on the accompanying CD-ROM.

The following discussion is all about using FTP software to put your files on a Web server.

### *Installing and setting up WS FTP*

First, buy a box of fudge brownies. I find this step to be critical to all following steps. If you can't eat fudge brownies, play some extremely soothing music.

Fudge brownies in hand, the first step is to install some software. On this book's CD-ROM is a program called WS FTP (Limited Edition) or WS_FTP95 LE. See the back of this book for installation instructions, and have a brownie.

Now start the program. A Session Properties dialog box appears, wanting to know a whole bunch of technical stuff, as shown in Figure 6-2.

Check your Internet Service Provider's (ISP) Web site for instructions on how users can transmit files to the ISP's Web server, or see whether you can get a technical-support person on the phone.

## Chapter 6: Serving Up Your Files to the Web 75

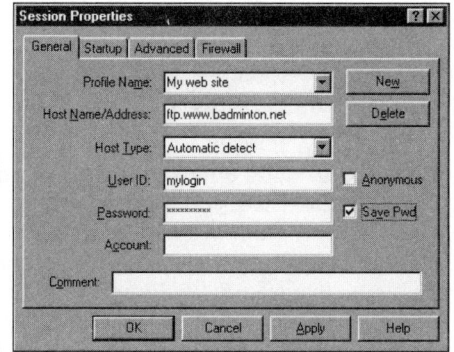

**Figure 6-2:** Wading through the geekspeak to victory.

Mindspring, the ISP on our CD-ROM that offers readers a special deal on Web sites, provides some instruction for customers on how to use WS FTP for uploading Web files. Customers can find their Web Help desk at http://webhelp.mindspring.com.

When you have found the instructions for putting files on your Web site, fill out the blanks in WS FTP's Session Properties dialog box, as follows:

- **Profile Name.** This box can contain anything that you want. I suggest that you use My web site, as shown in Figure 6-2.

- **Host Name/Address.** The entry in this box has to come from your ISP's Web site or from its Webmaster. The entry probably begins with ftp and ends with the Internet name (domain name) of the ISP whose Web server you are using, but don't guess at it. If you have your own domain name (such as www.blah.org), you will probably need to enter that domain name; in any event you will probably use a different Host Name/Address from those of other, less fortunate folks. (Such is the price of glory.)

- **Host Type.** Usually, if you leave this box alone (leaving the entry as Automatic detect, that is), everything is just ducky. Your Webmaster or your ISP's Web site may have something to say about the type of host that you have, however, in which case, choose that type from the drop-down list that you get when you click the box's down-arrow button. If you can't find the type specified in the instructions you received from your ISP or Webmaster, try using Automatic detect.

- **User ID.** For the entry in this box, check your ISP's Web site for instructions, or e-mail your Webmaster and ask, "What user ID should I use for FTPing to my Web folder?" Your user ID may be the same as your login, logon, or user name — the name that is associated with your account at your ISP. (If you don't remember your login, you probably can find it in whatever software does the dialing-up on your PC.) Your user ID also may be your e-mail address.

- **Password.** The entry in this box usually is the same as the password you use to connect to your account at your ISP. Check your ISP's Web site for instructions, or e-mail your webmaster and ask, "What password should I use for FTPing to my Web folder?" If you don't remember your login, you'll have to check with your ISP — probably by phone.

- **Save Pwd.** Click this check box to put a check in it if you want WS FTP to remember your password. Otherwise, you'll be prompted for a password whenever you connect to your Web site. If other people use your PC and dial-up connection, and you want to keep them from being able to fool with your Web site, leave Save Pwd unchecked.

- **Account.** You usually can get away with leaving this box blank. Ask your Webmaster whether you need a separate account name, but if he or she seems to be confused by the question, try leaving this box blank.

If you don't find the answers that you need to fill out the Session Properties dialog box on your ISP's Web site, try e-mailing the following message to `webmaster@your ISP's address` (such as `badminton.net`):

> Dear Webmaster: I intend to use an FTP program (WS FTP) to transfer files to my Web folder. I don't seem to be able to find the information that I need on your Web site. Can you please answer the following questions? What host name or address, host type, user ID, and password should I use? Do I need, in addition, to specify an account, and if so, what account should I use? Finally, what's the name of the folder that I should use on the Web server? Thanks, and I owe you a fudge brownie. Fondly, Me.

Open your box of fudge brownies and eat one an hour until you get an answer. (Or put on your headphones and play your soothing music loud enough to drown out your own grumbling.) If the Webmaster takes a while to respond, at least you won't care.

### Connecting to your Web-site folder

After setting up the Session Properties dialog box, click the OK button to connect to your ISP. (If the Session Properties dialog box is not on-screen, click the Connect button in the bottom-left corner of the WS FTP window.) Your PC probably launches your dial-up software automatically. If not, launch it yourself the same way that you do when you use your Web browser or e-mail software.

WS FTP may prompt you for a password at this point. Enter the password that your ISP or its Webmaster gave you. If all goes well, a bunch of technical goop flashes by at the bottom of the WS FTP screen, and one or more folders appear in the right pane of the WS FTP window.

Your objective is to open your personal Web site folder in the right pane. You can open a folder (if you have permission to open it) by double-clicking it.

## Chapter 6: Serving Up Your Files to the Web 77

From this point on, finding and opening your personal folder on the Web site is, unfortunately, another of those things for which you may need explicit instructions from your Webmaster or from a technical-support person at your ISP. You may need to open some folders before you find your own. Check your ISP's Web site for information on how the user folders (user directories) of the Web site are organized. If you don't find any instructions, following is the way things usually work (with lots of "maybes" and "probably").

- ✔ The program may list a lot of folders in the right pane (it may take a while before this list appears). If so, these folders probably are the ones for your fellow users of the Web server. Look for a folder that matches your user or account name at that ISP. Scroll down the list until you see your folder. Double-click that sucker to open it, and you're ready to start transferring files.

- ✔ If the program doesn't list a bunch of folders in the right pane, your folder probably is already open. Inspect the box labeled Remote System at the top of WS FTP's right pane. If your folder is open, that box should contain your folder name.

### Copying files and folders

If you succeeded in opening your Web-site folder (the box labeled Remote System at the top of WS FTP's right pane displays your folder's name), congratulations! Give yourself a fudge brownie, if you haven't eaten them all already; it's all downhill from here.

WS FTP makes it easy for you to clone from your PC to your Web-site folder — that is, to duplicate the exact file and folder structure. Copying everything that you want takes only a couple of button clicks. Following are the specific steps to take:

1. **Make sure that the left pane of WS FTP displays the folder on your PC where you keep your HTML Web files.**

    The box labeled Local System at the top of that window should display something like `C:\MyFiles\website` or whatever your folder is. If not, click the ChgDir button just below the Local System window and enter the proper folder description in the Input dialog box that appears.

2. **Select whatever HTML file(s) and associated folder(s) you want to add to your Web-site folder.**

    To select multiple files or folders, drag across them with the mouse or Ctrl+click them. To copy a single home-page document (and its associated graphics/audio files) named `index`, for example, click `index.htm` and then Ctrl+click the `index` folder, as shown in Figure 6-3. To copy all your Web-site files and folders, select them all. (Don't, however, highlight disk drives: the icons labeled a, b, c, d, and so on.)

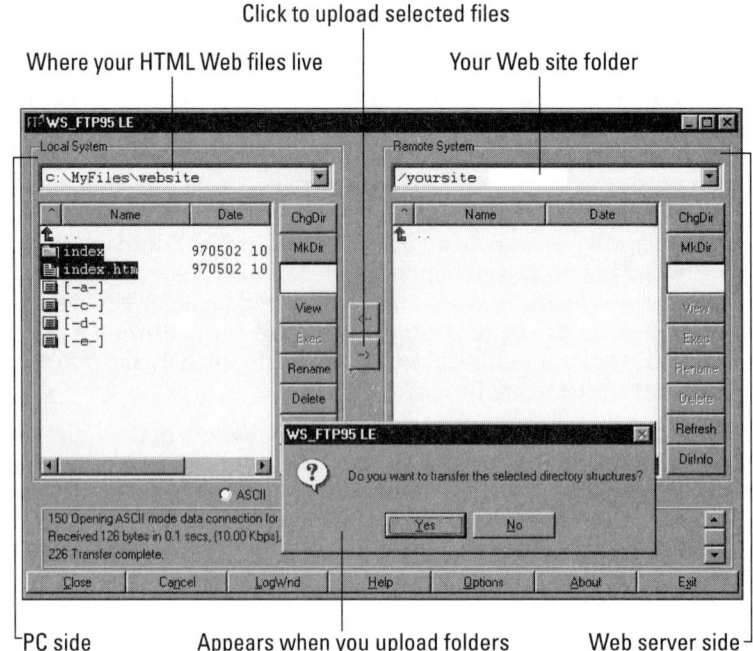

**Figure 6-3:**
A click of the button uploads everything that you select.

Callouts on figure:
- Where your HTML Web files live
- Click to upload selected files
- Your Web site folder
- PC side
- Appears when you upload folders
- Web server side

3. **Click the right-arrow button between the two windows in WS FTP (refer to Figure 6-3).**

   A WS FTP dialog box appears.

4. **In the WS FTP dialog box that appears, which asks** `Do you want to transfer the selected directory structures?`**, click Yes.**

   WS FTP takes a few seconds to transfer everything, during which time things flash by. Enjoy the show. You're done when your files appear in the right pane.

5. **Click the Exit button in the bottom-right corner of the WS FTP window.**

   Guess what — your files are now on the Web! Fire up your Web browser and take a peek.

Unless you purchased your own domain name (`www.me.com`), your URL (address) is something like `www.yourprovider.net/users/yourfolder`. Have another brownie.

> **TIP:** The absolutely safest procedure is to always copy your entire set of HTML files and folders from the PC to the Web-site folder. If you have many big files, however, that process gets terribly slow. The next-best solution is to always copy an entire document: an HTML file and its graphics/audio folder.

## Managing Files on Your Server

After a while, your Web-site folder begins to look a lot like my desk; it contains old stuff that should be thrown away, good stuff, stuff that should be put in a different folder, and so on. WS FTP can help you keep a tidier Web site.

When you are connected to your Web-site folder, the buttons to the right of the right pane of the WS FTP window allow you to delete files, rename files, or to add or remove folders (directories) at your Web site. Here's how to navigate the folders and use those buttons:

- To delete a file, click it and then click the Delete button.
- To rename a file, click the file and then click the Rename button. The Input dialog box appears. Enter the new filename.
- To add a folder within the folder that is currently displayed in the right pane of the WS FTP window, click the MkDir button; then enter the folder name in the Input dialog box.
- To open a folder on your site, double-click it.
- To go to the next-higher folder, double-click the green arrow at the top of the right pane.
- To move to a different folder, click the ChgDir button; then enter a new folder in the Input dialog box that appears.
- To remove a folder, first delete the files within it; then double-click the green arrow at the top of the right pane to see the folder icon. Click the folder icon; then click the Delete button.

Some servers insist that your HTML files must end in .html, not .htm. If you discover that this is the case for your server, you can use WS FTP's Rename button to change the ending to .html on your Web site. (And be sure to change any links in your Web pages that refer to .htm files.)

Changing things in your Web-site folder can be risky business; files are linked, and you risk causing hyperlinks or graphics to malfunction. Here are a few precautions:

- Go online, check all your documents, and test the links in your Web site after changing any files or folders there.
- If you delete or rename an HTML file, make sure that no other document on your site still links to it; otherwise, someone will click that link and get an error message. If your site has a document with a link to that deleted or renamed file, you need to open the document in WordPerfect, delete the link or edit it to point to the new filename, republish to HTML, and recopy the file to your Web site.

- If you delete a graphics file or a folder that contains graphics files, make sure that none of the remaining documents use that file or folder.
- If you rename any file or folder, change any other documents that contain links to that file (or to a file in the folder).

## Using index.htm for Home Pages and Folder Indexes

As the song "A Boy Named Sue" said so well, names are important. Your Web site can look more professional if you give your home page (and certain other documents) the distinguished name `index.htm` (or `index.html`). This choice of name is best done when you publish to HTML in WordPerfect, not when you click WS FTP's Rename button to rename your home page.

*Note:* This `index.htm` stuff is true for most Web servers, but not all. It depends on how the server is set up. If you named your home page `index.htm` and don't get the following results, feel free to use another name.

How does using `index.htm` make your site look more professional? Well, when you view the home page of some businesses, the URL (address) that you type in your browser usually doesn't look like `www.fooble.com/blah.htm`, right? No, the URL goes only as far as `www.fooble.com`. You don't have to type the home page's filename because (a) the Web weaver named the home page `index.htm`, and (b) most Web servers are designed so that if the URL doesn't give a document, the server looks in the folder for a file named `index.htm` (or `index.html`) and delivers that file. So by naming your home-page file `index.htm`, your visitor won't have to remember (or type) as much stuff.

You can use the same trick if you want to help people go directly to some folder on your Web site without going through your home page. Within your main folder, create folders for each particular category, such as `cats` or `dogs` on a veterinary Web site. In each folder, put a file, named `index.htm`, that provides hyperlinks to the other documents in that folder. This file acts like a miniature home page. Your visitor types `www.critturs.com/cats` to see the cat site (`index.htm` in the `cats` folder).

Apart from this `index.htm` stuff, another reason exists for adding folders. If several people are creating files for your Web site, using separate folders for each person's particular area allows everyone to use any filenames they want without overwriting everyone else's files.

**Chapter 6: Serving Up Your Files to the Web** 81

# Getting Visitors

"If you build it, they will come" (from the movie *Field of Dreams*) is a philosophy that apparently can get you visited by dead ballplayers. But will this philosophy get you live visitors on the Web? Oddly enough, it just may — after a fashion. If you build your site with Web search engines in mind, visitors eventually will find you. You may not attract the crowds that you would like to have, but people will come. To get the crowds, you also need to do some publicity footwork.

## Getting visitors through search engines

Some people find the idea to be a bit creepy to think about, but as you sleep, dozens (if not hundreds) of powerful programs, called search engines, are scanning nearly every single Web site on the Internet and making notes about what each site's documents contain. Creepy though they may seem to be, these engines are forces for good: They help Web surfers find the documents that interest them most.

Some popular search engines, directories, or robots are AltaVista, BigBook, Bigfoot, Excite, HotBot, Infoseek, Lycos, Magellan, OpenTextIndex, WebCrawler, and the famous Yahoo!. (Click the Net Search button in Netscape Navigator to see a large list of search engines.) If you haven't visited a search engine with your Web browser, you should. Two good starting places, which represent different approaches to Web searching, are Yahoo! (http://www.yahoo.com) and AltaVista (http://www.altavista.digital.com). Visitors can type a word or a phrase of interest, or choose a category of information, and the search engine returns lists of Web pages that fill the bill.

A search engine won't find your Web site immediately. It often takes days or even weeks for a search engine to find your new site. If you register your site with individual search engines and directories, you make sure that the site is listed as soon as possible. When these engines eventually discover your site, you can make their job more effective by paying attention to three elements of your pages: headings, titles, and keywords.

### Listing or registering your site

To make sure that your site is not ignored, register it with as many search engines and directories as possible. Go online with your Netscape browser, and click the Net Search button (or choose Directory⇔Internet Search) to see a list of these services. (If you use Microsoft's Internet Explorer, click Search.) Click the link to each service listed, and look for instructions on how to list or register your URL with that service.

## Headings

Headings are one part of your page that a search engine pays attention to. Some engines scan headings just because they are headings; others simply look for the first text in the document, which is likely to be your first, top-level heading.

Try to make your headings — especially the first heading on your home page — as descriptive as possible in as few words as possible. Try not to insert line breaks into your heading, because some search engines stop reading at the first line break. WordPerfect uses the first heading on your page as the title of the document unless you create a special title.

## Titles

A *title* is a description of a Web page that appears in the title bar (the top bar) of a browser. Search engines routinely read, record, and display the words used in titles, so for that reason alone, having a title on a Web page is a good idea.

Titles also are convenient for the visitor; they appear in bookmarks, and they appear when a browser user clicks the Go option in the browser to return to a previously viewed document. A title should be descriptive enough to help visitors remember what the page is about, even when they're not looking at your site. A poor title for the peach-pie pages of your Web site is "Peach"; a better title is "Iowa Express Pies: Peach Pies to Go."

If you think that the first heading in your document pretty much sums up the document, you don't need to do anything special to create a title. WordPerfect uses that heading to create the title for you. Often, however, the heading isn't really what you want for a title. To make a better title, follow these steps:

1. **Choose File⇔Properties.**

    The HTML Document Properties dialog box appears, displaying the Title tab.

2. **Click the selection labeled Custom title.**
3. **Type your title in the text box provided.**
4. **Click the OK button.**

    Now your title appears in the title bar of WordPerfect, just as it will in your visitor's browser.

## Keywords

When people use a search engine, they tell the engine to look for certain words or phrases that they are interested in (*keywords*). If your Web page — especially your home page — contains those words or phrases, the engine

## Chapter 6: Serving Up Your Files to the Web

lists your page among all the others that use those words. If a user submits many words, and if your page has all those words, the search engine generally lists your page near the top.

One way to make sure that your Web site is listed near the top is to make sure that the text on your home page contains all the words and phrases that your audience is interested in. Unfortunately, it's a pretty tough writing job to include all those words and phrases in the form of meaningful sentences without writing an enormous wall of boring text!

A better way to include all those words and phrases is to put them in the form of Meta text, which doesn't actually appear on your page and, therefore, doesn't have to be in sentence form. Here's how to include Meta text:

1. **Choose File**⇨**Properties.**

    Alternatively, right-click your document (anywhere but a graphic) and choose Properties from the shortcut menu that appears, or click the HTML Properties button in the Property Bar (the button near the left end of the bar, which looks like a calculator caught in a spider's web).

    The HTML Document Properties dialog box appears.

2. **Click the Advanced tab.**

3. **In the Meta info text box, type the following magical incantation:**

    ```
    <META HTTP-EQUIV="Keywords" CONTENT="keywords and phrases ">
    ```

    In place of the text *keywords and phrases*, type a list of the words and phrases that you think your prospective visitors may be searching for. Put commas and spaces between your words and phrases, as in the following example for an apple-pie-recipe page:

    ```
    apple pie, pastry, pastries, tart, dessert, fruit, baking
    ```

    Your list of keywords and phrases can be as long as you like. Include a variety of words that mean nearly the same thing, such as *video*, *cassette*, and *videotape*. Don't put quotes around individual words; put them around the list, as shown in Step 3.

4. **Click the OK button.**

Search engines are an important feature of the Internet for attracting visitors. Here are a few ways that you can help people who are trying to find you with search engines:

- WordPerfect's thesaurus can help you find additional words to list as keywords. Press the Esc key if you're viewing the Title dialog box at present; then type a word anywhere in your document, select the word, and press Alt+F1 to launch the Thesaurus. If you do that procedure for *pie*, for example, WordPerfect may list *pastry, quiche, tart,* and *turnover.* Click <u>C</u>lose to exit the Thesaurus and Ctrl+Z to undo your typing.

- If the word for multiple objects (such as *pastries*) isn't spelled like the word for a single object (*pastry*), include both words; otherwise, the single-object word usually will do.

- Use words that describe both actions and objects, such as *flying* and *airplane*.

- Don't repeat words in the hope that the search engine will list your site before someone else's site. Repeating *pie* 30 times does not make your site the number-one pie site.

- Besides putting keywords in your Web pages, try to make the first words of text that appear on your page highly descriptive. Search engines often display the initial text of a document, so initial text that reads *Worldwide express delivery of the finest fruit pies!* is more helpful to the viewer than *Everyone loves pie, the most traditional of American desserts.* If you start your page with an image that uses "alternate" text, that text may be what is shown.

## Links to your site and other publicity

If you want many visitors, you have to do more than register your site and build a Web site that shows up well in a search engine. One effective approach to publicity is to ask Web weavers of related sites to create links to your pages. You usually can reach the right person by looking for links to the Webmaster and then sending the Webmaster e-mail.

Most Webmasters ask that you return the favor by linking to their sites. You can put links to other sites directly into your text wherever those links seem to be appropriate. Remembering where these links are (so that you can test them periodically and keep them up to date) is a pain, however. A more manageable approach is to create a special page that contains links to related sites.

Other common ways to publicize your site include the following:

- Put your URL in your e-mail signature. If you're running a site for an organization, ask your colleagues to do likewise.

- Put a brief, one-time announcement in related mailing lists or newsgroups that you subscribe to, if other subscribers may truly be interested. Don't hype the site, and don't repeat the announcement; just provide the basic facts, or you'll turn people off.

✔ Advertise your site in any print advertisements, business cards, or other promotional literature that you distribute.

## Becoming www.me.com

If you share space on your Internet Service Provider's Web server, your address (or URL) shows it. If your provider, the Badminton Internet Access Company (BIAC), has an URL of www.badminton.net, your URL probably is something like www.badminton.net/users/jones. That URL indicates that your files are in the users folder of BIAC, inside the jones folder.

A URL like the preceding one carries no shame, but it doesn't put you up there with the big boys and girls. If you'd rather have an URL that's on par with, say, Microsoft's (www.microsoft.com), doing so is not hard — just a little expensive. You need two things: your own domain name (say, rutabagas.com) and a virtual Web address (also called a virtual domain) which is what allows you to become www.rutabagas.com. Your Internet Service Provider probably can get you everything that you need, for a service fee.

Domain names are registered with an organization called InterNIC. If you know your domain number (information that you can get from your provider), you can register a domain name yourself on the Web at http://www.internic.net. InterNIC charges $100 for two years at present. This procedure does not, however, automatically turn your Web site into www.rutabagas.com. You must also pay your provider to give you what is called a virtual domain or a virtual Web address so that you can tell people to go to www.rutabagas.com.

# Part II
# Text Tricks

### The 5th Wave　　　By Rich Tennant

"Hold your horses. It takes time to build a home page for someone your size."

## In this part . . .

Basic typing and formatting of text is easy enough in WordPerfect, if you're not particularly fussy about the results. You can "just do it" and, most of the time, your regular WordPerfect skills will see you through.

If, however, you want to use basic Web features like hyperlinks, if you care about the font, size, color, and position of your text on the page, or if you want a nice background or color scheme, you have to pick up a few new skills. Without knowing some of the peculiarities of Web text and WordPerfect, getting your text to look and work the way you want is a bit like doing origami with live bait.

# Chapter 7
# Helpful Hyperlinks

### In This Chapter
▶ Understanding what hyperlinks can do
▶ Using automatic hyperlinking
▶ Creating hyperlinks from text or graphics
▶ Linking between your Web pages
▶ Linking to pages elsewhere on the Internet
▶ Linking to specific locations within a document
▶ Using hyperlinks to view, download, or e-mail
▶ Editing and removing hyperlinks
▶ Testing hyperlinks
▶ Dealing with hyperlinks that have gone bad

*W*ithout hyperlinks (links, to their friends) the Web would fall apart. Moral decay would set in. Nothing would be connected, so there would be no Web in World Wide Web, and the Web would become a World Wide Bunch of Stuff, or WWBS. (Some cynics say that WWBS is what the Web is anyway, but good Web weavers try to prove them wrong.)

Hyperlinks are, of course, those helpful things that you click to move around on the Web, and they take different forms. Hyperlinks may look like underlined and colored text, buttons, or images with or without colored frames around them. Sometimes, hyperlinks are *clickable graphics:* cool-looking navigation controls and other images that link to different documents from different areas of the image. This chapter discusses the first three forms: text, buttons, and images. Clickable graphics (also called *image maps*) are a more advanced topic, so see Chapter 20 for information.

## How Hyperlinks Help

Hyperlinks have many uses. The three usual uses for hyperlinks are to perform jumps of certain types:

- To jump to other places on the Web
- To jump from page to page on your Web site
- To jump to specific places within a page

Sometimes, you don't jump anywhere when you click a hyperlink. Instead, you may do any of the following things:

- Start an e-mail message
- Download a file to your disk
- View a picture or movie
- Play sounds or music

You create all these different hyperlinks by using the same commands and dialog boxes in WordPerfect. The differences are just a matter of entering a slightly different link address.

As you create your hyperlinks, keep the following tips in mind:

- You don't do the underlining, boldfacing, or coloring yourself for a hyperlink. That appearance change happens automatically when you create a hyperlink.

- Don't say "Click here." People already know that they are supposed to click hyperlinks. Instead of using the words *Click here* for your hyperlinks, put hyperlinks in text that tells people something that they don't already know. Instead of typing **Click here for the events schedule** (here is hyperlinked), type **Our events schedule lists our trade shows and seminars for the next six months**.

- Just the text, ma'am — when you hyperlink from text, don't include the spaces before or after the text. Don't include ending punctuation unless you are hyperlinking the entire sentence.

- Don't use headings or large type for hyperlinks; the result usually is ugly and distracting. Hyperlink from normal text below the heading instead.

- If you use graphics for a hyperlink, provide something called "alternate" text in case the visitor's browser has graphics turned off. See Chapter 11 for instructions on creating "alternate" text.

# Using Automatic Hyperlinking

WordPerfect goes out of its way to make everyday hyperlinking to documents on the Web easy. To create a link to a document on the Web, just type its URL (its address), like this: www.snobble.com, followed by a space. WordPerfect automatically converts the text to a hyperlink to that Web site!

With automatic hyperlinking, the text in the document is the same as the URL — the text actually reads *www.snobble.com,* for example. If you prefer the text to read something like *Snobble Buggywhip Corporation,* you can edit the text — but first read "Editing and Removing Hyperlinks" later in this chapter.

Automatic hyperlinking works for other kinds of links, too. Any word that begins with `www`, `http`, or `ftp` is converted to an appropriate link. Text that begins with `mailto:` or that takes the form of an e-mail address (`___@___.___`) is converted to a mailto link. Mailto links are hyperlinks that, when clicked, launch the visitor's e-mail software and start a new e-mail message, with the given address filling out the To line.

If this automatic hyperlinking feature becomes a problem, you can turn it off. Choose Tools⇨QuickCorrect to display the QuickCorrect dialog box, and click the QuickLinks tab. At the bottom of the QuickLinks tab, click to clear the check box labeled Format words as hyperlinks when you type them.

# Creating Hyperlinks from Text or Graphics

Any text or graphic on your Web page can become a hyperlink when it grows up. Just follow these steps to turn a text or graphic into something you can click on to view another document:

1. **To use text for a hyperlink, select it; to use a graphic, click it.**

   Leading or trailing spaces in the text selection are best avoided.

2. **Choose Tools⇨Hyperlink.**

   Alternatively, for text, you can click in Web View the Hyperlink button in the Toolbar (the top set of buttons in WordPerfect). The Hyperlink button looks like a spider's web contemplating the purchase of a pair of granny glasses (actually, a pair of chain links). After you click the button, choose Create Link from the drop-down list.

   No matter which approach you take, the Hyperlink Properties dialog box appears (see Figure 7-1).

**Figure 7-1:**
Enter the name of the HTML file to which you're linking.

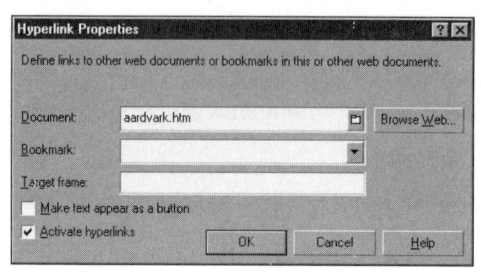

3. **Enter the filename of the HTML destination document (where the link is to) in the Document box.**

    If the destination document's file is in the same folder as this one, just enter its name and extension, as in `aardvark.htm`. For other documents, the process can be a bit tricky to do properly; see "Linking to other documents" later in this chapter.

    Don't click the tiny file-folder icon next to the Document box. Although this icon theoretically allows you to select your destination file by browsing, in reality, you end up with something like `C:\MyFiles\website\visit.htm` in the Document box. Such an URL works when you test your links on your PC but not when you put your files on the Web. Also, be careful not to link to WordPerfect documents (files that end in WPD).

4. **If you want to jump to a specific location in an HTML document, enter a bookmark name in the Bookmark box.**

    If you merely want to jump to the start of another HTML file, leave this box blank. Jumping to a location other than the start of a document can be a bit tricky; see "Hyperlinks for jumping to places within a document," later in this chapter.

5. **Click the OK button.**

Your hyperlink is ready. In fact, the link is *so* ready that if you click it, WordPerfect launches your Web browser and attempts to display the document that you linked to. This behavior is thoughtful of WordPerfect, but it can make editing the darn thing challenging: How do you edit text that you can't click? The answer lies in clearing the Activate hyperlinks check box (refer to Figure 7-3, later in this chapter). Simply choose Tools⇨hyperlinks again, click the check box to clear it, and click OK.

## Hyperlinking from graphics a different way

Another way to create a hyperlink for a graphic is to use the HTML Properties dialog box for graphics. This dialog box does exactly the same thing as the other approach, in which you choose Tools⇨Hyperlink. Here are the steps involved:

1. **Right-click the graphic and choose HTML Properties from the QuickMenu that appears.**

   The HTML Properties dialog box appears.

2. **In the Define mouse click action section, click Link.**

   A new Link tab appears at the top of the dialog box.

3. **Click the Link tab.**

4. **Enter the document name and/or bookmark information, just as you would by using the other approach (choosing Tools⇨Hyperlink).**

5. **Click the OK button.**

Hyperlinked graphics traditionally have a special border around them to show that they are hyperlinked. To be traditional, see "Graphics: beating the frame," later in this chapter.

## Linking to other documents

One of the fine arts of preparing documents for the Web is making links to other documents work properly regardless of where the documents are: on your PC, where you test them before making them public; on the Web; or some mixture of both. Getting links to work depends entirely on what you enter in the Hyperlink Properties dialog box (refer to Figure 7-3, later in this chapter).

Table 7-1 gives you some helpful suggestions for what to enter in the Document box in the Hyperlink Properties dialog box, depending on what you are linking from and linking to. The full details on linking in these various ways are given in the next few sections.

Here is how to use Table 7-1 to link to other documents:

- To link between documents in the same folder on your Web site, for example, use the form in the top row. Enter just the filename. (This method is the way to go if you're following the suggested procedures in this book.)

- To link to a document in a subfolder, use the form in the second row.

## Part II: Text Tricks

- To link to a document in a higher folder, use the third row.
- To link to a document somewhere on the Web, use the bottom row.

**Table 7-1  Examples of Linking from** `hither.htm` **to** `yon.htm`

| To Link Like This... | Enter Text Like This in the Document Box |
|---|---|
| Website / hither.htm / yon.htm | `yon.htm` |
| Website / hither.htm / morestuf / yon.htm | `./morestuf/yon.htm` |
| Website / stuff / hither.htm / morestuf / yon.htm | `../morestuf/yon.htm` |
| Website / hither.htm / Internet / http://www.sumwhere.net / yon.htm | `http://www.sumwhere.net/yon.htm` |

*TIP*

Table 7-1 can be useful for more than doing hyperlinks. The various ways of entering the address of a document shown in Table 7-1 are the infamous "URLs" of the Web. (See Chapter 1 and the sidebar "Becoming a Duke of URL" for more about URLs.) URLs are not only used for hyperlinks, they are used to link documents to the graphics files, audio files, and other files used internally by the document. When you publish to HTML, for instance, in the Publish to HTML dialog box, you enter an URL in the box marked "Location of graphics on Web Server" that describes where graphics files are for the document. This book has its own recommendation for that folder and the best form of URL to use to describe that folder: the form in the second row of Table 7-1 (minus the file name). If you wanted to use a different folder than the one this book recommends for your graphics files you could obtain the proper URL from Table 7-1, simply omitting the file name (the `yon.htm` part) and substituting your chosen folder name for the folder `morestuf`.

### Linking to other documents on your Web site

The suggestions in this book lead you to put all your HTML files in the same folder, both on your PC and on the Web site. If you are following those suggestions, linking to other documents on your Web site is simple. Select the text to be linked; choose Tools⇨Hyperlink; and in the Document box in the Hyperlink Properties dialog box, enter *only* the filename (including the `.htm`), as shown in the first row of Table 7-1 and in Figure 7-3.

## Becoming a Duke of URL

Here is the story behind all the confusing ways of filling the Document box described in Table 7-1. You can describe the address of a document that you want to link to in any of several ways, each way having its own pros and cons. These descriptions are the infamous so-called URLs, and they are used all over the Web wherever one Web file is linked to another for any reason.

*Absolute addressing* (such as `http://www.sumwhere.net/yon.htm`) describes a document on the Internet. If you use absolute addressing, you won't be able to test your links locally (from PC file to PC file). If you connect your PC to the Internet, however, you can test links from a PC file to a file that's on your Web site (or anywhere else on the Web). When all your files are on the Web, absolute addressing works well.

*Absolute local addressing* (such as `file://c:/myfiles/website/yon.htm`) describes a document on your PC's disk. (Local addressing is what results if you click the file-folder icon next to the Document box and specify a file in the dialog box that appears.) Local absolute addressing works well in WordPerfect for files on your PC. When you move your files to your Web site, which has no connection to files on your PC's disk, however, this link no longer works.

*Relative addressing* (such as `yon.htm` or `./morestuf/yon.htm`) describes a document's location in the folder tree relative to the current document. The symbol ./ means "Look in the current document's folder"; the symbol ../ means "Go up one folder"; the symbol ../../ means "Go up two folders"; and so on. When a name appears in slashes (as in /morestuf/) it describes a folder to be opened. This scheme works only within a disk or network, not across the Internet. By using relative addressing, you can develop and test an entire set of Web documents on the PC and then move them to the Web server without change. If you extract a single document from its environment (from someone else's Web site to your PC, for example) without its linked brothers, however, none of its links will work.

---

If you are linking to a document named `cookies` on your Web site, for example, enter the following in the Document box:

```
cookies.htm
```

If you're not following the suggestion to put all your HTML files in the same folder, see the other rows of Table 7-1.

Uppercase and lowercase don't matter on your PC, but they do on the Web, so this book recommends that you consistently use lowercase for every file that you create — and for folders, too. Also use lowercase when you create links.

> ### Your Web site and the art of linking
>
> Linking the documents on your site is a bit of an art. Following are some tips for linking your Web-site documents:
>
> - Include a clickable table of contents on your home page, with links to every important file on your Web site.
> - Put useful information right on your home page; don't make your home page just a table of contents. That approach forces your visitor to immediately click a link and wait to get information.
> - Put a link back to your home page on every other page.
> - Your site should require no more than two jumps to go from the home page to any other page.

The bottom line of Table 7-1 shows a link between a document on your PC and a document on some Web site. "Some Web site" includes *your own* Web site, too. You can link to other documents on your site that way instead of the way suggested in this section. You have to go online with your PC, however, to test that link from a file on your PC.

### Linking to documents on other Web sites

Linking to a document on another Web site is as easy as linking to a document on your own Web site, and maybe easier. The only difference is what goes in the Document text box in the Hyperlink Properties dialog box.

Select the text to be linked; choose Tools⇨Hyperlink; and, in the Document box in the Hyperlink Properties dialog box, enter an address exactly as you would put it in the Address, Location, or URL box of a Web browser. Unlike addresses in Netscape Navigator, however, this address should include the entire URL, including the initial `http://` stuff; don't start with the "www" part of the address.

If you are linking to a document named `cookies` on Fooble Corporation's Web site, for example, enter the following in the Document box:

`http://www.fooble.com/cookies.htm`

Rather than type the URL (a process that tends to generate mistakes, such as using lowercase instead of uppercase), click the Browse Web button in the Hyperlink Properties dialog box (when you are connected to the Internet) to launch your browser. Then, using your browser, view the page on the Web that you want to link to. When your browser begins to load the page, switch back to WordPerfect; you'll find the URL entered in the Document box.

**Chapter 7: Helpful Hyperlinks** *97*

*TIP* You can use the same approach to link to documents on your own Web site, instead of the relative URL approach (refer to "Linking to other documents on your Web site"). Just enter the absolute address (URL) of the document on your Web site. To test the links when you view a document on your PC, however, you need to connect your PC to the Internet.

*TIP* A shortcut way to link to a document on the Web is to simply type the document's Internet address (URL), followed by a space. Refer to "Using Automatic Hyperlinking" at the start of this chapter for more details.

## Hyperlinks for jumping to places within a document

Hyperlinks don't have to jump to another document; they can jump to a specially marked place in the current document — or in any other document, for that matter. Two steps are necessary for this kind of link:

- Marking the destination (the place to jump to)
- Creating the hyperlink

For quite a while, WordPerfect has had a bookmark feature that allows you to tag a location in a document with a name. Now that feature has been adapted for marking your destination in a hyperlink.

*TIP* If you have a long document, use these hyperlinks-within-a-document to create a clickable table of contents at the top. Create a bookmark at every major heading, list those headings at the top of the document, and turn each line of the list into a link to that heading in the document.

*TECHNICAL STUFF* The bookmarks used in Web files actually are called *named anchors* by the old sailors who write HTML by hand. To be technically accurate, you create bookmarks in a WordPerfect document, and they turn into named anchors when you create an HTML file.

### Creating the bookmark

The first step is creating a bookmark. The bookmark goes at your destination — the place that you want to jump to. Following are the individual steps for bookmarking (that's book*marking*, not book*making*, sports fans).

1. **Select (highlight) some text at the destination (the place that you want to jump to).**

    A heading is always a good choice for a destination.

**Part II: Text Tricks**

If you want a link that jumps to a bookmark in another document (call it the destination document), open the destination document and highlight the text. (If you have a Web-formatted WordPerfect file for the destination document available, open that file rather than the HTML file.)

2. **Choose Tools⇨Bookmark.**

   The Bookmark dialog box opens (shown in Figure 7-2).

Click to create a new bookmark

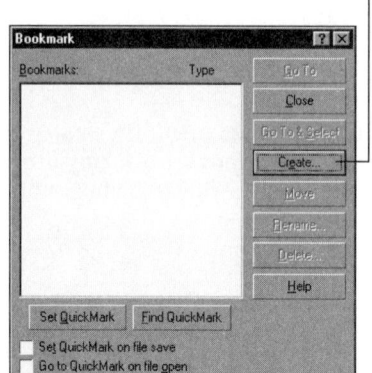

**Figure 7-2:** Creating a new bookmark.

An alternative way to open the Bookmark dialog box is to simply select your text and then choose Tools⇨Bookmark.

3. **Click the Create button in the Bookmark dialog box.**

   A Create Bookmark dialog box appears, suggesting a bookmark name copied from the text that you selected. You can use any name you like, but the suggestion WordPerfect makes is a good one that prevents confusion later.

4. **Click OK in the Create Bookmark dialog box.**

   Now you have your bookmark. Repeat Steps 1 through 5 for any additional bookmarks that you need.

5. **Save your work as a WordPerfect file by pressing Ctrl+S.**

6. **Publish the document to HTML.**

   To do so, click the Publish to HTML button on the toolbar (which displays a Web-ensnared document with a blue "o"). Or, if you prefer, choose File⇨Internet Publisher to display the Internet Publisher dialog box, then click Publish to HTML. See "Editing your Web document" in Chapter 3 for details on publishing to HTML.

### Linking to the bookmark

You've made your bookmark; now link to it! You can link to that bookmark from within the same document or from anywhere else. Creating a link to a bookmark is much like creating any other link.

Here are the steps to take:

 1. **Highlight the text (or click the graphic) that you want to turn into a hyperlink.**

 2. **Choose Tools⇨Hyperlink or click the Hyperlink button in the toolbar.**

    If you choose to click the Hyperlink button, choose Create Link from the drop-down list.

    In either case, the Hyperlink Properties dialog box appears.

 3. **If you're linking to a bookmark in the same document, leave the Document box reading <current document>.**

    If you're linking to a bookmark in some other document, refer to Table 7-1 earlier in this chapter for examples of how to describe that document in the Document box. If you are simply linking to a bookmark in another document on your Web site, and you are following this book's recommendation to put all your documents in the same folder, you can simply enter the file's name (such as `fooble.htm`).

    Don't click the file-folder icon to the right of the Document box (an action which displays a dialog box) to choose a document; the resulting link will fail!

 4. **Enter the bookmark name in the Bookmark box, as shown in Figure 7-3.**

    If you are linking to a bookmark in the current document, click the down-arrow button indicated in Figure 7-3 to see a list of available bookmarks. Click one of the bookmarks listed.

    If you are linking to a bookmark in some other destination document, no list of bookmarks is available within this dialog box. You must manually type the bookmark's name in the Bookmark box. If you don't remember the bookmark name, open the destination document in WordPerfect and choose Tools⇨Bookmark to see a list of bookmarks. Switch back to the document where you're creating the link, and enter the bookmark's name in the Bookmark box.

 5. **Click OK.**

    Your link is done. Cook up some more links, add eggs, and have breakfast.

Click for bookmarks in the current document.

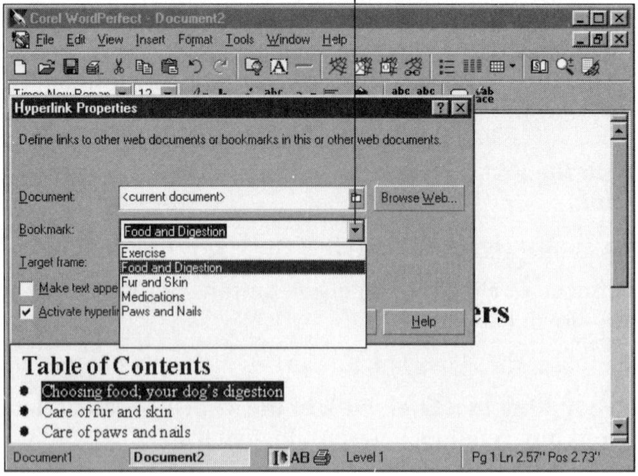


**Figure 7-3:** Linking Table-of-Contents text to a section in the same document.

# Using QuickLinks

If you need to make the same link repeatedly, the WordPerfect QuickLinks feature may save you time. QuickLinks can create a link automatically whenever you type a special keyword. If you want to link to the Acme Company's Web site whenever you mention its name, for example, your keyword is `Acme`, preceded by the at symbol (@), like this: `@Acme`. To create your own QuickLinks, do the following:

1. **Choose Tools➪Quick Correct.**

   The Quick Correct dialog box appears.

2. **Click the QuickLinks tab.**

3. **In the Link Word box, type the at symbol (@), followed by your keyword.**

   You can use multiple words, as in **@United Nations**.

4. **In the Location to link to box, enter the address of the document that you want to link to (such as `http://www.acme.com`).**

   Type the address that way if you want to link to a document on a Web server. To link to other documents (such as documents on your own server), type the address by using the other forms shown in Table 7-1 earlier in this chapter.

5. **Click the OK button.**

In your document, whenever you type @, followed by your keyword(s) and a space, WordPerfect removes the @ symbol and turns the text into the hyperlink that you specify. Cute!

## Clicking and Testing Your Hyperlinks

Test your links on the PC before you put your files on the Web server. If you discover you must correct and retest your links, the process is much faster and easier on your PC than on your Web server.

### Clicking and testing links in WordPerfect

When you create links in WordPerfect, WordPerfect makes the links *active,* which means that you can click links in WordPerfect to test them. You may, however, find the process to be rather odd.

When you click a link to an HTML file, WordPerfect reads that file into your Web browser — not into WordPerfect. When you click a link to a bookmark in the current document, you stay in WordPerfect.

Rather than leave all your links active, you can deactivate them in WordPerfect as the following section describes and then test them individually. To test a link when links are deactivated, click in the hyperlinked text (or on the hyperlinked graphic), then click the button shown in the left margin of this paragraph in the Property Bar.

### Deactivating and activating links in WordPerfect

Having active links in WordPerfect can be a problem when you need to edit the text in the link. Whenever you click the text to edit it, the link does its job and takes you somewhere else! To deactivate links in WordPerfect, choose Tools⇨Hyperlink to display the Hyperlink Properties dialog box. In the bottom-left corner of the dialog box that appears, click to clear the Activate Hyperlinks check box. Then click the OK button.

All of the links in your WordPerfect document will be deactivated. Deactivating links in the WordPerfect document has no effect on the HTML document.

The button shown in the left margin is a shortcut for switching your links between being activated and deactivated in WordPerfect. The button appears just above your document (on the Property Bar). It only appears, however, when your insertion point (the blinking cursor) is in hyperlinked text or a hyperlinked graphic is selected. If links are currently active, you'll have to move the insertion point into the hyperlinked text by using the navigation (arrow) keys on the keyboard, rather than clicking, in order to see the button.

### Clicking and testing links in your Web browser

To test links between documents, publish the documents to HTML and then open the .HTM files in your Web browser. Pressing Ctrl+O does the job in most browsers. See "Viewing Your Web Files in Browsers" in Chapter 3 for more details.

To test links to a bookmark in the current document, click the View in Web Browser button in the Toolbar to launch your browser. (The icon on the button looks like a document behind a spider's web.)

Always test your links after you copy your files to the Web server, too. Suppose that you copied the linked documents `bert.htm` and `ernie.htm` to your folder `users/einstein/` on a Web server named `www.badminton.net`. Go online with your PC; then, in your Web browser, enter the address `www.badminton.net/users/einstein/bert.htm`. After `bert.htm` downloads, click the link that is supposed to take you to `ernie.htm`, and see whether it works.

## Doing Things Besides Jumping

Jumping is nice. It's fun. It's aerobic. But hyperlinks can do other things than just jump a visitor from one HTML document to another on the Web; they can just as easily transmit files for images, videos, or sounds, or any other kind of file that you can name. Hyperlinks also can induce a visitor's browser to launch its e-mail program and address a new message to you.

### Viewing graphics, playing sounds

If a graphic image requires a large file, inserting that image into your Web document may not be a good idea; visitors will get very frustrated waiting for it to download. Instead, create a hyperlink from the document to the large graphic file. You could put a smaller version or sample piece of it (called a *thumbnail*) in the document and then link from that, or simply create a hyperlink from text. If a street map of New York City (`nycmap.gif`) is useful to your visitors, you could link from the words *large map of New York City* to the file.

The procedure for linking to a graphic file is identical to the process for linking to an HTML file. Here's how to link to a graphic or audio file:

1. **Follow the procedure given in "Linking to other documents on your Web site," but . . .**
2. **. . . in the Document box of the Hyperlink Properties dialog box, enter the name of your graphic or audio file.**

    For the map-of-New-York-City example, you would enter **nycmap.gif**.
3. **Put the file in the same folder as the HTML document that contains a link to the file.**

    You can use other folders, but refer to Table 7-1 for the correct way to write the link.

You can use the same trick for any file: .WAV files for sound, .AVI files for video, or even .WRL files for virtual reality! The server transmits the linked file to the visitor's browser. The browser then checks to see whether it knows what to do with the file, such as run a special plug-in or helper program. If the browser doesn't know what to do, it displays a dialog box and asks the human who's running the browser what to do.

## Downloading a file

Sometimes, you want to give your visitor a file, such as a compressed file or a program. Transmitting such a file is — in most cases — easy. Do exactly as described in the preceding section, "Viewing graphics, playing sounds." Put the file in the folder with your HTML document, and link from the document to the file.

*Note:* If your file is a binary file (not text), be aware that only certain binary-file types such as EXE or BIN files can always be safely transmitted to all visitors. For other types of binary files make sure that the file has one of the extensions that browsers typically recognize. A WordPerfect file, for example, with a .WPD extension, is a binary file that isn't recognized by most browsers. If you linked to a .WPD file, depending on your server and the browser downloading the file, the file may not download intact.

How do you know what file types you can safely use? You can't know for sure, but you can make an educated guess. In Netscape Navigator 3.01, choose Options➪General Preferences➪General to display the Preferences dialog box, and click the Helpers tab. Look down the Extension column to see the three-letter endings. If your file type is not listed, the file may or may not be transmitted properly.

In Communicator 4.01, choose Edit➪Preferences to display the Preferences dialog box. There, click Navigator Applications in the Category box, and click on application names in the Description box. As you do so, three-letter endings are displayed in the lower right of the Preferences dialog box (in the Extension field of the File type details area).

## Sending an e-mail message to you

One of the easiest and most common ways to get feedback from a Web site is to have your visitors send you e-mail. Sending e-mail is not as elegant as providing a form for visitors to fill out, but it's much less complicated.

The fastest way to create such a link (called a mailto link) is to simply type your (or anyone else's) e-mail address, such as `timleary@spacecadets.net`, followed by a space. WordPerfect automatically turns this text into a mailto hyperlink (refer to "Using Automatic Hyperlinks" at the beginning of this chapter).

If you don't want the text of the link to actually state your address, but instead want it to say `e-mail` me, for example, you can use another approach. Follow the same steps that you do to link to a document, but in the Document box of the Hyperlink Properties dialog box, use a mailto hyperlink instead of a filename. The hyperlink looks like this:

```
mailto:you@yourplace.com
```

Substitute your e-mail address after the `mailto` part.

# Editing and Removing Hyperlinks

Editing and removing hyperlinks would be an easy task but for one thing: To edit them, you have to click them or select them. If, however, hyperlinks are active when you click them, they do their hyperlinking thing! The trick, then, is to deactivate the links before editing them.

To deactivate links in WordPerfect, choose Tools➪Hyperlink to display the Hyperlink Properties dialog box. In the bottom-left corner of the dialog box, click the Activate hyperlinks check box to clear the checkmark there. Then click the OK button.

Chapter 7: Helpful Hyperlinks   *105*

Here's how to edit the link when it's inactive:

1. **Click anywhere within the linked text or click the linked graphic.**
2. **To edit the link, choose Tools⇨Hyperlink.**

    Alternatively, click the Hyperlink Edit button in the Property Bar. The Hyperlink Properties box appears, allowing you to change the link.

3. **To delete the hyperlink, click the Hyperlink Remove button in the Property Bar.**

    Deleting the link does not delete the text or graphic — only the link.

When you're done, you can reactivate the links if you want to try them in WordPerfect. Simply repeat the deactivation procedure and select the Activate Hyperlinks check box.

To move from link to link for editing purposes, use the Hyperlink Previous and Hyperlink Next buttons. They only appear when the insertion point (blinking cursor) is on hyperlinked text or a graphic.

# *Different Hyperlink Appearances*

Tired of blue text wherever you have a hyperlink? No problem. Choose some glitzy designer colors that go with your color scheme. In fact, for text-based hyperlinks, WordPerfect can take you away from underlined, colored text entirely and turn your text into a labeled button instead! For graphics-based hyperlinks, which traditionally include a frame, WordPerfect lets you set the frame width.

## *Colors: beating the blues*

Hyperlinks actually have three colors — one each for before, during, and after clicking. The during-clicking color is just a quick flash of feedback to tell the user that he or she has succeeded in clicking the text. The after-clicking color tells the user that he or she has explored this link already. The same set of colors is used for both text hyperlinks and the frame around graphics hyperlinks.

You set all three colors in the same dialog box that allows you to choose text and background colors for normal text. Choosing your link colors at the same time that you choose the colors for your normal text and for the document background is a good idea; see "Color Schemes and Dreams" in Chapter 9 for details.

## Graphics: beating the frame

A hyperlinked graphic traditionally has a "frame" around it — a border to indicate that it is hyperlinked. (Ordinary graphics in the WordPerfect tradition have also had borders, too, but those are different and fancier borders, controlled by different commands than the ones this section is discussing. See Chapter 13 for more about both kinds of border.)

WordPerfect doesn't automatically provide the traditional border when you hyperlink a graphic. You need to provide it. The color of the border for hyperlinked graphics is controlled in the same place as the color for hyperlinked text; see "Adjusting Text Color" in Chapter 9 for details.

The width of the traditional border is controlled in the special HTML Properties dialog box for graphics. WordPerfect initially sets the border width to zero when you hyperlink a graphic. Here's how to change the border width:

1. **Right-click your graphic image and choose HTML Properties from the QuickMenu.**

   The HTML Properties dialog box appears.

2. **Click the Image tab.**

   You find a Border width control that gives the width of the frame in pixels.

3. **Enter a new Border width number by typing it in the text box or by clicking the up- or down-arrow button next to the number.**

4. **Click the OK button.**

5. **To see your results, click the View in Web Browser button in the Toolbar.**

## Buttons

I'm sometimes accused of not having all my buttons. If that happens to you, too, try changing some of your hypertext links to buttons. It's not really appropriate to change a link to a button if it's simply an ordinary link to another document or a link in the middle of a sentence. But if something potentially exciting, annoying, or time-consuming happens when you click a particular link — such as playing a sound file of the Macarena (remember that?), downloading a program, or displaying a satellite image of the entire world — a button is a good choice.

Buttons are easy to create. When you create a hyperlink by using any of the methods described in this chapter, simply click the Make text appear as a button check box at the bottom of the Hyperlink Properties dialog box.

WordPerfect creates a small, hyperlinked graphic image of a button with your text on it — in reality, one of the WordPerfect text boxes. When you publish to HTML, the image ends up in your graphics folder as a small GIF file with a horrendously long name.

To edit the text of a button, position your cursor in the center of the button and click. A small editing window appears. Click Close when you're done editing. To do more formatting of appearances, read about text boxes in Chapter 11 and buttons in Chapter 12.

*TIP:* WordPerfect sizes the buttons by how much text you have. If you're arranging buttons in a neat array, as in a table, you may want them all to be the same width. A simple way to control your buttons' width is to add hard or nonbreaking spaces (press Ctrl+spacebar) to lengthen the text.

## When Hyperlinks Go Bad

Even with the best of intentions and care, hyperlinks sometimes don't work right. Even previously working hyperlinks can go bad. (This form of spoilage is not a matter of improper storage or shelf life; it's that people change things.) Following are some symptoms of bad links, possible reasons for the symptoms, and some suggestions for fixing the problem. To fix a link, edit the link as described in "Editing and Removing Hyperlinks," earlier in this chapter.

- **Links don't work when you click them in WordPerfect.** The links may not be active. Choose Tools⇨Hyperlink, and click to select the Activate hyperlinks check box in the dialog box that appears.

- **Links to other documents don't work when you preview a file by clicking the View in Web Browser button.** This situation is to be expected. You must publish to HTML and load the HTML file into your browser for links to work.

- **A link no longer works after you move files from the PC to the server.** Here are some possible reasons:
    - The folder structure (the directory tree) on the server is not the same as the one in which the document was created. Refer to Chapter 6.
    - The link is local, which means the link refers to a specific drive on your PC (such as C:\) that does not exist on your server. Edit the link according to Table 7-1, earlier in this chapter.
    - The link uses wrong-case characters (uppercase instead of lowercase) in the file or folder description; the case doesn't match the case of the characters on the server. Either rename the files or folders or change the link.

- **A link works on the Web but not on your PC.** The link probably uses absolute addressing, which means that the hyperlink uses an URL (such as `http://www.fooble.com/stuff.htm`) that refers to a document on a Web server. Try connecting your PC to the Internet.

- **A link used to work but doesn't now.** The HTML file that you are viewing was moved to another computer or folder, but the files that it was linked to were not. Alternatively, the file to which the link is supposed to take you (or its folder) was moved or renamed.

# Chapter 8
# Standard Styles and Alignment

*In This Chapter*
- Style
- Normal text
- Headings
- Address style
- Indented quotations
- Preformatted text
- Numbered lists
- Definition lists
- Line and paragraph spacing
- Justification (alignment): left, right, or center

Text on the Web is weird. Web text uses *styles,* which combine paragraphish things (such as line spacing, bullets, numbered lists, and indentations) with characterish formatting (such as bold, italic, and font size). If you've used styles in WordPerfect (or any other word processor), you have the general idea; if not, don't panic.

Web styles are different from word processor styles. Web styles leave the details up to the Web browser that's reading the file — not to the person who creates the document (you). The Web browser sees a Heading 1 style, for example; looks up what its user or designer specified for paragraph and character formatting for Heading 1; and does whatever that formatting calls for. Fortunately, even though the way that those styles appear on a Web browser is left up to the browser, most browsers today display them in basically the same way!

Web styles are your only tool for controlling paragraph formatting without resorting to hidden tables and other tricks. For headings, bulleted or numbered lists, indented text, and the like, Web styles are what you need to use. Web styles — plus ways to align paragraphs — are what this chapter is all about.

Keep in mind, however, that formatting on the Web is undergoing a revolution. New additions to HTML allow you to (within limits) control character formatting yourself. You can dictate font (typeface), font size, and color, as well as attributes such as bold and italic. Some of these new additions work only with certain browsers, as you see in Chapter 9.

## Choosing Style

You gotta have style, even if it's only Normal style. Style determines many things, but the two most important are paragraph formatting and the size of the text. So what style should you choose? Table 8-1 gives you some suggestions:

| Table 8-1 | What's Your Style? |
| --- | --- |
| *Your Text* | *What Style to Choose* |
| Regular old paragraphs | Normal |
| Headings | Heading 1 through Heading 6 |
| Lines with no spacing between | Address |
| Paragraphs indented left and right | Indented Quotation |
| Text that uses multiple spaces or tabs | Preformatted Text |
| Numbered lines | Numbered List |
| Bulleted lines | Bullet List |
| Indented paragraphs | Definition List |

### Giving text some style

WordPerfect gives you two ways to apply a style to text:

- Click the Font/Size button in the Property Bar (the big script *A*) and click a style in the drop-down list, as shown in Figure 8-1.

- Use the Font dialog box (redesigned for Web styles), shown in Figure 8-2. The commands that you use to display that Font dialog box are the same as ever: Press F9 or choose Format⇨Font.

**Figure 8-1:** The badly named Font/Size button shows plenty of style but no fonts or sizes.

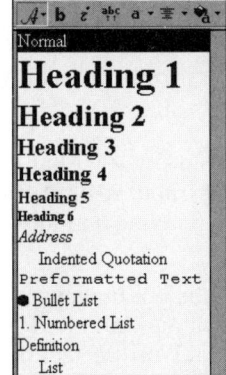

**Figure 8-2:** The Font dialog box with a Web-style facelift for Web text styles.

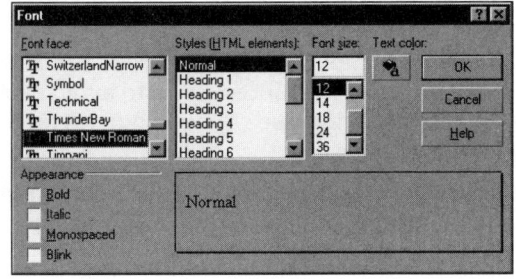

WordPerfect makes applying Web styles easy. Here are a few tips:

- You can tell what style a paragraph or line is in by clicking anywhere in the text and then looking at the status bar at the bottom of the WordPerfect window (unless the paragraph is in Normal style).
- You can apply a style either before you type text or afterward. To apply a style before you type, click where you want to type, choose the style (in the Font dialog box or from the Font/Size button's drop-down list), and start typing!
- To apply a style to a single line or paragraph, click anywhere in the paragraph or select the paragraph and then choose the style. Styles apply to the entire line or paragraph but no further.
- To apply a style to many lines or paragraphs, select the paragraphs first and then choose the style.

## Things that won't work

Following are a bunch of things that you might try to do in text styles, but that just won't work:

- Don't try to position text by entering multiple spaces! That method won't work in any style except the ugly Preformatted Text style. You can, however, use hard spaces (spaces where a line cannot wrap) by pressing Ctrl+spacebar.
- Tabs won't work for spaces within a line. Tabs do, however, control indentation in the Bullet List, Numbered List, and Indented Quotation styles, sort of the way that they do in normal WordPerfect documents.
- You can't create a first-line indentation for a paragraph (or the opposite, a hanging indent) by using just styles. You can, however, use hard spaces by pressing Ctrl+spacebar.
- Spacing after lines and paragraphs is not under your control, except that you can use a list style or the Address style to avoid using extra space. You can also add blank lines; see "Line and Paragraph Spacing" later in this chapter for details.
- Center and right alignment work only with Normal style, Address style, and the heading styles.
- You can specify the font (typeface), but it works only for Netscape Navigator users. Changing font size, however, has an effect in most browsers. See Chapter 9 for more information about fancy fonts.

## Normal Text

Normal is the best style to use for text in the body of a document. (Some people use headings to get beefier-looking body text, but because headings use bold type, headings generally look bad as body text.)

Most browsers put one line of space between paragraphs. Most new browsers allow you to control line height by choosing the size attribute (font size). Other browsers typically use 12-point Roman text for Normal style.

As is true of most Web text styles, you can indent Normal-style text only by using multiple hard spaces. Browsers ignore tabs and multiple ordinary spaces. To get indentations, you're better off choosing a list style or Indented Quotation style. To use tabs and multiple ordinary spaces (which is what you often get from converting a regular WordPerfect file to a Web-formatted file), you must choose Preformatted Text style.

## Headings

In most browsers, Headings styles are simply larger and bolder versions of whatever font the browser uses for Normal, including proportionally large spaces after the headings. Choose whatever heading level gives you the effect that you want; you don't have to start with Heading 1. I suggest that you use actual Headings styles for your headings, not large type sizes, bold text, or enlarged Normal text. This choice keeps you in good favor with folks who don't have new or highly sophisticated Web browsers.

## Address Style

Use Address style when you don't want spaces between lines in a list or between paragraphs. Most browsers display Address style as italicized text in the same font and size as Normal text. The important difference is that most browsers put a space between paragraphs in Normal style but not in Address style. So if you want lines to appear together (as you often do in an address) and don't mind italics, choose Address.

## Indented Quotations

Use Indented Quotation style if you want to center your paragraphs by indenting them from both the left and the right (without individually centering each line). You can start a new level of indentation by entering a Tab character at the start of a line. (Play with the indentations too long, however, and you may eventually confuse WordPerfect's overtaxed brain.)

This text style was created to make quotations stand out. Most browsers display the style in the same font and size as Normal text, only indented. In addition, Netscape Navigator pays attention to the typeface and size that you choose. Some browsers also italicize the text.

## Preformatted Text

Preformatted Text is the perfect style for people who are frustrated by trying to convert an existing document for the Web. If you have text from an existing document that uses many spaces and tabs, Preformatted Text style is your (somewhat unattractive) friend, which loves your text just the way it is and allows you to keep those spaces and tabs.

Don't panic if you appear to lose tabs and spaces when you copy, insert, or convert such a file to a Web document. The text may initially be in Normal style, which ignores white-space characters; try applying Preformatted Text style. You can also enter tabs in Preformatted Text style by pressing Ctrl+Tab. (The tabs end up as multiple spaces in HTML, however — not that it matters.)

Unfortunately for the aesthetics of your document, Preformatted Text traditionally is displayed in some unattractive *monospace* font (such as Courier), in which every character is exactly the same width. These days, however, you can apply a different font to Preformatted Text. Not all browsers recognize fonts, but the Netscape and Microsoft browsers do.

***Note:*** Don't confuse Preformatted Text style with the Monospaced appearance option in the Font dialog box, even though they look the same. Only Preformatted Text accepts multiple spaces and tabs. Accept no cheap imitations!

## Numbered Lists

Using Numbered List style for Web documents is much like using the numbered-list format in regular WordPerfect documents. As always in WordPerfect, you can either select a bunch of lines and then choose the style, or choose the style first and then type lines. To stop the line numbers, click the document at the point where you want the numbers to stop and then switch back to Normal style.

Numbered lists can be nested, too. Press the Tab key at the start of a line to begin a new, more-indented numbered list within the first list (or insert a Tab character at the start of an existing line). Press the Enter key to advance to the next numbered line in this new, indented list; you don't need to press Tab to indent each line. To return indentation to the next-higher level, press Shift+Tab at the start of a line.

Unlike normal WordPerfect documents, Web documents do not produce an outline format (1., a., i., and so on) when you indent by pressing the Tab key. Web documents use only regular numbers (1, 2, 3, and so on), regardless of the level of indentation.

One problem that I find with numbered and bulleted lists is that they provide no line spacing. You can fix this problem, where necessary, by inserting a line break and hard space at the end of a line. Choose Insert⇨Line Break and then press Ctrl+spacebar. (In WordPerfect, the hard space doesn't appear to be necessary, but you will see that it is necessary if you click the View in Web Browser button.)

## Chapter 8: Standard Styles and Alignment  *115*

## *Bulleted Lists*

Everyone loves bulleted lists. Using Bulleted List style is much like using Numbered List style. As you can with any style, either select a bunch of lines and apply the style, or choose the style and then type the lines. To stop the bullets, switch back to Normal text.

Bulleted lists can be nested. Press the Tab key at the start of a line (or insert a Tab character at the start of an existing line) to create an indented bulleted list within the first list. Each level of indentation gets a different style of bullet. Press the Enter key to move to the next bullet in this new, indented list; you don't need to press Tab to indent each line. Insert a Shift+Tab character at the start of a line to move up a level.

To add space after a line, add a line break and hard space. See the Tip in the preceding section for details.

## *Definition Lists*

Definition List style was designed for you to use when you have a series of topics, each of which is followed by an indented paragraph or two of definition or explanation, as shown in Figure 8-3. This style is also great just for creating indented paragraphs!

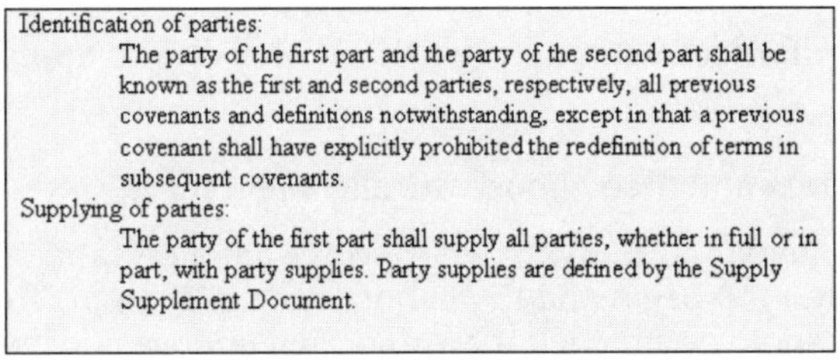

**Figure 8-3:** You, too, can create exciting documents with Definition List style.

```
Identification of parties:
    The party of the first part and the party of the second part shall be
    known as the first and second parties, respectively, all previous
    covenants and definitions notwithstanding, except in that a previous
    covenant shall have explicitly prohibited the redefinition of terms in
    subsequent covenants.
Supplying of parties:
    The party of the first part shall supply all parties, whether in full or in
    part, with party supplies. Party supplies are defined by the Supply
    Supplement Document.
```

To create the indented definition paragraphs, just add a Tab character at the beginning of a line. To take out the indentation, press Shift+Tab.

Like the Numbered List and Bullet List styles, this style jams paragraphs together. You can fix this problem, where necessary, by inserting a line break and hard space at the end of a line. Choose Insert⇨Line Break and then press Ctrl+spacebar, or insert a blank line and format the line in Address or Normal style. (Normal adds more space than Address does.)

## Line and Paragraph Spacing

If you feel like an out-of-control space cadet when you use Web styles, it's for a good reason: Spacing between lines and between paragraphs is actually not under your control in a standard HTML document. The Web browser decides how much space goes between paragraphs. You usually can cheat, however, by adding a blank line (pressing the Enter key) or inserting a line break (choosing Insert⇨Line Break). Here are two rules of thumb:

- Use a blank line (press Enter) to add space in any style but the Bullet List and Numbered List styles. (The blank line would be bulleted or numbered!)
- Insert a line break and hard space to add space at the end of a line in the Numbered List and Bullet List styles. (A line break alone appears to do the job in WordPerfect but doesn't do the job in the HTML document.)

## Achieving Alternative Alignments

You may think that you can just push text around in your document, making it center- or right-aligned, just as you can with a regular WordPerfect document. Not so fast.

You can realign only two text styles with impunity (or savoir faire, or whatever attitude you happen to have lying around): Normal text and headings. (List styles look terrible in anything but left alignment, anyway.)

As usual with WordPerfect formatting, you have two ways to apply alignment to text:

- Select some text and then choose the alignment for it.
- Click the document at the point where you want a certain alignment (such as Center) to begin and then choose the alignment. To stop that alignment at some point, click there and then choose another alignment (such as Left).

You also have two alternative places to go to get aligned:

- Choose Format⇨Justification and then choose Left, Right, or Center from the submenu.
- In the Property Bar, click the Justification button and then choose an alignment from the drop-down list that appears.

## Chapter 8: Standard Styles and Alignment 117

Alignment is a little unreliable in different circumstances. Here are a few of the places trouble can arise:

- WordPerfect may look as though it is happily left- or center-aligning nearly all styles of text in your document, but the HTML results tell a different story. To see how your HTML document looks in your browser, click the View in Web Browser button in the Toolbar (the document with a spider's web over it).

- Alignment is fairly new to the Web, and different browsers handle it differently and inconsistently. Publish to HTML and check your files in a popular browser other than your usual one.

- Older browsers may not pay attention to your alignment at all and make everything left-aligned!

### Center anything!

The current rules of HTML provide a way to center-align any text; any graphic; or anything else, for that matter. WordPerfect 8 doesn't give you that feature (probably because the feature is controversial). But you can cheat by entering a line of HTML in your document without WordPerfect knowing about it.

At the place where you want centering to begin, type the magic code <center>; then select it and choose Format⇨Custom HTML. The centering effect doesn't show up in WordPerfect, so to see the result, click the View in Web Browser Toolbar button. At the place where you want centering to end, perform the same trick, but use the magic code </center> instead.

# Chapter 9
# Frisky Fonts and Crazy Colors

*In This Chapter*
- ▶ Choosing your fonts
- ▶ Using bold and italic
- ▶ Using attributes other than bold and italic
- ▶ Changing text size
- ▶ Using color and background images
- ▶ Inserting special symbols
- ▶ Playing with fonts

Living with standard Web styles like those discussed in Chapter 8 can be pretty boring. In recent years, the Law of the Web has relaxed a bit, allowing Web designers to get comparatively frisky with formatting characters and using color. Now you can adjust text size, use colored text, use a solid color or an image for a background, use some special symbols, and (in Navigator and Internet Explorer) choose your fonts — not rocket science in the document-publishing world but an improvement in the Web world.

## Choosing Fonts

Netscape and Microsoft are first in line to get frisky with fonts. To date, the stern, definitely nonfrisky Law of the Web has been "Thou shalt not specify fonts in Web documents, as fonts are the exclusive choice of the browser user." Netscape and Microsoft have blown a giant raspberry at that Law and designed their browsers to accept your font choices in the Web page. Other browsers display the text in whatever font they are set up to use (most typically, Times Roman).

*Note:* The font is not actually transmitted with your document. This whole fontsy scheme relies on the person who's browsing your site to have the font you've chosen installed on his or her computer. To reach the broadest audience with your font selection, choose common fonts, such as Times Roman (or Times New Roman), Helvetica (or Switzerland), and Courier.

Choose and apply fonts in Web documents just as you do in normal documents; you can choose a font either before you type or afterward to selected text. To choose a font, you can use either the Font box in the Property Bar (the bottom row of buttons) or the Font dialog box (press F9 or choose Format⇨Font). Apply fonts after you choose a style; otherwise, the style dictates the font.

Font size initially comes from the Web style that you choose (such as Heading 1 or Normal), but you can change the size, if you like. Feel free to set font sizes as you normally would in a WordPerfect document (although fewer sizes are available).

If you do set font size, don't expect browsers to take the sizes given by WordPerfect literally. See "Text of all sizes," later in this chapter for details.

# Being Bold, Italic, Underlined, or Monospace

Feeling bold? Italian? Bold and Italian? On the Web, you can embolden or italicize text of any standard style — headings, Normal, Preformatted Text, whatever. You can combine bold and italic, too.

WordPerfect bold isn't really bold; it's *strong*. The difference sounds subtle, to be sure, but what it means is that whereas nearly all browsers display strong as bold, some browsers may display strong as italic, or display a different font, or display whatever the user chose! Likewise, WordPerfect italic is something called *emphasized*, and again, some browsers may not display it as italic.

## Bold and italic buttons

To use bold or italic type, click the buttons in the Property Bar (marked **b** for bold and *i* for italic), just as you would in a regular WordPerfect document. Notice that WordPerfect doesn't give you a button for underlining. On the Web, the underline is universally used to indicate hyperlinks. Underline something, and people may send you nastygrams that your links don't work. I suggest that you stay away from underlining.

## Font box freaks

As usual, WordPerfect gives you several ways other than Property-Bar buttons to change text attributes such as bold and italic. One way is to press F9 or choose Format⇨Font to display the Font dialog box and then click the Bold or Italic check box (see Figure 9-1).

**Figure 9-1:** Check your appearance in the Font dialog box.

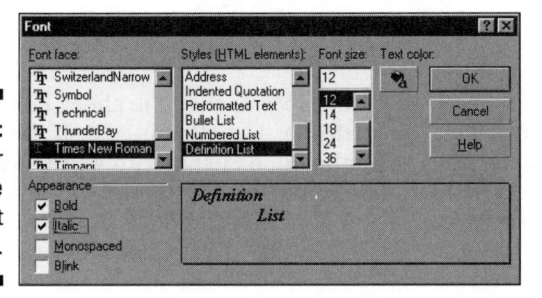

A couple of freaky appearance choices live in this dialog box, too: Monospaced and Blink. These oddballs are (and should be) rarely used. Browsers usually translate monospace type into Courier, in which each character gets exactly the same space in the line; you can apply it to any standard text style, such as Normal and the various Heading styles. Monospaced type provides all the ugliness of Preformatted Text without that style's useful capability to display tabs and multiple spaces.

The Blink option makes text flash on and off — but not in WordPerfect (where it just looks kind of fuzzy) or in any browser other than Netscape Navigator! This option is OK for text that is really important, but only if you use it on a page that is not going to be in front of your visitor for long. Blink is very annoying after a while.

# Accessing All Attributes

Web text can appear in all sorts of interesting and bizarre forms, called *attributes*. These attributes include familiar things (such as bold, italic, and underline), plus a few less familiar things (such as relative size, strikethrough font, and superscript or subscript).

WordPerfect hides these attributes in the Property Bar, in a tiny button that has a modest but bold **a** printed on it. Click that button and, as shown in Figure 9-2, a list of possible attributes comes tumbling down.

**Figure 9-2:** Where WordPerfect hides its attributes.

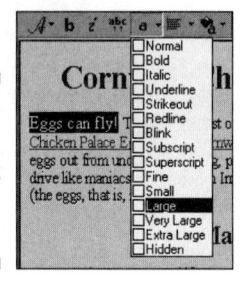

Click the check box of an attribute to select it; click the check box again to clear the check and deselect the attribute. The attributes near the top of the list (Bold through Blink) can be combined. As usual with WordPerfect formats, you can select text and then choose an attribute, or choose an attribute first and then type.

## Bold and italic again, and friends

The top half of the attribute list consists of some old and new friends. Like any collection of friends, not all of them are employed on a regular basis. But like any good collection of friends, most of them play well together; you can use them in combination. (Normal and Hidden play alone, however.)

Normal, Bold, Italic, and Underline should need no introduction, except maybe to say that Normal doesn't mean Normal style for text; it means "not having any attributes." (Makes me glad that I'm not considered to be Normal.) Also, don't use Underline; it makes your text look like hyperlinks to be clicked.

Strikeout, Redline, and Blink sound like three marginal ballplayers but actually are three marginal text attributes. Strikeout spikes a line through the middle of text and is not overly useful; Redline usually turns out to be just plain bold; and Blink is flashy but annoying (see "Font box freaks," earlier in this chapter).

Hidden is the most mysterious attribute; it makes your text go away entirely and irretrievably (unless you undo the change by pressing Ctrl+Z). My editor recommends that I use Hidden, however, so it must be great.

## Text of all sizes

The bottom half of the attribute list, from Fine to Extra Large, allows you to (drumroll, please) change the text size! Wow, what a space-age concept! Also, Subscript and Superscript attributes are available for you corporate folks who need to ™ and ® everything, as well as for the scientists and engineers among us who are typing endnotes and numbers raised to powers.

But notice in Figure 9-2 that all the sizes are relative, like "large"; no point sizes exist, as they do in a regular document. That omission exists because under the Law of the Web, true point size is the responsibility of the browser, so all you can do is use a smaller or larger size than Normal text. Most people leave their browsers' font preferences alone, so Normal text is 12-point for them.

"But," you should exclaim in confusion, "what about the regular Font Size box — the one next to the font selection box? How come the Font Size box uses point sizes?" That, pilgrim, is a good question. The complete answer is that WordPerfect's Font Size box is a benign fraud. Specific font sizes don't exist on the Web. The Font Size box is simply a WordPerfect way of trying to make word processing on the Web look like regular word processing. The Font Size box is, in fact, just another way to control relative font sizes that compete awkwardly with the relative font sizes in the attribute list.

The upshot of having these two ways of setting font size is the following rule:

Use either the relative sizes in the attribute list or the Font Size box. Don't combine the two.

## Text of All Tints

One nice thing about Web documents today is the fact that color is easy to use and universal. In the old days (a year ago or so), only Netscape browsers showed color text. Now Web weavers can go wild with text and background color!

And some people *do* go wild, unfortunately. Have you ever tried to read red text on a bright blue background? Afterward, you need to bathe your eyeballs in a warm herbal solution while someone massages your temples. Or what about reading light yellow hypertext on a white background? `Revolutionary new ____ cures _____ and grows ____!`, the hypertext may appear to say. What? Are the invisible words *diet, warts,* and *hair?* Or are they *fertilizer, lawn blight,* and *grass?*

**Part II: Text Tricks**

## Central color control

The central control for text and background color is in something called the HTML Document Properties dialog box. (Properties, of course, should never be confused with attributes, formats, styles, or appearances, right? Right.) So forget the dialog box's name and remember any of the three ways to find it:

- Choose Format⇨Text/Background Colors.
- Click the HTML Document Properties button (which appears to depict a cobwebby calculator) in the Property Bar. (This button does not appear when you have text selected.)
- Right-click any text or blank area of your document (not graphics) and then choose Properties from the shortcut menu that appears.

When the HTML Document Properties dialog box appears, click its Text/Background Colors tab, and you see something like Figure 9-3.

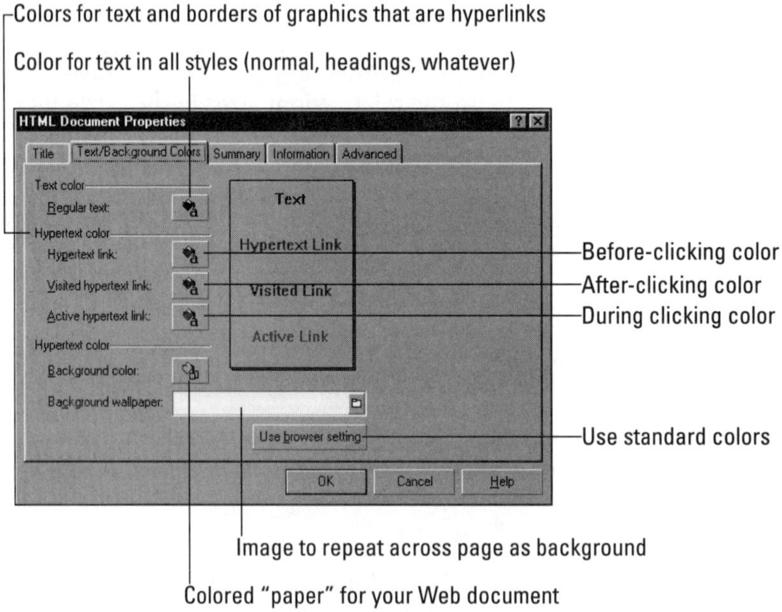

**Figure 9-3:** A text-coloring box that any kid or Web weaver (same thing) could love.

Colors for text and borders of graphics that are hyperlinks
Color for text in all styles (normal, headings, whatever)
Before-clicking color
After-clicking color
During clicking color
Use standard colors
Image to repeat across page as background
Colored "paper" for your Web document

To color any of the text types described in the dialog box (such as Regular text, which means "not a hyperlink"), click the button for that text type. (Buttons are called out in Figure 9-3.) A pretty multicolor box springs up, shown in many delightful shades of gray in Figure 9-4. Click any color displayed to select it. Colors that you have used recently are displayed across the top.

**Figure 9-4:** A lovely assortment of colors to choose among — trust me!

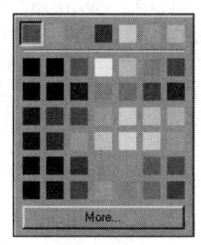

For more information on these colors, see upcoming sections of this chapter. First, though, ponder your color schemes and dreams with the help of the following section.

## Color schemes and dreams

Choosing colors is serious business. If you don't believe me, go to a paint center in your local hardware store and check out all the color schemes for house paint and trim.

Good designers think about all kinds of stuff when they choose colors. It's probably best not to inquire too closely exactly what they think about — but among their more useful ponderings is the mood, feeling, or attitude that the colors are likely to imply. Other, more practical issues include readability and clear color-coding of special information, such as hyperlinks. Following are some of the decisions that you, as designer, have to make and some of the implications of different choices.

### What text color on what background?

Because you can choose both background color and text color, you need to decide whether the text will be light on a dark background or the other way around. Most people find that dark on light is more readable and easier on the eyes. Given both combinations on a page, people's eyes may be first attracted by light text on dark but then drift toward dark text on light background. For a more dramatic look, use light text on dark, but don't be dramatic everywhere; drama gets tiresome fast.

For legibility's sake, use contrasting colors, but avoid using bright text colors with bright background colors. In particular, avoid using bright reds or yellows against bright blues or greens; these colors tend to vibrate visually. (If you're trying to convey an image of nervous excitement, of course, there you go.)

In general, for a more conservative appearance, use text and background colors that are all cool (blues and greens) or all warm (reds, yellows, and browns); for a more "in-your-face" appearance, feel free to mix 'em up.

If you choose a text color that goes well with a particular wallpaper background that you have chosen (*wallpaper* is an image that is repeated across the background of your page), choose a suitable background color, too. Some browsers have images turned off, and if you haven't chosen a background color, those browsers use standard gray. Your text may not be legible on gray!

### What colors look nice?

Deciding what looks nice for anyone in the entire world who might visit your site is a tough row to hoe. Even white is controversial. (In the Western world, white is associated with weddings, whereas in some Oriental countries, white is associated with funerals.) More to the point is what sort of image you want to convey. Here are some highly debatable and subjective suggestions:

- Primary colors — such as strong red, blue, green, and yellow — suggest playfulness or simplicity if used together, or directness and clarity if used singly.
- Pastels (chalky colors) suggest softness, tropical islands, spring, or dreaminess.
- Dark or muddy colors suggest solidity, secretiveness, earth, depth, or richness.
- Reddish colors suggest strong emotions or warmth.
- Bluish colors suggest passiveness, sky, water, or coolness.
- Greenish colors suggest nature; light blue-greens may suggest hospitals, though!
- Yellowish colors suggest light, warmth, or activity.
- Browns suggest earth, nature, security, or wholesomeness.

If you are doing work for an organization, your color scheme probably should use the organization's colors — the ones used in the logo, stationery, or newsletter. That task is a challenging one, however, because you are dealing in colors of light, and stationery deals in colors of ink. The person who designed your organization's printed materials may be able to help by giving you the CMYK colors, which you can enter in a custom palette. See "More colors: palettes for the picky," later in this chapter for details.

### Regular text color

The first color in the HTML Document Properties dialog box is Regular text color (refer to Figure 9-3). This color applies to all the text in your document (Normal-style text, headings, indented text, whatever) except hyperlinks (things that you click) and any spot color that you apply.

By *spot color*, I mean color that you choose to apply to particular blocks of text, using a completely different tool. See "Coloring selected text," later in this chapter for more information on the spot-color tool for text.

## Hypertext color

Hypertext colors apply to hyperlinked text (the text that you click) and also to the borders that usually appear around hyperlinked graphics. The middle three colors in the HTML Document Properties dialog box are the Hypertext Color options (refer to Figure 9-3).

Why three colors? The Law of the Web (the official HTML specification) specifies one color each for before, during, and after clicking. The during-clicking color is just a quick flash to tell the user that he or she succeeded in clicking the text. The after-clicking color tells the user that he or she has already explored this link. Following are some suggestions for choosing your hypertext colors:

- For the before-clicking color (Hypertext link), choose a color that contrasts with your background and is fairly bright. Colors in either the top row or the center columns of the color-selection panel tend to work well. (The before-clicking color is also used for "alternate" text when a graphic is used for a hyperlink.)

- For the after-clicking color (Visited hypertext link), choose a darker or lighter version of the before-clicking color. Darker is more conventional for visited links and so is more likely to be understood properly.

- The during-clicking color (Active hypertext link) could be anything, but a lighter version of the before-clicking color, or a slightly different color, generally gets the point across.

## Background color and wallpaper

Background color and wallpaper (an image that forms a continuous background) are controversial subjects among Web designers. Most designers prefer plain white for background color and use no wallpaper. That way, nothing distracts the reader from all the important stuff on the page.

### Color

Even if you want only a plain white background, you must specifically choose it, or you get gray. Choose your background color and/or wallpaper in the same place that you choose your text colors: the Text/Background Color tab of the HTML Document Properties dialog box (refer to Figure 9-3). Choose Format➪Text/Background Colors to open the dialog box.

In the Text/Background Color tab, click the paint can button next to the label Background color; then click a color in the panel that appears. Even if you plan to use wallpaper and not solid color, choose a background color. Refer to "Color schemes and dreams," earlier in this chapter, for suggestions about background and text color.

### Wallpaper

In place of a solid-color background, you can use an image, called *wallpaper*. Enter an image file in the Background wallpaper text box of the Text/Background Color tab, and your Web page suddenly has a clever appearance. Click the tiny folder button next to the text box, and a dialog box much like the WordPerfect Open box helps you select a background image. To remove wallpaper, delete everything in the Background wallpaper text box.

For more information on wallpaper, see Chapter 12.

Even if you use wallpaper, choose a background color. If people have images turned off in their browsers, the wallpaper won't show up, so you need a background that contrasts with your text. Also, because background color appears in the browser before the wallpaper does, choosing a background color that matches the predominant color in your wallpaper creates a nice, smooth-looking transition.

## Coloring selected text

If one color of text is nice, multiple colors are several times as nice. WordPerfect allows you to color individual letters, words, sentences, or any text whatever color that you like.

Simply select the text to be colored and then click the Font Color button on the Property Bar. Figure 9-5 shows the Font Color button (at top) and the text-color palette.

A good use of font color is to make your headings a different color from the body of your text. If you're in a giddy mood (and who could blame you, given all this color?), you can even color the letters of a word individually. In general, however, show some restraint: Two to four colors usually are plenty.

If you find the Font Color palette to be a little skimpy and want to create a custom color of your own, click the More button and then read the following section.

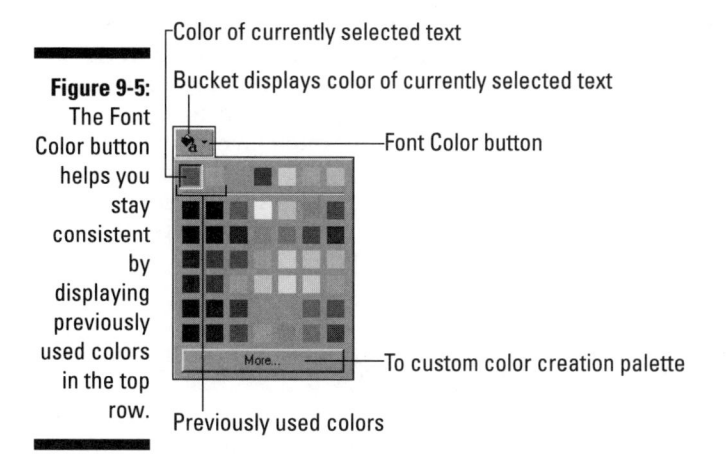

**Figure 9-5:** The Font Color button helps you stay consistent by displaying previously used colors in the top row.

- Color of currently selected text
- Bucket displays color of currently selected text
- Font Color button
- To custom color creation palette
- Previously used colors

## More colors: palettes for the picky

If you're trying to get just that right shade of magenta to go with your drapes or fingernails, WordPerfect allows you to create a custom color for text in your HTML document. You can choose among 16 million colors!

To make a custom color, click the More button in any palette that appears for text color. A Select Color dialog box appears. The most useful controls in that dialog box are shown in Figure 9-6.

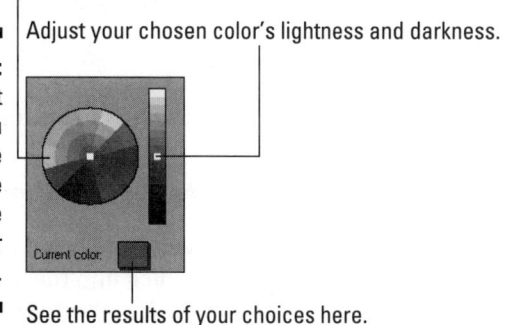

**Figure 9-6:** WordPerfect allows you to choose exactly the right shade of puce (or whatever).

- Click a color you like in the color wheel.
- Adjust your chosen color's lightness and darkness.
- See the results of your choices here.

Click the circle to select your color and then click the vertical bar to adjust the lightness or darkness. (You can drag the white square in these controls instead, if you prefer dragging to clicking.) Click OK when you're done, and your selected text is colored. (You can't see the color properly, however, until you click somewhere else in your document to get rid of the selection highlight.)

**Part II: Text Tricks**

> **TIP:** The Select Colon dialog box displays some other controls for color, most of which you won't ever need. But if you must match your company's trademark colors, you need to use certain controls: the Color model selection and the Color values numbers. Your trademark colors probably can be expressed in something called a CMYK color model, which gives you four numbers — one each for Cyan, Magenta, Yellow, and Black. Ask your logo designer for these CMYK values. Click the down arrow next to Color model and choose CMYK from the drop-down list that appears. Then enter the four numbers in the Color Model area of the dialog box.

## *Using Characters of All Kinds*

WordPerfect acts as though you can use any of its special characters in Web documents, but it just ain't so. WordPerfect allows you to insert those characters into the Web-formatted WordPerfect file, but when you publish to HTML, many of those characters don't appear.

You can, however, use some of the WordPerfect symbols. To insert a symbol, follow these steps:

1. **Choose Insert⇨Symbol.**

   Alternatively, click the Insert Symbol button — which by depicting the characters #* appears to be cursing in cartoon language — near the right end of the Property Bar.

   The WordPerfect Symbols dialog box pops up.

2. **Choose a Character Set at the top of the WordPerfect Symbols dialog box.**

   The Typographic Symbols and Multinational character sets (if installed) contain characters that you can use on the Web.

3. **To insert a character, click it and then click the Insert button at the bottom of the box.**

4. **Click the Close button to close the WordPerfect Symbols box.**

Figures 9-7 and 9-8 show the few special characters that the Law of the Web currently allows. If you need these characters, you'll find them in WordPerfect's Typographic Symbols and Multinational character sets. Not all the characters display properly in all browsers, but the newer browsers should do fine.

The WordPerfect Equation Editor also works fine on the Web. WordPerfect, in effect, takes a snapshot of the equation and produces the equation as a graphic file when you publish to HTML.

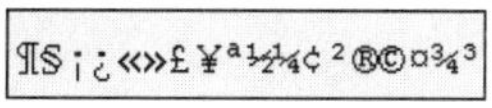

**Figure 9-7:** Web-usable characters in the Typographic set.

¶ § ¡ ¿ « » £ ¥ ª ¹ ¼ ¢ ² ® © ª ¾ ³

**Figure 9-8:** Web-usable characters in the Multi-national set.

Æ Á Â À Å Ã Ç Ð É Ê È Ë Í Î Ì Ï Ñ
Ó Ô Ò Ø Õ Ö Þ Ú Û Ù Ü Ý á â à
ã ä ç é ê è ð ë í î ì ï ñ ó ô ò ø õ ö ß þ ú û
ù ü ý ÿ

## When Fancy Fonts and Formats Go Bad

When text goes bad, things can get ugly. Following are a few puzzling uglies and what to do about them:

- **Italics can't be turned off.** The text may be in Address style, which always appears italicized. Press F9 and choose a different style for the text.
- **Blinking text doesn't blink.** In WordPerfect, text doesn't blink; it appears to be shadowed. Also, blinking is not an official standard, so non-Netscape browsers may not display it.
- **The chosen font isn't displayed in the browser.** Fonts (typefaces) work only in Netscape or Microsoft browsers, and then only on computers that have the chosen font (or one like it) installed.
- **The Font Size setting doesn't seem to work properly.** The Font Size setting is an illusion. The size of a font is actually determined by several different settings, including style and the attributes of relative size (such as Large). The situation is a messy one. Try making sure that the text attribute (set it by clicking the **a** button) is Normal.

# Chapter 10
# Tantalizing Tables

***

### In This Chapter
▶ Understanding weirdness in Web tables
▶ Creating tables
▶ Adding and deleting rows and columns
▶ Using the table Property Bar
▶ Sizing the table
▶ Controlling borders and space
▶ Positioning the table
▶ Aligning contents in cells
▶ Controlling row height and column width
▶ Splitting and joining cells

***

Tables are one of the most welcome recent additions to the Web. (It's hard to imagine what we all ate off before.) Tables are not just a way of displaying various types of nice, neat lists; Web weavers today frequently use tables to present an attractive smorgasbord of text and graphics on their Web pages. Figure 10-1 shows a simple example of the top of a home page that uses a table to control layout. Figure 10-2 shows a more conventional table.

**Figure 10-1:** A table can create a more precise layout.

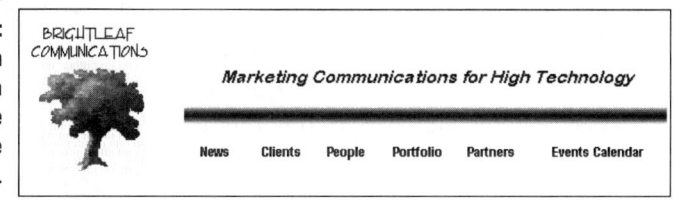

**Figure 10-2:** Your basic, everyday table.

| Product | Sales by Sales Channel | |
|---|---|---|
| | Direct sales | Distributor |
| Buggy whips | 25 | 125 |
| Unicycles | 5 | 85 |
| Atl-atls | 225 | 16 |

Although you can't really see anything that looks like a table in Figure 10-1 because borders are turned off, the text and graphics are actually in a table. For more information about using tables specifically for layout, see Chapter 17.

# What's Weird about Web Tables

Web tables are a bit unusual in certain ways. Here are a few of their peculiarities:

- Tables are new to the Web. Not all browsers support tables, and the ones that do support tables may display them somewhat differently.
- Table width can be set as a percentage of the browser's window or in pixels (dots on-screen).
- Column widths and heights depend strictly on the content and the width of the browser window. Despite the fact that WordPerfect gives you controls for width, you can't reliably set columns to a given width on the Web.
- Table borders appear to be raised above the page.
- Borders can be turned off entirely, so that you can use the table as a way to arrange text and graphics on a page.
- In Netscape and some other browsers, columns that have no contents disappear (except for their borders).
- Rows that have no contents also disappear.
- Cells that are not filled are raised to border level.

If you don't want to deal with all this weirdness, and want to present a table that looks just like the regular WordPerfect tables that you know and love, see "Cheating at the Table" at the end of this chapter. (Moralists, rejoice: There is a price to pay, however.)

## The Table Property Bar

WordPerfect, ever vigilant, is always changing its Property Bar (the bottom set of buttons) to suit whatever you are doing. When you click a table, the right end of the Property Bar gives you buttons for tables; Figure 10-3 shows some of the gems that you find there.

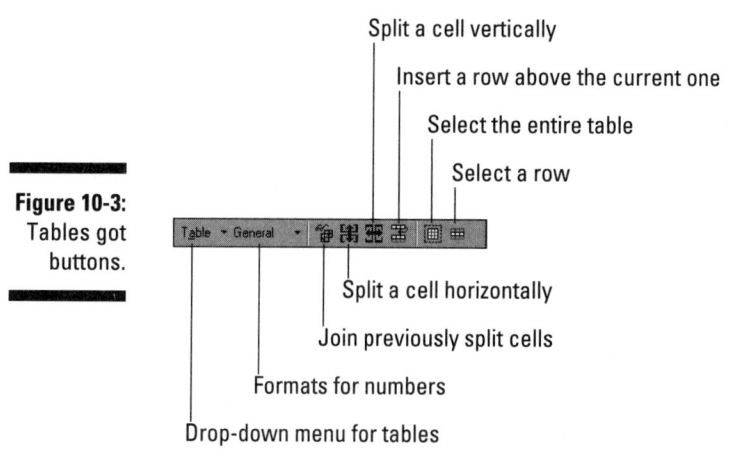

**Figure 10-3:** Tables got buttons.

Callouts: Split a cell vertically; Insert a row above the current one; Select the entire table; Select a row; Split a cell horizontally; Join previously split cells; Formats for numbers; Drop-down menu for tables

## Making a Table

To create a table for your Web-site surfers, begin the table as you would in a regular WordPerfect document. The two totally tubular ways to get tabular in WordPerfect are as follows:

- **The fast way:** Click the Table QuickCreate button in the Toolbar. This way, you make the table first and format it later.
- **The careful way:** Choose Insert⇨Table.

I suggest that you throw caution to the winds and use the fast way. Create a table in the usual WordPerfect Web format; then go back and format the table.

### The fast way

The fastest way to get a table is to click, hold, and drag the Table QuickCreate button in the WordPerfect Toolbar. Figure 10-4 shows you the button and the QuickCreate panel that springs forth from the button.

**Figure 10-4:** Click and hold the button, drag in the grid, and release it to make a table.

Click this button in the toolbar

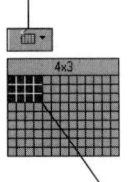

Drag to highlight the size of the table you want

Drag to highlight the number of rows and columns that you want; then release the mouse button. A nice, bordered, blank table appears in WordPerfect. To change the table's appearance, see the other sections of this chapter.

## The careful way

To carefully craft a table your way right from the start, choose Insert⇨Table; the HTML Table Properties dialog box springs up. See "Formatting the Entire Table," later in this chapter for instructions on using those controls.

Enter the number of columns and rows you want in the Columns and Rows boxes; then read further in this chapter for information on various types of formatting. When you're done specifying your table formats, click the OK button.

## Entering Stuff in the Table

You can put darned near anything in a table in addition to text — anything from pictures to movies to virtual-reality worlds — which is what makes tables so popular for controlling the layout of all the features on a page. But plain old text is still an important ingredient.

You can use any style of text you like in the cells of a table: Normal, headings, numbered lists, you name it. (Refer to Chapter 8 for the scoop on standard styles.) You can also use bold, italic, or font sizes to adjust appearances.

***Note:*** In initial releases of WordPerfect 8, the Tab key — which you press to indent in indented styles such as Definition List, Numbered List, Bullet List, and Indented Quotation — does not work. (Neither does Ctrl+Tab.) To use those lists in a table, create the indented list outside the table; then cut and paste it into the table. You need to cut and paste only one indented paragraph; pressing the Enter key at the end of an indented line spawns a new indented paragraph.

For the most part, you can use numbers in a Web document table just as you would in a regular WordPerfect table. You can't decimal-align numbers (align them so their decimal points line up). You can, however, still format the numbers as you like: with a fixed number of decimal places, as a percentage, as money, and so on.

Select any cell, row, or column or, to format the entire table, click anywhere in the table and then choose Edit⇨Select⇨Table. Immediately to the right of the Table button in WordPerfect's Property Bar is a Numeric Format button which displays whatever format is currently in use. Initially, the button displays "General," as shown in the left margin of this paragraph. Click that button and choose a new numeric format from the list that drops down.

You can insert graphics as well. Simply click the cell where you want an image to appear, choose Insert⇨Graphics, and then make your choice of graphic object from the submenu that appears. See Chapter 11 for more about the various choices.

## Formatting the Entire Table

The key to formatting the entire table (as opposed to individual rows, columns, or cells) is the set of controls shown in Figure 10-5. These controls appear when you create a table for the first time by choosing Insert⇨Table.

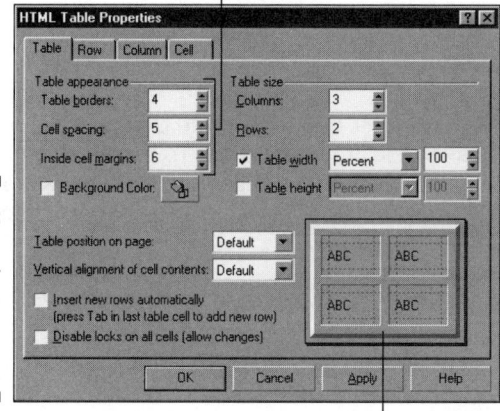

**Figure 10-5:** The controls for overall table formatting.

Any of the following methods display the dialog box shown in Figure 10-5:

- Click anywhere in the table and press Ctrl+F12.
- Click anywhere in the table and choose Table⇨Format from the Property Bar (the bottom row of buttons, not the menu bar).
- Right-click anywhere in the table and choose Format from the shortcut menu that appears.

The HTML Table Properties dialog box springs into action. Click the Table tab to access the controls shown in Figure 10-5.

## Adding or deleting rows or columns

The bottom of the table is the easiest place to add a new row. Just click the bottom-right cell of the table and press the Tab key.

WordPerfect also allows you to add a row or column next to any existing one. Click anywhere in the existing row or column and then choose Table⇨Insert to display the Insert Columns/Rows dialog box. Choose Columns or Rows, and enter the number of columns or rows that you want to add. Click Before or After to tell WordPerfect on which side of the existing row or column to put the new one. Then click the OK button.

The fast way to add a row is to add one above the "current" row (where the insertion point is). Just click the Insert Row button.

To delete a row or column, click anywhere in it and then choose Table⇨Delete to display the Delete Structure/Contents dialog box. Choose Columns or Rows. To delete additional following columns or rows, enter a number of rows or columns greater than 1. Then click OK.

## Sizing the table

Left to its own devices, WordPerfect creates a table that spans the entire width of the page and is as long as it needs to be. To use a table of more modest width or to specify a fixed width, click anywhere in the table, choose Table⇨Format (or press Ctrl+F12), and use the Table Size controls shown in Figure 10-6.

**Figure 10-6:**
Table Size controls are part of the overall table controls.

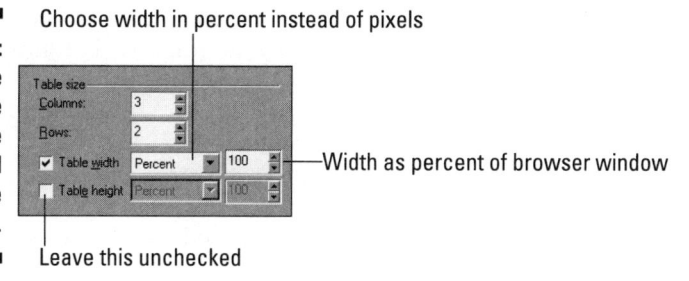

Choose width in percent instead of pixels

Width as percent of browser window

Leave this unchecked

You can adjust the number of rows and columns by changing the values in the Columns and Rows boxes, but that adjustment doesn't change the physical size of the table. You can set physical table width in Web documents in either of two ways:

- As a percentage of window size
- As a fixed number of *pixels* (dots on-screen)

Figure 10-7 shows a table set to 50 percent of window size. (If you also align the table to the right, text that normally would follow the table appears next to it.)

**Figure 10-7:** A smaller table can make for a nicer layout.

| Beverage Sales | Fall | Winter | Spring |
|---|---|---|---|
| Cocoa | 25,873 | 38,924 | 14,688 |
| Tea | 12,573 | 14,886 | 13,934 |
| Coffee | 60,183 | 58,925 | 58,824 |

Hot beverage sales over the 3-season period were more robust than usual due to the early onset and late departure of cold weather. The modest increase in tea sales may be due to the higher number of head colds.

Use the percentage method for everything except for graphics that you feel must be a particular size. For text, setting the width of the table in pixels just leads to confusion and moral decay. As you can see in Figure 10-6, the Table Size controls uphold the moral fiber of society by normally using Percent.

- To adjust width, enter a new percentage in the Table width box. If you enter, say, **50** (for 50 percent), your table occupies half the width of your visitor's browser window.

- The Table height box doesn't do anything useful — and can do some very confusing things — so leave it alone. The current state of the art in HTML provides no way to set table height; height adjusts to whatever is necessary to achieve the table width that you request.

Use the pixel method if you want to use a table to arrange graphics and are finicky about sizing your table precisely to your graphics. For information on using tables to arrange graphics and text, see Chapter 17.

## Controlling borders and space

Web tables give you precise control of borders and spacing. Tables on the Web have two kinds of borders:

- A rectangle around the entire table (called Table Borders, in WordPerfect)
- An additional rectangle around each cell (called Cell Borders, in WordPerfect)

You also can control the amount of blank space between the content of your cells and the border. In WordPerfect, this space is called Cell Margins.

Figure 10-8 shows the controls for borders and spacing, with arrows pointing to the areas of the table they affect. The dialog box conveniently displays a sample area where you can see the results as you adjust the borders or spacing.

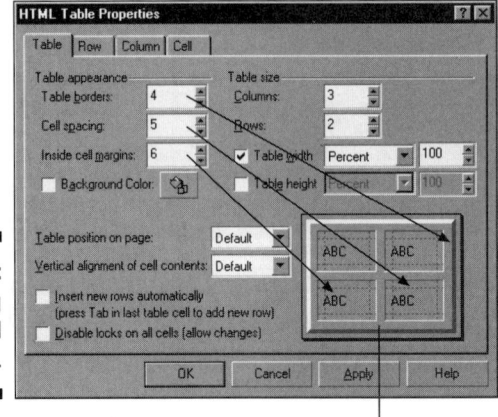

**Figure 10-8:** Adjusting borders and spacing.

To make all borders disappear, click the text box labeled Table borders and enter **0**. (If you are using a background color for a row, column, or multiple cells, some gap in color always appears between cells. Set Table borders to 0 and Cell Spacing to 1 to eliminate borders and minimize gaps.)

To widen the borders, enter larger values. The value that you enter gives width in pixels (dots on-screen).

To adjust the space between the contents of your cells and their borders, click the text box labeled Inside cell margins and enter a value. (This value, like the border values, is in pixels.)

## Positioning the table left or right

Like an illustration, a table can be positioned against the left or right side of the browser window. When you use positioning, however, first set the width of the table to something less than 100 percent.

Click anywhere in the table and then call up your old pal the HTML Table Properties dialog box. (Choose Table⇨Format.) In the Table tab (refer to Figure 10-8), set the table width to less than 100 percent, and choose Right or Left from the Table position on page drop-down list.

***Note:*** Text wraps around only right-aligned tables, not left-aligned ones. Put the text for wrapping after the table, not before it. Early releases of WordPerfect 8 don't display text wrapping to tables, but you can click the View in Web Browser button (the document-behind-a-web icon) and check the result in your browser. Don't accidentally right-align tables of 100 percent width, or the subsequent text may overwrite the left side of the table!

# Selecting Rows, Columns, and Cells

You can select cells by dragging in WordPerfect tables, but shortcuts exist. Here's a quick review of how to select rows, columns, cells, or an entire table:

- To select a column, move your mouse pointer toward the top edge of any cell in that column; when the pointer turns to an up arrow, double-click. Alternatively, click any cell of the column and then click the Select Row button (the button at the far right end of the Property Bar).

- To select a row, move your mouse pointer toward the left edge of any cell in that row; when the pointer turns to a left arrow, double-click. Alternatively, click any cell of the row and then click the Select Row button (the third button from the right end of the Property Bar, which is the bottom set of buttons).

- To select the entire table, click the Select Table button.

To select just one cell, perform either of the first two actions, but single-click instead of double-click.

You don't have to select a row or column to format it. Just click any cell of the row or column that you want to format, choose Table⇨Format to display the HTML Table Properties dialog box, and then click the Row or Column tab.

## Aligning Contents in Their Cells

Just as you can in regular WordPerfect documents, you can align the contents of cells left, right, or center within the cells. You can also align the contents vertically: top, center, or bottom.

*Note:* Vertical alignment has no effect unless blank space appears in the cells above or below the contents. That event occurs only when something tall appears in another cell of the row.

Here are the steps to follow for aligning contents within their cells:

1. **Select whatever cells, rows, or columns you want to align, or the entire table, if you like.**

2. **Choose Table⇨Format.**

    The HTML Table Properties dialog box springs into action.

3. **Click the Row, Column, or Cell tab, depending on whether you are aligning the contents of a row, a column, or an individual cell.**

    If you're working on the entire table, I suggest that you choose the Cell tab.

4. **To align contents horizontally, click the box labeled Horizontal and then choose Left, Right, or Center.**

5. **To align contents vertically, click the box labeled Vertical and then choose Top, Bottom, or Center.**

You can set the vertical alignment of all cells in the table at the same time; the control for doing so is in the Table tab of the HTML Table Properties dialog box. This control, however, works only on cells for which you set the vertical alignment to Default in the Row, Column, and Cell tabs (all three!).

## Sizing Columns, Rows, and Cells — Not!

The Law of the Web says that you can't size individual columns, rows, or cells. Your Web-site visitor's browser decides the sizes of these elements. The browser simply divides the available space among the columns. The browser tries to divide space evenly among the columns, but if any cell's contents are too wide to fit in an equal share, its column gets more space.

The more text appears in any cell of a column, the wider the column becomes at the expense of the other columns. If the text gets too wide to fit in the browser's window, the browser wraps the text around in the cell, making the row higher.

## So what are those width and height controls for?

WordPerfect tries to give you some control of row and column sizes through controls similar to the ones that you use in normal WordPerfect document tables. (The Column width control of the Column tab in the HTML Table Properties dialog box is one example.) Because this approach doesn't conform to the current HTML standard, the results are unreliable, but it may give you some control in Netscape Navigator. Someday, HTML rules for tables may allow these controls to work universally.

## So how can I control width and height?

You can increase column width by using nonbreaking (hard) spaces; to add a hard space, press Ctrl+spacebar. A modern browser won't wrap text at nonbreaking spaces. By substituting nonbreaking spaces for regular spaces, and by adding nonbreaking spaces before or after text, you can force a cell to be wider by preventing line wrap.

Likewise, you can increase row height by using a Heading style, by choosing a larger type size, or by adding manual line breaks (choose Insert⇨Line Break) to force a line of text to wrap. The use of large graphics also increases column width and row height.

To decrease the width of a column or the height of a row, make other columns or rows bigger by using the techniques in the preceding two paragraphs. You can even add blank rows or columns for the sole purpose of squishing the others.

# Using Borders and Fills — Not!

Borders and fill don't work for tables on the Web. But if you want fancy tables, see the last section of this chapter, "Cheating at the Table."

## Splitting Cells

Tables sometimes need to undergo *mitosis,* which means "splitting of cells." (*Mitosis* is a great word. You can get the day off from work by calling in and saying, "I've got to stay home and take care of my mitosis." Be prepared to answer a few questions later, though.)

Splitting (or its reverse, which is joining) of cells allows you to create tables like the one shown in Figure 10-9. Figure 10-9 shows a conventional table in which splitting or joining is necessary, but splits and joins are also essential for the less-conventional task of performing complex page layouts of text and graphics. See Chapter 17 for more information about complex layouts.

**Figure 10-9:** Joining the animals in their family.

Table was originally 3 by 4 rows

| Family | Animal | Track pattern |
|--------|--------|---------------|
| Mustelid | Fisher | Bounding |
|  | Long-tailed weasel |  |
|  | Short-tailed weasel |  |

Three cells joined in two places

I created the table in Figure 10-9 by starting with a three-column by four-row table. Then I used WordPerfect's join feature to merge three cells into the one cell for Mustelid and did likewise with the cell for Bounding. Joining cells is slightly simpler than splitting them. To join cells, select them and then choose Table⇨Join⇨Cell.

I could just as easily have started with a three-column by two-row table and split the center cell of the bottom row into three rows. To split a cell, click that cell and then choose Table⇨Split⇨Cell to display the Split Cell dialog box. Choose Columns to create multiple columns in that cell or Rows to create multiple rows. Enter the number of rows or columns that you want to create; then click OK. Figure 10-10 shows the splitting process in the Split Cell dialog box.

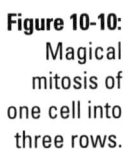

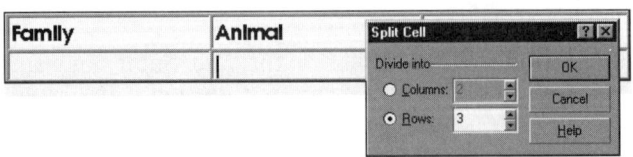

**Figure 10-10:** Magical mitosis of one cell into three rows.

Another way to split or join is to use the QuickSplit or QuickJoin button shown in Figure 10-11. They appear near the right end of the Property Bar.

**Figure 10-11:** Quick but sticky buttons for splitting and joining.
— QuickJoin
— QuickSplit row
— QuickSplit column

These buttons are what I call "sticky": you click them and they remain enabled until you click them again. The following steps will explain further:

1. **Click a button.**

    Your tool is enabled.

2. **Do your work, as follows:**

    • If you're using QuickSplit, click a cell to split it in two even parts.

    • If you're using QuickJoin, drag over multiple cells to join them.

3. **Click the button again.**

    The tool is disabled.

The QuickJoin and QuickSplit tools are great when you are trying to use a table to control layout. Lots of splitting and joining goes on.

# Attractive Tablecloths: Background Color

WordPerfect offers a slick trick that is not standard under the most recent rules of HTML but that works in Netscape Navigator and Microsoft Internet Explorer: background color for the table.

You can set background color for the entire table or for rows, columns, or individual cells. Select the cell, row, column, or individual cell that you want to color; then choose Table⇨Format to display the HTML Table Properties dialog box. Choose the Table, Row, Column, or Cell tab of the dialog box, and find the background color check box. Click the paint can icon next to the check box and then choose a color from the palette that appears.

> **TIP:** In early releases of WordPerfect 8, setting color in the Table page of the HTML Table Properties dialog box did not work. The workaround is to select the entire table and then use the background color control in the Row, Column, or Cell tab.

## Cheating at the Table

If you would really not rather deal with the peculiarities of Web tables, but just want to display a table more or less as it looks in WordPerfect, you can cheat: Create a text box and put a table there! WordPerfect turns the table into a graphic image. By doing this, of course, you make your document slower to download on the Web, because graphic images require comparatively large files. The tradeoff is yours to make.

Choose Insert⇨Text Box and a blank Text Box Editor screen takes over your WordPerfect window. Use the usual WordPerfect table controls, such as the Table QuickCreate button described earlier in this chapter, to create a table. You can apply fill patterns and do more of the usual dressy WordPerfect stuff than you can in Web tables. Click the Close button when you're done. When you publish to HTML, the table appears as a graphic image.

# Part III
# Getting Graphical

## The 5th Wave          By Rich Tennant

"Can someone please tell me how long Bud's Lunch Truck has had his own page on the Web?"

## In this part . . .

Rick Smolan, noted photographer and author, talks about "Painting on the Walls of the Digital Cave" — a phrase that seems to sum up a lot of what's happening on the Web. The Web, for better or worse, has gone graphical: and we're all spitting digital paint over our, um . . . digital hands to put graphics on our Web pages.

If you're ready to make your mark, this is the part where you get your hands dirty. Here's how to insert graphics, position and size them, use them for jazzier text, use them for banners, backgrounds, bullets, and buttons, publish them to HTML, and keep them from clogging up the works in the process.

# Chapter 11
# General Graphics

*In This Chapter*
- Putting graphics in documents
- Inserting WordPerfect Clipart
- Inserting other kinds of graphics
- Creating cool "graphical" text with TextArt
- Creating more graphical text with WordPerfect text boxes
- Sizing and positioning graphics
- Using "alternate" text
- Publishing to HTML with graphics

Do you know your graphical aptitude? No? Horrors. Take a short magazine-style quiz. Complete the sentence "A Web page without graphics is . . ."

. . . like a day without sunshine.

. . . like a breath of fresh air compared with Web pages that take a day to download.

. . . like, totally bogus, man.

Give yourself 3 points for each answer that you chose, because graphics are both a blessing and a curse to the Web. Graphics add color, excitement, and sometimes even (gasp!) information. Graphics also present a real challenge to Web designers who need to create the right kind of graphics and make sure that those graphics display properly and efficiently.

WordPerfect helps you create and use many types of graphics, which lifts part of the curse. WordPerfect allows you to use nice features such as TextArt, captions, and text boxes. The program even gives you a vast Scrapbook of clip art (called "Clipart") on your hard disk and on the installation CD-ROM.

But along with more power comes more responsibility (and a few complications). Use the power of graphics wisely, Luke Webweaver. Make sure that you read about using "alternate" text and publishing to HTML with graphics.

## Putting Graphics in Documents

Simply inserting graphics into a Web document is not much different from inserting graphics into any other WordPerfect document. The commands and buttons are the same, and the result looks about the same — while you're in WordPerfect, at least. The main and most convenient controls for inserting graphics into a Web page are

- The Clipart button in the Toolbar
- The Insert⇨Graphics command
- The Text Box button in the Toolbar

Knowing WordPerfect, I suspect that it probably gives you a half-dozen other ways to insert graphics, too; I'll let you know when I find them.

### Deciding where to insert a graphic

You can insert a graphic anywhere. But if a graphic illustrates something that's discussed in text, the best place to insert it usually is the beginning or the end of a paragraph. Create a blank line and insert the graphic there, if the graphic is to stand alone with no text alongside. See "Vying for Position" later in this chapter for more information on positioning graphics.

### Types of graphics that you can insert

You can insert all kinds of stuff. Click the beginning or end of a paragraph, choose Insert⇨Graphics, and then choose any of the following options from the submenu:

- **Clipart.** Insert WordPerfect picture files from WordPerfect's Scrapbook of images on your hard disk and the WordPerfect CD-ROM.
- **From File.** Insert any drawing or image file from any disk on your computer.
- **TextArt.** Use the WordPerfect TextArt tool to create swirly, cute text.
- **Draw Picture.** Use WordPerfect's drawing tools to create a WordPerfect picture.

- **Chart.** Graph data in your document as a bar chart, line chart, or other type of chart.
- **Acquire Image.** Scan something in with your scanner. (You may have to choose Select Image Source first if you have more than one scanner driver.)

You may also copy and paste an image from any other Windows program into your WordPerfect document. Just to complete the list of graphics that you can put on a Web page, although WordPerfect text boxes and embedded objects such as spreadsheets are not graphics, you can also insert them into your document. When you publish to HTML, WordPerfect takes a snapshot of the text box or object and creates a graphic for your Web page.

HTML documents can't use WordPerfect graphics directly. WordPerfect converts these graphics to Web-compatible bitmap files (such as GIF and JPEG) when you publish to HTML.

If you use WordPerfect graphics, save your work as a WordPerfect document in addition to publishing an HTML document. Use the WordPerfect document — not the HTML document — for future editing. Graphics in HTML documents are harder to edit than the WordPerfect graphics.

As you undoubtedly recall from installing WordPerfect, your license from Corel to use its graphics online has certain limitations on image size (in pixels) and stipulates certain legalese in your documents.

## Inserting Graphics from WordPerfect's Scrapbook

WordPerfect 8 comes with an enormous and — yes, even useful — library of clip art (or Clipart, as Corel calls it)! Some of the clip art is installed on your hard disk, but most of it lives on your installation CD-ROM (for which we who are running short on disk space are thankful). Together, for some reason, it's called the Scrapbook.

To use the Scrapbook, just follow these steps:

1. **Click the Clipart button in the Toolbar or choose Insert⇨Graphics⇨Clipart.**

   The Clipart button is the quickest approach.

   After a brief pause, the Scrapbook appears, looking like Figure 11-1. The Scrapbook, which is a visual gallery from which you can copy artwork into your document, initially displays the Clipart collection on your hard disk.

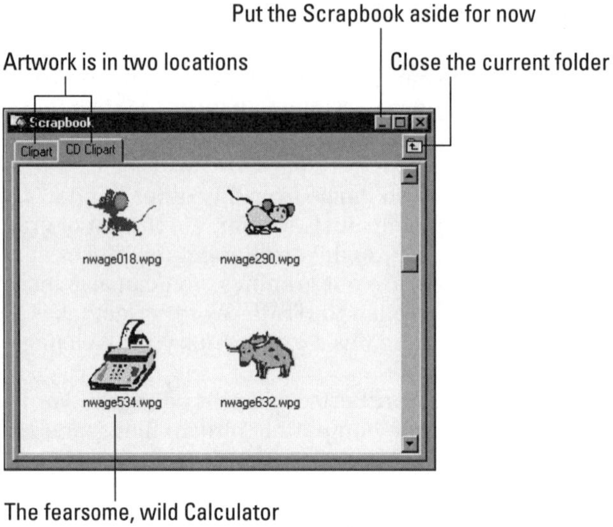
Put the Scrapbook aside for now
Artwork is in two locations
Close the current folder
Scrapbook
Clipart
CD Clipart
nwage018.wpg
nwage290.wpg
nwage534.wpg
nwage632.wpg
The fearsome, wild Calculator

**Figure 11-1:** Some fierce critters in the CD-ROM Clipart wild animals selection.

2. **To see more images, click the CD Clipart tab near the top of the Scrapbook; then double-click any file folders that look interesting.**

   To close a folder and look in other folders, click the tiny file-folder icon in the top-right corner.

3. **When you find an image you want, right-click it and then choose Copy from the QuickMenu that appears.**

4. **Drag the Scrapbook window out of the way or minimize it (click the – button in the top-right corner of the window).**

5. **Click the place in your document where you want to insert your graphic.**

   If the graphic goes with text, the best spot usually is the beginning of the paragraph.

6. **Press Ctrl+V to paste the graphic.**

   An alternative to copying and pasting is to simply drag the graphic, kicking and screaming, out of the Scrapbook and into your document approximately where you want it. This method makes for sloppy positioning, but if you're going to attach the graphic to the paragraph, sloppiness doesn't much matter (see "Vying for Position" later in this chapter).

You're done. Well, you're done if you like the result. If not, you may still need to indulge in sizing, positioning, and half a dozen other gerunds. To size the graphic, drag one of the tiny squares (*handles*) around it. To move the graphics, either drag it or cut and paste it. See "Sizing up Graphics and Other Boxes" and "Vying for Position" later in this chapter for details on sizing and positioning.

Use Clipart to brighten your document the same way that you would in a paper document. Virtually all the standard features of WordPerfect are available to you, including the usual drawing tools and the Image Tools Palette. You can also combine graphics with other features, such as tables and WordPerfect text boxes. To position Clipart precisely, for example, put it in one cell of a table, with text in other cells. The example shown in Figure 11-2 uses one of the images called "Ender" from Clipart in a one-row, three-column table.

**Figure 11-2:** Clip art can put your Web pages in the ivy league.

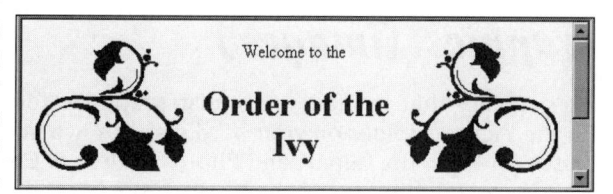

Chapter 13 gets into more fine points of graphics, but just for the record, here's how I created the graphics in Figure 11-2. After inserting the left image, I copied it by pressing Ctrl+C and then pasted it on the right side by pressing Ctrl+V. I flipped the image by right-clicking it and then clicking the Flip Left/Right button in the graphics Property Bar. I right-aligned the image by clicking the Justification button in the Property Bar.

## Inserting All Kinds of Other Graphics

WordPerfect 8's Scrapbook is a great source of graphics, but what if you want to use other, non-Scrapbook files? For non-Scrapbook files, insert the graphic by choosing the command Insert⇨Graphics⇨From File.

That command gives you WordPerfect's familiar file-opening dialog box, which allows you to choose your graphics file. You can also insert WordPerfect Clipart (the same files that appear in the Scrapbook) and other graphics, if you can find them on your hard disk or on the CD-ROM.

Figure 11-3 shows you where WordPerfect's other graphics are installed on your hard disk (assuming that you performed a standard installation). You can find more graphics on your CD-ROM.

**Figure 11-3:**
Where Corel keeps graphics on your hard disk.

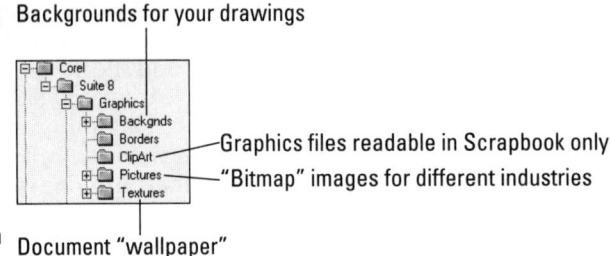

- Backgrounds for your drawings
- Graphics files readable in Scrapbook only
- "Bitmap" images for different industries
- Document "wallpaper"

```
Corel
 └─ Suite 8
     └─ Graphics
         ├─ Backgnds
         ├─ Borders
         ├─ ClipArt
         ├─ Pictures
         └─ Textures
```

## Bitmap graphics (images)

Some of the other graphics that you find are bitmap graphics. You can find bitmap images in the Pictures folder on your hard disk (shown in Figure 11-3) and the Photos folder in the Clipart and Photos folders of Corel's Library CD-ROM. You can tell bitmap images by the three-letter ending of their filenames. BMP, GIF, JPG, PCX, TGA, and TIF are among the most common file types (or *formats*, in geekspeak).

*WARNING!*
If you use files that end in GIF or JPG, you may need to take one extra step when you publish your document to HTML (see "Publishing to HTML with Graphics" at the end of this chapter).

Bitmap images are made up of color dots, not the lines, curves, and fills of WordPerfect graphics. Scanning produces bitmap images, as do programs such as Paintbrush and Photoshop. Bitmap graphics have two potential problems, from the point of view of a Web-page designer:

- ✔ They lose quality if you enlarge them beyond their original sizes.
- ✔ They are difficult to edit (change shapes, remove elements, or change individual areas of color).

To acquire an image by using your scanner, choose Insert⇨Graphics⇨Acquire Image. At that point, your usual scanner driver software takes over.

## The usual drawings and charts

You can create drawings and charts in a Web document just as you do in a regular document. WordPerfect's drawing and charting software is so full-featured that this book just doesn't have enough room to discuss it and still include stuff that's especially useful for Web work (such as TextArt). For basic drawing and charting instructions, see *WordPerfect 8 For Windows For Dummies*.

A nice feature for Web designers is the fact that the backgrounds of drawings and charts are transparent: Whatever background color or wallpaper your document uses shows right through. This effect gives the elegant impression that charts and pictures are drawn directly on the "paper" of your document, not pasted on.

## Creating Cool Graphical Text

One way to get past the limitations of standard Web text styles is to use pictures of text! The folks at Corel realized that some of WordPerfect's great text features, such as text boxes and TextArt, can't be implemented as actual text in Web documents, so instead, they cleverly programmed WordPerfect to take a snapshot of these features from the screen and automatically create a graphic image when you publish to HTML.

### Terrific TextArt

TextArt not only creates pictures from text, but also allows you to create all kinds of special text effects, such as bends, rotations, fills, shadows, and 3-D effects. TextArt's new 3-D features can even create text that looks like photographs of solid text carved out of various materials; see Figure 11-4 for an example.

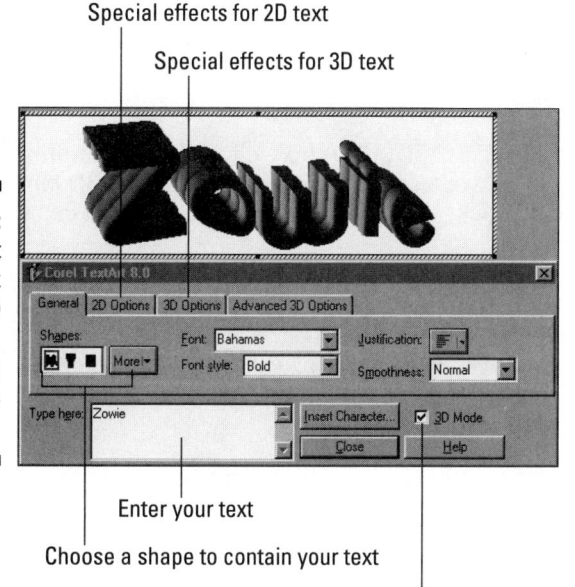

**Figure 11-4:** The TextArt dialog box (bottom) gives you amazing graphics (top).

Special effects for 2D text
Special effects for 3D text
Enter your text
Choose a shape to contain your text
A checkmark here disables 2D and enables 3D

Choose Insert⇨Graphics⇨TextArt to open the Corel TextArt dialog box. The general idea is to type some text in the Type here box and choose a shape for it from the Shapes box (click the More button to see additional shapes). Then you can fiddle with all kinds of fine points of appearance by using the other controls in the various tabs of the dialog box.

TIP

Select some ordinary text before launching TextArt, and that text is used for TextArt.

At any time while you are fiddling, you can change the size and proportions of the graphics box in which your TextArt appears. Just click on the handles (black squares) around the edge of the box and drag. The TextArt dialog box remains on-screen.

Some of the controls — such as Font, Font Style (for example, Bold), and Justification — are familiar from your ordinary text work; others are pretty far out. Following are some tips for using these controls.

Here's what the controls do in the General tab shown in Figure 11-4:

- **Shapes.** Choose the shape into which your text will be molded. If the shape has several sections (as shown in Figure 11-5), enter several lines of text in the Type here box.
- **Smoothness.** Specify how not-jagged the edges of your text are. Choose Normal, High, or Very High.
- **Insert Character.** Insert those special WordPerfect characters and symbols (including many that you can't use in regular text on the Web).
- **3D Mode.** Click this check box to create text that looks chiseled or cut out of something solid (refer to Figure 11-4). Clicking the check box enables the two 3-D tabs of the dialog box and disables the 2D Options tab.

For special effects on regular, flat (2-D) text, click the 2D Options tab; TextArt presents the controls shown in Figure 11-5. (If the 3D Mode check box contains a check, click to remove the check so that you can use 2-D text.)

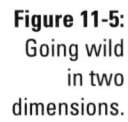

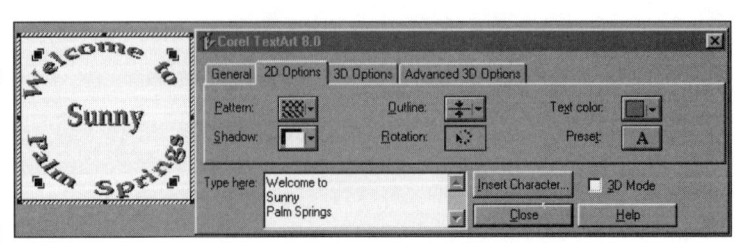

**Figure 11-5:**
Going wild in two dimensions.

## Chapter 11: General Graphics 157

Here are some tips for using 2D Options:

- **Pattern.** Creates a two-color patterned fill for 2-D text; choose the pattern and the two colors here.
- **Shadow.** Controls how much shadow appears behind 2-D text; also controls the color of the shadow. Choose a darker shade of your document's background color to make text float over your background.
- **Outline.** Controls the thickness and color of the outline around 2-D text.
- **Rotation.** Rotates your text. Click this button and drag the handles (large black squares inside the graphics box, braced by lines that look like eyebrows). Dragging rotates the text within the dimensions of the graphics box. Enlarge the box to a square (by dragging its handles) to rotate with less distortion.
- **Text color.** Color filling the center of the text, surrounded by the outline.
- **Preset.** Choose among a gallery of predesigned styles and then adjust them with the controls.

For the ultimate in coolness, click the 3D Mode check box and then click the 3D Options tab. Figure 11-6 shows this tab of controls. To save time and effort, click the Preset button and check out the prebuilt styles.

*WARNING!*

If your PC isn't particularly fast when you work with graphics, it will be amazingly slow when you work with 3D TextArt.

**Figure 11-6:**
Going wild in three dimensions!

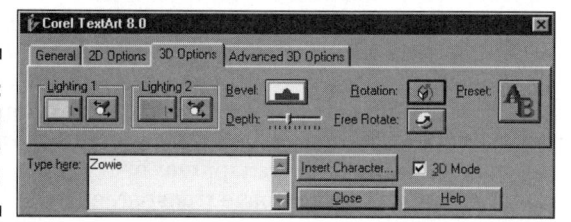

Here are the controls for creating wild and crazy 3D text:

- **Lighting 1 and Lighting 2.** Colored lights that illuminate the text and supply its colors. (The text has no color of its own.) In each pair of buttons, click the left button to choose a color. Click the right button to choose a direction for the light by observing how the light strikes a set of sample illuminated bumps. Choose different directions for Lighting 1 and Lighting 2.

- **Bevel.** Gives text an interesting contour in the thickness direction. Shapes shown look like cross-sections of wall molding, if you're a hardware-store junkie. Figure 11-4, shown earlier in this chapter, uses the three-bump shape (last in the list).
- **Depth.** Slide the slider to the right for thicker text and to the left for thinner text.
- **Rotation.** Choose the rotation and tilting of your text from a set of samples that display various rotations of the letter *E*.
- **Free Rotate.** Crosshairs appear on the TextArt like a sniper's scope. Position the hand-shaped mouse pointer over the horizontal crosshair and drag sideways to rotate text left or right. Position the pointer over the vertical crosshair and drag vertically to adjust the tilt of the text.
- **Preset.** Choose among a set of predesigned 3D shapes and appearances, and then adjust them with the controls.

The following controls appear in the Advanced 3D Options tab:

- **Textures.** Choose a surface texture (a kind of bumpiness) for the surfaces that comprise the front, back, and bevel (thickness) sides of your text.
- **Quality.** For Web documents, higher DPI slows WordPerfect and doesn't add much to the result. The higher the number of bits for Color (8, 16), the better the shading looks, but the bigger the file is.

Whenever you create a graphic that includes text, be sure to add "alternate" text in case your Web-site visitor isn't using graphics or the Internet is having a slow day. See "Adding 'Alternate' Text for Graphics-Free Browsing" later in this chapter for instructions.

*Note:* The image created by 2D TextArt has a transparent background. Any background color or wallpaper in your document shows right through the text. 3D images don't automatically have transparent backgrounds. See Chapter 13 for information on making an image transparent.

## Tasteful Text Boxes

Besides TextArt, another tasteful way to fake text in Web documents (getting past the limitations of HTML text styles) is to use the WordPerfect text boxes. Text boxes make great sidebars for Web pages.

WordPerfect text boxes turn into graphics when you publish to HTML, so you don't have to worry about Web text styles. You can use any font, style, symbol, border, or fill that you like. In Figure 11-7, a sidebar about the cheetah uses 14-point Casablanca type and a green border. You can even apply a shadow to make the WordPerfect text box float over your page.

**Figure 11-7:**
Be a cheetah: Create fake text fast by using WordPerfect's text boxes.

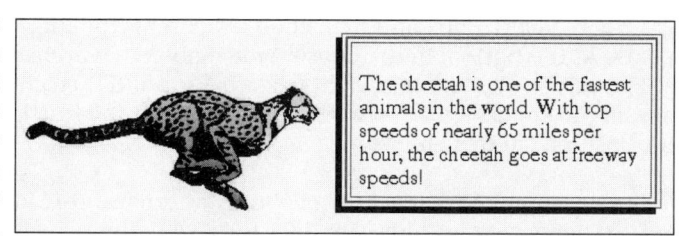

> The cheetah is one of the fastest animals in the world. With top speeds of nearly 65 miles per hour, the cheetah goes at freeway speeds!

**WARNING!**

Don't get carried away and try to use WordPerfect text boxes for everything on your page. With all those graphic images, your page will take so long to download that no one will bother reading it.

In case you haven't tried WordPerfect text boxes before, here are some instructions and hints:

 1. **Click the Text Box button in WordPerfect's toolbar.**

    WordPerfect displays the Text Box Editor window in place of your document. Don't worry, WordPerfect didn't close your document.

 2. **Choose a font, size, and style.**

 3. **Enter your text.**

    Feel free to add any WordPerfect text formatting that you like: center alignment (click the Justification button in the Property Bar), use bold or italic style, or color for your text (press F9). Apply formatting just as you would for regular WordPerfect text.

 4. **Click the Close button.**

    Your text box appears with a transparent background, so your document background color or wallpaper shows through. The effect looks to the visitor as though you have overcome the font limitations of HTML (except that download times are much slower with graphics)!

 5. **To add a custom border or a colored fill, right-click the WordPerfect text box and choose Border/Fill from the Quick Menu that appears.**

As you can with any WordPerfect box, you can size the text box afterward. Just right-click to display handles; then drag any handle.

**TIP**

If you try to select a WordPerfect text box by clicking it, you often enter the Text Box Editor instead! (Click the Close button if that happens.) That mistake occurs because you clicked the center of the box. To select a WordPerfect text box, carefully position your mouse pointer over the box edge — where the pointer is an arrow, not a vertical bar — and click. Alternatively, right-click the WordPerfect text box and then choose Select Box from the QuickMenu that appears.

You can rotate or position a text box. To rotate by quarter-turns (90-degree intervals), right-click the box and then choose Content from the QuickMenu that appears. At the bottom of the Content dialog box that appears, select a rotation. To position the text box, right-click the box and then choose Position from the QuickMenu that appears; then follow the instructions in "Vying for Position" in this chapter.

When you use graphics to display text, include "alternate" text for the times when the Internet is running slowly and for folks who don't have graphical browsers! Refer to "Adding 'Alternate' Text for Graphics-Free Browsing" later in this chapter for instructions.

## Sizing up Graphics and Other Boxes

Graphics of any kind — TextArt, text boxes, and hypertext formatted as buttons — are all various forms of boxes to WordPerfect. The easiest way to size any box is to click it and drag the little black squares (handles) that appear around the box. Some boxes (namely, text boxes and hypertext buttons) surprise you by opening an editing box when you click their centers, so click their edges instead. Here are the two dragging rules:

- To keep the correct proportions (height and width), drag a corner handle.
- To change width or height independently, drag a center handle on any side.

For more precise control of the size, right-click the graphic or other box and then choose Size from the Quick Menu that appears. A Box Size dialog box pops up, displaying controls for width and height. To keep the box in proportion, click Maintain Proportions for one dimension (either Width or Height) and then adjust the other dimension.

Don't take the dimensions in the Box Size dialog box too seriously. The Web has no inches. Unfortunately, WordPerfect offers no way to set dimensions in the only way that matters on the Web: in pixels. On my PC, 1 inch corresponds to 92 pixels; your mileage may differ.

If an image looks speckly after you shrink it, you probably need to shrink the original image before you insert it into WordPerfect (see "Using Photo House for Transparency and Other Effects" in Chapter 13).

When you size a GIF or JPEG image in WordPerfect, you don't actually affect the image file that goes out on the Web; you change only the size of the image as it is displayed in the browser. To actually change the size of the image file by using WordPerfect, you can induce WordPerfect to make a new

GIF file by making some small change with WordPerfect's Image Tools Palette or use Corel Photo House (or one of the tools on the CD-ROM) to change the image file. See "Publishing to HTML with Graphics" later in this chapter for more information.

## Vying for Position

You can't position graphics with all the flexibility and elegant text wrapping that is possible in regular WordPerfect documents. In truth, the only positions that you can actually achieve (without yoga training) for graphics or other boxes (such as text boxes) are the following:

- **Positioned against the left or right edge of the page.** This positioning also allows text to flow (or wrap) alongside your box. You achieve left or right alignment by using *paragraph attachment*, in WordPerfect terminology. You can also center a graphic that uses paragraph attachment, but text won't wrap around the sides. See "Left or right, with text alongside" later in this chapter for more on paragraph attachment.

- **Positioned left, right, or center, but standing alone.** If you want your box to stand alone (no text on either side), put it in a line (paragraph) by itself. Position the box at the left edge, right edge, or center of the document by using paragraph attachment. Alternatively, don't fool with the attachment at all; simply align the paragraph left, right, or center.

- **Floating along in the line of text, just like a character or word.** You have some control of how high or low the box sits on the line. A box inserted this way is *attached to a character*, in WordPerfect terminology. When you initially insert a graphic, WordPerfect uses character attachment. See "In line with the text" later in this chapter for more on character attachment.

You may be able to position your graphic or other box simply by dragging it. Try dragging, and if you don't get the results that you want, use the more detailed instructions in the following sections.

## Left or right, with text alongside

To position a graphic left or right and have text flow alongside, attach it to a paragraph. Glue it to the paragraph this way:

1. **Create or insert your graphic anywhere within the paragraph.**

    If you already have a graphic elsewhere in your document, you can drag it to this paragraph now or wait until you complete the following steps to drag it.

2. **Right-click the graphic (or other box) and choose Position from the Quick Menu that appears.**

    The Box Position dialog box springs into action.

3. **For the Attach box to option, choose Paragraph.**

    The Box Position dialog box now looks something like Figure 11-8.

**Figure 11-8:** The buck wraps here. Paragraph attachment allows text wrapping.

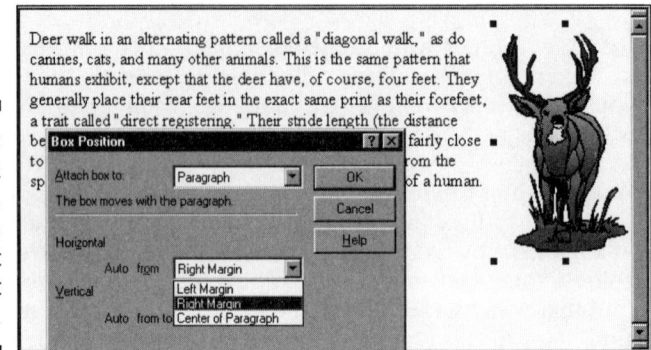

4. **In the Horizontal section, choose Left Margin or Right Margin from the Auto from drop-down list.**

    You can choose Center of Paragraph and your graphic will, in fact, be centered, but text will not flow alongside the graphic. If you want your graphic to break up the paragraph, for some reason of your own, choose Center of Paragraph.

5. **Click the OK button.**

When the graphic is paragraph-attached, you can drag it to any other paragraph, and the horizontal alignment that you gave it (left, right, or center) still applies.

## Left, right, or center, but standing alone

It's lonely at the top, but standing alone is a good idea for graphics that serve as a top banner or as a horizontal line across the document. To ensure that a graphic or other WordPerfect box stands alone, with no text wrapping around it, put it in a paragraph by itself. (The job often is easier if you make paragraph marks visible on-screen. Choose View➪Show ¶.)

To create a new paragraph exclusively for your graphic, click the end of an existing paragraph and then press the Enter key. Now your insertion point (the blinking vertical bar) is on a line by itself. Use the steps listed in the preceding section to position your graphic the way you want.

**Chapter 11: General Graphics** *163*

*TIP* Alternatively, you can just use the text alignment of the paragraph to align the graphic. As long as you haven't changed the graphic's attachment to Paragraph since you inserted it, you can align the graphic by choosing Format⇨Justification and then choosing Left, Right or Center from the submenu.

## In line with the text

When you insert a graphic, WordPerfect inserts it just like a letter or number into the line of text. Sometimes, this form of insertion is exactly what you want. You may, for example, want to put a small graphic image right in line with the text. I say "small" because if you put a tall image in line with the text, and if you have more than one line, you make a large, ugly gap in the paragraph's line spacing. The most common uses for this sort of positioning are using a custom bullet symbol for indented lists, inserting a small chunk of cool Text Art instead of boring real text, and inserting a graphic with some special symbols (such as an equation from the Equation Editor) that can't be represented in HTML text.

If you don't have your graphic in the document yet, click where you want your graphic to appear and then insert it by choosing Insert⇨Graphics. However you insert your graphic, WordPerfect automatically assumes that you want your graphic to be in line with the text, so you're done. Well, you're done if you like the way that the graphic sits on the line of text (its vertical position). If you don't like the graphic's vertical position on the line, take the following steps.

If the graphic is already elsewhere in the document, leave it there for now. Perform the steps that follow, and when you're done, you can drag the graphic into position.

1. **Right-click the graphic (or other box) and then choose Position from the Quick Menu that appears.**

    The Box Position dialog box springs into action.

2. **For the Attach box to option, choose Character, as shown in Figure 11-9.**

3. **Choose a line alignment by clicking Top, Centered, Bottom, or Content baseline.**

    Your choice moves the graphic up and down on the line of text. A sample picture in the Box Position dialog box helps you see the result of your choice.

    • I've found Content baseline to be one of the most useful choices; it puts the image itself (not any white-space border that may be present) on the baseline. (A *baseline* is the imaginary line that text sits on; the tails of characters such as *y* and *g* hang below it.)

**Figure 11-9:** For a good time, form an attachment to a character.

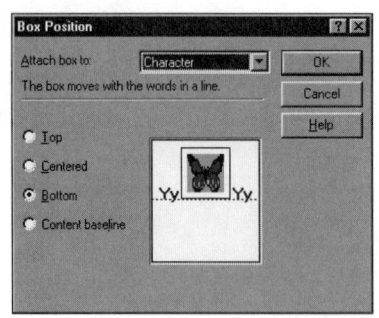

- Bottom makes the entire graphic, border and all, stand on the baseline.
- Top makes the graphic hang down (aligns the top of the graphic with the baseline of the text). I've never found Top to be a useful choice.
- Centered centers the graphic on the baseline of the text.

  **4. Click the OK button.**

Now the graphic is essentially part of the text. The graphic flows and wraps wherever the text does (depending on how wide the browser window is), so you can't force it to stay in any position on the page. If the graphic is higher than the text, it forces greater space between the lines. (You can use larger text to help fill that space, if you like.)

If you need to move the graphic, just drag it. The insertion point (the dark vertical line) moves as you drag to show you where the graphic will go when you release the mouse button.

# Adding "Alternate" Text for Graphics-Free Browsing

Until the day when everyone has high-speed modems and can always download from the Web at, say, 100KB per second (or until Honolulu freezes over, whichever comes first) Web surfers are occasionally going to turn the graphics off on their Web browsers. Some folks never view graphics at all. All surfers have experienced the World Wide Wait problem, when the Net is so slow that you'd rather have the graphics mailed to you. If you're waiting for a graphic with essential information, such as instructions or a description of a link, this wait is infuriating.

## When to use alternate text

The solution to all these problems is "alternate" text — the text that (on the better-designed Web pages) you see in place of graphics when you have turned off your browser's graphics or while you're waiting for graphics to download. You should unquestionably use alternate text in your Web documents for the following sorts of graphics:

- ✔ In graphics that are hyperlinked (that intend to be clicked), your alternate text should say what the link is to.
- ✔ In graphics that contain text, your alternate text should be the same as the text in the image.

You can use alternate text for any graphic, but if the graphic is just there for fun, the text (such as *Picture of my dog*) is less essential. Still, if the image is really cool, you may want to tell people about it so that they can choose to view it.

## How to apply and test alternate text

To apply alternate text to a graphic, right-click the graphic and then choose HTML Properties from the QuickMenu that appears to display the HTML Properties dialog box. Click the Image tab (if that tab is not already on top). In the Alternate text box, type your alternate text. Click the OK button when you're done.

*TIP*

All kinds of other interesting Web features lurk in the HTML Properties dialog box. See Chapters 13 and 20 to learn more.

To test your alternate text in a browser, turn off the browser's automatic image loading. In Navigator 3.*x*, click Options and then click the Auto Load Images check box to clear it. In Navigator 4.0, choose Edit⇨Preferences, click Advanced in the Category box, and then click the Automatically Load Images check box to clear it. In Microsoft Internet Explorer 3.0, choose View⇨Options and, in the General tab, click the Show Pictures check box to clear it.

Now try viewing your document. (Click the View in Web Browser button in WordPerfect, or publish to HTML and load the file into your browser.) If your images still appear (not the alternate text), close the browser and reopen it (or clear the memory cache, if you know how to do that).

## Publishing to HTML with Graphics

When you publish to HTML a document that uses graphics, all kinds of stuff goes on. For the most part, you don't have to be concerned. Complex decisions are made and actions are taken on your behalf by WordPerfect. Most of those decisions aren't too critical. If the decisions are wrong, you just get a document in which the graphics are a little funky-looking or one that takes a long time to download. Chapters 13 and 14 can help you with those problems.

Some of the decisions that are left to you, however, can result in graphics not appearing at all! You need to either (a) walk the straight and narrow path that this book lays out for you or (b) understand what's going on in all its gory detail.

### Walking the straight and narrow path

The easiest and safest way to make sure that your graphics work properly when you publish a document to HTML is to publish as Figure 11-10 shows. Figure 11-10 shows someone publishing a document called coolpage. Notice that all the lines end with the document's name.

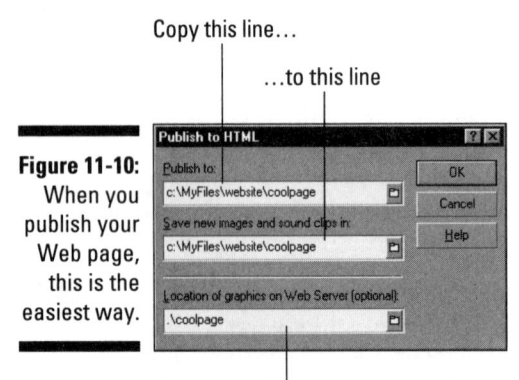

Copy this line...

...to this line

**Figure 11-10:** When you publish your Web page, this is the easiest way.

Enter .\ and the document name here

> **WARNING!** The straight and narrow path probably sounds like — and probably is — your best bet, but you never know. *Tempus fugit*, all is flux, and stuff like that. In later releases of Word Perfect 8, Corel may decide to change the way that these details work, in which case Understanding What's Going On may become Necessary. *Caveat emptor. Nolo contendre.*

Here are the steps that keep you on the straight and narrow path when publishing a document that contains graphics:

## Chapter 11: General Graphics    167

1. **Click the Publish to HTML button in the toolbar.**

   Or, if you prefer, choose File➪Internet Publisher to open the Internet Publisher dialog box, then click the Publish to HTML button.

   The Publish to HTML dialog box appears, with some initial suggestions already entered in the first two text boxes. The first time you publish the document, ignore those suggestions.

2. **In the first text box, enter the path to the place on your PC where you want your HTML Web file to go, ending in the name of the file.**

   You can add the .HTM extension, if you like, but I suggest that you don't for now. (Click the file-folder icon if you would rather choose a path and filename by using a dialog box like the WordPerfect Save As dialog box.)

   As Figure 11-10 shows, I suggest that you put your HTML Web files in a folder called website inside the MyFiles folder. (WordPerfect creates any folder that you specify, if it's not already there, when you publish to HTML.)

3. **In the second text box, simply copy the first box, as Figure 11-10 shows.**

   To copy, select the text in the first text box. (Leave out the .htm extension, if one is present in that box.) Press Ctrl+C, then press Tab to move to the second box. Press Ctrl+V to paste.

4. **In the third line, begin with a period and a slash (. /) and add the name of your creation (such as coolpage), with nothing after it at all.**

   Notice that the recommended slash is the forward slash (/), not the backslash (\). The backslash works for most situations, but not all.

Now your HTML documents are ready to be loaded into your browser and tested on your PC (as described in Chapter 3). After you test them, copy them to your Web site as described in Chapter 6. If you have used GIF or JPEG graphics, before you test your files, see "If you have used GIF or JPG graphic files" later in this chapter.

*Note:* Often, you'll make a few edits and republish before you finally close the file. When you republish during the same editing session, WordPerfect adds .htm to the end of the first line and a slash (\) to the end of the second line. Adding .htm is OK; adding .htm means the same thing as not adding .htm. Just click the OK button.

In the example in Figure 11-10, the top box creates a file called coolpage.htm. The second box creates a folder called coolpage and puts your graphics files there. The third box tells the browser that wherever it finds coolpage.htm, it should find a folder called coolpage and look there for graphics.

## If you have used GIF or JPG graphic files

In publishing, WordPerfect usually takes a hands-off position on any GIF and JPG files that you have inserted into the document; it doesn't publish them unless you have modified them in WordPerfect. If you have inserted graphics files ending in GIF or JPG — and if you haven't changed the image by using WordPerfect's Image Tool Palette, borders, or captions — you need to perform one more step by copying those files. Copy the files to your graphics publishing folder (the folder that you entered in the second text box of the Publish to HTML dialog box).

*Warning!* Don't copy the GIF or JPG file if you have added a caption, a WordPerfect border, or a fill in your document, or if you have used WordPerfect's Image Tools to modify the image. In those cases, WordPerfect realizes that you have made modifications and publishes a modified GIF in your folder. If you copy the original file to that folder, you may smoosh (replace) the modified image.

Following is one way to copy a file in Windows 95:

1. **Double-click the My Computer icon in Windows 95 and then browse to find the GIF or JPEG file that you used.**

2. **Click the file and then press Ctrl+C to copy it.**

3. **In the My Computer window, browse until you open the folder that you specified in the second text box of the Publish to HTML dialog box.**

4. **When you open the correct folder, press Ctrl+V to paste the file.**

WordPerfect doesn't copy unmodified GIF and JPG files for you, because GIF and JPG are the "official" graphics file formats of the Web. WordPerfect apparently figures that if you're using those kinds of files, you know what you're doing, and it's not about to mess you up by making copies that you may not want.

## Understanding what's going on

When you publish your Web-formatted WordPerfect document to HTML, you end up with more than just the HTML file (`blah.htm` or `blah.html`); you also end up with separate graphics files, one for each different graphic image that you use.

### Where the graphics files go

To allow a Web browser to find the graphics files and place them in your document, the HTML document contains links — pointers to the graphics files. If your graphics files get separated from the HTML file or get placed in the wrong folders, the links just won't work. (For more information on preventing this problem, see Chapter 3.)

WordPerfect helps you keep your graphics files together when you publish to HTML. The program allows you to specify a folder for what I call the *outgoing* graphics files — the ones that are going out on the Web. (The outgoing files are copies of the graphics that you used in your Web-formatted WordPerfect document, but in the correct format for the Web.)

The second text box of the Publish to HTML dialog box tells WordPerfect what folder to use for your outgoing graphics files on your PC. You can put your outgoing Web graphics files in any folder you like, but my suggestion is to put them in a folder alongside the HTML file and with the same first name as the HTML file. In Figure 11-10 earlier in this chapter, for example, I told WordPerfect to create a folder called coolpage in the same folder where I was putting my coolpage HTML file.

WordPerfect provides the entry in the third box of the Publish to HTML dialog box so that you can choose what folder your graphics files are going to be in — not on your PC, but on your Web server. WordPerfect gives you this entry because — heck, you could copy the graphics files to any old folder. The folder may not even be on your own Web site.

What, in fact, the third box does is tell WordPerfect how to write the HTML file's links to the graphics files. Links are addresses called URLs — the same URLs that you use for hyperlinks or that you enter in your Web browser to view a page on the Web. You can write URLs in many ways. For an overview of different kinds of URLs, see Table 7-1 in Chapter 7, which discusses hyperlinks.

Only two ways of writing URLs, however, create links that work both on the PC (where you're testing your files) and on the Web server — a result that I'm striving to achieve in this book. One way is to use a separate folder for the graphics of each document and then use the relative URL that is described in Chapter 7, like the one shown in Figure 11-10 earlier in this chapter (`./coolpage`). The other way is to put nothing in the third text box of the Publish to HTML dialog box and, in the second box, to tell WordPerfect to put your graphics files in the same folder as your HTML file (say, `C:\MyFiles\website`). I recommend the first way, because it gives you a separate folder for each HTML document, thereby ensuring that you don't accidentally overwrite graphics files that are used by other HTML files.

### What graphics files WordPerfect produces

Although you may not be able to tell by looking at the result in a Web browser, the graphics that you see on your Web page aren't necessarily the same as the ones that you started with. The Web can accept only certain graphics file types (formats). Whenever you use a file type or format that isn't directly Web-compatible (such as Clipart and other .WPG files), WordPerfect has to translate the image to a file format that is Web-compatible. For all practical purposes, those formats are limited to GIF and JPEG (JPG). WordPerfect limits itself to creating GIF files unless you request JPG, putting the GIF files in the graphics folder that you specify when you publish to HTML.

If you insert a GIF or JPG image file in the first place, WordPerfect usually doesn't publish (copy) these files. WordPerfect avoids copying those files because it suspects that you may not want copies — that you may, for example, intend to reuse a GIF or JPEG from another document. If you modify an image from a GIF or JPG file, however, WordPerfect does publish a modified GIF file (not JPG) in its stead.

Trade-offs exist in choosing GIF or JPG, and you do have choices. You can convert an image to GIF or JPEG before you insert it into your document, using the programs that come with WordPerfect and on this book's CD-ROM. You can also choose which of the two formats WordPerfect uses when it publishes to HTML by using the HTML Properties dialog box. (Right-click the graphic, choose HTML Properties from the QuickMenu, click the Publish tab in the HTML Properties dialog box that appears, and check off JPEG or GIF.) For more information on choosing GIF vs. JPG, see Chapter 14.

# Chapter 12
# Building Blocks: Banners, Backgrounds, Bullets...

*In This Chapter*
- Downloading from the Web
- Inserting lines (bars)
- Creating banners
- Using backgrounds (wallpaper)
- Creating bullets
- Beautifying buttons
- Creating control strips and panels of buttons

Although "banners, backgrounds, and bullets" sounds like the building blocks of political revolution, it is simply a list of some common graphical building blocks of Web pages. (If you are creative, however, you can get some revolutionary — or even revolting — results.) I call these elements building blocks because some of them are so standardized that you can buy or download collections of them to sprinkle on your Web pages.

An amazing quantity of building blocks is available for free on the Web. A good start is Yahoo!'s listings. Point your browser to www.yahoo.com and click the following categories in successive pages: Choose Computers and Internet, then World Wide Web, then Page Design and Layout, and finally Graphics. In the Graphics category, you'll find interesting categories of building blocks, including Backgrounds and Icons (Yahoo!'s term for bullets and lines, or bars). You may find Animated GIFs and Transparent Images to be interesting, too, although they offer more tools than they do actual examples.

## Downloading Building Blocks from the Web

Every book on Web design mentions that you can download stuff from the Web, but few books tell you how to do that! How to download is not obvious.

To download a graphic image from the Web, take the following steps:

1. **Find a page that displays a graphic image that you like and have permission to use.**
2. **Right-click the image (in Navigator or Explorer).**
3. **From the shortcut menu that appears, choose Save Image As (in Netscape Navigator) or Save Picture As (in Microsoft Internet Explorer).**

   A conventional Save As dialog box appears, allowing you to complete the process.

4. **Select the folder where you want to store the image file.**
5. **Click Save.**

*TIP:* If the file that you download is a GIF or JPG file (and it probably is), download the file to the folder that you use for graphics when you publish to HTML. If you are publishing your document to `C:\MyFiles\website\coolstuf.htm`, for example, you're probably using the folder `C:\MyFiles\website\coolstuf` for your graphics. Download the file to (or later copy it to) that folder. If you forget to do this, your graphic will not appear in your HTML document.

*WARNING!*

### Free lunches may cause indigestion

Just because something is advertised as free doesn't necessarily mean that you can use it legally. Some people who advertise free images have carelessly made collections of image files copied from rightful owners. Look for reputable original sources, not amateur collections of other people's work. Never use any image file from a Web site without explicit permission from the file's true owner.

Also be wary of downloading self-extracting compressed files that end in .EXE from anyone but a reliable software vendor. Such files are programs, and if they are not actually what they are advertised to be, they could be viruses or programs that may harm your PC.

# Lines

For a well-disciplined, toe-the-mark kind of document, use some nice straight horizontal lines to divide one topic from the next. (Such lines are also called *bars* or *separator bars* on the Web.) Documents that are actually long lists of stuff — such as sales offices by country or job listings by category — often benefit from lines between categories. WordPerfect's regular old horizontal line does that job just fine.

For a more undisciplined, trip-gaily-over-the-mark kind of document, you want cute, colorful, wavy, frivolous lines — sort of party lines. You've seen these lines; now use 'em yourself. Party on!

## The same old line

For a boring but convenient horizontal line, use the WordPerfect regular old horizontal line. Click the end of a paragraph to put a line immediately at the end of the paragraph. Alternatively, press Enter to make a blank paragraph for the line, creating space above and below the line. Then choose Insert⇨Horizontal Line, press Ctrl+F11, or click the Horizontal Line button in the WordPerfect Toolbar. (The button displays a horizontal line; remember that you can pause the mouse cursor over any button to check its identity.)

The joy of this line is that it always extends across the full width of your document, no matter how wide a Web surfer sets a browser window. One problem with the line is that it appears as a lightly indented line on the Web, with a faint shadow, so certain backgrounds make it hard to see.

**Note:** In early releases of WordPerfect 8, horizontal lines are difficult to delete. Choose View⇨Reveal Codes to open the WordPerfect secret code window, find a tiny box there labeled Graph Line, and drag it into the document window to delete it. Then choose View⇨Reveal Codes again to close that ugly window.

**Note:** WordPerfect doesn't display spacing around lines and other icons exactly as it appears in a Web browser. Check whatever you do by clicking the View in Web Browser button in the Property Bar (the document-behind-a-web button).

Microsoft's Internet Explorer offers what this book refers to as a *stupid browser trick* — a trick that allows it to display colored lines but that doesn't work in other browsers. Instead of using the WordPerfect line, type **<HRCOLOR=*name*>**, but for ***name*,** substitute any of the following: **AQUA, NAVY, BLACK, OLIVE, BLUE, PURPLE, FUCHSIA, RED, GRAY, SILVER, GREEN, TEAL, LIME, MAROON, WHITE,** or **YELLOW.** (You don't need to use capital letters.) Highlight what you typed and then choose Format➪Custom HTML to format the line as HTML code. You won't see the result until you view your published HTML document in Internet Explorer.

## Party lines

For a horizontal line with a less-buttoned-down look, you basically can insert any wide, skinny graphic. The Web offers vast quantities of suitable lines (also called bars or rules) for free. You can also make a line with any of the WordPerfect graphics tools — insert an empty squashed-flat text box with an interesting fill or border, for example. See the list of tips for squashing a text box later in this section.

The drawback of using a graphic image as a line is that you can't make the graphic span the width of the browser window automatically, as the standard line does. Instead, click the graphic and then drag the tiny black handles on the left and right sides to make it the same width as the other graphic elements on your page, such as your banner.

Repeated use of a graphic line in WordPerfect can make a document big, fat, and slow to download on the Web. See Chapter 14 for suggestions on using repeated graphics.

Any alignment (justification) will do, but most lines look best centered. I recommend that you put the graphic in a line (paragraph) by itself to make centering easier and then center-align the paragraph just as you would text. Select the graphic and then choose Format➪Justification➪Center.

You can choose to insert ClipArt, choose Insert➪Graphics➪From File if you have downloaded something from the Web, or create your own line with WordPerfect's Draw tool or Text Box tool. I find the Text Box tool to be the easiest choice. Following are a few tips:

- ✔ Use a text box with no text but with a border and/or a fill. Figure 12-1 shows a chicken-wire horizontal line created as a text box, to go with the eggy theme of the subject. Such lines are a bit thick, as lines go, but otherwise not bad.

- ✔ Don't worry about the initial size of the graphic that you create. Shrink or stretch the graphic box by dragging the black handles around it.

- ✔ Create "alternate" text of a series of dashes (————) for your horizontal line image in case someone has graphics turned off. See Chapter 11 for instructions on using alternate text.

# Chapter 12: Building Blocks: Banners, Backgrounds, Bullets... 175

TextArt box, no text, no border, "chain link" fill

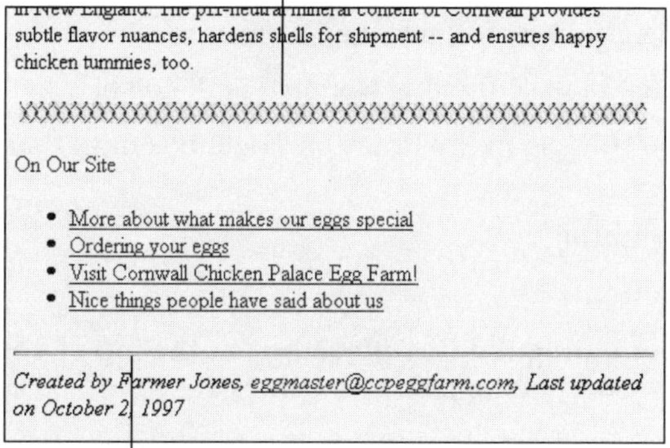

> in New England. The pH-neutral mineral content of Cornwall provides subtle flavor nuances, hardens shells for shipment -- and ensures happy chicken tummies, too.
>
> XXXXXXXXXXXXXXXXXXXXXXXXXXXXXXXXXXXXXXXXXXXXX
>
> On Our Site
>
> - More about what makes our eggs special
> - Ordering your eggs
> - Visit Cornwall Chicken Palace Egg Farm!
> - Nice things people have said about us
>
> Created by Farmer Jones, eggmaster@ccpeggfarm.com, Last updated on October 2, 1997

**Figure 12-1:** Borders keep the chickens in line on the egg-farm page.

Standard horizontal line

To create your own cool line with a Text Box, try the following example. Create a center-aligned paragraph; then perform the following steps:

1. **Choose Insert⇨Text Box.**

   The Text Box Editor appears.

2. **Click the Close button.**

   Your document reappears

3. **Right-click the rectangle that's now in your document and then choose Border/Fill from the QuickMenu that appears.**

   The Box Border/Fill dialog box appears.

4. **Click one of the borders displayed in the dialog box, if you like, to have it appear doubled in your line.**

   I prefer to choose the None option in the top-left corner.

5. **Click the Fill tab of the Box Border/Fill dialog box.**

6. **Click any fill style.**

   I suggest that you choose the first gradient fill (which starts dark at the bottom and gradually fades to light at the top). If you choose a different fill, skip to Step 9.

7. **If you chose the gradient fill, proceed as follows:**

   Click the Start Color button and then choose a color from the palette that appears.

   Do the same for the End Color button.

## Part III: Getting Graphical

Click the <u>A</u>pply button to see the effect in the (temporarily-too-thick) line in your document.

 8. **If you chose the gradient fill, proceed as follows:**

    Click the Advanced tab of the Box Border/Fill dialog box.

    Click the tiny up triangle in the Rotation Angle box until that angle reads 90.

    Click the <u>A</u>pply button.

 9. **Click the OK button.**

10. **In your document, drag the tiny black box at the top of your new graphic downward to make a skinnier line.**

No matter how you create a line, when you're done, check the results in a Web browser by clicking the View in Web Browser button in the toolbar.

## Vertical lines

The Web provides no official way to create vertical lines, but if you feel that you really need a vertical line, you can build one by using the WordPerfect graphical tools, such as Draw. You can also use a horizontal line that you pick up on the Web.

If you picked up a horizontal line from the Web, or if you created one with Draw, you can rotate the line into a vertical orientation with the following steps:

 1. **Click the horizontal-line image to select it.**

 2. **Stretch the graphics box the line appears in vertically by dragging the tiny black square (handle) on the top of the image upward to the full height that you want.**

    Stretching vertically gives you space for rotating the line.

 3. **Right-click the graphic and then choose <u>I</u>mage Tools from the Quick Menu that appears.**

    The Image Tools palette appears.

 4. **Click the <u>R</u>otate button in the Image Tools palette.**

    New handles appear inside the box, near the corners of the box, bracketed by tiny brackets.

 5. **Drag any of these new handles to rotate the bar to a vertical position.**

 6. **Click a side handle of the box and drag it inward to shrink the box.**

## Chapter 12: Building Blocks: Banners, Backgrounds, Bullets... 177

If you created a horizontal line by using a text box, you can make it vertical by changing its dimensions. Take the following steps:

1. **Right-click the text box, and choose Size from the QuickMenu that appears.**
2. **In the Box Size dialog box that appears, set the Width to a very small value, such as 0.25 inch, and the Height to whatever height you need, such as 4 inches.**

To position a vertical line alongside the text, you must attach it to the paragraph, not to a character. (See Chapter 11 for information on positioning.) You can also position a vertical line between two chunks of text if you use a three-column, one-row table. Put the text in the left and right columns, and put the vertical line in the middle column. Leave the column widths alone, no matter what they look like! You can see the real result by viewing the document in your Web browser.

## *Banners*

A *banner* is the main graphic that you see at the top of most Web pages — a sort of widish advertising graphic or logo. Sometimes, banners also contain buttons and stuff to click *(navigation controls),* but mostly, they don't. Navigation controls usually are separate from the banner but are cleverly tiled alongside the banner and other elements to look like one seamless top thingy.

Many banners are stunningly executed by cunningly clever designers who use numbingly tricky tools that you probably don't have and wouldn't want to take the time to learn, anyway. Fortunately, WordPerfect offers some fairly simple solutions for creating banners. Don't create a banner, however, until you decide on your document layout and know just how big the banner should be. Banners do not have to occupy the entire top of the document; they are often placed in a table to help control the arrangement of graphics and text. See Part IV for layout considerations.

The secret to interesting banners is combining graphics with text. Figure 12-2 shows some examples.

WordPerfect provides several tools that you may find to be useful for creating banner art:

- **TextArt,** which makes artistic, graphical text. See Chapter 11 for more information on using TextArt. You can box the text, if you like, by adding a border or background.

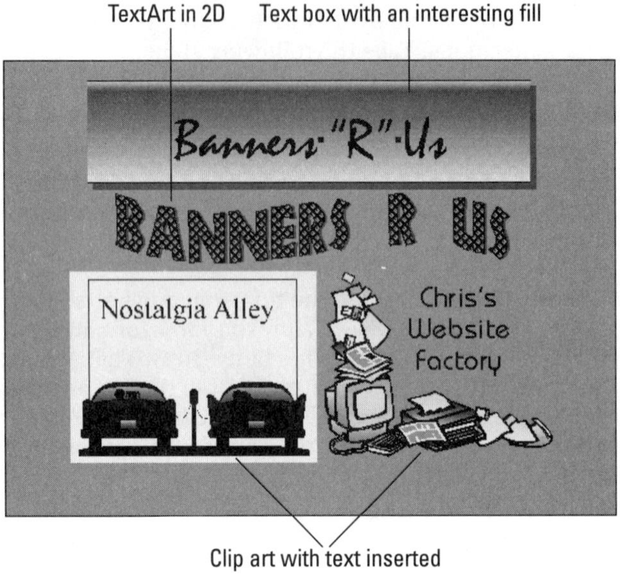

**Figure 12-2:** Having a banner day with clip art, text boxes, and TextArt.

- TextArt in 2D
- Text box with an interesting fill
- Clip art with text inserted

- ✓ **WordPerfect text boxes,** which allow you to put any kind of text or graphic in a nice rectangle with a border and/or fill. See Chapter 11 for information on text boxes. You can even put TextArt in a text box (and ship it Federal TextPress?).

- ✓ **ClipArt,** upon which you can overlay your own text. Double-click the image to launch WordPerfect Presentation software and then insert a box or line of text or even TextArt. Figure 12-3 shows an example. You can add backgrounds and borders afterward by choosing Graphics⇨Border/Fill.

# *Interesting Backgrounds (Wallpaper)*

A background image that underlies everything on your Web page is what WordPerfect calls *wallpaper*. This element is called wallpaper and not a background image because browsers make it look continuous. If the image is smaller than your visitor's Web-browser window, the browser repeats the image horizontally and vertically like a set of tiles, but with no space between the tiles.

WordPerfect provides wallpaper images that are specially designed to work like real wallpaper. These images are carefully crafted so they can go side by side and never show a "seam." (Programs such as Adobe Photoshop have tesselation features that can help you create seamless images from regular ones.)

### Chapter 12: Building Blocks: Banners, Backgrounds, Bullets... 179

**Figure 12-3:** Editing ClipArt to add text.

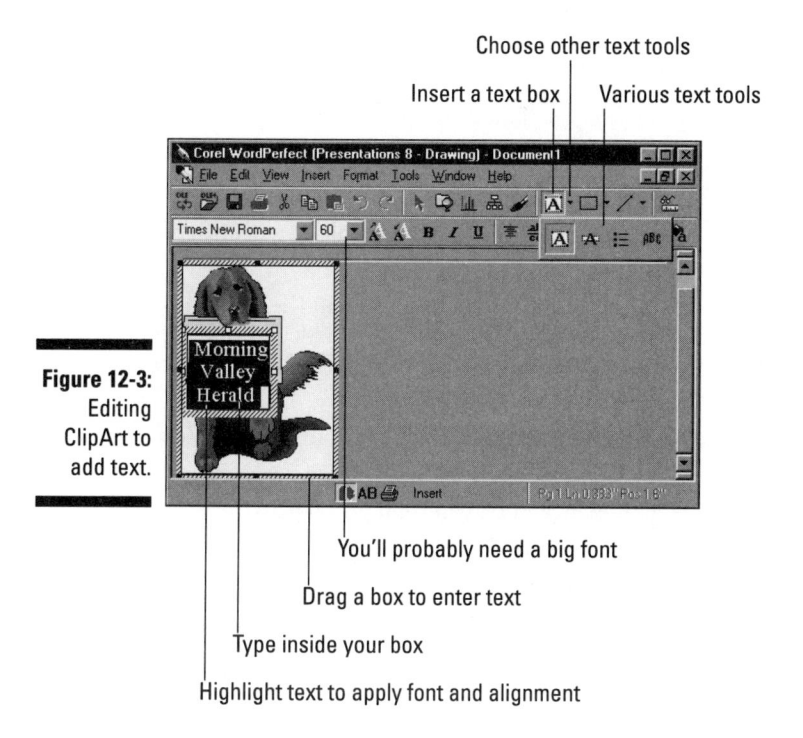

Callouts on figure:
- Choose other text tools
- Insert a text box
- Various text tools
- You'll probably need a big font
- Drag a box to enter text
- Type inside your box
- Highlight text to apply font and alignment

Backgrounds were popular when they first came out but are less so now. Designers found that unless a background was very subtle, it distracted from the Web page's contents. You be the judge.

Unlike regular wallpaper, Web-page wallpaper is actually fun to apply (you can change your mind without incurring the Wrath of Spouse). Set up wallpaper by using the same dialog box in which you choose font color and background color: the HTML Document Properties dialog box. Before applying wallpaper, choose a background color of a hue and darkness similar to the wallpaper that you want. That way, if a visitor to your Web site has graphics turned off, your chosen text colors are still visible.

The following steps will help you apply wallpaper to your Web document:

**1. Choose Format⇨Text/Background Colors.**

Alternatively, click the HTML Document Properties button (it looks like a cobwebby calculator in the Toolbar) or right-click your document and then choose Properties from the QuickMenu that appears. Whatever. Then click the Text/Background Colors tab in the HTML Document Properties dialog box that appears.

To remove wallpaper, delete everything in the Background Wallpaper text box. (A fast way is to click the start of the stuff in that box, press Shift+End, and then press Delete.)

**Part III: Getting Graphical**

2. **Click the tiny file-folder icon at the right end of the box labeled Background Wallpaper to browse for a nice background picture.**

   The Background Wallpaper dialog box appears.

3. **Click the Toggle Preview On/Off button so that you can preview any images you click on.**

   (The button is just to the left of the yellow folder with the red checkmark.)

   WordPerfect takes you to its Textures folder (in the Graphics folder where Corel Suite 8 is installed on your hard disk). In that folder, you find folders for images related to Fabrics, Food, Nature, Paper, and other subjects.

4. **Choose one of the bitmapped (made of dots) images, which are mostly of the BMP type.**

   You can choose images from elsewhere, if you like.

5. **When you find an image that you like, click the Select button in the Background Wallpaper dialog box.**

   The HTML Document Properties dialog box shows you how your selected text colors look on your new background image. Figure 12-4 shows an example.

6. **Click the OK button in the HTML Document Properties dialog box.**

If you decide to take images from somewhere other than the Textures folder, be careful. Here are some caveats for using other images for wallpaper:

✓ WordPerfect won't accept WordPerfect graphics (.WPG files) for a background.

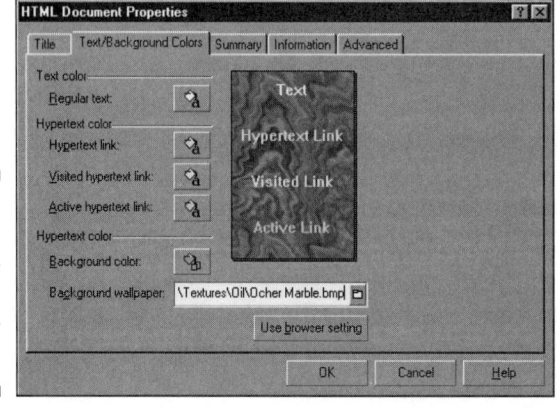

Figure 12-4: Checking text for legibility on the new wallpaper.

- If you use a GIF or JPG file (which are file types that you often find on the Web), you need to download or copy that file to the graphics folder that you are using for HTML documents. Refer to Chapter 11 for more details.
- Ordinary images (images that aren't seamless) create a repetitive pattern across the screen. To avoid making this pattern visible, you need an image as large as the largest window that you expect a visitor to use.

*Technical Stuff:* When you publish to HTML, WordPerfect converts the BMP (or DIB) background image that you choose to a GIF file and puts it in the folder with the rest of your graphics.

If you want people to be able to read your text easily, be careful about what image you use for wallpaper. The Jelly_Bean.bmp background in the WordPerfect Food folder, for example, is cute, but it's so contrasty that no text, light or dark, shows up well on it. In general, the best wallpaper images are

- Low-contrast (no very dark or very light colors)
- Light (whitish) in color, with a dark text color
- Seamless
- Free of text or other large or distracting elements

For graphics tips that you can use to improve wallpaper images, see Chapter 13. Often, reducing the contrast, making the image black-and-white, embossing, and other tricks can make an image work better as wallpaper.

*Technical Stuff:* A popular trick is to create one or more vertical stripes as a background. A stripe can run continuously down the left side of the page, for example, perhaps imitating the binding of a spiral-bound notebook. Such stripes are made from a thin, wide image — wider than most people's browser windows so that the image doesn't appear to repeat horizontally. Only a small part of the image — the leftmost inch, for example — forms the visible stripe as the image is repeated hundreds of times down the page. The rest of the image typically is white and forms the main background. The file size of the image is small, and the image is downloaded only once, so you achieve a nice background without slowing download times.

# Boffo Bullets

Not since the American Revolution have folks been quite so interested in making their own bullets. You can, of course, use the ordinary black bullets that come with Bulleted List style text, but how boring! If you don't mind boring, simply highlight the text to be bulleted and then click the Insert Bullet button. Refer to Chapter 8 for more details.

**Part III: Getting Graphical**

> **WARNING!** Standard bullets may be boring, but they need less downloading time than other bullets do. If you create your own bullets (or any other repeated graphic), see Chapter 14 for tips on reducing downloading time for your Web document.

Just how do you persuade your bulleted text to exchange its boring bullets for boffo bullets? You don't. You don't use Bulleted Text style at all. You simply insert tiny pictures in front of ordinary text! The WordPerfect ClipArt feature offers many interesting graphics that you can use. (Refer to Chapter 11 for a discussion of inserting ClipArt.) Alternatively, you can insert a symbol by using TextArt. You can also find bundles of boffo bullets on the Web; refer to the first section of this chapter for suggestions.

> **TIP** Try inserting a 2D or 3D TextArt bullet. Click the Insert Symbol button in the TextArt dialog box; then find and insert the black-dot symbol.

A few tricks make using graphics for bullets easier. Figure 12-5 provides tips and examples at the same time.

Custom bullets should use character attachment. Fortunately, character attachment is what WordPerfect normally uses anyway when you insert graphics. Character-attached graphics can be adjusted vertically on the line of text for a better appearance in certain instances. Refer to Chapter 11 for more information about attachment and positioning.

> **WARNING!** If you use bullets gleaned from the Web, they may well be graphics in GIF or JPG format. If so, and if you have not modified those bullets within WordPerfect, you must copy those files to the graphics folder that you are using for HTML documents. Refer to Chapter 11 for more information about publishing with graphics and to Chapter 14 for a way to reduce downloading time when using bullet graphics.

**Figure 12-5:** Taking a few bullets from ClipArt is fairly painless.

- Shrink your chosen graphic by clicking it and dragging the tiny square in any one of the corners toward the center of the graphic.
- To put space before or after the bullet, use Ctrl+spacebar.
- To give a bulleted paragraph the indented appearance of regular bulleted text, create a table and turn off the borders. Put the bullet in the left column and the text in the right.
- Copy and paste the graphic to your other bulleted lines. This repetition can make your page large and slow to download, however. See Chapter 14 for tips on avoiding the problem.
- Center the graphic vertically on the line if there's no danger of text wrap.

## Basic and Beautified Buttons

Buttons add a certain "Push my buttons; I'm an electronic appliance" appearance to Web pages, which is particularly useful for creating navigation controls. WordPerfect makes basic buttons fairly easy to create, and with a few tricks, you can beautify your buttons.

### Basic buttons and icons

The buttons and icons that you see on Web sites look as though they must be special fancy thingamabobs, but in fact, they often are nothing more than small individual graphics with hyperlinks. For graphics that make pretty good icons, see Chapter 11's discussion of the WordPerfect Clipart collection. (Icons are symbols that don't look like actual physical buttons.) For the basics on applying hyperlinks to graphics, see Chapter 7.

*TIP:* If you create buttons in WordPerfect and use the same buttons over and over again, see Chapter 14 for tips on reducing downloading time for your Web document.

To make buttons that look more like the buttons on electronic appliances, you can use the WordPerfect special Make Text Appear As Button option when you create text hyperlinks. The section "Different Hyperlink Appearances" in Chapter 7 tells you more about that feature.

*TIP:* You can adjust the size of buttons, as you can any other graphic, but adjusting the width can cause text wrap, which in turn changes the height! To return to a uniform height, right-click a button, choose Size from the QuickMenu that appears, and in the Box Size dialog box that appears, set the Height setting to, say, 0.5 inch. Repeat for all your buttons.

### Beautified buttons

WordPerfect's regular buttons are boring, gray rectangles with text. How about adding a little color and maybe using graphics instead of text, as shown in Figure 12-6? (Well, you'll have to take my word for the color.) Adding color and graphics is easy to do, because the WordPerfect buttons are nothing more than text boxes with a particular border and fill!

Changing the color of a button is an easy job. Just perform the following steps:

**Figure 12-6:** A bunch of beautified buttons.

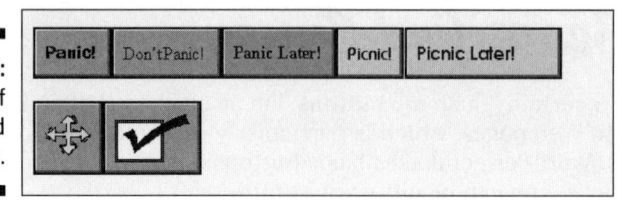

| Panic! | Don'tPanic! | Panic Later! | Picnic! | Picnic Later! |

 1. **Right-click your boring button and then choose Border/Fill from the QuickMenu that appears.**

    The Box Border/Fill dialog box appears.

 2. **Click the Fill tab.**

 3. **Click the paint can button labeled Foreground and then choose a new color from the palette that appears.**

 4. **Click the Apply button to check the appearance of the button in your document.**

 5. **Click OK when you're done.**

Changing the content on the button from text to graphics is almost as easy; do it this way:

 1. **Click the text in the center of the button.**

    Now you're in the Text Box Editor. Your document disappears, but don't panic.

 2. **Delete the text and insert graphics (Clipart, TextArt, or any other form of graphics).**

    The commands and controls for inserting graphics are the same as those that you use when you're working in the main document.

 3. **Click the Close button in the Text Box Editor window.**

You may need to adjust the dimensions of the button after changing to a graphic. Click the outer edge of the button to select the button and then drag any of the tiny black squares on the sides of the button to adjust dimensions. Alternatively, right-click the button and then choose Size from the QuickMenu to display a dialog box that allows you to set size precisely.

You can use a nicer font on your button by editing the button text. Follow the first three steps in the preceding list for inserting graphics. When you're in the Text Box Editor, select the text and choose a different font. Click the Close button when you're done.

## Keeping Your Buttons Together

A row of buttons looks nice, but if your visitor is using a narrow window, the buttons wrap to the next line and possibly mess up your layout. The best way to prevent a row from breaking is to place all the buttons in a single-cell (1x1) table. For best results, use a table set to a width of 100 percent and a border of 0.

## A right-handed control panel

A one-cell table can also help you put your buttons in a control panel on the right side of your page. Figure 12-7 shows that effect and also shows how text can wrap around the table on the left side.

**Figure 12-7:** A single-celled organism helps keep controls under control.

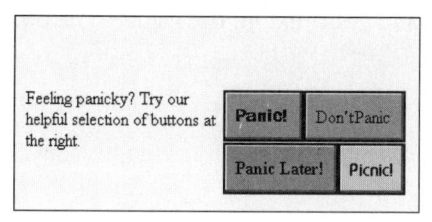

Here are the steps to take to create a right-handed control panel:

1. **Create a single-cell table.**

    (Refer to Chapter 10; click the Table button and drag to 1x1.)

2. **Cut and paste your set of buttons into the cell.**

3. **Insert line breaks (choose Insert⇨Line Break) between buttons where you want to break a row into two rows.**

4. **Choose Table⇨Format on the Property Bar.**

    The HTML Table Properties dialog box springs gracefully upon the scene.

5. **Set Table borders to 0.**

6. **Set Table width to less than 100 percent (say, 40 percent).**

7. **Set Table position on page to Right.**
8. **Click OK.**

    You may need to repeat Steps 4 through 8 and fiddle with the table width a few times to get things to work right.

To have text wrap, put the text immediately after the table. Choose View⇨Show ¶ to make sure no blank lines or paragraphs are between table and text. Click the View in Web Browser button (the document behind the Web) to check your results.

## A left- or right-handed control panel

Oddly, you can't have the controls on the left by using a single-celled table — just the right. If you want to have controls on the left, create a two-celled table (2 columns x 1 row) of 100 percent width.

Put your controls on the left and your text on the right. (The other way around also works.)

# Chapter 13
# Better, Fancier Graphics

*In This Chapter*
- Creating captions
- Using WordPerfect's graphical borders and fills
- Using HTML borders and spaces
- Making graphics fade in during downloading
- Flipping, rotating, brightening, and contrasting
- Using and creating see-through graphics
- Using Photo House for transparency and other effects

If you add a WordPerfect caption or a border to a GIF or JPG image, or if you use WordPerfect's Image Tools palette to modify the image, WordPerfect realizes that you have made modifications and publishes a modified GIF in your graphics folder when you publish to HTML. As a result, you don't need to (and should not) copy the original GIF or JPG file to the graphics folder, as you normally would for unmodified GIF or JPG images. See "Publishing to HTML with Graphics" in Chapter 11 for more discussion of this confusing stuff.

## Creating Captions

When it comes to graphics, WordPerfect leaves no stone unturned — and leaves no excuse for uncaptioned Web graphics, either. You can put a caption on any of WordPerfect's boxes, including ClipArt or other graphics, TextArt, or text boxes. For Web documents, WordPerfect gives you captions exactly like those for regular documents but achieves them in a wonderfully sneaky way. HTML doesn't quite yet provide a way to do captions with actual text, so WordPerfect simply creates a caption as it always has and then, when you publish to HTML, takes a picture of the caption! The program converts the caption to graphics as part of the graphic that it's captioning.

WordPerfect's captioning is a regular Arnold Schwarzenegger of a feature — too big to fit into this book and more muscular than nearly anyone needs on a regular basis. Following are a few of the captioning features:

- ✓ You can position a caption anywhere around the outside of the figure, running vertically or horizontally, inside or outside the border of the graphic.
- ✓ You can offset a caption from the position that you give, in inches or percentage points, in either direction.
- ✓ You can make captions as wide as the graphic (or as tall, for vertical captions) or any percentage of the graphic's width.
- ✓ You can left-align, center, or right-align the caption.

Here's how to apply a caption, without any of the fancy stuff:

1. **Right-click the graphic (or other box) that you're captioning and then choose Create Caption from the QuickMenu that appears.**

   Don't panic because your document disappears; you're now in the Caption Editor window.

2. **Delete the text** Figure 1 **in the window and type your own text.**

   Feel free to use any font or color that you like. Heck, insert a ClipArt or TextArt image, too, if having one in your caption suits you!

3. **Click the Close button at the top of the Caption editor window.**

To edit your caption, right-click the graphic again, but this time choose Edit Caption from the QuickMenu. You land back in the Caption editor for a repeat performance.

To position or remove your caption, right-click the graphic and then choose Caption from the QuickMenu. (Alternatively, left-click your graphic and then choose Graphics⇨Caption from the Property Bar.)

An enormous Box Caption dialog box appears, displaying lots of stuff to fool with, all related to the features just listed (in the bullets that appeared a few paragraphs ago). The Edit button in that dialog box takes you to the Caption editor window. To remove your caption altogether, click the Reset button in the Box Caption dialog box. (Click OK in the query box that appears.) Click the OK button when you're done in the Box Caption dialog box.

Figure 13-1 in the following section shows an example caption centered along the bottom of the image. You can see that because WordPerfect makes the caption part of the image, the HTML Vertical space appears outside the caption. (Although an HTML border is not used in the example in Figure 13-1, if it were, it too would appear outside the caption.)

# Using WordPerfect's Graphical Borders and Fills

WordPerfect's border and fill feature is another Schwarzeneggian doodad like its caption feature, with dozens of options. All its regular borders and fills (backgrounds) work on Web pages. Add to these regular borders the special borders that HTML documents use, and you've got more borders than Aunt Suzy's Discount Rooming House. Figure 13-1 shows how the various borders and fills can add up to create the effect that you want.

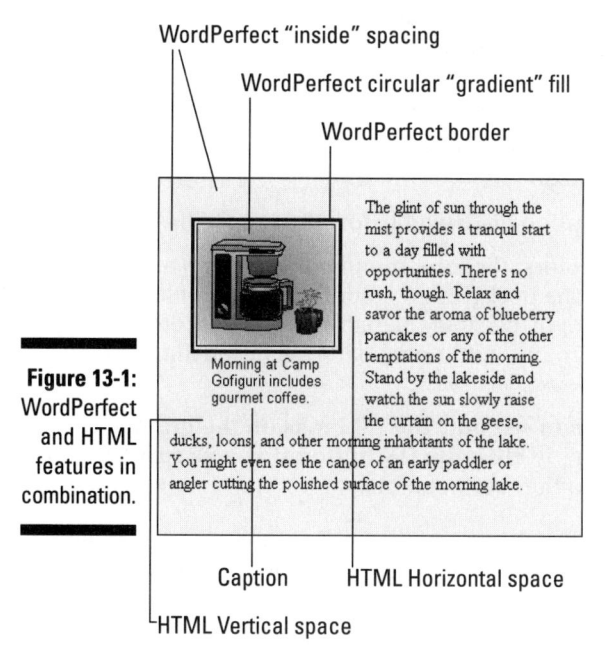

**Figure 13-1:** WordPerfect and HTML features in combination.

*Labels:* WordPerfect "inside" spacing; WordPerfect circular "gradient" fill; WordPerfect border; Caption; HTML Horizontal space; HTML Vertical space

*Caption text in figure:* Morning at Camp Gofigurit includes gourmet coffee.

*Body text in figure:* The glint of sun through the mist provides a tranquil start to a day filled with opportunities. There's no rush, though. Relax and savor the aroma of blueberry pancakes or any of the other temptations of the morning. Stand by the lakeside and watch the sun slowly raise the curtain on the geese, ducks, loons, and other morning inhabitants of the lake. You might even see the canoe of an early paddler or angler cutting the polished surface of the morning lake.

For now, focus on WordPerfect's ordinary borders and fills, and tackle the HTML borders in the next section. Here are the steps for applying WordPerfect borders and fills to Web graphics:

1. **Right-click the graphic and then choose Border/Fill from the QuickMenu.**

    The Box Border/Fill dialog box puts in an appearance, with the Border tab displayed.

2. **Choose a border style from the roughly 40 available styles.**

    The dialog box displays your chosen border on a sample area of the dialog box.

Scroll down the list to see more choices. The first style (the one in the top-left corner) removes any border. Choose a color, line style, and drop shadow for the border, if you like, by clicking the buttons with those labels.

*Note:* Light gray areas become transparent.

3. **Click the Apply button to see how the border looks on the graphic in your document, or simply click the OK button if you're sure of your choice and need no fill.**

4. **Click the Fill tab at the top of the dialog box if you want a background behind the graphic.**

   A list of fills is displayed, the same way that borders are displayed in the Border tab. The first fill (the one in the top-left corner) is no fill, which provides a transparent background for the image that your document background or wallpaper shows through.

5. **Click a fill that you like and observe its effect in the sample displayed in the dialog box.**

   Notice the brief description displayed below the list of fills.

   Fills are made of two colors: the foreground color (shown as black in the selection list) and the background color (shown as white in the list). Choose new colors by clicking the paint-bucket buttons labeled Foreground and Background. Additional patterns lurk behind the Pattern button.

6. **Click the Apply button to see how the fill looks on the graphic in your document, or simply click the OK button if you're sure of your choice and need no further refinements.**

To adjust spacing between the image and its border, apply a shadow, fine-tune a gradient fill, or apply rounded corners to the border and fill, click the Advanced tab in the Box Border/Fill dialog box. Following are some of the Advanced things that advanced beings may want to do:

- ✔ To adjust spacing between the graphic and its border, click the Inside button and then choose a space width from the list that appears.

- ✔ The Outside spacing, which normally adjusts space between the box and the text, actually has no effect in Web documents (at least, in early releases of WordPerfect 8). Instead, a special HTML spacing feature controls that spacing (see the following section).

- ✔ To make the box look like it's floating over the page, add a drop shadow by clicking the Color button and then choosing a darker version of your background color from the palette that appears.

- ✔ Set the width of the shadow by clicking the Width button and then choosing a line width from the selection of lines that is presented.
- ✔ Create a rounded border by increasing the value in the Corner Radius box.
- ✔ If you chose a gradient fill in the Fill tab, you can fiddle with it by using the Vertical and Horizontal offset and Rotation angle settings. The sample in the dialog box reveals the effect.

Click the Apply button to see how the result looks on the graphic in your document. Click the OK button when you need no further refinements.

> An important, nonobvious control is the Discontinue button in the Border tab. That button removes all WordPerfect border and fill settings and restores a transparent background if the image previously had one.

# Using HTML Borders and Spaces

WordPerfect's borders and spacing controls are fairly comprehensive for ordinary documents, but they don't do everything for HTML Web documents (the files that your visitor actually sees on the Web). HTML Web documents have two border-related features that the WordPerfect Border/Fill controls don't control (at least, in initial releases of WordPerfect 8):

- ✔ Spacing between the graphic and the text
- ✔ The HTML border (an optional border that surrounds your entire graphic, including the existing WordPerfect border)

*Note:* You can't see either of these HTML document features in WordPerfect; you must view the document in a Web browser to see their effect.

To control Web borders and spacing, right-click your graphic (or other box) and then choose HTML Properties from the QuickMenu. The HTML Properties dialog box springs into action. Click the Image tab of that dialog box to get to the controls shown in Figure 13-2.

Adjust the values in the Horizontal space and Vertical space boxes to determine the space, in pixels (screen dots), between the outside of the graphic and any text in the same paragraph. (A caption, if you use one, is part of the graphic.) For an example, see the lovely white horizontal and vertical space in Figure 13-1 earlier in this chapter. The spacing in that figure is set to 20 pixels both horizontally and vertically.

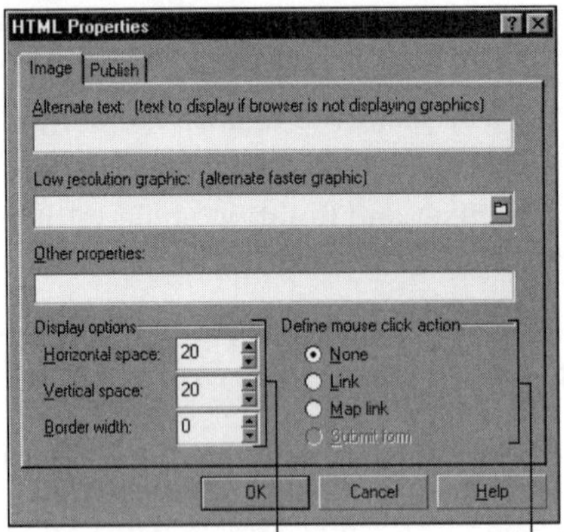

**Figure 13-2:** Web border and spacing controls.

Set spacing and border
Linking affects border color

Adjust the value in the Border width box to determine — you guessed it — the width (or thickness, if you prefer) of the line used for the Web border. The values in the Border width, Horizontal space, and Vertical space controls are also in pixels. Zero width turns the border off.

The color of the border depends on whether the graphic serves as a hyperlink (something that you click to go to another location). You can tell that a graphic is hyperlinked if either Link or Map link appears (refer to Figure 13-2). If the graphic is hyperlinked, the colors used for the border are the same as the colors used for hyperlinked text. (Refer to Chapters 7 and 9 for details on colors and hyperlinking.) If the graphic is not hyperlinked (that is, if None is chosen in the Define mouse click action section), most browsers display a border in black.

To create a hyperlink, click Link in the Define Mouse Click Action section shown in Figure 13-2. A new Link tab appears in the HTML Properties dialog box; click that tab and enter your hyperlink, as discussed in Chapter 7. You can change the color of the border by using the text and background color controls discussed in "Hypertext Color" in Chapter 9.

# Making Graphics Fade in During Downloading

The sad truth of the Web is that graphics can take a long time to arrive at a browser. The big philosophical question that arises, then, is which is better: looking at a blank spot in the document while the graphic is transmitted or watching the image gradually form (*fade in*)? If you'd like your graphics to be of the fade-in variety, all you need to do is tell WordPerfect to create a form of GIF graphics called "interlaced" when it publishes to HTML.

The control to create interlaced GIF graphics is a simple check box in the Publish tab of the HTML Properties dialog box. Here's how to use that control:

1. **Right-click the graphic and then choose HTML Properties from the QuickMenu that appears.**
2. **When the HTML Properties dialog box appears, click the Publish tab.**
3. **Click the Interlaced check box on the Publish tab.**

*Note:* You can't force images to fade in; you can only give your visitors the opportunity to view the graphic in this way, because final control rests with each visitor's browser. Most browsers are set up to fade in from the start. (Otherwise, in Netscape Navigator 3, the user chooses Options⇨General Preferences and, in the Images tab, sets Display Images to While Loading for the graphic to fade in during downloading.)

# Flipping, Rotating, Brightening, and Contrasting

WordPerfect has built-in image tools that perform several useful tricks on inserted graphics. To access the image tools, right-click the graphic and then choose Image Tools from the QuickMenu that appears. An Image Tools palette floats on-screen, displaying the buttons shown in Figure 13-3.

Following are notes on the most useful of these buttons:

- Flip the image horizontally (upside down) or vertically (left to right) by clicking the Flip buttons.
- Rotate the image by first clicking Rotate; then drag any of the new handles (tiny corner squares) that appear around the image and drag. Drag the tiny plus sign (+) that appears in the middle of the image to move the center of rotation.
- Brighten or darken the image by clicking the Brightness button; then choose a brighter or darker icon from the palette of butterflies that appears.
- Adjust contrast the same way by clicking the Contrast button.

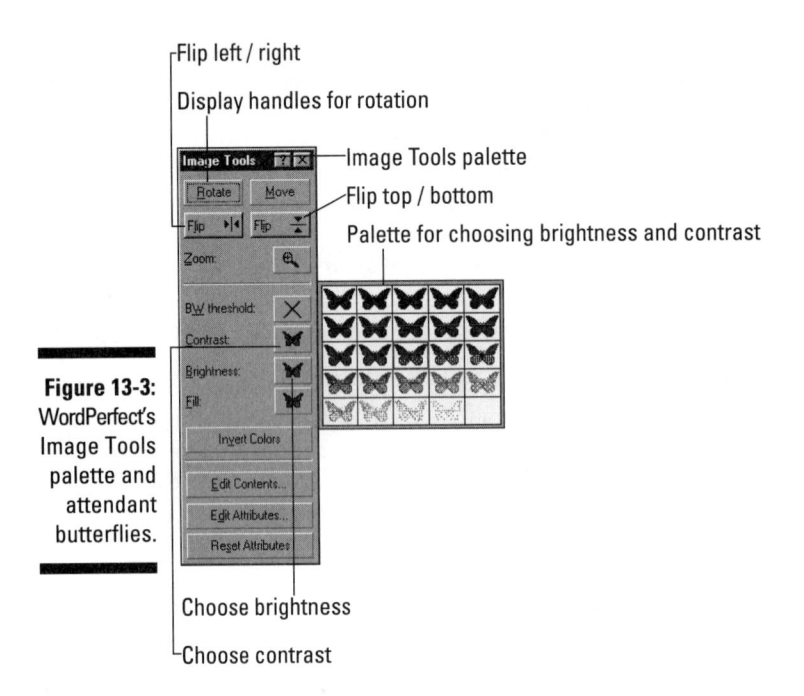

**Figure 13-3:** WordPerfect's Image Tools palette and attendant butterflies.

Labels on figure:
- Flip left / right
- Display handles for rotation
- Image Tools palette
- Flip top / bottom
- Palette for choosing brightness and contrast
- Choose brightness
- Choose contrast

These tools work on various inserted graphics, such as WordPerfect Clipart, text boxes, drawings, TextArt, and bitmap image files (such as BMP images inserted from the WordPerfect Pictures folder).

# Using and Creating See-Through Graphics

The concept of see-through graphics originated with stained-glass windows, in which it served a lofty purpose. After a brief, infamous fling with vinyl swimwear in the '60s, the concept has reemerged on the Web in a more moderate role. On the Web, the concept is sedately called transparency (it's more of a peekaboo effect, actually).

With a transparent background, an image appears to have been cut out and pasted on the document background. No rectangular background area surrounds the graphic, as though it were drawn on a separate piece of paper and pasted on. In truth, the image's background color is electronically designated to be transparent so that the browser displays the document background instead.

## Transparency using ClipArt and other WordPerfect artwork

When you publish ClipArt to HTML, WordPerfect preserves the transparent background that ClipArt normally has. WordPerfect also preserves any transparency that's present in other WordPerfect graphics: drawings, text boxes, and TextArt. (3-D TextArt backgrounds normally are not transparent, however.)

When it comes to transparency on the Web, you're the boss. You can create a transparent background where one doesn't currently exist, for example. You're not limited to making background color transparent, either; you can make any color appear to be transparent. You won't see the result in WordPerfect; you see it only when you view your document in a Web browser. You can also turn transparency off.

Figure 13-4 shows the effect of changing the color that is designated to be transparent. The image on the left is my own fine-art creation with the transparent background that WordPerfect normally gives drawings. In the center is the identical image with the eye color transparent; on the right, the body color is transparent.

**Figure 13-4:** Achieving the Cheshire Cat effect with transparency.

Transparent background | Transparent eye color | Transparent body color

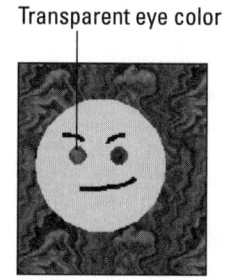

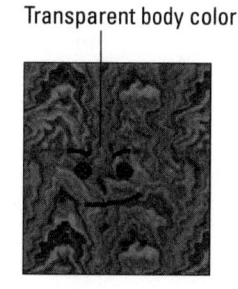

To change transparency when you're using a WordPerfect image (WPG file or an image that you create in WordPerfect), follow these steps:

1. **Right-click the image and then choose HTML Properties from the QuickMenu that appears.**

    The HTML Properties dialog box appears.

2. **Click the Publish tab.**

3. **Select GIF and Transparency, if they're not already selected.**

    If you hope to turn a transparent area to solid gray, click Transparency to *de*-select it and then click the OK button.

4. **Click the paint-bucket button labeled Transparency, and from the palette that appears, choose the color that you want to make transparent.**

   The trick is that you have to know precisely what color, of all the possible colors in the the WordPerfect palette, is used in the image. If the image is ClipArt, you can try to guess. If you created the image, you may remember which palette color you used. Otherwise, see the sidebar "What color is that?" later in this section.

5. **Click the OK button in the HTML Properties dialog box.**

6. **Click the View in Web Browser button (the document-behind-the-web icon) to see the result.**

If you need to repeat these steps to get things to work right, each time you view the file in the Web browser, you may need to click the Reload button in the browser to see the latest graphic.

## Transparency using BMP and scanned-in images

In theory, WordPerfect can create transparent Web graphics from BMP images or a photograph that you scan into your document. Simply choose one of the colors in the image to become transparent and follow the procedure for WordPerfect files given in the preceding section. (Transparency won't show up in WordPerfect; click View in Web Browser to see the result.)

---

### What color is that?

If you don't know what color is being used in ClipArt or other WordPerfect graphics, you can find out. (The technique does not work, however, for photographic or bitmap images, such as BMP files.) Follow these steps:

1. **Double-click the graphic to get access to the graphics tools.**

2. **Right-click the graphic and then choose Separate Objects from the QuickMenu that appears.**

3. **Click the object that contains the color in question, and observe the paint can icons in the Property Bar.**

4. **Click the paint can of the color that resembles the one you're trying to identify.**

5. **In the palette that appears, observe which color is selected (or select a new one) and remember its position.**

6. **Click outside the graphic to exit drawing mode, and try again to set transparency.**

In reality, many bitmap-image files are tricky to use for creating transparent images. These images are tricky because they are made up of dots of various colors, not solid areas of a single color. Even if an area looks like one color, it's often not. If you choose a single color to be transparent, you usually succeed only in creating many transparent dots, making your image look as though it has been gnawed by mice.

The trick, then, presuming that you are not into the mouse-gnawed look, is to get a solid, uniform color over the portion of the image that you want to be transparent. Several approaches can be effective; you may need to use them in combination to get a result that you like.

### Using WordPerfect's Image Tools to get a uniform color

WordPerfect's Image Tools can help you get uniform color in some images. If you want transparency where an image is a nearly uniform white or light gray, try increasing the contrast or brightness of the entire image and then choosing white as the transparent color. If the area that you want to be transparent is dark, increase contrast or reduce brightness to darken the dark to black, and then choose black as the transparent color. To try this approach with the WordPerfect built-in image tools, refer to "Flipping, Rotating, Brightening, and Contrasting" earlier in this chapter.

The downside of this approach is the fact that it affects the entire image. When you succeed in making the background a uniform white (or black), the object that you're interested in is often mangled.

### Using other image tools to get a uniform color

Apart from adjusting contrast and brightness, WordPerfect's Image Tools are limited in how much they can help you achieve a uniform color. Other tools, however — especially Corel's Photo House — can do a great deal. The following section deals with using Photo House for some of these jobs.

A simple brute-force approach to getting a uniform color in an area of a BMP file is to load the file into Windows' Paint program (which comes with Windows 95) and paint over an area! Delete the BMP image from your document first. Then, in Windows 95, choose Start⇨Programs⇨Accessories⇨Paint. Open the BMP file by choosing File⇨Open. At the bottom of the Paint window, click a nonsubtle color, such as red, yellow, green, blue, black, or white. Pick any color that you'll be able to recognize in the WordPerfect color selection palette and that's not used anywhere in the image. Using the brush tool, paint over the area that you want to be transparent. Save the file; insert it into your document by choosing Insert⇨Graphics⇨From File; and make the color transparent, as described in the preceding sections.

## Using Photo House for Transparency and Other Effects

You can go only so far in WordPerfect to achieve transparency and other special effects with graphics. Photo House and the graphics tools on this book's CD-ROM can help you work around WordPerfect's limitations. You can either work on the graphic before you insert it into your document or work on the GIF or JPG file that WordPerfect creates when you publish to HTML. (For backgrounds, work on the image before you apply it to the document.) Photo House works only on bitmap files (such as BMP, GIF, TIF, and JPG), but it can convert WordPerfect artwork and other nonbitmap formats to bitmap form. See "Opening and importing files" later in this chapter, and "Convert File Types Using Graphics Tools" in Chapter 14.

To start Photo House, click the Corel Photo House icon in the Corel DAD (Corel's answer to Microsoft's MOM). The DAD is the box of stuff located at the far right end (or bottom) of your Windows 95 Start bar. (Pause your mouse pointer over any icon to see a description of what it is.) If you don't have DAD installed, choose Start➪Corel WordPerfect Suite 8➪Corel Photo House.

*Note:* If you can't perform either of these actions, you probably need to install Photo House! Insert the WordPerfect Suite 8 installation CD-ROM and do a custom installation of only Photo House. What? No installation CD-ROM? Check your company network for Photo House or try one of the other fine tools on this book's CD-ROM.

### Opening and importing files

To open or import a file in Photo House, choose File➪Open, browse to the folder where the image file hangs out, click the file, and then click the Open button to open the file.

In the Open dialog box, click the Preview check box. Now you can click any bitmap file (BMP, JPG, GIF, TIF, and some others) and see the image that it contains. If the file is not a bitmap graphic, such as a WPG file, you can't preview the file — just open it.

An Import into Bitmap dialog box asks you for instructions on exactly how to convert the image to bitmap form. Unfortunately, hollering "Just do it, darn it!" into your disk-drive slot doesn't work. (I tried.) Just clicking OK and hoping for the best isn't a good idea, either. Figure 13-5 shows the dialog box with suggested settings.

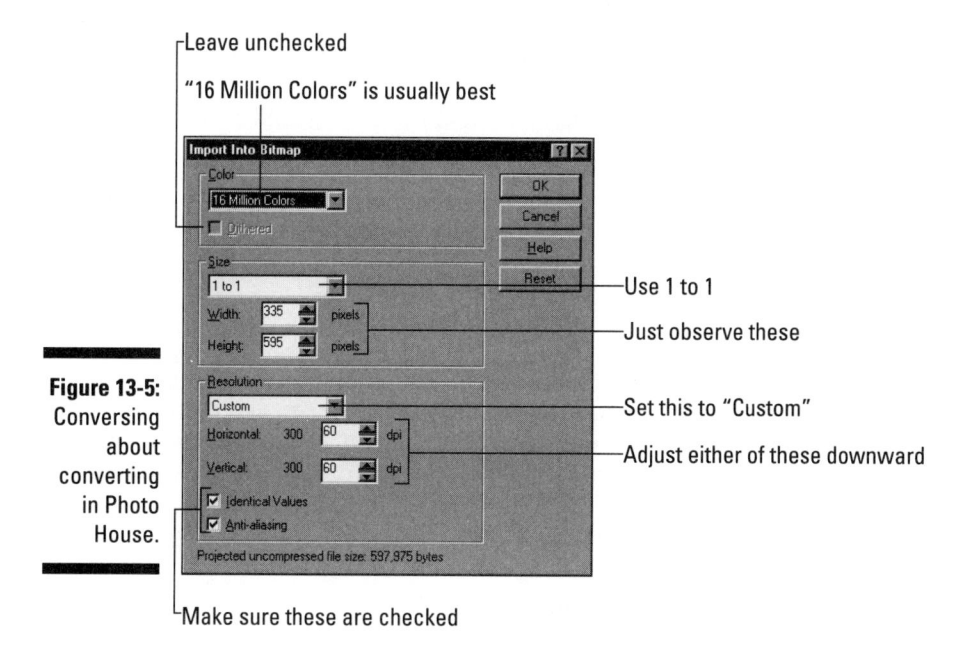

**Figure 13-5:** Conversing about converting in Photo House.

- Leave unchecked
- "16 Million Colors" is usually best
- Use 1 to 1
- Just observe these
- Set this to "Custom"
- Adjust either of these downward
- Make sure these are checked

The main problem with opening nonbitmap graphics in Photo House is that the program makes an enormous image unless you step in. Usually, the best solution is to choose 16 Million Colors in the Color drop-down list; choose Custom in the Resolution drop-down list; and adjust either the Horizontal or Vertical value while observing the Width and Height values.

Stop adjusting resolution when the image size meets your needs; an image smaller than a Width of 800 pixels and a Height of 600 pixels usually is a good idea. (Also, your license from Corel probably restricts online sizes to 768 × 512 pixels if you're using Corel artwork! Check your license for restrictions.) Click OK when you're done. Then go get lunch or take a nap, because you may have a long wait for results!

If you choose fewer than 16 Million Colors in the Color drop-down list, and the result is an image with ugly bands or blocks of color, close the image window (and don't save the image). Try again with Dithered deselected in the Import into Bitmap dialog box.

## Saving files

Before saving a file, check the palette of your image. If the palette is incorrect, the format that you want doesn't even appear as an option in the Save As dialog box. The rules for palette settings in Photo House are these:

- To save a GIF file, you must use an image with a 256-color (or smaller) palette.
- To save a JPG file, you must use an image with 16 million colors.

Choose Image⇨Image Properties to display the Image Properties dialog box. In the Color mode box, choose the number of colors you want. Then click OK. If you chose 256 Colors or fewer, don't panic if your image looks cruddy afterward. Choose View⇨Zoom 100%. If the image still looks cruddy, you can panic.

Second, choose the size of your image, in pixels. Choose Image⇨Image Properties again to display the Image Properties dialog box. Make sure a check appears in the Maintain aspect ratio check box to avoid distorting the image; then adjust either the Width or the Height (in pixels). How big is a pixel? The answer depends on the computer. Many PC monitors are 800 pixels wide by 600 high these days.

Finally, save the file as the file type that you want. Here's how:

1. **Choose File⇨Save As in Photo House.**

   The Save As dialog box appears.

2. **Open a folder for your graphic.**

3. **In the Save as type box, choose the format that you want.**

   Your choice may be CompuServe Bitmap (GIF), for example, or JPEG Bitmaps (JPG).

4. **Enter a name for the file.**

   Preferably, enter a short, simple name (eight letters or numbers, with no spaces or punctuation).

5. **Click the Save button.**

What happens now depends on what file format you chose in Step 3.

If you chose GIF in Step 3, the Transparent Color dialog box appears. Take the following steps to create your GIF file:

1. **Click 89a Format.**

2. **Click Interlaced Image if you want the image to be capable of fading in on the Web.**

3. **Check the Transparent Color check box for a transparent image; then, in the palette that appears, click the color that you want to make transparent.**

4. **Click OK.**

If you chose JPG in Step 3, the JPEG Export dialog box appears. Take these steps to create your JPG file:

1. **Drag the sliding control labeled Quality Factor to the right for a lower-quality but smaller file; drag it to the left for a higher-quality but bigger file.**
2. **Click OK.**

You are done! In WordPerfect, insert your new file into the document by choosing Insert⇨Graphics⇨From File.

## Creating a uniformly colored area for transparency

Bitmap images are tricky when you want to make a colored area transparent. Such areas often are not made up of a single color — which, because transparency can be assigned to only a single color, is what you need. If you have Corel's Photo House installed on your PC, it can help with transparency by replacing a range of colors with a single color. Photo House provides several ways of doing the job; I find that using the fill tool works best.

In Photo House, choose File⇨Open to open your image file. Before doing anything else, choose Image⇨Image Properties to display the Image Properties dialog box; choose 16 Million Colors for the Color mode; then click OK.

*TIP*

The following procedure works better if you boost the contrast of the image a bit beforehand. Choose Image⇨Touch-up Effects⇨Brightness/Contrast/Intensity. In the dialog box that appears, drag the Contrast slider to the right and click Preview to see the effect. Click OK when you're done.

A column of tools runs down the center of the Photo House window. Click the Change Colors tool at the bottom of the column, and in the Paint Color palette that appears, choose a striking color that is used nowhere in your image — preferably one that has a simple name, such as Blue. I find that Magenta often is a good choice. This color is your painting color. (You select that color as the transparent color later.)

Click the spilling-paint-bucket icon in the center column, and your mouse pointer becomes a fill painting tool. Click the area that you want to make transparent; then position the tip of the spilling-paint-bucket mouse pointer quite near, but not on, the object that you want to remain opaque. When you click, a portion of that area is painted in your chosen color.

If the color solidly fills a well-defined area along the edge of the object, with few speckles, you're doing well. Figure 13-6 shows a good result, in which the paint fills everything but the object, its shadow, and the upper corners.

**Part III: Getting Graphical**

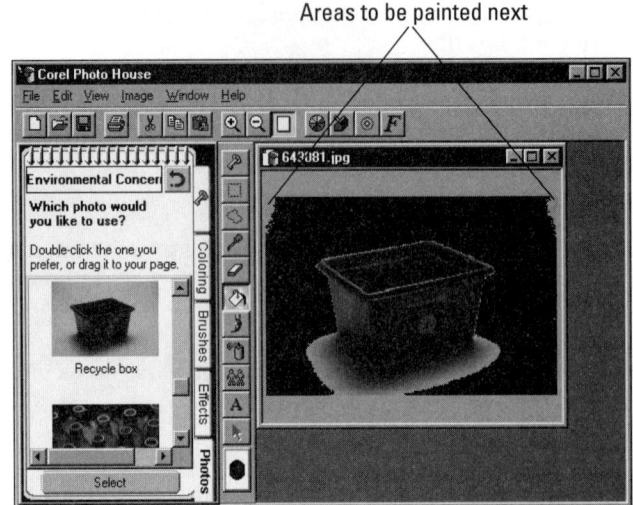

**Figure 13-6:** Painting over a range of colors in Corel Photo House.

Areas to be painted next

If the paint color leaks into the wrong place, you need less of something called color tolerance. If the color leaves many spots and speckles uncovered, you need more color tolerance.

To try again with more or less color tolerance, press Ctrl+Z to undo your first try; then click the Color Tolerance Dialog button in the row of buttons across the top. (The button looks like a bull's-eye, with concentric circles of color.) The Color Tolerance dialog box, shown in Figure 13-7, appears. Change the tolerance setting by typing a new value, clicking the up/down arrows next to the value, or sliding the slider. Click OK when you're done.

**Figure 13-7:** Improve your tolerance here.

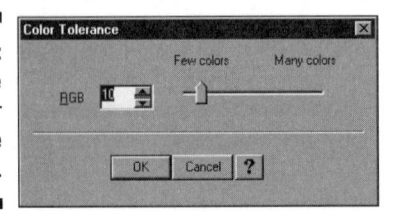

Try repeatedly painting and undoing, using different tolerances, until you get a clearly defined paint area with few speckles, no matter how small the area. Then repeat the process in the remaining area that you want to make transparent, each time moving farther out from the object and painting another band. When you have painted as much as possible with the paint can fill tool, click the brush tool and paint the remaining spots.

## Photo catalog

Anything called "Photo House" ought to be prepared to cough up a few photos — and sure enough, Corel supplies a modest catalog of 'em. Click the Photos tab of the cute spiral-notebook window in the left pane of the Photo House window. In the Catalog listing that appears, double-click a category. If you see a photo that you like, double-click it or drag it into the right pane. Photo House photos are of the JPG file type, the most efficient type of file for color photographs.

## Special effects

Photo House offers a bunch of rip-snorting special effects, plus a few that are just plain useful. Following are a few tips for using these effects.

Click the Effects tab on the spiral-bound notebook in the left pane. The notebook displays a list that includes the Touch-Up and Cool & Fun categories. (If the notebook shows only Touch-Up or Cool & Fun, click the U-turn arrow to the right of the category name.)

Click a category to choose it, and you see an illustrated gallery of special-effects tools. Following are some general instructions for using these tools:

- Many effects don't work on a 256-color image (typically, GIF). Choose Image⇨Image Properties to display the Image Properties dialog box; then choose 16 Million Colors for the Color mode.
- Double-click an effect or drag it to the right pane to use it.
- You can adjust all effects by using your choice of adjustment controls: a slider or a pair of up and down arrows that you can click.
- All effects use a Before and After window. Click Preview to see the result of your current settings in the After window. Click Reset to return to the original settings.
- Click OK when the After image looks the way you want it, or click Cancel to give up without any changes.

Photo House's Fun & Cool effects do some attractive, general graphics stuff. I'll leave you on your own to use the Fun & Cool effects. The Touch-Up effects have some special uses for Web work. Here are a few tips for using Touch-Up effects:

- **Brightness/Contrast/Intensity.** Scanned photos tend to be a bit low-contrast; this effect can brighten them. Also, increased contrast makes creating transparency easier for any image; often, it can push a range of light or dark colors to uniform white or black.

- **Reduce Speckles.** This effect makes images fuzzier as you use lower settings of the control labeled Threshold, helping reduce speckles. The effect also makes creating transparent areas easier.

  Some speckling can't be removed this way, because it's not the fault of the image. The speckling results from displaying a large bitmap image as a small graphic in the document or from using a View setting other than 100% in Photo House. Try reducing the image size as described in "Saving files" earlier in this chapter.

- **Replace Colors.** This effect works a bit like the paint-fill and color-tolerance tools described in "Creating a uniformly colored area for transparency" earlier in this chapter, but it affects the entire image at the same time. (The eyedropper picks your color from the Before image, and the Range control works like the color-tolerance tool.) The effect can be useful for creating a uniformly colored area, as well as for changing colors for aesthetic reasons.

- **Simplify Colors.** This effect can make photos look like abstract art. The effect also reduces low-contrast speckling and tends to create areas of uniform color, which aids in creating transparent areas.

# Chapter 14
# Speedier, Smaller Graphics

*In This Chapter*
- Reusing graphics
- Choosing and converting file types
- Reducing image size
- Reducing color depth
- Adjusting JPG compression quality
- Using sequential images in Netscape Navigator

*O*ne of the chief causes of the World Wide Wait (in which Web pages appear on your screen roughly as fast as moss grows on a rock) is big, fat, and, therefore, slow graphics. Part of the problem is that some designers rely on graphics for too much of their page content. The other part is poor graphics-file hygiene: transmitting redundant images, using an inappropriate file type, or using more colors or more pixels than are really needed. This chapter gives you tricks for turbocharging your Web graphics: achieving the high-speed downloading that makes your Web site shine above the commonplace byte-guzzler.

In many of the procedures in this chapter, the object is to make graphics files smaller. You need a window open on your outgoing graphics folder to see whether you're succeeding. (*Outgoing graphics folder* is my name for the folder that you designate for graphics when you publish to HTML.) Double-click the My Computer icon in Windows 95, browse your way down to that folder, and then click View⇨Details in that window to see file sizes in the Total Size column.

The tools that you may need are Corel's Photo House (part of the WordPerfect 8 Suite) or one of the tools from this book's CD-ROM: Lview Pro or Paint Shop Pro. Instructions for starting Photo House are in Chapter 13. Instructions for installing and starting Lview Pro and Paint Shop Pro are in the appendix.

## Reuse and Rejoice!

If you're using a graphic repeatedly — as a bullet, for example, or a banner — why should you waste your Web-site visitor's time by transmitting the same graphic over and over again? Unless you are careful, that's exactly what WordPerfect does; the program creates a separate, identical file for each place in which you use the same graphic and then transmits all the files! The result can be very time-consuming. But to paraphrase an old environmentalist friend, "Rejoice! Graphics are reusable!" Figure 14-1 shows a simple example in which a graphic is repeated.

**Figure 14-1:** These bullets cost 2K each until they were reused.

☑ Make sure top is securely fastened.
☑ Include biohazard label.
☑ Do not sniff contents.
☑ Avoid cheese sandwiches.

The solution has three parts:

1. Use a GIF or JPG file for the graphic.
2. Put the graphic in the outgoing graphics folder.
3. Insert the graphic from that folder into your document.

### Getting a GIF or JPG graphic

You may already be using a downloaded GIF or JPG file from the Web for your graphic. If you were clever, you downloaded the file directly to your outgoing graphics folder. If you didn't do that, copy the file from wherever you stored it by choosing Edit⇨Copy and Edit⇨Paste in the My Computer window.

If you're not currently using a GIF or JPG file for your graphic, you can create a GIF or JPG file from just about any other type of graphic file by using either Corel Photo House (refer to Chapter 13) or one of the tools on this book's CD-ROM. See "Convert File Types by Using Graphics Tools," later in this chapter for the basics.

## Inserting the GIF or JPG graphic

Insert the graphic into your document from the outgoing graphics folder by choosing Insert➪Graphics➪From File. After inserting the graphic, copy it by pressing Ctrl+C; click the document where you want the graphic to appear; and paste it by pressing Ctrl+V. Paste as many copies as you like! Now the graphic will be downloaded to the Web site visitor only once, saving lots of time, and any changes that you make in the graphic automatically show up everywhere!

*TIP*

If you copy and paste that graphic to other documents on your site, it still is downloaded only once! (This statement assumes that you are following this book's publish to HTML and Web-site folder recommendations or that you know your way around graphics links and URLs.)

## Using ClipArt bullets

If you want to use WordPerfect ClipArt as a bullet, you first must convert it to a GIF or JPG file. You can do the conversion manually, importing the graphic into Photo House or Paint Shop Pro and saving it as GIF or JPG, or you can perform the following trick:

1. **Insert the ClipArt into your document only once — the first time you use it.**

2. **Publish to HTML.**

    When you publish, WordPerfect spits a GIF file into your graphics folder.

3. **Choose Insert➪Graphics➪From File.**

    The Insert Image dialog box appears.

4. **Turn on the Preview feature (click the button to the left of the yellow file folder that has the red check).**

5. **Find the GIF file that looks like your original graphic (it has a name like** `wpdoc0{image0}.gif`**) and double-click it to insert it.**

    If you have several of these files, find the most recent one.

6. **Copy and paste the file as many times as you like!**

# Publish to JPG or GIF

When you use WordPerfect for Web publishing, it normally creates GIF files to go on the Web. WordPerfect can, however, produce JPG files instead, if you say so. GIF and JPG are very different kinds of files, offering different

## Give me GIF

GIF files were the original graphics files of the Web. Pretty much every graphic was GIF, which remains the most commonly used graphics-file format on the Web today. Here are the advantages of GIF over JPEG:

- Smaller files (if the image is not a color photograph or realistically shaded color artwork)
- Clearer display of text
- No loss of detail or distortion of color
- Capability to provide images that fade in slowly
- Capability to provide images that have transparent backgrounds or other regions

## Make mine JPG

JPG (or JPEG) files, pronounced *jay-peg*, are relative newcomers to the Web world. These files are, however, the files of choice sometimes because they are smaller than GIF files if the image is a color photograph or realistically shaded artwork. The advantage can be as much as 20 to 1 over GIF files, but more typically is between 4 and 10 to 1.

The disadvantage of JPEG files is that they tend to lose small details. The files also get blurry around sharp edges, as in text. (You can trade off compression quality for smaller file size in some graphics tools, such as Photo House or Lview Pro, but not in WordPerfect, which uses a fixed, fairly high compression quality.) Figure 14-2 shows a comparison of GIF and JPG, using very-low-compression quality JPG to illustrate the differences.

**Figure 14-2:** A 19K GIF file on the left and a 5K JPG file on the right.

## Choosing JPG

The normal choice for WordPerfect, GIF, may be the best choice, especially if the graphic has broad areas of uniform color or is black-and-white or gray. If the graphic is in color and has realistic shading or a photographlike appearance, a nice JPG file may just make things go faster. Here's how to choose JPG:

1. **Right-click the image and then choose HTML Properties from the QuickMenu that appears.**

   The HTML Properties dialog box appears.

2. **Click the Publish tab.**
3. **Click JPEG in the Output format section.**
4. **Click OK.**
5. **Check appearances by clicking the View in Web Browser button (the document-behind-a-web icon).**

Viewing in the Web browser on your PC doesn't reveal the speed difference, however. To see whether a significant advantage exists, you must either try the document on the Web or compare file sizes. (The smaller file is the faster one.)

*Note:* Even if you perform the preceding steps, WordPerfect does not publish a JPG file if you created the graphic in the document by inserting a GIF file. Neither does WordPerfect do the opposite: create a GIF from a JPG. At least, those statements are true of early releases of WordPerfect 8. To create a GIF from a JPG or vice versa, use Corel Photo House or one of the graphics tools on this book's CD-ROM.

## Convert File Types by Using Graphics Tools

Sometimes, the best way to create faster, smaller graphics files is to insert a different type of file — and use a special graphics tool to create it. If you are currently inserting a GIF file in your document, for instance, converting it to a JPG file and inserting that file instead allows you to achieve smaller file size by trading off (reducing) compression quality. Several graphics tools allow you to choose the right trade-off for you. Likewise, if you are currently inserting a BMP file or WordPerfect ClipArt image, converting them to GIF and inserting the GIF file instead may allow you to create a smaller file by trading off (reducing) the color depth or image size (resolution).

WordPerfect itself allows you to choose between publishing GIF and JPG files, but that's all that it does for file conversion. It cannot perform the trade-offs described in the previous paragraph. Corel Photo House and the graphics tools on this book's CD-ROM can all convert files from one type to another and also allow you to make trade-offs. These tools have various advantages and disadvantages:

- All of these tools can read and write bitmap formats: GIF, JPG, BMP, and others.
- Photo House and Paint Shop Pro can read WordPerfect graphics (WPG and other non-bitmap graphics) and convert them to bitmap form.
- Lview Pro and Paint Shop Pro give you a great deal of control over the conversion process and the quality of the resulting file.

When you convert an image to a different file type, you have a choice of creating a new incoming file or an outgoing file. An *incoming file* is a file that you insert into the document; it can reside in any folder on your PC or company network. An *outgoing file* is the one that WordPerfect publishes in the folder that you choose for graphics when you publish to HTML. In general, you are better off creating a new incoming file, which you insert in place of the original one.

In all these graphics tools, the basic procedure for conversion is the same: Open the file by choosing File⇨Open, choose File⇨Save As, and save it in whichever format you like in the Save As dialog box. Some tools display another dialog box during the process of saving, allowing you to make various adjustments. In other tools, adjustments require a separate step before saving. See the following sections for specific instructions on adjusting image size and quality.

## Reduce Image Size or Resolution

A simple way to make graphics download faster is to make them smaller. A graphic reduced 25 percent in width and height cuts the file size nearly in half. You can resize any image that you inserted into a document by clicking it and dragging the corner handles that appear or by choosing Graphics⇨Size. Refer to Chapter 11 for the details.

GIF and JPG graphics are special. Resizing the image in WordPerfect does not reduce the file size if you inserted GIF or JPG graphics; all that resizing does is squeeze the same file into a smaller box! You need to create a smaller image in terms of length and width, measured in pixels (dots on-screen).

Because image size and file size are independent of each other with GIF and JPG, if you do create a smaller GIF or JPG image in terms of pixels, you can still use the same size box in WordPerfect! The pixels expand to fill the box; the image just looks grainier (lower-resolution). If your image can tolerate that sort of treatment, this method is one way to accelerate downloading without reducing apparent size.

Here are the ways to reduce the pixel dimensions (and, therefore, the file size) of GIF and JPG graphics:

- To create a smaller graphic in Corel Photo House, see Chapter 13.

- To create a smaller graphic in Lview Pro, open the file by choosing File⇔Open; choose Edit⇔Resize (or press Ctrl+R) to display the Resize Image dialog box; drag either the Cols or Rows slider to the left; click OK; and then choose File⇔Save.

- To create a smaller graphic in Paint Shop Pro, open the file by choosing File⇔Open; choose Image⇔Resize to display the Resize dialog box; click Custom Size and, below that label, enter either a new width (the number on the left) or height (the number on the right). Then click OK. Save the file by choosing File⇔Save.

After you create a smaller graphic, delete the old graphic from your document and insert the new one so that you can see the result. You can expand the new box to the original size, if you like, although the resulting image is grainier (lower in resolution).

As you do with all GIF and JPG graphics that you insert into a document, you also need to copy the new file to the outgoing graphics folder. See Chapter 11 for details.

If the idea doesn't boggle your mind too much, you can downsize the GIF or JPG files that you copied to your outgoing folder without changing the images that you inserted into your document. The result is lower-resolution graphics on the Web without the trouble of reinserting and sizing the images in your document.

# Reduce Color Depth

If you're not after realism, or if the image doesn't appear to use many colors, try reducing the so-called *color depth* (palette size) to get a smaller file. Use Photo House or other graphics tools to create color-reduced GIF files. You can use existing GIF or BMP files, or WordPerfect ClipArt, to create the files. When you are done, delete the original BMP, GIF, or ClipArt graphic from your document; then insert the new GIF file in its place.

**Part III: Getting Graphical**

Figure 14-3 shows the effect of reducing color depth from 256 to 16 to 2 (black and white). In each image, the graphics software used a process called *dithering,* in which a color is achieved by using dots of various other colors (sort of like an Impressionist painting).

Here's how to reduce color depth by using the graphics tools that you have lying around:

- In Corel Photo House, open the file by choosing File⇨Open; then choose Image⇨Image Properties to display the Image Properties dialog box. (Refer to Chapter 13 for information on importing WordPerfect graphics.) Choose 16 Color or Grayscale in the Color mode box. Click OK. Then, if you like the result, save the file by choosing File⇨Save.

- In Lview Pro, open the file by choosing File⇨Open; then choose Retouch⇨Color Depth to display the Color Depth dialog box. Click Palette image; then click either Windows Palette (16 colors) or Custom Number of Colors and try a number between 16 and 256. If you don't like speckles in your image, click to clear the Enable Floyd-Steinberg Dithering check box. Then click OK. If you like the result, save the file by choosing File⇨Save; otherwise, choose Edit⇨Undo and try again.

- In Paint Shop Pro, choose Colors⇨Decrease Color Depth and choose one of the options presented to you. Click OK in the Decrease Color Depth dialog box that appears. If you like the result, save the file by choosing File⇨Save; otherwise, choose Edit⇨Undo and try again.

As you do with all GIF and JPG graphics that you insert into a document, you also need to copy the new file to the outgoing graphics folder. Refer to Chapter 11 for details.

**Figure 14-3:**
From left to right, file size drops from 100 percent to 80 percent to 20 percent.

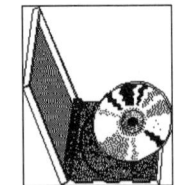

## Adjust JPG Compression Quality

You can create JPG images in different levels of something called *compression quality:* a number that measures the quality of the image. The lower the compression quality is, the smaller the file size and the lower the visual quality. Lview Pro and Paint Shop Pro can help you choose the compression-quality level that's right for you. Here's how to adjust compression quality:

- In Corel Photo House: Please see Chapter 13.
- In Lview Pro: With the JPG file open, choose File⇨Properties; then click the JPEG tab in the Properties dialog box. Whoa — all kinds of stuff here! Ignore everything but Compression Quality, and drag the slider left for reduced quality/file size or right for the opposite effect.
- In Paint Shop Pro: Choose Preferences⇨File Format Preferences to open the File Preferences dialog box. Click the JIF/JPG Preferences tab, and adjust the Compression Level spin control to a higher number to get a smaller, lower-quality file.

## Use a Stupid Browser Trick

WordPerfect supports a trick that — like all this book's stupid browser tricks — is not particularly stupid but has limited value because it works in only one vendor's browser: Netscape Navigator, in this case. The idea is to transmit a low-quality image as a temporary placeholder for a high-quality image that, given the speed of the Web, may be a while in coming.

You can create a poor-color (low-color-depth) or grainy (low-resolution) version of your high-quality picture of Mount Rushmore, for example, and connect both images to your document by using the browser trick described in this section. Visitors to your site get the general idea of faces carved in rock when the first image downloads, but they may not be able to tell whether they're seeing Teddy Roosevelt or Bullwinkle the Moose until they see the second image.

To make a low-quality but fast-downloading copy of an image, you can use the methods described in this chapter to do any of the following things:

- Make a small GIF file (reduced width and height in pixels)
- Make a file in JPG format
- Make a GIF file with reduced color depth

Using Photo House or one of the graphics tools from this book's CD-ROM, open the file, make whatever adjustments to quality you choose, then choose File⇨Save As instead of File⇨Save to create a second, lower-quality file with a different name (preferably, using all lowercase letters). Save the low-quality photo to the outgoing graphics folder that you use for publishing to HTML.

After you have created a low-quality image, the following steps then link the low-quality image to the high-quality image already in your Web document:

1. **Right-click the high-quality image in your document and then choose HTML Properties from the QuickMenu that appears.**

   The HTML Properties dialog box appears.

2. **In the Low resolution graphic box of the Image tab, enter a relative URL for the lower-quality image.**

   In other words, enter a line that looks like this:

   ```
   ./folder/filename.ext
   ```

   Replace `folder` with the name of your outgoing graphics folder (such as `index`) and `filename.ext` with the full name (including extension) of your new, low-quality image file. Make sure that you match the case (lowercase or uppercase) of letters in your new file.

   Do not use browse (that is, do not use the tiny file-folder icon) to enter the line in Step 2. In early releases of WordPerfect 8, at least, this feature has many bugs.

3. **Click OK.**

4. **Publish to HTML.**

Load your HTML file into your browser to test the result. Don't click the View in Web Browser button to test the result.

On your PC, images load so much faster than on the Web that you may not be able to tell whether the feature is working. Click the Reload or Refresh button in your browser repeatedly and watch closely, or try putting your document on the Web. If the feature doesn't seem to work on the Web, check your browser's options or preferences to make sure that it is displaying images during loading, not after loading.

# Part IV
# Wayout Layouts and Dazzling Designs

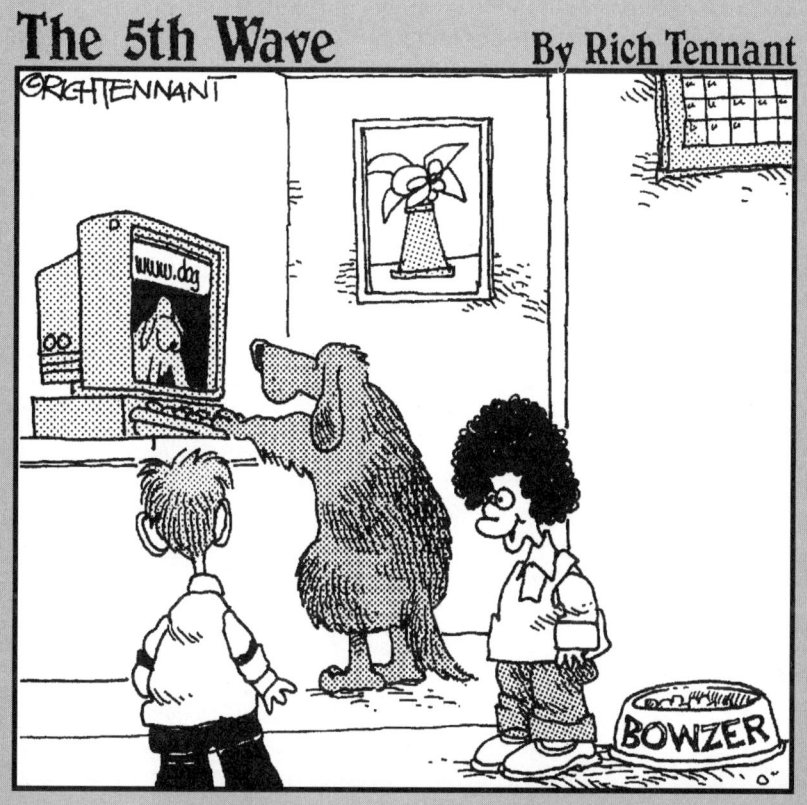

## The 5th Wave                By Rich Tennant

"He's our new Web Bowzer."

## In this part . . .

Okay, you put words and pictures on paper, but somehow it just doesn't look as cool as the Web sites from the big boys. Well, of course it doesn't! You don't have a million-dollar budget and a staff of designers, programmers, and other techno-*artistes*!

But despair not. If you have the time to sketch and fiddle around with your ideas, WordPerfect can help you create a fine-looking site that nearly any Web-weaver would be proud of. Here are some of the secrets of arranging text and graphics on the page, fine-tuning their appearance and position, and even surpassing the limitations of WordPerfect by using frames. And, if all that fails, Part IV ends with a chapter on "Lazy Layouts and Indolent Authoring" using the Perfect Expert and files from the CD.

# Chapter 15
# Quick Tricks for Layout and White Space

### In This Chapter
▶ Positioning graphics
▶ Using WordPerfect text boxes
▶ Breaking text to resume after a graphic
▶ Using text tricks for white space
▶ Using browser tricks for white space

The big new feature of the Web that makes layout possible is tables. (*Layout,* by the way, simply means controlling the position and alignment of text and graphics). Chapter 17 goes into detail on using tables for layout.

For people who don't want to deal with tables, however, tricks with alignment and white space do the job without much hassle. Such basic tricks are what this chapter is all about.

## Positioning Graphics: An Overview

For the full scoop on positioning graphics on the page, see Chapter 11. Right now, I just want to give you an overview of the ways that graphics can be positioned.

Horizontal positioning of graphics is limited to aligning them left, right, or center on the page. You must attach graphics to a paragraph to position them horizontally.

If graphics are aligned left or right, text flows around them. If graphics are center-aligned, text doesn't flow on either side but breaks instead and resumes after the graphic.

Graphics can also be attached to a character, which basically means that they move around with the text — like leaves in an autumn stream, if you're in that kind of mood. Because these particular leaves usually are taller than the type, you get to decide how high they float with respect to the text baseline (the imaginary line on which text sits). Graphics can float in the following ways:

- Sticking up above the surface of the text, called *bottom alignment* because the bottom of the graphic is aligned with the text baseline
- Halfway sunk into the text, called *center alignment* because the center of the graphic is aligned on the text baseline
- Totally submerged, called *top alignment* because the top of the graphic is aligned on the text baseline

## *Using Text Boxes: An Overview*

WordPerfect's Text boxes are one way to achieve sidebars or to force the layout to be exactly what you want. For full details, refer to Chapter 11, but the basic idea is that WordPerfect turns its text boxes into graphics, complete with any border or fill that you want. Just about anything can be put into a text box that can be put into a document: tables, graphics, or clip art. In theory, you could create an entire page as a text box. You also can use text boxes for any other chunk of text, such as sidebars, headings, and titles. You align text boxes just as you do any other graphic.

You can even turn text boxes sideways! Right-click the text box, choose Content from the Quick Menu, and then choose 90 degrees, 180 degrees, or 270 degrees in the dialog box that appears.

The trade-off of using text boxes is that graphics take a great deal of file space, so documents that use text boxes are slow to download. In addition, anyone who does not have browser graphics turned on won't see the boxes. (You can minimize the latter problem by using "alternate" text; refer to Chapter 11.)

## *Breaking Text to Resume After a Graphic*

One layout trick on the Web allows you to insert a line break that causes text to resume after a left- or right-aligned graphic, instead of flowing around the graphic. Figure 15-1 shows the way that text normally flows around a graphic. Figure 15-2 shows the effect that you may want to achieve instead.

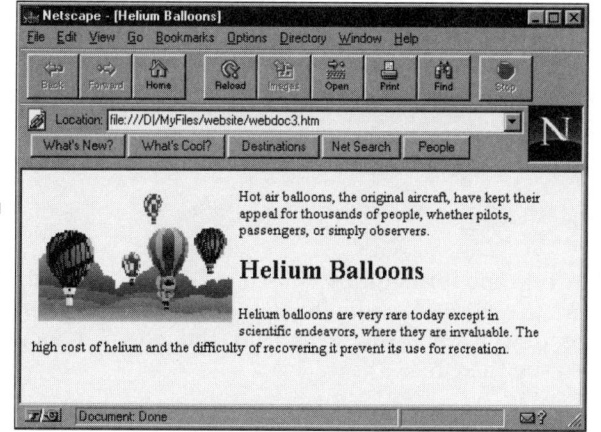

**Chapter 15: Quick Tricks for Layout and White Space** *219*

**Figure 15-1:** Text flows around a left-aligned graphic in Navigator.

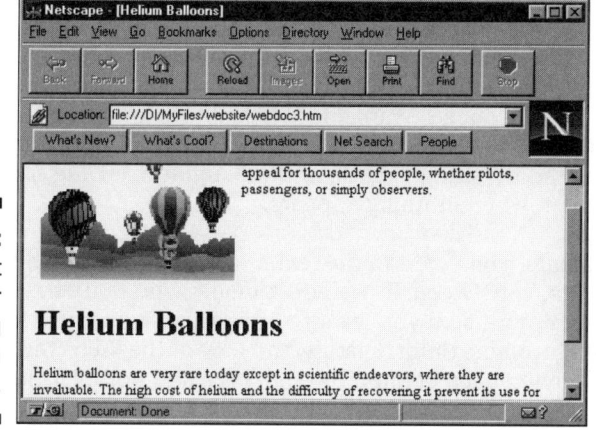

**Figure 15-2:** The result in Navigator of resuming text after a graphic.

Figure 15-3 shows how to achieve the effect: by adding HTML code to your document. Add the code just before the text that should follow the graphic.

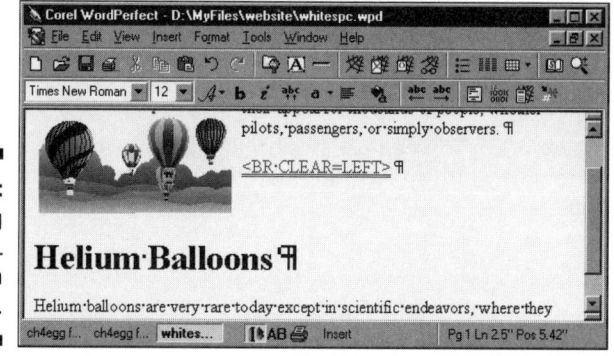

**Figure 15-3:** Adding HTML code in WordPerfect.

In WordPerfect, type the following magic text (HTML code) for a left-aligned illustration:

```
<BR CLEAR=LEFT>
```

For a right-aligned illustration, type this text:

```
<BR CLEAR=RIGHT>
```

Then select the code and format it by choosing Format➪Custom HTML. Figure 15-3 shows the result. You don't see the result in WordPerfect; you have to click the View in Web Browser button (the icon of a document behind a web) to see the effect.

# Using Text Tricks for White Space

"Don't look at the doughnut; look at the hole" is a wise old saying that has never made any sense to me whatever, with one exception: when I'm drawing a picture or laying out a document. Artists and graphic designers may refer to the hole in a doughnut as white space. (At least, they may if you bribe them to do so by, say, giving them the doughnut.) *White space* is the part of a document where nothing appears.

In paper documents, you position the text and graphics, and white space is just what happens in between. In Web documents, you don't have many ways to position things, so if you want to adjust the layout, you may need to actively add white space. Unfortunately, the Law of the Web (the HTML specification), having been created by engineers and not by artists, largely frowns upon adding white space, so Web weavers must use a few tricks.

## Text tricks for horizontal spacing

The classic old white-space trick that everyone uses in paper documents (even though they really shouldn't) is adding spaces. For years, conventional wisdom has said, "This trick just plain doesn't work on the Web. Neither does adding tabs. Web browsers have firm instructions to ignore multiple spaces and tabs, so forget it."

Well, it ain't so anymore. You can use nonbreaking spaces (press Ctrl+spacebar) to add white space. (Repeated regular spaces and tabs are, however, still ignored.)

## Chapter 15: Quick Tricks for Layout and White Space 221

Another, older trick is using the Preformatted Text style of paragraph (click the big script *A* button and then choose the style from the drop-down list that appears). In this style, you can use all the spaces and tabs you want, and the browser cannot ignore them. Unfortunately, with Preformatted Text, you're using the ugly, nonproportionally spaced Courier typeface for all the rest of the text in your paragraph. You can apply a different typeface (font) to text in Preformatted style, but because typefaces are a Netscape extension to HTML, non-Netscape users may still end up seeing Courier.

Figure 15-4 shows both of these tricks for creating white space. The figure shows an image being positioned that is attached to a character, in WordPerfectspeak. (Right-click the image and then choose Position from the Quick Menu to check the attachment method.)

**Figure 15-4:**
Two ways to nudge things horizontally.

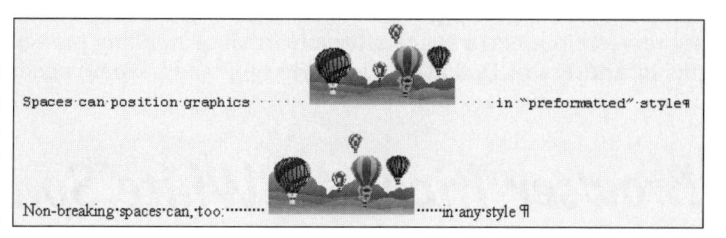

Choose View⇨Show ¶ to view the space characters, as I did in Figure 15-4, which makes positioning easier. Don't try to be too precise, however; something unexpected always changes positioning slightly in people's browsers.

Here are a few points to keep in mind when you are adding white space to a document:

- Different fonts (and, therefore, different Web styles, font selections, or font sizes) cause different spacing.

- Nonbreaking (hard) spaces often prevent wrapping to the next line. (The browser won't break the line at a hard space.) Don't add so many spaces that your visitor is forced to scroll horizontally to see whatever it is that you're positioning.

- Regular spaces in Preformatted Text style will wrap if your visitor's browser uses a small window, thereby ruining all your careful positioning.

### Text tricks for vertical spacing

The old trick of adding blank lines (blank paragraphs) or line breaks to adjust vertical spacing works nearly as well on the Web as on paper. Simply click the end of a paragraph (or just after a graphic), press Enter once to get a blank paragraph, and press Enter again to begin typing the next paragraph. Alternatively, choose Insert⇨Line Break instead of pressing Enter to add a blank line.

Blank lines and paragraphs don't give you perfect control, however, because technically, line spacing still is up to the Web browser. The best way to control how much space a line takes is to choose a Web style (click the big script *A* button) or a font size. The bigger the font that you use for a style, the greater the vertical spacing.

Most browsers put extra space after a Normal or heading paragraph. Paragraphs in Address or Definition List style typically have no space afterward.

## Stupid Browser Tricks for White Space

Besides the standard tricks for layout that this chapter has presented so far, Netscape and Microsoft provide a few tricks of their own. Remember that browser tricks work only in these specific browsers named, so if you use them, some people miss the tricks.

### Netscape spacers

Netscape Navigator has a special feature for space cadets: the spacer. Spacers come in three flavors: horizontal, vertical, and block (which provides a rectangle of space). WordPerfect doesn't provide a command to insert a spacer, so you have to enter the HTML code yourself. You won't see the result in WordPerfect; you have to click the View in Web Browser button (the icon of a document behind a web) to see the effect.

#### Horizontal space

To add space before or after text or a graphic, type the following code in your document where you want the space to appear:

```
<SPACER SIZE=pixels TYPE=HORIZONTAL>
```

In place of `pixels`, enter a number; this number is the width of the space, measured in dots on-screen. (Most PC screens are about 800 dots wide.) Select the text and then choose Format⇨Custom HTML.

### Vertical space

The code for vertical space is practically identical to the code for horizontal space. To add space above or below text or a graphic, type the following code in your document where you want the space to appear:

```
<SPACER SIZE=pixels TYPE=VERTICAL>
```

In place of `pixels`, enter a number; this number is the width of the space, measured in dots on-screen. (Most PC screens are about 600 dots high.) Select the text and then choose Format⇨Custom HTML.

### Horizontal and vertical space

To create a rectangle of white space, around which text wraps as though the space were a left- or right-aligned graphic, type the following code in your document where you want the space to appear:

```
<SPACER TYPE=BLOCK HEIGHT=pixels WIDTH= pixels ALIGN=LEFT
       (or RIGHT)>
```

Substitute numbers for `pixels` as you do for horizontal and vertical space, as described in the preceding two sections. After `ALIGN=`, use either `LEFT` or `RIGHT`. Select the text and then choose Format⇨Custom HTML.

## Microsoft margins

Microsoft Internet Explorer allows you to add margin space above or to the left of your document. This idea is a good one, because extra margin space often makes your page more readable.

WordPerfect doesn't give you a command to control this feature, but you can enter the HTML code that does the job. Enter the following text at the top of your document:

```
<BODY LEFTMARGIN=pixels TOPMARGIN=pixels>
```

In place of `pixels`, enter a number; this number is the width of the margin, measured in dots on the screen. (Most PC screens are 800 pixels wide by 600 high.) Feel free to set pixels to zero if you want to jam something flush against the left side or top.

Select the text and then choose Format⇨Custom HTML. You won't see the result in WordPerfect, but click the View in Web Browser button (the icon of a document behind a web) to see the effect.

# Chapter 16
# Initial Layout and Design

*In This Chapter*
- ▶ Thinking about your design
- ▶ Sketching a layout
- ▶ Analyzing your sketch
- ▶ Creating some simple layouts

Many Web pages are created by just knocking around. That approach works fine for personal or other informal pages, but for an organization's Web site, it leaves things looking pretty ragged. A little forethought goes a long way toward a more professional appearance.

Don't try to fine-tune your layout and design before you actually try your ideas, however. The Web has a way of introducing surprising problems that may prevent you from getting exactly what you had in mind.

## Thinking about Design

I like to think about stuff on a Web page as falling into three categories (or, as Julius Caesar probably would have observed, "*Omnes Webpagines in partes tres divisae,*" which would have sounded much more impressive). Those three categories are content, identity, and controls.

### Contemplating your content

*Content* is the stuff that your visitor is actually looking for — the unique information that a page carries. You should first think about content of your entire Web site. If you haven't already considered what content your Web site will have and how it will be organized in pages, check out Chapter 1 for some suggestions.

**Part IV: Wayout Layouts and Dazzling Designs**

Once you have figured out what the content of your Web site will be, begin thinking about the individual pages. Every Web page contains a bunch of stuff that you can consider to be the *components* of the page. The usual components are (from top to bottom):

- A banner, which is made up of a logo and other graphics
- A top heading, which often is part of the banner
- A set of controls across the top, down the side, or across the bottom and sometimes part of the banner
- The body text and graphics
- Occasionally, a background graphic
- Custom bullets, separator bars, and other graphical building blocks
- A signature line with the date, your name, and your e-mail address

## *Deliberating about identity*

*Identity* is marketing jabber for your logo, banner, and other personal or corporate text or images, plus fonts, color, and the overall look and feel, which together make your page say, "I am Joe Blotz's Web page" (which, if you're Joe Blotz, is a good thing). The idea of having identity ingredients throughout your site is to make sure that your Web-site visitor recognizes each page as being one of yours, and also — mysterious but true — to make your site more professional-looking and memorable.

The most obvious identity elements of your Web site are the various parts of your document banner — both graphics and text. Figure 16-1 shows a simple Web-site banner. Document banners (or parts of them) should be repeated on the other pages of your document.

**Figure 16-1:**
A banner contains the most obvious components of identity.

## Considering your controls

*Controls* are the links that your visitor clicks to get to the various pages (or bookmarked sections) of your Web site. To work well, controls need to be clear, consistent, and easily accessible.

### Text or graphical controls?

Some fancy sites go to great lengths to make stunning graphical controls (*mapped images*) — an act which, frankly, rarely helps anyone except the artist who was hired to do the job. These controls are single images in which clicking different parts takes the visitor to different documents. Simple text hyperlinks usually are just as effective, are easier to create, don't consume as much downloading time, and don't disappear when graphics are turned off on the visitor's browser.

Mapped images make the most sense when you're presenting information about something physical. You may want your visitor to click locations on a globe to find your sales offices, parts of the body to see medical information, or screen features to see pictures of the software that you're selling.

Graphical controls in the form of icons make sense when you're trying to reach an international audience. Graphical controls are also sensible choices if you want to emulate some other control system that your visitor is familiar with, such as a TV remote control, a light switch, or a telephone.

A compromise between using mapped images and using text is to use a separate image for each control button and then use "alternate" text for each image. That way, if the visitor has turned graphics off, he or she can still use the controls. This approach also prevents you from having to create image maps, which can be a tedious process.

### Okay — who stole the remote?

If you think that trying to keep your TV remote control from sneaking between the sofa cushions is a tough job, try finding a way to keep Web-page controls handy for your visitor. On a well-designed (translation: short) home page, this accomplishment should not be a challenge; there should be little room for a control to hide. On longer pages, putting the controls at the top and bottom is a reasonable solution. (The visitor can always press Home or End on the keyboard in order to get to the controls.)

To offer your visitor maximum convenience, you can resort to using frames, which allow your visitor to scroll the document while keeping the control section in sight. Frames are neither standard under the Law of the Web (the HTML specification) nor particularly convenient for the Web weaver. Frames do work, however, in both Netscape Navigator and Microsoft Internet Explorer. For information on using frames, see Chapter 18.

## Pondering readability

Two somewhat conflicting design concerns are impact (grabbing the reader's attention) and readability. For readability's sake, observe my Six Suggestions (like the Ten Commandments, only easier to obey):

- Don't use too many different typefaces (fonts) or Web styles; two or three ought to do the job.
- Use only a few colors, unless you're looking for a very playful style.
- Use a color scheme, not just colors. Consider matching the color of your text to colors that predominate in your graphics. If you're showing a Caribbean beach scene, for example, you may try to match your text color with one of the colors of the water.
- Don't cram too much onto a page by using tiny type. The page will end up looking like a bottle of Dr. Bonner's Castile Soap or a computer-supplies catalog.
- Use "alternate" text for graphics, in case the visitor has graphics turned off.
- Don't put all your text in bold (or in one of the Heading styles).

## Developing a consistent style

Foolish consistency may be the hobgoblin of little minds (which is why I keep harping on it), but a modicum of consistency is a good way to make your site more attractive and readable. (If you don't have a modicum, a *soupçon*, dash, or thimbleful will do.) Following are a few design attributes where consistency counts:

- Position or alignment of text and graphics
- Typeface (font) and size
- Color
- Document organization
- Banner and controls

One secret to a professional-looking Web site is working out a style for every type of information that appears repeatedly on your pages. You should have no *mavericks* — text or graphics for which you decided the paragraph style, font, alignment, size, or position on the spur of the moment.

## Sketching a Layout

Layout designers who work with paper documents create grids to help them keep a consistent layout. A grid identifies the common elements of each page and says exactly where each element should appear. The designers who do this are trained, highly paid professionals (well, they're trained professionals, anyway), so the rest of us ought not to try this grid stuff at home.

Oh, what the heck — try designing on a grid anyway, but don't take it too seriously, because you simply don't have as much control on the Web as you do on paper. Sketch your page layout, figuring out what should line up with what, where things should be centered or aligned right, where you want extra space, and what heading level or text size you want. Figure 16-2 shows a simple sketch.

The sketch gives you an idea of where you need to invest in special layout tricks (such as tables) or white-space tricks (such as nonbreaking spaces) to deal with browser wrap. (Browser wrap is not to be confused with Bowser Wrap, which is used for doggie bags.)

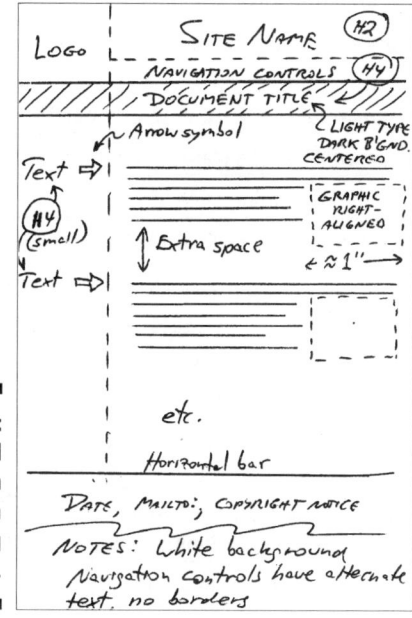

**Figure 16-2:** A general page sketch provides a starting point.

## Analyzing Your Sketch

If you are laying out a print document with a page-layout program, moving from a sketch to software is simple. Because the Web doesn't allow precise positioning, the process of going from plan to practice is not so simple. Using your Web-page sketch and Table 16-1, decide how you're going to achieve the layout that you want.

**Table 16-1          How to Achieve Various Layout Effects**

| Effect | What to Use |
|---|---|
| Headings | Any of the Heading styles |
| Bullets | Bullet List style (or insert your own bullet graphic) |
| Numbered list | Numbered List style |
| Alignment left/right/center | Paragraph alignment (Format⇨Justification) |
| Left indentation | Definition List, Numbered List, or Bullet List style |
|  | Nonbreaking spaces (Ctrl+spacebar) |
|  | Preformatted style, with spaces |
|  | Table with text in column 2 and white space in column 1 |
|  | Insert white space (refer to Chapter 15) |
| Right indentation | Insert white space (refer to Chapter 15) |
| Left and right indentation | Indented Quotation style |
| Graphics left/right with text wrap | Attach to paragraph by using left or right alignment |
| Columns | Table |
|  | Multicolumn layout (Netscape only) |
| Alignment left/right/center in table | Choose Table⇨Format, choose the Cell or Column page; then choose a Horizontal alignment |
| Sidebar | Text box |
|  | Single-cell table, formatted less than 100 percent wide, with Table position on page set to Right |
| White space | Various tricks (refer to Chapter 15) |
| Buttons | Choose Make text appear as button in the Hyperlink Properties dialog box |
| Controls that stay on-screen | Frames (see Chapter 18) |

## Identify browser wrap problems

Browsers wrap stuff as readily and comprehensively as fast-food joints wrap burgers. As is true of fast-food establishments, it's not always easy to keep browsers from wrapping your stuff. To have it your way on the Web, you need to keep an eye out for critical areas of your design, such as the following:

- Text that should not wrap can be spaced with nonbreaking (hard) spaces (press Ctrl+spacebar).
- A row of hyperlinks (as in your controls) will wrap in small browser windows, even if you use nonbreaking spaces between the hyperlinks. If hyperlinks must stay in a row, insert a wide blank graphic or line of nonbreaking spaces above or below the hyperlinks, in the same cell, or anywhere in that column.
- Anywhere that text must appear down the side of a document (or in other types of columns) is an area that requires either a table or one or more WordPerfect text boxes.

## Anticipate table troubles

Tables are the most useful layout tools to come down the road yet for Web weavers. Simply remove their borders, and tables form a nice, invisible layout grid.

Tables aren't, however, the ultimate answer to layout problems. Tables are kind of squishy on the Web, adjusting their column width and row height according to their contents. You can set the total width of a table in pixels, but column width is another story. Following are a few table tips to keep in mind:

- Not every browser displays tables! (Most of the biggies do, however.)
- Browsers distribute the available window width among the columns, according to what columns have the most stuff in them. You can't control column width easily.
- You can't easily mix skinny and fat rows in a single table. To get a skinny row or skinny horizontal line between rows, for example, you usually must split the table in two.
- Tables can be as simple as one or two cells, so if a one- or two-cell table will help you control your layout, go for it! A single-cell table can be right-aligned and serve as a sidebar, for example.

### Try your ideas

Don't get too analytical with all this pondering and sketching; try your idea out! Most of Web design is a process of trial and error.

When it comes to Web-page layout, and especially layout that uses tables, WordPerfect is not exactly WYSIWYG (What You See Is What You Get). Make a practice of clicking the View in Web Browser button regularly to check the results of your efforts in a real browser. (The View in Web Browser button is the document-behind-a-web icon.)

## Creating Some Simple Layouts

Keep things simple! A page layout that relies on multiple tables or tricks is going to drive you nuts. In fact, try to construct your page without using any tables or white-space tricks, if possible.

In a simple layout, most of the challenge is alignment, particularly aligning elements in the banner at the top of the page. The following sections provide some tips for creating simple left- or center-aligned pages, their banners, and their navigation controls.

### Pages that go with the flow

Some of the best pages on the Web don't fight the natural text-wrapping and space-compressing inclinations of Web browsers. These pages don't force stuff into tables, push it around with white-space tricks, or dictate the fonts; instead, they combine left, right, and center alignments, and they use the standard Web styles. The following sections describe a few such simple layouts, and how to . . . um, lay them out.

### Basic left- or center-aligned pages

Left- or center-aligned (or -justified) layouts are among the easiest and most effective designs on the Web. The left-aligned layout is what you get without even trying, so I won't belabor the obvious by explaining how to do it.

The center-aligned layout is great for home pages and other documents with a minimum of text. This type of layout gets annoying if you have a great deal of text, however, unless you're delivering poetry. A centered layout often looks something like Figure 16-3.

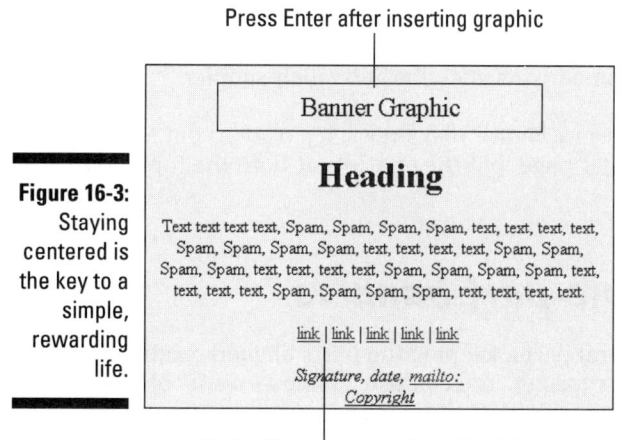

**Figure 16-3:** Staying centered is the key to a simple, rewarding life.

[Banner Graphic — Press Enter after inserting graphic]

**Heading**

Text text text text, Spam, Spam, Spam, Spam, text, text, text, text, Spam, Spam, Spam, Spam, Spam, text, text, text, Spam, Spam, Spam, Spam, text, text, text, text, Spam, Spam, Spam, Spam, text, text, text, text, Spam, Spam, Spam, Spam, text, text, text, text.

link | link | link | link | link

Signature, date, mailto: Copyright

Vertical bar character (usually Shift + \)

To center-align, simply select center alignment before you start typing. Choose Format⇨Justification⇨Center (or click the Justification button in the Property Bar and then choose Center from the drop-down list that appears). Alternatively, you can type everything, select it all, and then choose center alignment.

The only tips for basic left- or center-aligned pages are to put the banner graphic in a paragraph by itself (otherwise, it may end up in a line with the heading, if a visitor uses a wide window) and to use the vertical-bar character to separate your text hyperlinks. (Using the vertical bar as a separator has become kind of a convention in arrays of text links. A vertical appears as a solid bar on the Web, not as the divided bar that you often see on the PC screen.)

Common variations on the theme include centering the banner graphic and left-aligning the text. It doesn't matter whether you left-align the graphic by putting it in a left-aligned paragraph or by using left-aligned paragraph attachment.

## Simple, text-based navigation controls

To allow your visitor to browse your entire Web site, you want to provide *navigation controls* — links that take the visitor to your other pages. The easiest form of navigation controls is text hyperlinks. (Chapter 7 describes how to create the linking part.)

Increasingly, Web sites put the navigation controls in a frame down the left side of the page, where they stay conveniently on-screen while the user scrolls a page. A simpler alternative than using frames is creating a table

**Part IV: Wayout Layouts and Dazzling Designs**

with a long column on the left for controls and another column on the right for text. Yet for most sites, putting the controls across the top (and/or bottom) of every page is nearly as effective and much simpler.

For a short page, like the one Figure 16-3 shows, it's okay to put the controls at the bottom. For a longer page, put the controls at both the top and the bottom.

## Simple multiple-part banners

When a banner has several parts, keeping the parts aligned can be a bit like keeping worms in a berry basket. You can use a table as a sort of sloppy straitjacket (see Chapter 17). You don't need to resort to using a table, however, for banners that have only a few elements.

### Two-part banners

Figure 16-4 shows text next to a graphic in four possible positions — which depend, oddly, on how the graphic, not the text, is positioned. You can substitute character-attached graphics for the text in Figure 16-4 and Figure 16-5, which appears in the following section; the same techniques for positioning hold true.

To create a two-part banner as in Figure 16-4, insert your graphic at the beginning of your heading; don't put it in a separate paragraph. Then position the graphic using character attachment as described in the following steps:

1. **Right-click the graphic and then choose Position from the QuickMenu that appears.**

   The Box Position dialog box appears.

2. **Click the selection box marked Attach box to, and choose Character.**

   (Character may already be chosen.)

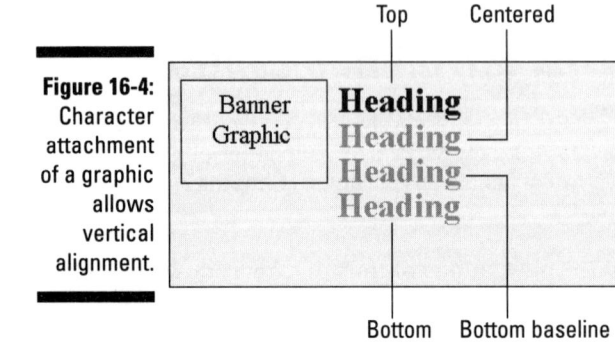

Figure 16-4: Character attachment of a graphic allows vertical alignment.

3. **Finally, choose Top, Centered, Bottom, or Content baseline for the different alignments that Figure 16-4 shows.**

    (Content baseline aligns the baseline of the text with the bottom of the graphic, ignoring any border that may be set in the graphic's HTML properties.)

4. **Click OK.**

### Three-part banners

To put more than one line of text next to the graphic, as shown in Figure 16-5 (or to add graphics where Figure 16-5 shows text), you must use paragraph attachment for the graphic(s). WordPerfect initially uses character attachment when you insert graphics. Here's how to switch from character attachment to paragraph attachment:

1. **Right-click the graphic and then choose Position from the QuickMenu that appears.**

    The Box Position dialog box appears.

2. **Click the selection box marked Attach box to, and choose Paragraph.**

3. **Choose Left Margin in the Horizontal selection box to achieve the left-aligned graphic that Figure 16-5 shows. (Right Margin also works nicely.)**

**Figure 16-5:**
Paragraph attachment permits additional elements alongside the graphic.

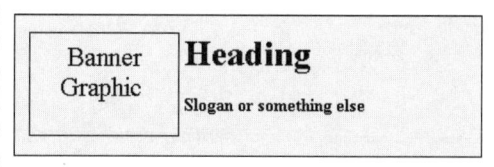

| Banner Graphic | **Heading** |
| | Slogan or something else |

With paragraph attachment, text that follows the graphic always begins at the top of the graphic. You have no choice of vertical alignment. If you want to move the text down, however, click before the text and then press Enter to add blank lines (which can be formatted in different Web styles to adjust their height), or choose Insert⇨Line Break.

# Chapter 17
# Doing Layouts by Using Tables

*In This Chapter*
- Creating a table for layout
- Removing table borders
- Setting table width
- Walking through an example

Ironically, for a truly way-out layout, you need order and control! You need to cause text and graphics to line up in some way. (And stay there! Good boy! Sit!) The human eye seems to crave organization, whether that organization is horizontal, vertical, or (in the case of, say, *Wired* magazine) in another orientation. On paper, documents with text pasted on like ransom notes are currently in vogue in some circles, but they don't cut the mustard for most readers.

The Web doesn't have any features for arranging things precisely on the page — say, two inches from the left and three inches from the top — but it does allow you to make tables. The rows and columns of Web tables provide a soft, squishy kind of alignment, but that alignment is enough for you to do things in an attractive way.

The use of tables for controlling the layout of a Web page opens up infinite possibilities, so this chapter can show you only some of the basic settings, tricks, and pitfalls. The chapter also takes you through an example of going from sketch to actual Web page.

If you need a refresher on creating and formatting tables, refer to Chapter 10 first.

Your carefully constructed layout may be wasted on some of your Web site visitors, or worse: the layout will be utterly garbled. Although most popular browsers can handle tables now, not all browsers can. Older browsers in particular ignore the table structure, displaying only the text and graphics. Be sure to check your layout in a browser that does not support tables to make sure your pages are understandable.

## Creating a Table for Layout

The basic idea of this chapter is to create a giant table to hold your Web-page stuff in a grid, but to make the borders of the table invisible, so that you don't appear to be using a table. (Sneaky, huh?)

You can create a table for layout either before you get started or after you've been playing around with your Web page in WordPerfect. You can always cut and paste the stuff that you've already created into the table. Go to the top of the document (press Ctrl+Home) to create your table.

*REMEMBER*

To create a table, choose Insert➪Table and use the HTML Table Format dialog box that appears. Alternatively, click and hold the Table button in the Toolbar (its icon looks like a tiny white grid), and in the tiny drop-down box that appears, drag to highlight the number of rows and columns that you need. The details for creating tables are in Chapter 10.

Personally, I don't have the patience to sit down and figure out exactly how many rows and columns I need to lay out a document using a table. Most tables that are used for layout are not simple "Y rows by X columns" tables, anyway, but use split and joined cells. I simply eyeball my layout sketch and create a table that seems to roughly fit the bill. Adding or deleting rows or columns, or splitting or joining cells, is easy enough after you create the table. Creating a single table for the entire page generally is the best way to start.

If that approach is too vague for you, your first job is to figure out how many columns you need. Start with a rough sketch of your layout on paper, as shown in Figure 17-1.

Then draw vertical lines to define your columns, using the following suggestions:

- ✔ Find the more-or-less obvious columns. If text or graphics seem to line up in columns, draw vertical lines between the columns.
- ✔ Find any ordinary, left-aligned (justified) text that's indented from the left edge of the page. Draw a vertical line along the left edge of the paragraph.
- ✔ Likewise, find any right-aligned text that is indented from the right edge of the page, and draw a vertical line along the right edge of the paragraph.
- ✔ Find any center-aligned text that's not centered on the page, and draw vertical lines along the left and right side of the text.
- ✔ If parallel lines are close, replace them with a single line.

To figure out how many rows you need, draw horizontal lines wherever paragraphs in one column align side by side with paragraphs in another column.

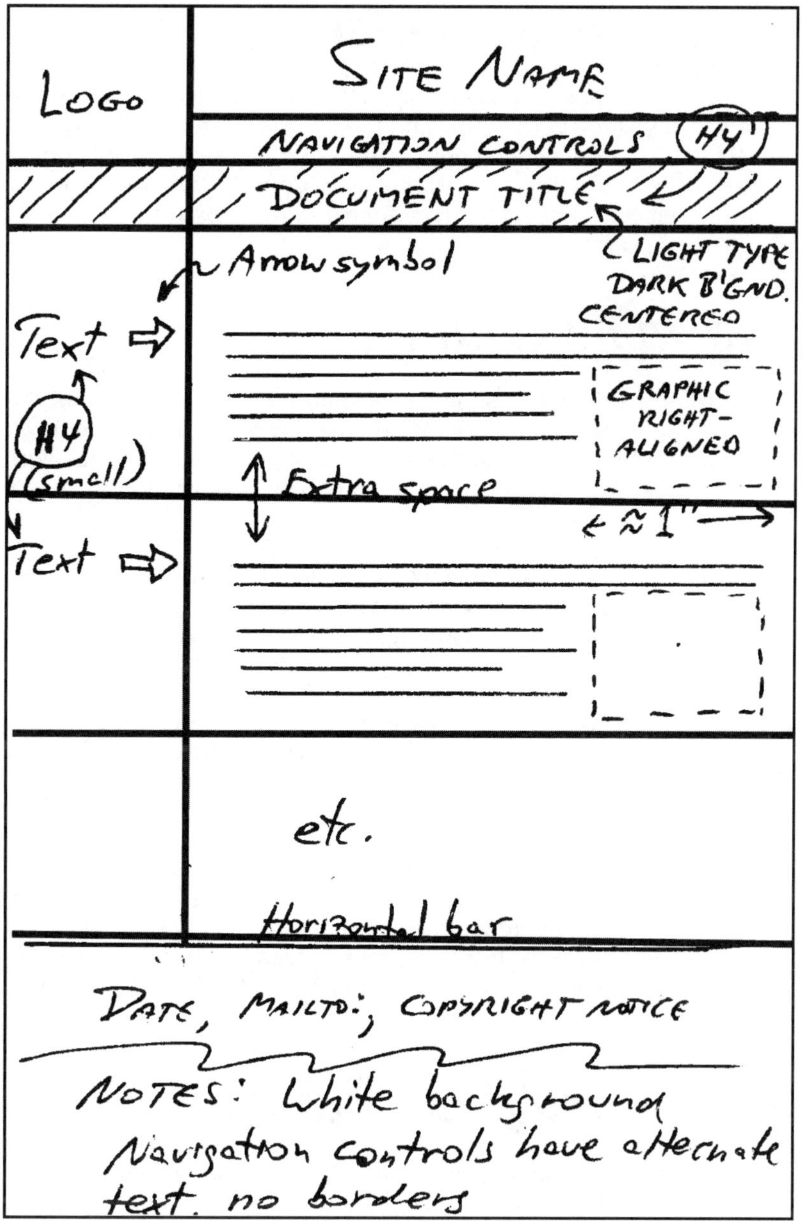

**Figure 17-1:**
A rough sketch of a layout, with columns and rows ruled on it.

Notice that, as in the Logo section of Figure 17-1, rows don't continue all the way across in some places. Likewise, columns may not extend all the way down. Those places are created when you either split or join cells, rows, or columns.

## Removing Table Borders for Layout

In general, when you use a table for layout, you want to turn off its borders. Click anywhere in the table and then choose Table⇨Format to display the HTML Properties dialog box. In the Table tab, set the Table borders value to zero. Click the OK button when you're done. WordPerfect shows dotted lines between cells, but no borders appear in the browser.

## Setting Table Width

Most of the time, you should size your table at 100 percent of the browser-window width, simply because everything on the page usually goes into the table; nothing is outside the table. When you create a table, WordPerfect initially uses 100 percent as the table size, so normally, you don't even have to think about width.

You can also size the table by using a fixed width, in pixels. A fixed width gives you a bit more precise control of column widths, spacing, and alignment. A popular width is about 500 pixels — a width that fits comfortably into the window that most browsers use when you launch them.

To set table width, click anywhere in the table and then choose Table⇨Format to display the HTML Properties dialog box. In the Table tab, next to the label Table width, choose pixels, not percentage, and enter a width in pixels.

If you do choose a fixed width in pixels, you must make sure that any graphics that you place in a row fit into the width you choose. Making graphics fit can be difficult, because WordPerfect describes graphics' sizes in inches, not pixels! If the graphics exceed the table's width, WordPerfect automatically resets the table to 100 percent of browser-window width.

## Walking Through an Example

Often, the best way to learn something is to watch someone else do it, especially when you have many details and fine points to master — and particularly when the task is subject to as many individual choices as Web-page design offers.

I wish that I could let you watch over my shoulder while I lay out a page, but the following discussion is the next-best thing. The example starts with a sketch and proceeds through the creation of the page, illustrating many of the little issues that arise and how to deal with them. I suggest that you follow along in WordPerfect, introducing your own variations on the design as you go.

### The sketch

The sketch shown in Figure 17-1 earlier in this chapter shows some tentative columns and rows in heavy black lines. This layout is not perfect, but then again, it doesn't have to be. As you proceed with a layout, you have to make adjustments for the reality of how browsers display tables, text, and graphics.

Stick a coffee stirrer or whatever you have on hand into the book at Figure 17-1 so that you can refer to the sketch easily.

### The table

Before creating the table, I set the background color. I like a plain white background. Choosing Format⇨Text/Background Colors, I click the Background color button in the HTML Document Properties dialog box and then choose white from the palette that appears.

Referring to my sketch (Figure 17-1), I conclude that I should start with a table of two columns, and at least six rows will do the job. I click the Table button in the Toolbar and drag to a 2 x 6 table, and the table shown in Figure 17-2 appears. As Figure 17-2 shows, columns in Web tables in WordPerfect start out evenly balanced (of equal width) — and, oddly, remain so, despite the table contents. In a Web browser, a table behaves differently, adjusting column width to the contents.

**Figure 17-2:** A 2 x 6, 100-percent-width table.

I leave the borders on for now. A border makes seeing what's happening easier when I preview my work in my Web browser.

### The logo

I refer to the identity or banner graphic as the logo, but the graphic doesn't have to be a logo; it can be any graphic that you want to appear atop all your Web pages. For this example, I use one of the WordPerfect images.

First, however, notice from the sketch in Figure 17-1 that the logo spans two rows of the table. This situation is my cue to join two cells. I drag across the top two cells in the left column and then click the QuickJoin button in the Property Bar.

Clicking the cell in the top-left corner, I choose Insert⇔Graphics⇔From File and in the dialog box that appears, I select the HOTAIR.WGP image from the WordPerfect ClipArt folder. Figure 17-3 shows the result.

**Figure 17-3:** Joining two cells creates a logo space two rows high.

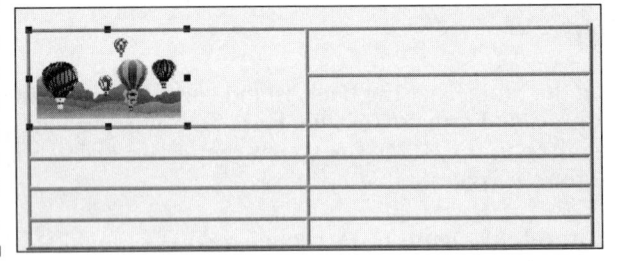

This would be a good time to check the size of the logo and adjust it, if necessary. To adjust size, right-click the graphic and then choose Size from the QuickMenu that appears to display the Box Size dialog box.

### The site name

The Web-site name in this layout goes in the top-right cell of the table. I chose the name Buoyant Adventures for this example, and I'll try formatting it in the Heading 1 Web style. I make sure not to press the Enter key at the end of the line, because that action adds extra line spacing that I don't want.

Figure 17-4 shows the result, including line wrapping to two lines. I'm not immediately worried about the line wrapping because WordPerfect doesn't provide variable column width the way that browsers do.

**Figure 17-4:**
The title appears to line-wrap in WordPerfect.

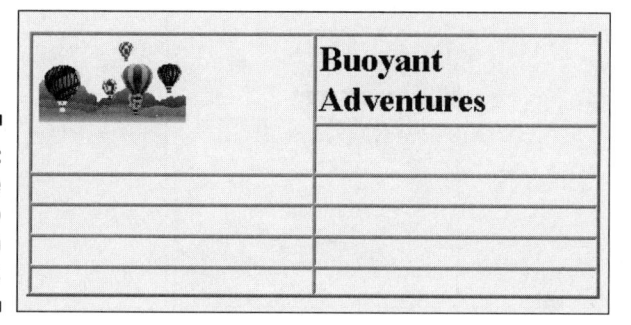

If the text is actually likely to wrap to two lines in a browser, I need to take some action to control the layout: either prevent the line from wrapping or force it to wrap. A simple solution — if it doesn't make the page too wide — is to use a hard space between the words *Buoyant* and *Adventures* (by pressing Ctrl+spacebar). Another solution is to insert a line break between the words, thereby forcing the title to line-wrap.

At this point, I check the results in my browser by clicking the View in Web Browser button. As Figure 17-5 shows, the title works just fine in a standard-width window; no wrapping occurs. Also notice in Figure 17-5 that the empty cells of the table do not appear, even though they do appear in WordPerfect.

**Figure 17-5:**
Viewing your work in a browser reveals the truth.

## Navigation controls

In this example, I'm placing the navigation controls at the top of the page in the cell below the site name and using plain old hyperlinked text. I'll try using Normal style and see how things look. I prefer that the links not line-wrap between the words, so I use hard spaces there. As I did with the site name, I avoid pressing Enter at the end of the line.

As Figure 17-6 shows, lines wrap between the links but not at the nonbreaking spaces in the middle of the links. I confirm the line wrap by viewing the result in my Web browser.

**Figure 17-6:** Controls line-wrap between links, but not midlink.

If I decide that I don't like having the controls line-wrap, I need to protect the width of their cell by making some other cell in that column unbreakable. One approach is to put a nonbreaking space in the site name between *Buoyant* and *Adventures,* by pressing Ctrl+spacebar, and then to see whether the width of the site name is enough to keep the control line from breaking. As it is, I don't mind if the controls line-wrap.

## Document name

The sketch in Figure 17-1 shows that each page of this Web site has a document name in light-colored text on a dark background. Heading 4 is the suggested style.

First, I will set the background color. Clicking the cell under the control row, I choose Table⇨Format from the Property Bar and then click the Row tab in the HTML Table Properties dialog box. Clicking the button next to the label Row background color, I choose a blue background.

Now I add a document name for the home page in the cell under controls. I cleverly enter the text **HOME PAGE** (being careful not to press Enter afterward, to avoid excess line spacing) and then choose the Heading 4 Web style. Finally, I highlight the text, click the Font Color button in the Property Bar, and choose white from the drop-down list.

The result looks pretty good in WordPerfect, but Figure 17-7 shows the result when I view it in the Web browser. A large blue space appears below *HOME PAGE,* and even though I specified a blue background for the entire row in WordPerfect, the blue background doesn't appear in the empty cell below the logo graphic.

**Figure 17-7:** Slightly incorrect results show up in the Web browser.

Blue should appear here    Too much space

The problems come from two areas:

- Heading styles automatically provide space below the text (and WordPerfect doesn't display the space).
- WordPerfect displays empty cells; Web browsers don't.

The fixes for these problems are simple. First, I choose for the *HOME PAGE* text a Web style that doesn't provide extra space: Definition List. Second, by pressing Crtl+spacebar, I put a hard (nonbreaking) space in the blank cell so that the cell's background is displayed.

## Aligning banner elements

So far, I've been leaving the text in this banner left-aligned, but the sketch calls for center alignment of this text. Now is a good time to align all the text at the same time.

I drag across the top three cells of the right column to select them. Then, choosing Table⇨Format from the Property Bar and clicking the Cell tab in the resulting dialog box, I choose a Horizontal alignment of Center. I choose Cell formatting rather than Column because according to the sketch, the rest of the right column is to be left-aligned, not centered.

## Left- and right-column text

According to the sketch, the left column of this page is to provide a margin in which topics are called out. The text is to use Heading 4 Web style with the Small attribute. Arrow symbols are to point from the topic to the corresponding text in the right column. Each topic-text combination goes in its own row.

Entering the text is straightforward enough. After typing it, I simply highlight the left-column text; apply the Heading 4 Web style to it; and then apply the Small attribute (by clicking the *a* Font Attribute button in the Property Bar and choosing Small from the drop-down list). The text in the right column I leave in Normal style.

Oops! After previewing the document in the browser, I realize that Small is too small. I return the Font Attribute to Normal. WordPerfect isn't WYSIWYG when it comes to fonts. This sort of difference between WordPerfect and reality is why continually clicking the View in Web Browser button is a good idea.

## Arrow symbols

The arrow symbols are a bit tricky; the Web doesn't allow many special symbols. Also, I want to left-align the text but right-align the arrows in the column.

Hmmm. I could create tiny text boxes containing a WordPerfect symbol, which theoretically would solve both problems. Alternatively, I could insert a ClipArt arrow. (Either way, the result is a graphic, which could be paragraph-attached to the topic text and then right-aligned.) Tiny graphics often are tricky to size and to align with the regular text, however.

I opt for another solution. To position the arrows, I will create a new column exclusively for the arrows. For each arrow, I will insert a Web-standard symbol from WordPerfect's Typographic symbol collection.

To create the new column, I select the bottom three cells of the left column and then click the QuickSplit Column button in the Property Bar. (Alternatively, you can choose Table⇨Split⇨QuickSplit Column from the Property Bar menu.)

To insert the symbol into the new column, I choose Insert⇨Symbol. For the Set, I choose Typographic Symbols, and I select symbol number 4, 10. To give the arrow a little spacing, I put nonbreaking spaces before and after the symbol. Figure 17-8 shows the rather ugly result in WordPerfect.

Fortunately, the result is pretty nice in a Web browser. I click the View in Web Browser button and get a page like the one shown in Figure 17-9.

## Removing the border

The border has served its purpose: helping me see where the cell boundaries are in my Web browser. It's time to turn off the border and see how things look. I choose Table⇨Format from the Property Bar and set Table borders to 0.

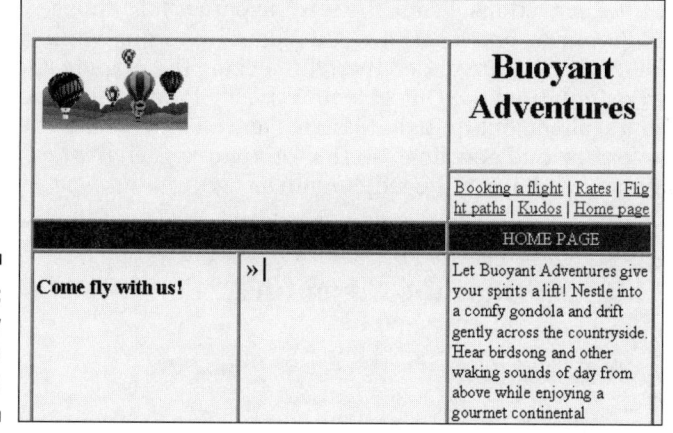

**Figure 17-8:**
Ugly result in WordPerfect.

**Figure 17-9:**
Nice result in a Web browser.

When I check the page in a Web browser, I see that the result is not bad. I have a few things to clean up, and the appearance is not quite dramatic enough for a home page, but on the whole, things are working well.

I find that I still don't have a continuous background of blue across the page title row, as I wanted. A tiny white line appears between the cells. You should be able to remove this line by setting Cell Spacing (a table-format setting) to 0. In my version of WordPerfect Suite 8, this only makes matters worse; setting Cell Spacing to 1 produces the best results, but still does not eliminate the thin white line. If you need to solve a problem like this white line, see the suggestion in the section "Cleanup and troubleshooting," later in this chapter.

## Illustrations

The sketch in Figure 17-1 shows illustrations hovering at the bottom-right corner of the paragraphs, with text wrapping around them. You can't quite do this positioning on the Web. The closest that you can come is to put graphics in the top-right corners of the paragraphs.

To insert the illustrations, I click the leading paragraph; choose Insert⇨Graphics⇨From File; and insert a cloud illustration from WordPerfect's Graphics/Pictures/Nature folder. By right-clicking the graphic and then choosing Position from the QuickMenu, I specify Paragraph attachment and set Horizontal alignment to Right Margin. Figure 17-10 reveals the result in a Web browser: A cloud now floats in the top-right corner. (*Note:* I fiddle with the paragraph headings in the left column as I go.)

**Figure 17-10:** Paragraph attachment helps float a cloud graphic.

## Bottom stuff

A good way to end a home page is a call to action (in which you suggest what to click next). I put a suggestion in the final paragraph and a link in the text to make it easy for the visitor to follow up.

On a page in which the controls are at the top, repeating the controls at the bottom is a good idea, if the page is a long one. (Copying hyperlinks can be tricky; I suggest using the WordPerfect Reveal Codes, if you're familiar with them. Highlight your selection not by using the mouse, but by holding down the Ctrl key and then pressing the right- or left-arrow key. This procedure helps you make sure that you select all the hypertext codes.) The example home page is short, so repeating the controls is not necessary here.

A good Web page includes the date on which it was created and a mailto link to the creator or Web weaver. A centered line of text outside the table does the job here. Usually, a horizontal line separates this information from the body of the page.

## Cleanup and troubleshooting

Visually, this home page is nice but lacks a dramatic entrance. I insert a row below the document-name bar *(HOME PAGE)* and add a centered Heading 2 title above the text column. (See Chapter 10 if you don't know how to insert rows, and refer to Chapter 8 for informatiom on styles and alignment.) Figure 17-11 shows the more-or-less final product.

**Chapter 17: Doing Layouts by Using Tables** *249*

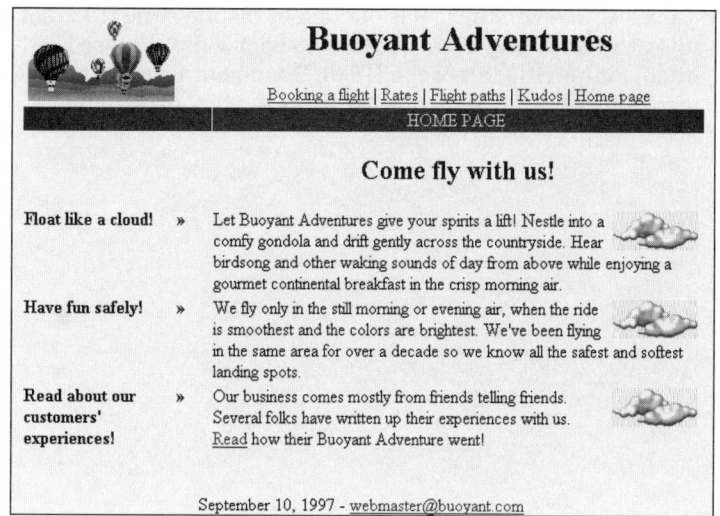

**Figure 17-11:** A pretty good realization of the original sketch.

The page could benefit from a more open feeling. I could put blank rows containing hard spaces between the existing rows of text, or I could increase the Inside Cell Margins (a table-format setting).

Also, the annoying tiny white line mentioned earlier, which appears between cells in the colored document name row, is still there. You can solve this peculiarity of early releases of WordPerfect Suite 8 only by editing the HTML code itself. If you have this problem and are comfortable with using Windows' WordPad, open your HTML file in WordPad, search for `CELLSPACING="something-or-other,"` and change it to read `CELLSPACING="0"` (a zero, not the letter O). Save the file and reload it into your browser. If you edit your Web file in WordPerfect, you need to repeat this step afterward.

Controlling layout is tricky, even with tables. Moreover, WordPerfect is not trouble-free when it comes to Web tables (especially in initial releases of WordPerfect 8). Following are a few tips for avoiding or shooting trouble:

- Avoid pressing the Enter key at the end of text in a table, unless you want the extra space that a paragraph mark brings. Choose View⇨Show ¶ so that you can see paragraph marks.

- Inserting rows at a place in the table where the number of columns changes sometimes strains WordPerfect. The program survives, but your table may need repairs.

- If text or graphics suddenly lose their alignment, check to see whether the column width is set at some number of pixels. (Choose Table⇨Format, and in the HTML Table Properties dialog box, click the Column tab.) If column width is set, click to clear the Column width check box. WordPerfect has a tendency to try to set column widths, and it just doesn't work well.

- Check to see whether your document displays the title that you want in the title bar of your browser (the top bar). If not, choose File➪Properties; then, in the Title tab of the HTML Document Properties dialog box, click Custom title and enter a title in the box provided.

# Chapter 18

# Layout with Browser Tricks: Frames and Columns

*In This Chapter*

▶ Using frame-based home pages from the CD-ROM
▶ Hyperlinking: The frame name game
▶ Netscape's multiple columns

Although it boggles the imagination to think that the citizens of the Web (who are known for being conservative and rule-abiding) might adopt methods that are not Officially Sanctioned, that is exactly what has happened with frames. The frame is a browser trick for layout (an HTML extension) that Netscape invented, which isn't official HTML (at this time) but which both Netscape and Microsoft support. A second, unrelated HTML extension — multiple columns — currently is supported only by Netscape (which invented it). This chapter is about these browser tricks that are increasingly commonplace on the Web.

Frames are sort of like picture-in-a-picture television, except that they don't cost as much. Frames are subwindows within the browser window. Each frame can contain its own HTML document or graphic, which stays put even if other frames ebb and flow. The most common uses for frames are to create stable, supportive, and loving homes for navigation controls and for banners. Navigation controls typically appear in a frame down the side of the document, and the banner typically appears in a frame across the top of the window.

Frames are not without problems. Although users of both Netscape and Microsoft Web browsers can see frames, users of others browsers cannot. Also, some people dislike frames and turn them off on their browsers.

Also, WordPerfect does not support frames, so if you want them, you could work in the HTML language itself. You could also juggle flaming marshmallows in your underwear. Fortunately, neither act is necessary. This book's CD-ROM provides a small but tasteful collection of basic frame designs that you can install on your hard drive and use.

## Using Frame-Based Home Pages from the CD-ROM

When you're looking at a frame-based Web site, you're looking at several documents at the same time:

- A single page (usually, the home page) that creates the frames but provides little, if any, content.
- The individual HTML documents (or graphics) that fill the frames. I call these files the *content* files.

First, you need to install the files from the CD. See the instructions in the back of this book for installing the files from the CD-ROM. After you have installed the files, find the folder called `Author's Files from CD\frames` on the disk drive where you installed those files. In that folder, you find several ready-to-use, frame-based home pages, with dummy content files to fill the various frames. You don't edit these files at all; you just provide new content files. Here's how to use them:

1. **Launch your Web browser.**

2. **Press Ctrl+O, and in the dialog box that appears (which has a different name for different browsers), browse to the folder** `Author's Files from CD\frames` **on your hard drive.**

    Your browser displays an index of folders.

3. **Browse the available home pages by opening the folders and clicking any file named** `index.htm`.

    Each frame on the home page tells you what content file is used to fill that frame. The home page in the `3part_A` folder, with its dummy content, looks like Figure 18-1.

4. **When you find a home page that suits your Web site, copy it to the folder on your hard drive where you keep your HTML Web files.**

    An easy way to copy is double-click the Windows 95 My Computer icon, click your chosen file, choose Edit⇨Copy, browse to the destination folder on your hard disk, and then choose Edit⇨Paste.

    Do not use WordPerfect to edit the `index.htm` file (except as ASCII text)! The program does not know how to handle frames (at least, in early versions of WordPerfect 8) and ruins the file. You don't need to edit the files from the CD-ROM to use them!

5. **Publish your own content files to the same folder, using the same names displayed by the dummy content files in your Web browser.**

Publish your graphics files as you normally do. If you are publishing `c:\myfiles\website\banner.htm`, for example, put your graphics or audio files in the `c:\myfiles\website\banner` folder.

**Figure 18-1:** One of the frame-based home pages from the CD-ROM.

Your file **banner.htm** goes here.
If you put a graphic 75 pixels high in **banner.htm**, it will fill this frame.
For hyperlinking, this frame's name is **banframe**.

Your file **navigate.htm** goes here.
A graphic 100 pixels wide will fill this column.
For hyperlinking, this frame's name is **navframe**.

Your file `content.htm` goes here.

For hyperlinking purposes, this frame's name is **main**.

Click for a brief lesson in hyperlinking

## Whittling your own custom frames

If your technical skills are up to hacking in HTML code, you can customize frame pages that you installed from the CD-ROM. View or edit the HTML code by choosing File⇔Open in WordPerfect, and in the Convert File Format box that appears, choose ASCII DOS Text instead of HTML. Commands appear between < and > symbols. HTML commands between `<NOFRAME>` and `</NOFRAME>` appear only in browsers that don't have frame capability.

One `FRAMESET` command divides the screen horizontally (`COLS`), and another divides it vertically (`ROWS`). Either command could come first. Insert the command `FRAMEBORDER="0"` into the `FRAMESET` command to turn off borders. The list of numbers after `COLS=` or `ROWS=` gives the sizes of the columns or rows in pixels. Each number in the list creates one row or column. The * (asterisk) means "all remaining available space."

`FRAME` commands say what document to load by using `SRC="file"`. The frame names are provided by `NAME="name"`. To adjust white space around the inside of the frame, use `MARGINWIDTH` and `MARGINHEIGHT="pixels"`. To prevent scrolling bars from appearing, insert `SCROLLING="NO"` in the command. To prevent the user from resizing the frame by dragging the separator, insert `NORESIZE`.

When you save the file, choose ASCII DOS Text. If you choose File⇔Save As to save the file, you subsequently need to close the file and then rename it to remove the .TXT extension that WordPerfect applies. When you're testing your work in Netscape Navigator, clicking Reload doesn't reload the frames file, just the contents. Click the Location window and press the Enter key instead.

After creating the content files, open the home page (`index.htm`) in your Web browser and see how you've done. If you gave your files the correct names, your new content files take the place of the dummy files in the various frames.

*Note:* If you use the `index.htm` files from the book's CD, folks who can't see frames will be presented with a choice of which content file they want to see. (I built that feature into the `index.htm` files.) This solution isn't ideal, but it works.

## Hyperlinking: The Frame Name Game

Hyperlinking between the documents on a Web site becomes a challenge when you add frames. After all, the new document could appear in any of the frames. The burning question that you are undoubtedly asking yourself is "How do you indicate where the new document should appear when the link is clicked?"

The answer is that each frame has a name. The frame name for the main frame is, naturally, main! (To paraphrase a dame, "The name of main stays mainly with the frame.") This name game is my bane! My brain has gone insane! Again! . . . *Whack!* . . . Whew. Thanks. I hate it when that happens. Okay, where was I?

Each frame has a name, hidden within the HTML file that contains the frames. (That file is `index.htm` for the frames from the CD-ROM.) When you create a hyperlink in a frame-based Web site, you can specify a target frame for that hyperlink by using the frame's name. (Notice back in Figure 18-1 that the samples from the CD-ROM tell you what each frame is named so that you can target your hyperlinks properly.) Figure 18-2 shows a hyperlink targeting the main frame.

**Figure 18-2:** Targeting the main frame, where most content is displayed.

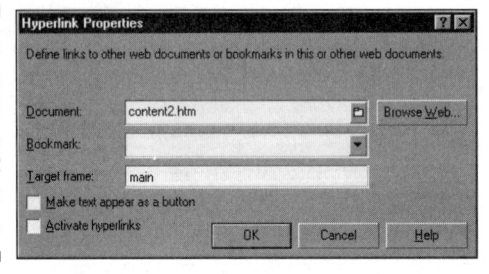

Netscape reserves certain names for doing special targeting. All these names begin with the underscore character (_). If you use the following names in the Target frame box, various useful things happen:

- `_self` targets the same frame as the current document (the one that you're working on).
- `_blank` opens a new Navigator window with the new document in it.
- `_top` gets rid of the frames and puts the new document in a normal, unframed Navigator window.
- `_parent` does something rather too complicated and insufficiently useful to bother explaining.

# Netscape Multiple Columns

Multiple columns qualify for this book's stupid browser trick category because they're cute but of limited usefulness. You can create multiple-column documents for Netscape Navigator users but (at the moment) for nobody else. Other browser vendors may adopt columns over time, if Web weavers decide that they like columns and start using the feature. In the meantime, bear in mind that non-Netscape users see your document only in a simple one-column format.

If you want a newspaper- or magazinelike appearance for your document, as Figure 18-3 shows, consider using multiple columns. You can control the number of columns, the spacing between them, and the column width in pixels. You can even change the number of columns in the middle of the document.

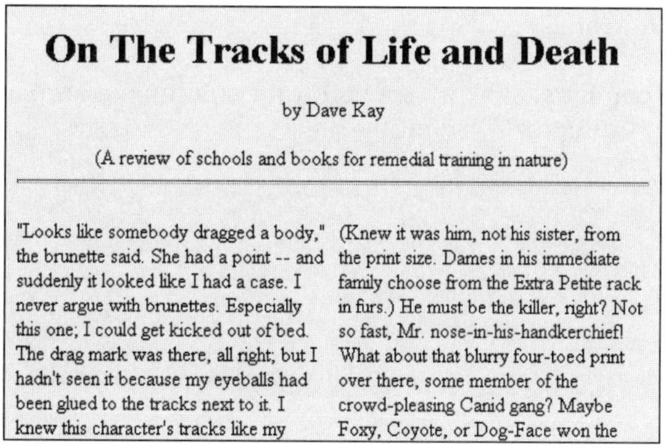

On The Tracks of Life and Death

by Dave Kay

(A review of schools and books for remedial training in nature)

"Looks like somebody dragged a body," the brunette said. She had a point -- and suddenly it looked like I had a case. I never argue with brunettes. Especially this one; I could get kicked out of bed. The drag mark was there, all right; but I hadn't seen it because my eyeballs had been glued to the tracks next to it. I knew this character's tracks like my (Knew it was him, not his sister, from the print size. Dames in his immediate family choose from the Extra Petite rack in furs.) He must be the killer, right? Not so fast, Mr. nose-in-his-handkerchief! What about that blurry four-toed print over there, some member of the crowd-pleasing Canid gang? Maybe Foxy, Coyote, or Dog-Face won the

**Figure 18-3:** Switching to two-column format.

## Part IV: Wayout Layouts and Dazzling Designs

In WordPerfect, starting from the point at which you apply it, the column format continues until you discontinue columns or change the format. So click where you want multiple columns to begin and then choose Format➪Columns➪Format. (The Department of Redundancy Department has been busy.) The Web Columns dialog box, shown in Figure 18-4, leaps into action.

**Figure 18-4:** A dialog box that presents less control than meets the eye.

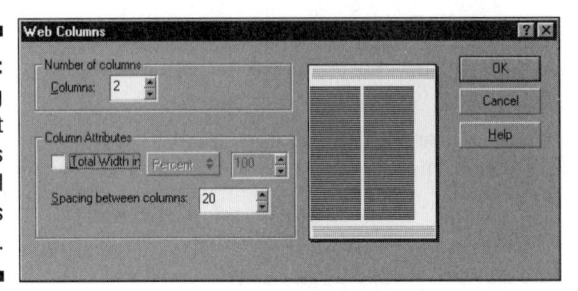

The dialog box does its job well in most areas of control. You can choose a number of columns in the Columns box and adjust the gap between the columns (in pixels) by using the Spacing between columns box.

In initial releases of WordPerfect 8, setting the Total Width as a percentage does not work in the HTML document. (This method appears to work in WordPerfect.) You can, however, set Total Width in pixels. Total Width refers to the width of all your columns, including the spaces between them. You can't set column widths individually.

The columns come out fairly equal in length. You can't control how or where the text column wraps except by temporarily discontinuing or changing column format. If you do change the number of columns or discontinue columns in the middle of the document, the text preceding that point quite logically column-wraps.

To discontinue columns, click where you want columns to stop and then choose Format➪Columns➪Discontinue.

# Chapter 19

# Lazy Layouts and Indolent Authoring

**In This Chapter**
▶ Running the PerfectExpert
▶ Using files from the CD-ROM

*I*n the *...For Dummies* spirit of not doing any more work than is actually necessary, here is one of the shortest chapters of the book. The publisher wants every paragraph to have at least two sentences, so I will next say that this chapter is about ways to make Web pages without working hard. Have at it. I'm taking a nap.

## *Perfect Indolence*

For folks who just want to knock out a basic Web page and don't want to sweat the small stuff, WordPerfect has just the tool: the PerfectExpert. (For no good reason, my perverse brain continues to recall this tool's name as the PerfectIdiot, but really, it's not — it's a nice little feature. I just had to get that phrase out of my system. Thanks.) To enjoy the services of the PerfectExpert, choose File➪New.

Figure 19-1 shows the PerfectExpert dialog box that appears. As shown in Figure 19-1, choose Web Publishing from the drop-down list at the top of the Create New tab. Click the Create button.

The PerfectExpert switches WordPerfect to Web view and sits expectantly to the left of your document window, as Figure 19-2 shows, providing a set of buttons to click in the order (more or less) in which you want them. (I used those buttons to create the charming poem that appears on the right side of Figure 19-2.)

**Part IV: Wayout Layouts and Dazzling Designs**

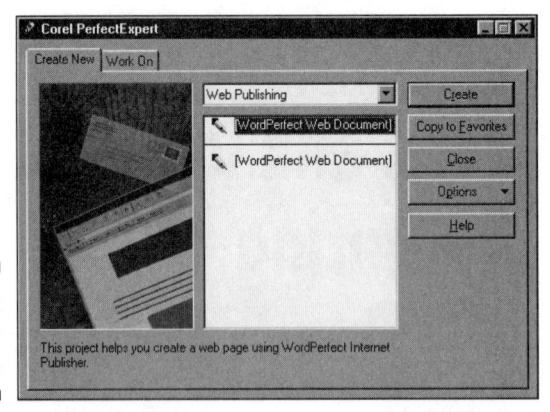

**Figure 19-1:** Finding the right expert.

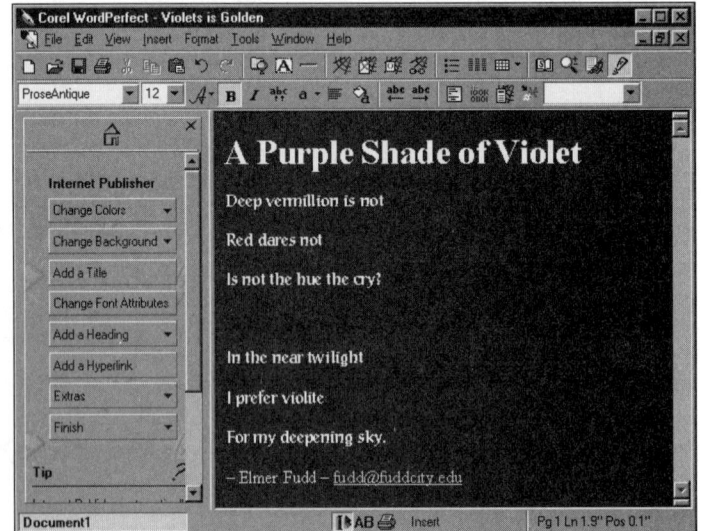

**Figure 19-2:** Perfectly straightforward authoring.

If you start with the top button and proceed down the list (going back and forth as needed to, say, add more headings), you end up with a Web document. Amazing.

As you probably realize, all these buttons are simply shortcuts to standard WordPerfect Web features, but what's bad about that? If you have any questions about what's going on or want to do something fancy, simply see the appropriate section of this book. Table 19-1 lists the buttons, what they do, and where to go in this book to read more.

## Table 19-1    Behind the Buttons

| Button | About the Button | Where to Read More |
|---|---|---|
| Change Colors | Chooses a color scheme for text and background, based on the background that you choose | Chapter 9 |
| Change Background | Chooses background wallpaper | Chapters 9 and 12 |
| Add a Title | Creates a title for the title bar | Chapters 4 and 6 |
| Change Font Attributes | Presents the Font dialog box | Chapters 8 and 9 |
| Add a Heading | Applies a Web Heading style | Chapter 8 |
| Add a Hyperlink | Creates a hyperlink for selected text or graphic | Chapters 7 and 11 |
| Extras | Inserts graphics, lines, bulleted or numbered lists, or a table | Chapters 8, 10, 11, and 12 |
| Finish | Check results in a browser or publish a Web document | Chapter 3 |

When you're done with the Expert, click the scribbly X in the top-right corner of the Expert panel. You don't have an incredibly sophisticated Web page by today's standards, but you do have a Web page, and you can proceed to make it as sophisticated as you like. I suggest that you save your work as a WordPerfect document, in addition to publishing it as a Web document.

# Lazy Layouts

Another lazy approach to creating a Web page is to start with one of the partially prefabricated documents from this book's CD-ROM. See the instructions in the back of this book for installing the CD-ROM. Prefabricated documents end up on your hard drive in the folder named `Author's Files from CD`. For some frames-based pages, see the `Frames` folder and Chapter 18. For straightforward pages, see the folder named `Starters`. You'll find some basic pages in the `Vanilla` folder. For a couple of cooler ideas, see the `ChocoSwirl` folder. For an unconventional page, see the `FunkyMonkey` folder.

### Gazing languorously upon two examples

Figure 19-3 shows the rather unconventional `goldenbook.htm` file in the `FunkyMonkey` folder. This file uses a trick that is deceptively simple to implement. A skinny strip of background wallpaper creates a booklike page; the text uses an exotic font in a gold color to create the illusion of a gold-leaf embossed book cover. (The font really is too exotic to use on the Web if you want to be sure that most other people see it.) Figure 19-4 shows a more conventional (and more useful) Web page design from the `Vanilla` folder.

### Opening the starter files

Many of the starter files on this book's CD-ROM are HTM (HTML) files, not WordPerfect files, which means that you can view them in your Web browser to see which ones you like before you open them in WordPerfect. (Viewing these HTM files in a Web browser first is a good idea because browsers display Web files more accurately than WordPerfect does.) Chapter 3 tells you how to view HTM files in a Web browser.

To use a starter file, open it in WordPerfect. If a WordPerfect file is provided (a WPD file of the same name as the HTM file), open that file instead of the HTM file.

If you open an HTM file, WordPerfect will convert the file from HTML to a Web-formatted WordPerfect document. Chapter 3 provides suggestions for working with a document that started its life as an HTML file.

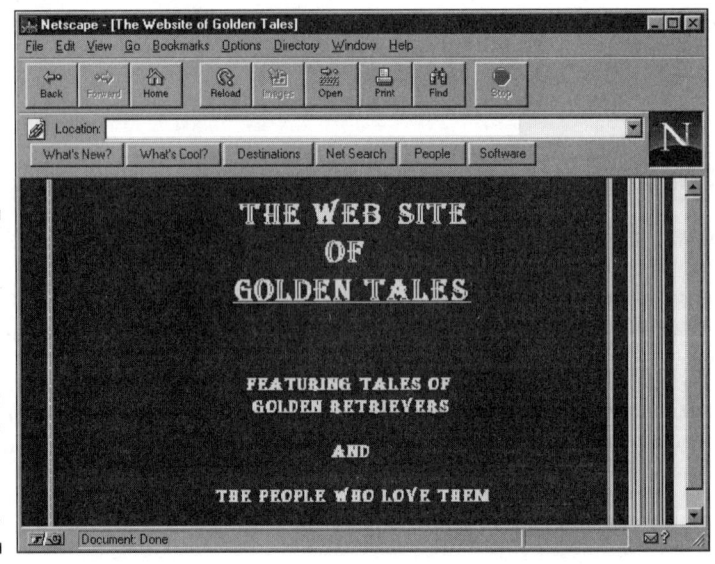

**Figure 19-3:** Fun with backgrounds in `goldenbook.htm` from the `FunkyMonkey` folder.

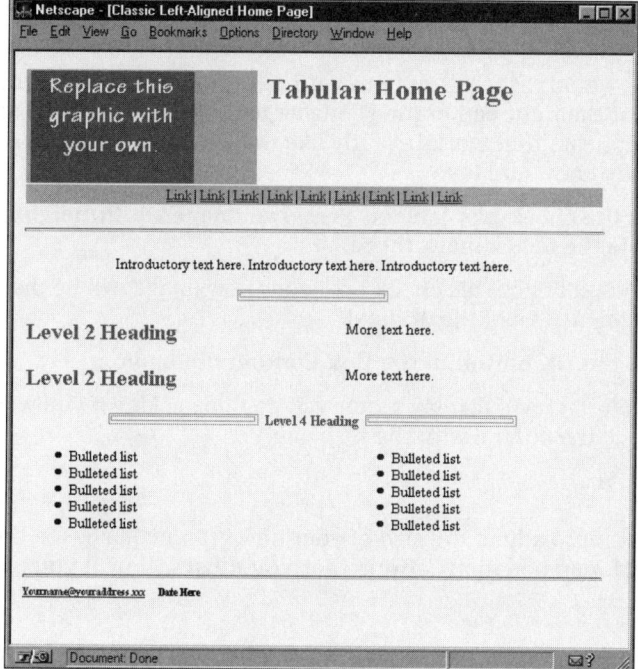

**Figure 19-4:** A more conventional Web page, `home-tab.htm`, in the `Vanilla` folder.

## Changing text, graphics, and hyperlinks in web documents

To use the starter files from the book's CD-ROM (or to use existing Web files from any other source, such as your company's Web server), you must replace the text with your own text, do likewise with the graphics, and edit the hyperlinks.

Performing these replacements and edits ranges in difficulty from simple to tricky. To replace normal (non-hyperlinked) text, simply select the original text (highlight it) and type your new text. You cannot, in most instances, replace existing graphics with ClipArt or TextArt without losing the original size and positioning. You can, however, replace existing graphics with a graphics file, such as a WPG, BMP, or GIF file. To replace graphics with a graphics file without distortion, and without losing the size and position of the original graphic, do the following steps:

1. **Right-click the original graphic.**
2. **Choose Content from the QuickMenu that appears.**

    A Box Content dialog box comes to your aid.

3. **Enter your new graphic file's filename and path in the Filename text box.**

   If you would rather browse to your new graphic file, click the file-folder icon at the right end of the Filename text box. An Insert Image dialog box appears that works exactly like the File Open dialog box you already know and love.

4. **Click the check box labeled Preserve image width/height ratio to enable the check mark there.**

   If you don't click this check box, your new image will be distorted to fit the dimensions of the original.

5. **Click the OK button in the Box Content dialog box.**

   WordPerfect will display a query dialog box asking if you want to replace the old file with the new one.

6. **Click Yes.**

You may want to adjust the size of your new graphic. If so, see Chapter 11. Chapter 11 also has instructions that you must follow if you use a JPG or GIF file.

The third change you need to make is to edit your hyperlinks, which can be a tricky job. See Chapter 7 for instructions. You will need to change the text of the hyperlinks as well as the address you are linking to.

# Part V
# Beyond WordPerfect: Web Site Sizzle

The 5th Wave — By Rich Tennant

"Here, boy."

## In this part . . .

To really whoop it up on the Web, you need to go a bit beyond WordPerfect. While WordPerfect remains your good buddy for actually creating the Web documents, the sizzle itself requires a few extra tools or typing a few short lines of HTML gobbledygook. This part gives you painless ways to add cool features like clickable graphics, sound, animation, scrolling marquees, time-sequenced "slide shows" and other special effects.

If you program, or know someone who does, there's help for you, too: most importantly, how to create forms to gather names and other information from your Web site visitors. This part also shows you how to hook up your Web pages to Java applets and JavaScript — the latest all-singing, all-dancing technology that probably, someday, is going to run everything from telephones to Tinker Toys.

# Chapter 20
# Graphics That Really Click

### In This Chapter
▶ Understanding clickable graphics
▶ Using tools for clickable graphics
▶ Using Live Image
▶ Using Corel Presentations

*A*nyone who has spent a few minutes on the Web has run into *clickable graphics;* clicking a certain part of an image takes you to document A, and clicking another part takes you to document B. It's a tidy way of creating a graphical control panel without piecing together lots of separate images. You can use a clickable graphic in your Web document, too, if you're willing to step outside WordPerfect for a while to do some work.

Clickable graphics are often overused or misused, however. Some sites create a clickable graphic that fills the home page, sort of like a giant hyperlinked magazine cover. Large graphics take aeons to download, leaving the visitor clueless and powerless until the process is done.

Don't make the same mistake. Use clickable graphics only where they make sense. Maps or pictures of physical objects are the best applications. Don't forget that when you create a control panel by using only a clickable graphic, people who have turned graphics off no longer have any controls! If you instead make a control panel from multiple separate graphics (or text), each one can display alternate text and still function if graphics are turned off.

## Understanding Clickable Graphics

Clickable graphics are images that have certain *hot areas* — places that, if you click there, you jump to another document (or exercise some other kind of link, such as a mailto link).

### Whose side is your image map on, anyway?

Image maps come in two varieties, which are distinguished by where they live: in the HTML file that gets downloaded to your visitors or as a separate map file on the Web server. These two forms are called *client-side* and *server-side* image maps. The more recent (and, generally, more useful) form is the client-side map that becomes part of the HTML file. Most, but not all, contemporary browsers offer client-side image mapping. That form is the one that this chapter leads you through.

---

How does this magic work? How does the browser know what address to go to when you click a hot area of the graphic? The chunk of HTML that does the trick is called a *map*, and the job that it performs is called *image mapping*. If you had to write a map yourself, you might call it a nap instead, because writing it would be really, really boring. Fortunately, software exists in which you simply draw a line around an area of the graphic and say what address on the Web the area should connect (or map) to.

Unfortunately, WordPerfect 8 is not cartographically inclined (it doesn't create maps). If you want an image map, you have two choices:

- Hack one yourself (write the HTML) and format it as HTML in WordPerfect. This choice falls in the "I'd rather juggle flaming marshmallows in my underwear" category, if only because image mapping is incredibly tedious.
- Add an image map to your HTML file after you publish the file, using a separate tool. This choice falls in the "Boy, am I glad I bought this book" category.

This book warmly adheres to the "Flaming marshmallows, Non-juggling of" rule, which means that you should look elsewhere if you want to hack your own HTML code. Check out *HTML For Dummies* (IDG Books Worldwide and soon to be galaxywide) by Ed Tittel and Steve James.

## Using Tools for Clickable Graphics

To create a clickable graphic in your Web document, you use a separate software tool. You can download several tools from the Web, but you already have two at your fingertips:

**Chapter 20: Graphics That Really Click** *267*

> ✔ Live Image, which you can install from the book's CD-ROM. (The version on the CD-ROM is a time-limited evaluation version; for long-term use, you need to buy the tool from its vendor.) Live Image allows you to define areas in a variety of shapes and simply installs the map right in your HTML document. You don't need to do anything further in WordPerfect.
>
> ✔ Corel Presentations, which is part of the WordPerfect Suite 8. Corel Presentations plays a special program called a macro to perform crude but workable image mapping. The macro, which is limited to mapping rectangular areas of the graphic, creates a separate file for the map. Putting the image and the map file together requires several steps.

For minimum pain and strain, try the Live Image software from the CD-ROM and then spring for the few bucks required to buy this nice program. The Corel solution is workable but not especially fun 'n' easy.

## Using Live Image

Live Image operates directly on the HTML file that you publish from WordPerfect. After you use Live Image on your HTML file, you don't have to do anything further about image mapping in WordPerfect. If you need to go back and edit your Web document in WordPerfect, however, open and edit the HTML file — not the WPD file — to retain the image map. Otherwise, you overwrite the HTML file that contains the map when you publish to HTML. Follow these steps to use Live Image:

1. **Publish your document to HTML, and close the document in WordPerfect.**

   *Note:* If the HTML file is open in WordPerfect, Live Image can't open the file and won't be able to do its job.

2. **Launch Live Image by choosing Start⇨Programs⇨Live Image⇨Live Image.**

   The Welcome to Live Image dialog box appears, starting you down the path of creating a map for an existing HTML file.

3. **Click OK.**

   The Create a New Image Map dialog box appears.

4. **Click Next to continue down the path of creating a map for an existing HTML file.**

   The New Map in Existing HTML - Step 1 dialog box appears.

5. **Click the HTML file that you just published; then click Next.**

   You see the New Map in Existing HTML - Step 2 dialog box.

**Part V: Beyond WordPerfect: Web Site Sizzle**

6. **Select the graphic that you want to image-map; then click Next.**

   *TIP*

   Figuring out what image you want simply by reading the filenames may be hard. If so, click a file in the New Map in Existing HTML - Step 2 dialog box; the Preview window in the dialog box may show you the image that you clicked.

   After you click Next, you see the New Map in Existing HTML - Step 3 dialog box.

7. **Click Finish.**

   Your graphic image appears in the Live Image window.

8. **Choose one of the blue drawing shapes on the buttons at the left end of the Toolbar shown in Figure 20-1.**

   The button that is selected in Figure 20-1 is the most useful one for most graphics.

Choose a shape for your "hot" area.

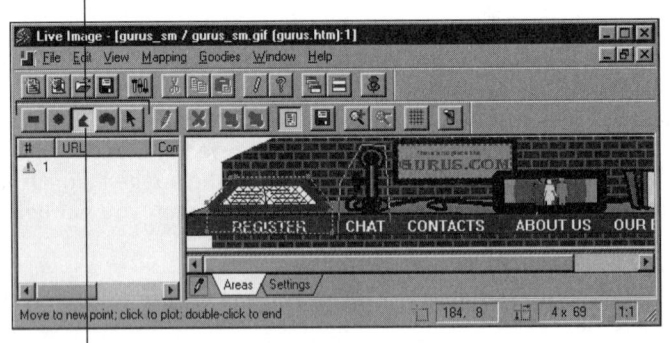

**Figure 20-1:** Defining hot areas.

Define a complex polygon shape.

9. **Click various points around the area that you want to make hot.**

   As you click, a line connects those points to form a shape.

   When you have completed a closed shape by clicking on the starting point, the Area #1 Settings dialog box appears (see Figure 20-2), inquiring about a URL, a possible target frame, and an optional comment.

10. **In the URL to activate when this area is clicked text box, enter the Web address of the document that you want to jump to.**

    See the sidebar "A review of royalty: Types of URLs," later in this section for a refresher on entering Web locations.

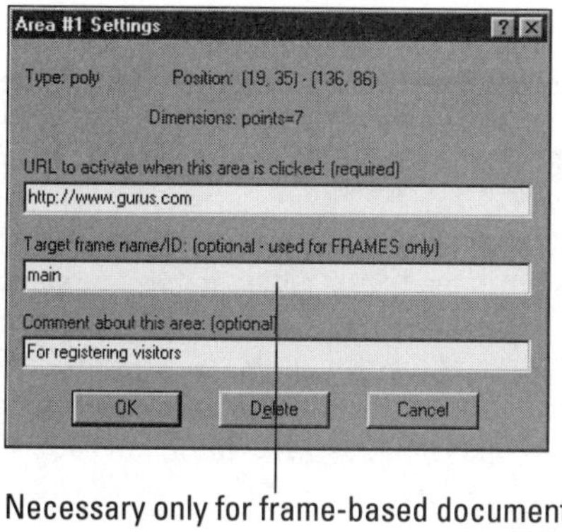

**Figure 20-2:**
Setting the address, or URL, usually is the only requirement.

Necessary only for frame-based documents

11. **If the document that you are working on is used in a frame-based Web site, enter the target frame's name in the Target Frame Name/ID text box.**

12. **Click OK.**

    Your settings appear in the area on the left side of the Live Image window, and the shape that you defined for those settings is cross-hatched.

13. **Repeat Steps 8 through 12 for other areas (Area #2, #3, and so on).**

    Use the same shape tool or a different tool, starting with Step 8.

14. **After you define all the hot spots in your graphic, save your work by choosing File➪Save or by clicking the floppy-disk button in the Toolbar.**

Live Image creates a modified HTML file, which now performs image mapping! To test the result, choose Goodies➪Test Map. The Test the Map dialog box appears, displaying all kinds of information on ways to test your image map. I suggest that you choose The Second and then click OK. That choice launches your browser with your HTML document already in it. Connect to the Internet and try clicking the image!

If you find an error in a link, return to Live Image and click the arrow button in the Live Image Toolbar. Double-click any hot spot to edit the link information. To modify the outline of a shape, position your mouse pointer over any point in the outline and drag the point to move the outline. You can also move an entire shape simply by dragging it.

> ### A review of royalty: Types of URLs
> 
> To jump to any document on the Web, enter the full URL, as in `http://www.gurus.com`. To jump to a document on your Web site, just enter its full filename (such as `ourbooks.htm`), assuming that the document is in the same folder as the document that you're working on. To jump to a bookmark (or named anchor) in another document, append its name to the URL in either of these formats: `http://www.gurus.com#goodstuff` or `ourbooks.htm#msworks`, in which the bookmark name follows the # sign. For other possibilities, refer to Chapter 7.

## Using Corel Presentations

Use Corel Presentations for image maps only if you can't or don't want to use Live Image. The process has three steps. First, Corel Presentations plays a macro (a sort of program) that helps you create image maps. These maps are separate HTML files that you then insert into your document by using WordPerfect. Finally, you connect the graphic to the map by using the HTML Properties dialog box for graphics.

### Creating the image-map file

Corel Presentations is part of WordPerfect Suite 8; it may not be installed on your system. If not, get the CD-ROM and perform a custom installation, checking only Corel Presentations in the check boxes.

Before using Corel Presentations, publish your document to HTML in the usual way. Make note of the folder in which you're publishing your graphics (the second text box in the Publish to HTML dialog box). After you have published your document to HTML, take the following steps to create an image-map file:

1. **In Windows 95, choose Start➪Corel WordPerfect Suite 8➪Corel Presentations 8.**

   Click OK if an initial dialog box appears, mumbling about color schemes.

2. **Choose Tools➪Macro➪Play to display the Play Macro dialog box.**

3. **Double-click `Imgemap.wcm`.**

   The Create HTML Image Map Code dialog box appears.

4. **Click the tiny file-folder icon at the far right end of the Enter Bitmap text box, and browse to the folder to which you published the graphics for your HTML file.**

    To make finding the correct file easier, click the Toggle Preview On/Off button in the Open dialog box (the white-document button next to the yellow-folder-with-red-checkmark button).

 5. **Double-click the file that you want to image-map.**

    If WordPerfect created the file, it has a terrible name like `wpdoc0{image0}.gif`.

    You return to the Create HTML Image Map Code dialog box.

 6. **In the Save file(s) to text box, enter the location where your HTML document is stored; then click the OK button.**

    If you're following this book's recommendations, that location is `c:\MyFiles\website`.

    When you click OK, things flash by on-screen; your image appears; and you see the Image Map Macro dialog box.

 7. **Click OK.**

    Somewhere on-screen, an Image Map dialog box appears; find it but do nothing with it yet.

 8. **Click the image and drag diagonally across the first area that you want to link.**

    Press Esc if you make a mistake.

 9. **Find the little Image Map Macro dialog box on your screen and click the Set Map button.**

    The Link to URL dialog box appears.

10. **Enter the location (URL) of the document that you want to link to from this first area of the graphic.**

    Refer to the sidebar "A review of royalty: Types of URLs," earlier in this chapter for a refresher on entering Web locations.

11. **Repeat Steps 8 through 10 of this process until you set a URL for each part of the graphic that you want to link.**

12. **Click the Done button in the Image Map dialog box.**

    The Create Image Map Is Finished dialog box appears, telling you proudly what Presentations has accomplished.

13. **Click OK.**

Now you're done with Presentations; put it away and return to your document in WordPerfect.

## Inserting the image map into your document

If you used Presentations to create your image-map file, the file is named `bitmap.htm` and is located in the folder where you publish your Web documents. Now you need to insert the file into your document. Follow these steps:

1. **Press Ctrl+End to go to the end of your document; then choose Insert⇨File.**

    The Insert File dialog box appears.

2. **Browse to the folder where you publish your HTML Web documents (such as `c:\MyFiles\website\`) and double-click the file `bitmap.htm`.**

    The Convert File Format dialog box appears.

3. **Do *not* choose ASCII DOS Text, as WordPerfect most likely suggests; click the text box and choose HTML instead.**

4. **Click OK.**

Quite possibly, nothing will appear in your document at this point. In that event, the image map has been inserted, but it's formatted as hidden. (Choose View⇨Reveal Codes to see all the extra stuff.)

## Linking the image map to the graphic

If you used Corel Presentations 8 to make your image map, the final job is connecting the graphic to its map by using the map's name (not its filename). The macro in Corel Presentations 8 names all its image maps bitmap, so here is how you connect to a bitmap:

1. **In WordPerfect, right-click the graphic and choose HTML Properties from the QuickMenu that appears.**

    The HTML Properties dialog box appears.

2. **Click Map Link in the bottom-right corner.**

    A new tab appears in the dialog box, labeled Map Link.

3. **Click the new Map Link tab.**

4. **In the Name text box of the Map Link tab, enter** bitmap.

    The File text box should already say `<current document>`.

5. **Click the OK button when you're done.**

Now if you publish to HTML again and open the HTML file in your Web browser, the image should be mapped. Click the graphic to test the links.

# Chapter 21
# Documents That Sing and Dance

**In This Chapter**

▶ Singing documents (audio)
▶ Dancing documents (animated GIFs and videos)
▶ Documents with 3-D stuff (VRML)
▶ Documents that use Java applets and JavaScript

It's time for the fun stuff. You've sweated through line spacing, hyperlinking, formatting, styles, fonts, and tables, and now it's time to party. Wanna sing? Add sound. Wanna dance? Add an animation or video. Wanna get real? Add 3-D virtual-reality worlds. To complete the all-singing, all-dancing cast of toe-tapping technology, throw in some Java and a few stupid browser tricks from Chapter 23, and you have a Web site that's capable of inducing a migraine in a 12-year-old Nintendo player. Go for it, I say.

## Singing Documents

Mr. Gutenberg probably is spinning in his grave, but documents can now sing, play music, talk, and make rude noises. At least he's spinning to a funky beat.

Sounds come in various forms on the computer; files called WAV, AU, and MIDI are among the most common. WAV and AU files are sound recordings and are quite large compared with MIDI files of the same duration. MIDI files are, in essence, a musical score that tells the software what notes to play. Corel provides a small collection of these files in the `corel/suite8/sounds` folder. You can hear most of these files simply by opening them in your browser (I enjoy simply dragging them to the browser).

Before you attempt to use any audio files in your document, you must have the file in the correct location. Copy your WAV, MIDI, or AU file (a file that ends in one of those sets of letters) to the outgoing graphics folder — where you publish your graphics files when you publish the current document to HTML. If you're following the recommendations of this book, for the document `c:\MyFiles\website\index.htm`, the graphics folder is `c:\MyFiles\website\index`.

## Click-to-play sound

If you are going to include sound on your Web site, the most user-friendly approach is to design the page so that the visitor clicks something to play the sound. That way, the user specifically chooses to play the sound and can't blame you if that sound wakes the baby or scares the dog. Add some explanatory text or a graphic to indicate that the reader should click to play a sound.

Creating click-to-play sound is no more complicated than creating the hyperlink that you're probably already familiar with. In fact, all you are doing is hyperlinking to a sound file rather than another HTML file.

Refer to Chapter 7 if you need details on hyperlinking. Here are the basics for linking to an audio file (not to be confused with an audiophile):

1. **Select the text or graphic that you want the user to click.**
2. **Choose Tools⇔Hyperlink.**

    The Hyperlink Properties dialog box swings into action.

3. **In the Document text box, instead of entering an HTML file, enter the WAV, MIDI, or AU file that you have copied to your outgoing graphics folder.**
4. **Click OK.**

    Figure 21-1 shows the correct URL for a file named `welcome.wav` in the folder for `index.htm` (a home page).

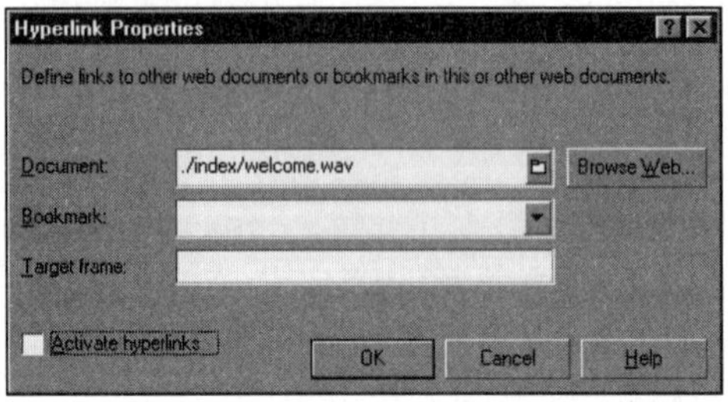

**Figure 21-1:** Linking to the welcome.wav file.

## Background sound

Background sound is sound that plays automatically when the page is loaded. Be careful not to annoy the visitor, as musical tastes vary from "Weird Al" Yankovic to the Mormon Tabernacle Choir. (For some of us, the ultimate musical experience is both parties in concert together.)

WordPerfect has no features for creating background sound, so you have to hack it yourself in HTML. Not to worry, however — the process is simple. Enter the following secret code anywhere in your document (say, at the bottom):

```
<EMBED SRC="./yourfolder/yourfile.xxx" HIDDEN=TRUE
           AUTOSTART=TRUE>
```

You can use capitals or not, as you like, for the non-italicized text. Substitute the name of your outgoing graphics folder for *yourfolder* and the full name of the audio file for *yourfile.xxx*. (As always, when linking to a file in a Web document, be careful to enter all upper- and lowercase letters in their proper case.) Select the line you have typed and then choose Fo_r_mat➪ _C_ustom HTML. Publish the result to HTML, load the HTML document file into an audio-capable browser, and enjoy the music. (At this writing, the View in Web Browser button doesn't do the job for background sound.)

## Inserted sounds

The good news is that WordPerfect comes complete with a sound-insertion feature. *In theory,* here's how that feature works:

Choose _I_nsert➪_S_ound; then click _I_nsert in the dialog box that pops up. Click the tiny file-folder icon in the next dialog box to browse to a WAV or MID (MIDI) audio file. Click the OK button, and viola — I mean voilà — you have the sound of a viola (or whatever) in your WordPerfect document. Click the tiny speaker symbol to play the sound.

You can even test the HTML result right there on your PC by clicking the View in Web Browser button; it works like gangbusters.

The bad news is that inserted sounds don't work if you publish to HTML — at least, in early releases of WordPerfect 8, they don't. WordPerfect doesn't properly handle the link to the sound file. In fact, several parts of this feature are so flawed that you may not even be able to insert the file in the first place. So forget about "inserting" sound until Corel fixes the feature.

The final word is, who cares? Inserted sounds are only click-to-play sounds that use a special speaker graphic. Do your own click-to-play sounds instead!

### Controlled sounds in Netscape Navigator

One way to keep your visitor in control of the sound experience — and also to indicate that a sound is available — is to provide a sound-control console with play, stop, pause, and volume controls. Figure 21-2 shows two consoles that are available in Netscape Navigator. (Microsoft Internet Explorer launches its own sound-playing console automatically, outside the Explorer window, whenever a sound file is played.)

**Figure 21-2:** Netscape's CONSOLE and SMALL-CONSOLE.

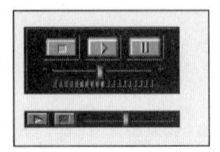

WordPerfect provides nothing to accomplish this effect, so you have to hack your own HTML. At the position in your document where you want the console to appear, type the following line:

```
<EMBED SRC="./yourfolder/yourfile.xxx" HEIGHT=60 WIDTH=144
            CONTROLS=CONSOLE>
```

Substitute the name of your outgoing graphics folder for *yourfolder* and the full name of the audio file for *yourfile.xxx*. Select the line and choose Format⇨Custom HTML. For the skinnier console in Figure 21-2, substitute SMALLCONSOLE for CONSOLE and change the HEIGHT setting from 60 to 15.

## Dancing Documents

Care to dance? Now your Web page can wiggle with the best of them. Add animation or a movie to liven up the page or illustrate some "moving" concept. Often, animations are used for banners that change text periodically, but they can be used for darn near anything that moves.

### Animated GIFs

GIF files don't necessarily have to contain just a single image; they can contain many images that appear in sequence, like frames in a movie. This effect is what is called an animated GIF file.

## Chapter 21: Documents That Sing and Dance 277

Animated GIFs are widely offered for downloading on the Web. Point your browser to www.yahoo.com and click the following categories in successive pages: choose Computers and Internet, then World Wide Web, then Page Design and Layout, and finally Graphics. After clicking Graphics, you see a category called Animated GIFs. Remember not to publish anything without explicit permission to do so.

*[On the CD icon]* This book's CD-ROM contains a trial version of an excellent and inexpensive tool called the Ulead GIF Animator, which, among its many talents, can help you create your own animated GIF. (You have two weeks after installation to see whether you like the tool, after which you need to purchase a license.)

Another excellent and inexpensive GIF animator is the GIF Construction Set. You can find this shareware program at http://www.mindworkshop.com (or go to www.shareware.com and search for GIF Construction Set). The folks at Alchemy Mindworks are the kind of free-spirited souls who say things like "Abuse of our e-mail resources may result in legal action or a leather-winged demon of the night dining on your pancreas" on their Web site and throughout their literature. They were too free-spirited to want their program to appear on this book's CD-ROM, however (even though I had already written about their tool), so go visit the Alchemy Mindworks Web site if you want to try the software.

Leather-winged demons aside, all you now need is a series of original bitmap images to string together to form an animation. How the heck do you do that? One answer is to create a temporary Web document that contains a WordPerfect graphic: ClipArt, TextArt, drawings, or even text boxes. These graphics are made of individual parts that you can move or rotate; you can also change their color. By copying and pasting the graphic, and changing these parts slightly each time, you can easily create a series of images to use in your animation, as Figure 21-3 shows.

**Figure 21-3:** Making the telephone "ring" visually.

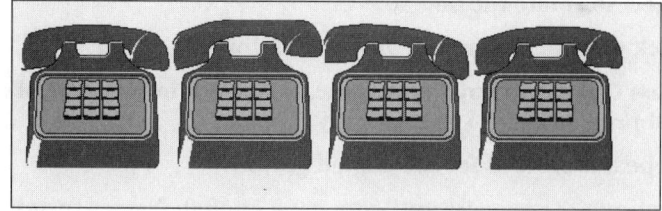

*[Tip icon]* You can make some cool animations with exceptional ease by using WordPerfect text boxes and TextArt! To animate ordinary text as a marching marquee, create a series of text boxes, making slight changes in each one in terms of text position, font, or text color. You can animate TextArt the same

way, including making some outstanding, rotating 3-D text by adjusting the rotation slightly each time. The images you create become a series of graphics files, which you can then string together to form an animated GIF file using one of the tools from this book's CD-ROM.

For samples of the original WordPerfect documents, the resulting GIF files, and the animated GIFs themselves, install this book's CD-ROM using the instructions in the back of the book. Then see the Author's Files from CD\GIF Animania folder on your hard drive. To see examples of the techniques that this section presents, load `animdoc.htm` into your Web browser from the folder.

Here's how to create the series of images by inserting and modifying Clipart:

1. **To begin editing the graphic, double-click it.**

    You now are using the WordPerfect drawing editor, so various graphics tools and the Graphics button appear along the WordPerfect Toolbar and Property Bar.

2. **Choose Graphics⇨Separate Objects to break the graphic into its components.**

3. **Click the selection tool (the black arrow in the toolbar); then click the part of the graphic that you want to change.**

    You may now drag that part to a new position (if your animation requires the part to change its position, and not simply rotate or change appearance).

4. **Choose Graphics⇨Rotate.**

    A collection of hard-to-see gray arrows appears around the selected object.

5. **Drag any of the hard-to-see gray arrows that appear around the object to rotate the object.**

6. **Click outside the graphic to exit the drawing editor.**

7. **Press Ctrl+C to copy the graphic; then click to the right of the graphic and press Ctrl+V to paste a copy.**

8. **Repeat Steps 1–6 for the copied graphic.**

9. **Continue the process until you have enough frames to suit you.**

    If you don't have any other guidelines, assume that you need ten copies of the graphic per second of animation.

Before you publish to HTML, set the temporary document's background color to whatever color you want to use as the background for the animated images. Then publish your temporary document to HTML. Each graphic becomes a separate GIF file that you can load into your GIF animation software.

## Animation with Ulead GIF Animator

*ON THE CD*

Install Ulead GIF Animator from this book's CD-ROM and then launch it from whatever program group you installed it in. Ulead's GIF Animator offers a convenient set of wizards, which I suggest that you use. Here is how to use the Wizards:

1. **Launch GIF Animator, and the Startup Wizard dialog box appears with some choices. Choose the Animation Wizard.**

   You can also rouse the Animation Wizard by choosing it from GIF Animator's File menu at any time.

   The Select Files dialog box appears.

2. **Click the Add Image button.**

3. **Browse to the outgoing graphics folder (the folder where you published the graphics files from your temporary document).**

   You see a bunch of GIF files with numbered names like `wpdoc0{image0}.gif`, `wpdoc0{image1}.gif`, and so on.

4. **Select all those GIF files in order by Ctrl+clicking them or by dragging a rectangle around their names from top to bottom.**

5. **Click the Open button.**

   Check the order in which the files now appear in the Select Files dialog box. You can rearrange their order by dragging them.

6. **Click the Next button to move to the Source Type dialog box.**

7. **For most animated WordPerfect art, choose Text-oriented (No dither).**

   For 3-D TextArt or other images that look like photographs, choose Photo-oriented (dither).

8. **Click the Next button to proceed to the Frame Duration dialog box.**

9. **Accept the dialog box's suggestion by clicking its Next button.**

   GIF Animator suggests a frame duration of $1/4$ second, which usually works pretty well for WordPerfect art. Feel free to adjust the slider to faster or slower, though.

10. **Click the Finish button.**

    GIF Animator displays your animation and then stops. To replay the animation, choose View➪Start Preview (or click the Start Preview button); to stop, choose View➪Stop Preview (or click the Stop Preview button).

GIF Animator initially creates an endlessly looping animation. Such animations are annoying, but on the other hand, single-run animations require a great many images to achieve a useful length. To adjust how many times your animation loops, follow the instruction in the callouts of Figure 21-4. In the white box on the left side of the GIF Animator window, click the line that says Global Information. Then look for the gray area of the window marked Looping and click to clear the Infinite check box. In the box below that check box, enter the number of times that you want the animation to loop.

If the background of any of your frames is black, it's probably transparent. To make the background opaque, click the frame's filename in the white box on the left side of the GIF Animator window; then find and clear the Transparent index check box. Alternatively, to make the other frames transparent, click their filenames and then select the same check box.

At this point, you can simply save your GIF by choosing File⇨Save. To make the animation faster to download and more clean-looking, however, first choose File⇨Optimization Wizard and then click Next in each wizard window to accept all its fine suggestions. When you're done, the wizard proudly displays your shorter, faster, newly optimized GIF file. Click the Save As button, and save your work.

If you want to view your animation in a browser, simply open the GIF file in the browser (it doesn't have to be in a document). Insert the animated GIF file into your actual document (not the temporary one where you made the individual frames of the animation), as you would any other GIF file.

## Animation with GIF Construction Set

Download and install GIF Construction Set (the 32-bit version), and launch it by choosing Start⇨Programs⇨GIF Construction Set 32⇨GIF Construction Set 32. Then choose File⇨Animation Wizard. The Animation Wizard does a fine job of stepping you through the process with clear instructions, so I won't repeat them here, but here are a few tips for some of the steps:

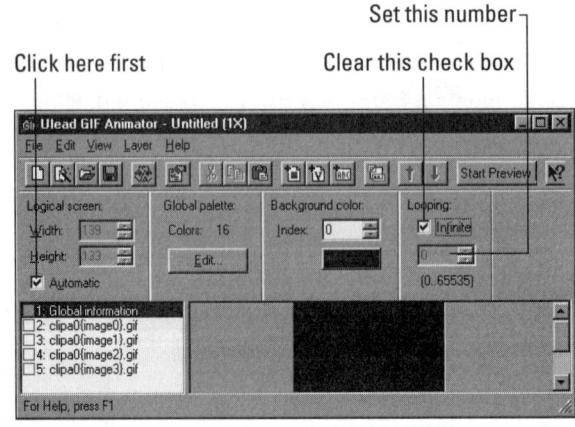

**Figure 21-4:** Loop control in Ulead's GIF Animator.

## Chapter 21: Documents That Sing and Dance 281

- Indefinitely looping animations are tedious; but single-run animations require a great many images to achieve a useful length. If you're unsure what to choose, choose Animate Once and Stop. Then see the tip near the end of this list that provides instructions on looping a given number of times.

- Images that result from using most WordPerfect graphics are (in terms used by GIF Construction Set) "drawn" or "drawn in 16 colors." 3-D TextArt is, however, "photorealistic."

- A short delay — say, $^{10}/_{100}$ of a second — is often a good choice for animating WordPerfect graphics. (You won't actually get that speed, but you won't slow the animation, either.)

- When you are asked to select files, look in the folder where you published the graphics files from your temporary document. You see a bunch of GIF files with numbered names like `wpdoc0{image0}.gif`, `wpdoc0{image1}.gif`, and so on. Double-click each of these files in numerical order. Then click the Cancel button in the Open dialog box.

- After you click the Done button, you see a techie-looking window. Simply click the View button to see your animation. (Press the Esc key to stop a loop.)

- To add a loop of a given number of repetitions, click Insert; click Loop; click Edit; and then set the number of iterations. (Pay no attention to the note about Netscape.)

- Save your work by choosing File⇨Save. A good place for the file is the outgoing graphics folder for the document in which you want to use it.

After you create the new GIF file, save your temporary document as a WordPerfect document to make future edits possible. Insert the animated GIF file into your actual document (not the temporary one), as you would any other GIF file.

## *Video (movies)*

Many Web browsers today can display several forms of video (movies), but bear in mind that displaying video on a Web page remains a dicey proposition. Not all computers are powerful enough to display good video. Several kinds of video files exist, and not all browsers are equipped to display all the kinds. What's more, video files tend to be enormous and take a long time to download.

The three most popular file formats for video are MPEG, AVI, and QuickTime. Your Web-site visitors may well need additional software (plug-ins) besides the standard browser to view these files. In general, PC users are somewhat more likely to be able to view AVI files; Mac users, to view QuickTime movies; and workstation users, to view MPEG movies.

You can make videos appear in a window on a Web page, but because video files take so long to download and may require software that your visitor does not have, displaying video in a window generally is not a good idea at this time. Instead, simply hyperlink some text or a graphic on your page to the video file. Only if the visitor clicks the hyperlinked text or graphic is the file downloaded to the visitor's browser. The procedure is exactly the same as linking to a sound file, except that you link to an AVI, QT or MOV (QuickTime), or MPG (MPEG) file. Refer to "Click-to-play sound," earlier in this chapter for instructions.

If you really want to put video in a window on your Web page, and if you have the file in AVI format, consider converting it to an animated GIF file. Ulead's GIF Animation tool and GIF Construction Set software both do good jobs of converting AVI files to animated GIFs. The quality is significantly reduced in the process, but so is the file size. The gavel.avi file in Corel's movies folder, for example, is reduced from 401K to 256K when GIF Construction Set converts it to an animated GIF file.

## *Converting AVI to GIF in Ulead's GIF Animator*

Converting an AVI file to GIF in the Ulead GIF Animator is quite painless. Use the following steps:

1. **Choose File⇨Animation Wizard.**

    The first of many dialog boxes named Select Files appears.

2. **Click the Add Video button.**

3. **Browse to any AVI file and double-click it.**

    (Corel provides some AVIs in its `corel/suite8/movies` folder; I like using `currency.avi`.)

4. **Click the Next button in the Select Files dialog box.**

    The Source Type dialog box appears.

5. **Choose Photo-oriented for an AVI that looks realistic, as though it was taken with a camera. For clip-art-like images or images that feature mostly text, choose Text-oriented.**

6. **Click Next again; then click Finish.**

At this time, consider optimizing the file with the Optimization Wizard. See the end of the earlier section, "Animation with Ulead GIF Animator," for information on the Optimization Wizard. Not all AVI conversions can be easily optimized, however.

## Converting AVI to GIF in GIF Construction Set

To convert an AVI file to a GIF file, first install GIF Construction Set, if you have not done so already. Then follow these steps:

1. **Launch the GIF Construction Set program.**

   If you followed the standard GIF Construction Set installation, choose Start▷Programs▷GIF Construction Set 32▷GIF Construction Set 32.

2. **Choose File▷Movie to GIF and browse to select your AVI file.**

   The Movie options dialog box appears (see Figure 21-5), allowing you to choose how you want to compromise quality: through dithering or remapping.

   GIF files can have only 256 colors, whereas AVI can have 16 million. To bridge the gap, GIF Construction Set must either use dots of varying colors to approximate a color in the original file *(dithering)* or choose as close a single color as it can find among the 256 *(remapping)*. Narrow down your choice to the two dithering options if you wish to sacrifice image clarity for color accuracy, or to the two remapping options if you wish to sacrifice color accuracy for clarity. To narrow down your choice to one option, you must choose a palette. For better viewing in Netscape Navigator, choose Netscape 216-color palette. Otherwise, choose 256-color orthogonal palette.

   Your final option is looping, in which the movie repeats endlessly (sort of like cable TV programming). To loop endlessly, click the Loop check box.

   Click OK in the Movie Options dialog box and sit back for a long wait. When GIF Construction Set finally displays a window full of techie-looking stuff, it's done with the conversion.

**Figure 21-5:** Choose your compromises in GIF Construction Set.

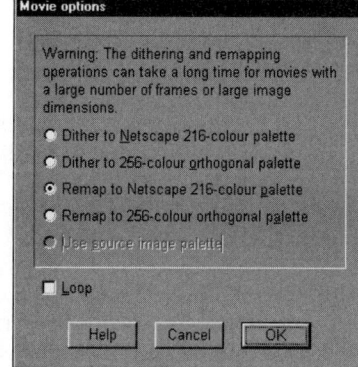

Save your work by choosing File⇨Save. A good place for the file is the outgoing graphics folder for the document in which you want to use it.

# Documents with 3-D Stuff in Them

To get truly weird, you can create three-dimensional objects, or virtual-reality worlds, for your Web site. These objects are not simply images, but 3-D objects that you can walk around (or through) and worlds you can navigate through, just like in a video game.

To view these worlds, Netscape Navigator for the PC uses a Live3D plug-in; you may have to download the plug-in separately from Netscape, depending on what version of Navigator you are using. Other browsers also typically need plug-in software. Navigator helps you acquire the software that it needs from the Netscape Web site if you try to view a 3-D world without the software.

Creating objects and worlds requires either writing computer code known as VRML (Virtual Reality Modeling Language) or getting hold of a VRML authoring tool. To find VRML software, try the Netscape VRML Resources Page, which at this writing is `http://home.netscape.com/comprod/products/navigator/live3d/vrml_resources.html`.

To learn more about viewing and building VRML worlds of your own (without having to learn the VRML language), pick up a copy of *VRML and 3D on the Web For Dummies* (IDG Books Worldwide) by Doug Muder and yours truly.

You can find VRML authoring tools in either of two states of maturity: VRML 1.0 (in which you can create shapes and worlds) and VRML 2.0 (in which you can also animate your world and add sound and stuff). Some authoring tools that are inexpensive, fun, and fairly easy to use include 3D Website Builder (see `www.virtus.com`) and Virtual Home Space Builder (see `www.paragraph.com`).

You can sometimes find free VRML objects and worlds on the Web, in files that end in WRL, WRZ, or GZ. A few possible sources are `www.viewpoint.com`, `www.paragraph.com`, and `www.caligari.com`. If permission to use a model is granted, download it into the outgoing graphics folder where you publish your graphics to HTML. The model may be in the form of a ZIP file, which you need to unzip with WinZIP.

To use VRML worlds on your Web site, either link to them as this chapter describes for click-to-play audio files or write the following stuff in your Web document:

```
<EMBED SRC="./yourfolder/yourfile.wrl" HEIGHT=200
WIDTH=200>
```

Substitute the name of your outgoing graphics folder for *yourfolder* and the full name of the VRML file for *yourfile.wrl*. Select the line and choose Format➪Custom HTML. Then publish to HTML and view the result in Netscape Navigator.

## Singing, Dancing, Java-Stimulated Documents

Java, to hear all the hype from techie types and their marketing minions, is the answer; it doesn't matter what the question is. Soon, everything from toasters to toddlers will run on Java. (Personally, I currently run on French roast.)

Java is a programming language. Programmers use this language to write programs that run only in certain warm, supportive environments, such as inside Java-enabled Web browsers. (You can't run Java programs right in Windows, for example.) These programs come in various forms:

- Java applets (which have nothing to do with Apple computers)
- JavaScript (a mutant form of Java)
- Java beans and other cute names, which currently don't have much to do with the Web

A Java program allows a document to be more *interactive:* to respond to inputs by the viewer in ways other than the usual, which is downloading a file (HTML, audio, or other) in response to a click. A Java program can, for instance, sense the mouse position even if the mouse is not being clicked and can display something about the item on the page that the mouse is passing over. A Java program also can do calculations or other processing based on information that the viewer provides. The viewer can enter mortgage information, for example, and the program can calculate a payment schedule. A Java program can even do complex things over the Internet, such as running an online live chat room.

### Java applets

Java *applets* are common forms of programs used on the Web. WordPerfect has a special feature that allows you, too, to use applets.

Frankly, obtaining and customizing applets is tricky. Applets are not really ...*For Dummies* kinds of features, so be warned that if you use them, you have to wade through some technical stuff at some point. Still, applets are cool enough that you may want to try them anyway.

Creating an applet takes a programmer. When programmers create applets, they usually design the applets to accept custom instructions from Web-page designers (like you). An applet that displays a graphical banner with text and animated fireworks, for example, might allow you to choose what text is displayed, what font size and color to use, and what dimensions to make the banner.

Therefore, using an applet involves two steps: creating the applet and giving it your custom instructions. A programmer creates an applet by writing in the Java language and then compiling the program into a binary (computer-readable) file. When you see the applet, it consists of one or more separate files called class files, plus possibly a few other graphics or sound files. You put the custom instructions in your HTML document invisibly by choosing WordPerfect's Insert⇨Java command. (The instructions are not visible in a browser.)

For the entire scheme to work, the HTML file and the applet files must all be on the Web server. Most of the time, the files are in the same folder, but that arrangement is not necessary as long as the HTML file knows where to get hold of the applet files.

When you have the class file and its associated files, WordPerfect provides a way for you to enter the custom information in your HTML document. You have to know what sort of information the applet wants, of course.

### *Applets: How to get 'em*

You could learn the Java language, obtain a Java Development Kit (JDK) or other Java development tool set from Microsoft or www.javasoft.com, and write your own applets. You could also juggle angry cats in your underwear.

A second (and nearly as painful) approach is to obtain from the Web free Java source code (files written in the Java language) from the nice people who offer it. Then, using your handy JDK tools, you compile these files into the actual applets.

A milder form of this amusement is to obtain some form of program that allows you to assemble a program out of dialog boxes, text, graphics, and other components and then spits out Java applets as its output. Tools such as Microsoft Visual J++ and Symantec's Cafe Lite are reputed to be worthwhile. Still, using them is programming.

> ## Using FTP software to download
>
> Some Web sites may advise you to use FTP software rather than your browser to download applets and may give you a link address that looks something like `ftp://ftp.frenchroast.com/pub/java/coolapp.zip`. Fortunately, you have WS_FTP on this book's CD-ROM, so you can do as these sites suggest. Launch WS FTP and enter the company's domain name (such as `frenchroast.com`) in the Host Name/Address text box of the Session Properties dialog box. Unless the Web site gives you a login and password, click the Anonymous check box and enter your e-mail address for Password. (Otherwise, enter the login for User ID and the password for Password.) Finally, click the OK button.
>
> If you succeed in connecting, you can browse to the correct folder given in the link address. In the right pane of the WS FTP window, for a link address of `ftp://ftp.frenchroast.com/pub/java/coolapp.zip`, open the pub folder and then the java folder. Click the file (say, `coolapp.zip`). In the left pane, browse to the folder where you want to keep the downloaded file. Finally, to download the file, click the left-arrow button in the column between the two WS FTP panes. Click the Close button when you're done.

I (and the other bottom-feeders in the Java food chain) get applets from the Web. Set your browser to www.yahoo.com, and navigate your way through these categories: Computers and Internet, Programming Languages, Java, and Applets. In the Applets category, you find links to many applets and companies that make applets. You can download and use a fair number of applets for free. Just be careful who you get applets from, because badly or maliciously written applets are capable of making life unpleasant on your PC.

To use an applet, you need two basic things:

- The class file (usually *something*.class) and any associated files for the applet, such as graphics or sound files.
- Documentation that describes what sort of custom information (parameters or HTML tags) to give to the applet. Documentation may be right on the Web page or in a downloadable ZIP, TXT, or DOC file. A sample HTML file will do, instead of documentation.

Exactly how to obtain these files sometimes is obscure. Here are a few ways to get applets on the Web:

- Follow a link to the source of the applet. This source may include the class and documentation files that you need; it may instead just be files in the Java language (*something*.java), for which you need special tools. In the latter case, forget it.
- Follow a link to download a ZIP file that contains everything, including documentation and class files. You need a program called WinZIP to decompress the file.
- Follow links to a documentation file, plus a ZIP file described as being for Netscape Navigator or a CAB file for Internet Explorer. CAB and ZIP files for a given browser are compressed packages that you put on your Web site in their entirety; you don't need to decompress or unzip them. These ZIP or CAB files may, however, be in one big master ZIP file along with the documentation, which you need to unzip.

### *Using applets by copying from a sample HTML file*

If you have a sample HTML file that uses the applet, open the HTML file in WordPerfect, but choose ASCII DOS TEXT instead of HTML when the Convert File Format dialog box appears. Then follow these steps:

1. **Copy the class files (usually *something*.class) and any associated graphics or audio files to the folder where you publish your HTML Web file.**
2. **In the sample HTML file that's open in WordPerfect, select the block of text that starts with** `<APPLET CODE=` **and ends with** `</APPLET>`**; then press Ctrl+C to copy it.**
3. **Open the Web document to which you want to add the applet in WordPerfect, or start a new Web document.**
4. **Click where you want the applet to appear; then press Ctrl+V to paste it.**
5. **Select all the gobbledygook that you just pasted and choose Format⇔Custom HTML.**

At this point, the basic stuff that you need to use the applet is in your document. If you publish to HTML, putting the HTML file in the same folder with the applet files, you're done. Try the HTML file in a Java-enabled browser, such as Navigator or Internet Explorer. (The browser may need to go online to the Web, for reasons known only to itself or the applet programmer.)

Unfortunately, the WordPerfect version of your Web document now looks ugly and remains so as long as you continue to save it and edit it as a WordPerfect file. You may, however, decide to perform your edits in the HTML file from now on. If you do so, the ugly gibberish is replaced by a nice tidy applet window (canvas), and you can use the WordPerfect Insert⇔Java⇔ Modify Applet command (described in the following section) to customize the operation of the applet.

If you choose, instead, to edit the ugly WordPerfect version of the document in order to customize the operation of the applet, edit the red, double-underlined text that has been formatted as Custom HTML. The things that you modify are in quotation marks. Assuming that you can see through the technospeak, you can learn what things can be changed to by reading either the applet's documentation or the comments placed right in the red text.

### *Adding or customizing applets with WordPerfect's applet feature*

When you have the applet files, open the documentation file (if one exists) for reference. Then follow this procedure to install a new applet in your document or modify the behavior of an existing one:

1. **If you haven't already done so, copy the class files (usually *something*.class) and any associated graphics or audio files to the folder where you publish your HTML Web file.**

2. **Open your Web document or start a new Web document.**

3. **Click where you want the applet window (canvas) to appear and choose Insert⇨Java⇨Create Applet.**

   (If you're modifying an applet that's already installed in your document, choose Modify Applet instead of Create Applet.)

   The Create (or Modify) Java Applet dialog box appears (see Figure 21-6).

4. **In the Class text box, enter the full name of the class file (such as dostuff.class).**

   If you're modifying an applet, a name already appears in this text box.

5. **Consult the documentation to find out what width and height the applet needs, and enter those values in the Width and Height boxes.**

6. **To add space around the applet canvas area, increase the values for Horizontal Space and Vertical Space.**

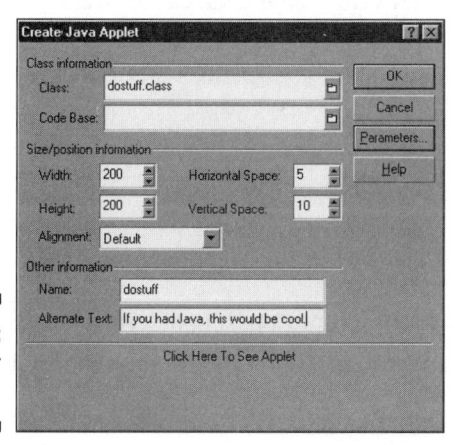

**Figure 21-6:**
Going for Java.

7. **Consult the documentation to find out what the name of the applet is (if one exists); then enter that name in the Name text box.**

    Be careful to duplicate uppercase and lowercase letters precisely.

    If you're modifying an applet, a name already appears in this text box.

8. **Enter some text in the Alternate Text box to amuse people who don't have Java-enabled browsers.**

9. **Click the Parameters button.**

    The Java Applet Parameters dialog box appears (see Figure 21-7).

Figure 21-7: Adding yummy parameters to your Java.

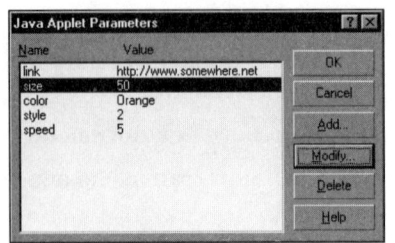

10. **Consult the applet documentation for information on parameters.**

    Each parameter has a name and can take on certain values — numerical or text. These different values are how you customize the applet for your own use.

11. **For each new parameter that must be set, click the Add button in the Java Applet Parameters dialog box or press the Enter key.**

    If you are modifying the parameters of an applet that you installed earlier, click the Modify button instead.

12. **In the tiny dialog box that appears (see Figure 21-8), enter the parameter name and your chosen value; then click OK or press the Enter key.**

Figure 21-8: Adding or modifying parameters.

13. **Repeat Steps 11 and 12 until all parameters are set.**

14. **Click the OK button in the Java Applet Parameters dialog box.**

15. **Click OK in the remaining dialog box.**

    You should see a rectangle in your document that includes the words *Java Applet* and the name of the applet's main class file.

Publish to HTML, putting the HTML file in the same folder with the applet files. Open the HTML file in a Java-enabled browser, such as Navigator or Internet Explorer. (The browser may need to go online to the Web, for reasons known only to itself or the applet programmer.) You will either be amazed or incredibly frustrated.

## *JavaScript*

JavaScript is, in many ways, more useful than Java for the Web-page designer. JavaScript is a programming language that you can write into your Web page, so you don't need special tools, as you do with Java. JavaScript can't do everything that a Java applet can, but it can open and otherwise control windows and frames; perform calculations; display things in the browser window; respond to clicks and data entries; and more.

Unfortunately, JavaScript is too complicated to explain in this book. If you have some experience with programming, you may be able to pick up a few hints from the following two examples. A quick way to start learning is to check out Netscape's JavaScript Guide, which (as of this writing) is at this URL:

```
http://home.netscape.com/eng/mozilla/3.0/handbook javascript/
```

If the guide has been moved when you look, just search the Netscape Web site for JavaScript Guide.

Be aware that many non-Java browsers are still in use, and their users cannot see anything that you do in JavaScript.

### *Entering JavaScript in your document*

If you decide to learn JavaScript and want to enter it in your document by using WordPerfect, you have to use a few tricks. Follow these steps:

1. **Type the JavaScript initially as regular text.**

2. **Follow the opening statement with a weird, incomplete-looking line, as follows:**

   ```
   <SCRIPT LANGUAGE="JavaScript">
   <!@hy anything you want or nothing here
   ```

   The preceding weird line that begins with <!, and the similar line that precedes the closing </SCRIPT> statement, keep JavaScript from appearing as text in non-Java browsers.

3. **Precede the closing** `</SCRIPT>` **statement with a full HTML comment line, like this:**

   ```
   <!-- anything you want or nothing here -->
   </SCRIPT>
   ```

4. **Format all your JavaScript by choosing Format➪Custom HTML; then format it in the Web by using Preformatted Text style.**

   If you do not use Preformatted Text style, you cannot include any line breaks!

5. **Change the text attribute to hidden, if you want to keep the code from cluttering your WordPerfect screen.**

The following sections provide two examples of JavaScript. The first example is simple and actually useful; the second one is more complex and has real value only as a learning aid. The actual JavaScript begins with `<SCRIPT LANGUAGE="JavaScript">` and ends with `</SCRIPT>`.

You can install these JavaScript examples to your hard drive from this book's CD-ROM. The installation instructions are in the back of this book. The examples are installed in the Author's Files from CD\JavaScript folder on your hard drive. You can insert the examples into your document by choosing Insert➪File.

### Opening a second window with a document in it

The following code opens a second browser window, 100 pixels wide by 50 pixels high, and loads the document window.htm into that window (the window name NavigationControls is an internal name for reference by other JavaScript code):

```
<SCRIPT LANGUAGE="JavaScript">
<!--
window.open('window.htm,'NavigationControls','width=100,height=50')
<!-- -->
</SCRIPT>
```

You can change the size of the window by editing the width and height values. You can also change the name of the HTML document that's loaded into the window from window.htm to anything else you want. If the other document is not in the same folder as the one that you're putting this code in, you need to consult Table 7-1 in Chapter 7 for strange prefixes that need to appear before the document name.

### Performing a calculation on user input

You can actually do something with text or numbers that a user enters. Following is a document that contains a crude calculator, which performs a not-very-accurate multiplication or division function on two numbers entered by the user. The JavaScript part comes first, followed by an HTML form.

Several things are going on in this chunk of JavaScript:

- The browser reads the JavaScript and runs it, but doesn't run the functions until they are called by another statement.
- The form has a name that I assigned to it: userinput.
- The various inputs in the form have names, which are also defined as variables in the beginning of the script and given initial values.
- The action begins when the user clicks the Do It button, which is defined by a statement in the form area. A function called onClick reacts to the button click and calls the calc function, which I created in JavaScript.
- The calc function makes a decision based on whether the user entered an asterisk (*) for multiplication. Then the function calls either the multiply function or the divide function.
- The values entered by the user are stored in variables whose full names start with the word document (meaning the current document in the browser window) and continue with .userinput (meaning the name of the form in which they were entered), .inputval1 (the name of the variable), and .value.

Following is the code that implements a crude calculator in JavaScript:

```
<SCRIPT LANGUAGE="JavaScript">
<!--Persuade non-JavaScript browsers that code is comment
document.write("Enter two numbers and * for multiply, / for
     divide:");
var inputval1=0.00;var inputval2=0.00;
var operator="+";

function multiply(){
document.write("<P>Here is the product: ",
     document.userinput.inputval1.value*document.userinput.
     inputval2.value, "</P>");
}

function divide(){
document.write("<P>Here is the result: ",
     document.userinput.inputval1.value/
     document.userinput.inputval2.value, "</P>");
}

function calc(){
if (document.userinput.operator.value=="*") multiply();
else divide();
}
```

*(continued)*

*(continued)*

```
<!--End of faux comment here: -->
</SCRIPT>

<FORM NAME="userinput">
<P>First number: <INPUT NAME="inputval1" TYPE="text" SIZE =
    "10" MAXLENGTH="10"></P>
<P>Enter "*" or "/"<INPUT NAME="operator" TYPE="text"
    SIZE="1" MAXLENGTH="1"></P>
<P>Second number:<INPUT NAME="inputval2" TYPE="text" SIZE =
    "10" MAXLENGTH="10"> </P>
<INPUT NAME="doit" TYPE="button" VALUE="Do It"
    onClick="calc()">
</FORM>
```

# Chapter 22
# Forms and Feedback

***

## In This Chapter

▶ The sad truth about forms
▶ Copying or borrowing an existing CGI script
▶ If CGI scripts are not for you
▶ How forms and scripts communicate: names and values
▶ Creating a form
▶ A cheesy JavaScript compromise
▶ Forms and tables

***

So now you have a Web site. What has it done for you lately? If the answer to that question is "Not much," the reason may just be that you're not using your site well. Web sites aren't much more than electronic bumper stickers unless they actually give you something: information. The lack of any means of feedback or other information from visitors is what keeps most homegrown Web sites from being truly useful to their owners.

For you, the Web weaver, the easiest way to get feedback is to have the visitor e-mail you. For the visitor, however, the easiest way to give feedback is to enter data in a form, just like a paper form. So what do you do? Read on.

## The Sad Truth about Forms

To make entering data fun 'n' easy for folks who surf the Web, the architects of the Web created a whole bunch of data-entry gizmos. You can put these gizmos (sometimes called *widgets*) on a Web page to create a form area: buttons with text on them, pictures that work like buttons, boxes for inputting text or numbers, checklists (for choosing several things in a list), menus, and option lists (for choosing one thing in a list).

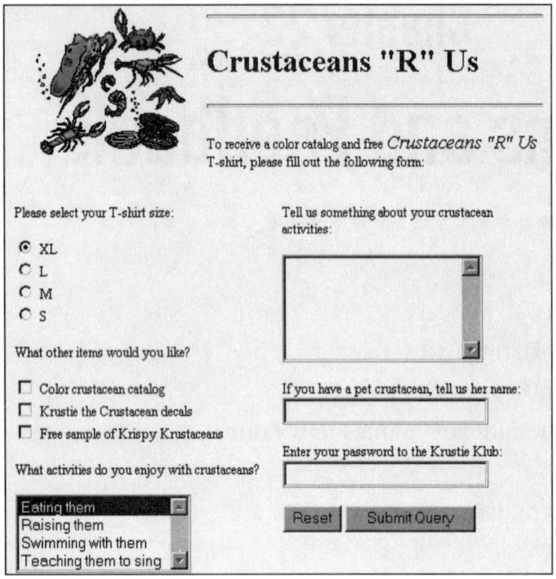

**Figure 22-1:** A form for visitors to fill out.

Sounds great, right? We should all run right out and put forms on our Web sites, right? But of course, there's a catch. Using forms requires much more than just creating a regular Web page. Here's what you need to do to use a form:

- Create the form on one of your Web pages for people to enter information.
- Put a program (called a CGI script) on your Web site to receive information from that form and either e-mail it to you or collect it as a data file.
- If the information isn't e-mailed to you by the CGI script, read and delete the data file periodically.

The first and last jobs are within reach of the amateur Web weaver. The second job, however, usually falls into the "you probably would rather wrestle rabid weasels in your underwear" category. (*You* being in the underwear, not the weasels. Hmmm. Try saying "Web weavers wrestle rabid weasels" five times.)

Weasels aside, the bottom line is: On most Web sites, you can't expect to use forms without help from a programmer. You can create the forms, all right; WordPerfect can help you do that. The problem is creating and installing a CGI script to match your form. Even if you download a prebuilt, tested CGI script from the Web and use it as it is, so many things can go wrong simply in installing it on your Web site that you need a programmer. Your Internet service provider may even charge you for reviewing the CGI script to make sure that it won't foul up the works.

What kind of programmer do you need? CGI scripts can be written in several languages, most commonly Perl but also C and a few others. The language depends largely on what kind of computer the server runs on. If you are sharing space on your Internet service provider's Web server, the language probably is UNIX. In that case, you most likely need someone who's experienced in UNIX and Perl — and, in particular, in writing CGI scripts. In other words, any random 12-year-old ought to serve just fine.

> With some Internet service providers (ISPs), including MindSpring (the ISP represented on this book's CD-ROM), you can escape the need for a programmer. These ISPs offer standardized ways to put forms on your Web site. For more about MindSpring's standardized forms see "Using Standardized Forms at ISPs," later in this chapter.

## Copying or Borrowing an Existing CGI Script

Unless you are a programmer, the chances of your being able to get a prebuilt script to run properly on your Web site are slim to none. Nonetheless, getting a CGI script, as opposed to creating it, is a possible option. The Web offers many scripts, but all need some form of customization or custom installation to run on each individual site. For scripts and information on scripts, check out the following URL:

```
http://www.yahoo.com/Computers_and_Internet/Internet/
         World_Wide_Web/CGI___Common_Gateway_Interface/
```

If you can find someone else on the same Web server who will allow you to copy a script, and also provide some guidance on how to customize and install it, your odds get even better. The script needs to be customized, however; otherwise, all your data goes to the person who gave you the script. Conceivably, someone on the Web server that you share is using a script that you can share as well. All that you need to do at that point is direct your form to use that script and set a hidden input value to your e-mail address. This scheme typically is available only when your organization owns its own Web server.

## Why You Still May Care about Forms

Don't give up yet. You may still be able to use forms if any of the following statements are true:

- Your ISP provides standardized forms, or offers MIT's *cgiemail*. (See "Using Standardized Forms at ISPs," at the end of this chapter.)
- Your Web site already uses forms, you just need to add or modify one.
- You've found an experienced CGI script programmer with whom you can work.
- You are secretly a CGI script programmer or aspire to become one.
- You don't care about feedback from visitors, but you're a programmer and want to use the various form gizmos to create a useful interactive Web page (such as a mortgage calculator or random horoscope generator) in JavaScript (or VBScript).
- You are fond of weasel-wrestling or don't wear underwear.
- You can write some JavaScript or VBScript and don't mind using a slightly cheesy approach.

Hence, this chapter mostly discusses forms. If at this point, forms have lost their appeal to you because of the difficulty of using a CGI script, at least read the next section. That section, "If CGI Scripts Are Not for You," discusses using e-mail for feedback. If you're ready to charge ahead and use forms, skip the next section.

### A few modest proposals for getting feedback

If your site is for a business or an organization whose work involves any sort of outreach to other people (such as a church or volunteer organization) you should at least be soliciting visitors' names and addresses by e-mail. People rarely dispense personal information without some sort of quid pro quo or payback, of course, so you need to figure out what that payback is. (Also, it's a good idea to commit yourself to *not* share that information with anyone else and to *not* send the visitor e-mail, other than what the visitor asks for.)

Some of the possible incentives that you can provide for leaving information on your site are a brochure, a coupon, a T-shirt, a chance to win something, a downloadable something-or-other, a subscription to your newsletter, an e-mail notice when your organization does something important, a free ticket to your seminar series, admission to a trade show, or credit toward the visitor's first order with you. To arrange for a downloadable something-or-other to be presented when a form is submitted, speak to your CGI script programmer.

## If CGI Scripts Are Not for You

If CGI scripts don't appear to be your cup of tea (or tangle of weasels), you should still provide some way for people to e-mail you easily. The absolutely simplest way to do that is (and this is cute) to just type your e-mail address on your Web page! This simple trick is one of the nicest conveniences of WordPerfect 8.

If you type any e-mail address in WordPerfect (in Web view) and follow it with a space, WordPerfect automatically converts the address to a mailto hyperlink. When your visitor clicks that link, an e-mail program on the visitor's computer launches (in most cases) with your e-mail address already in place. (Success depends on how the computer is set up and what browser is used.) At the very least, your visitor sees your address and can manually enter it in an e-mail program.

If you want to make the fact that you're using a mailto link less obvious, you can hyperlink a graphic or other text to a mailto URL; see Chapter 7 for more information. That way, your visitor can click something that says `Request your free T-shirt!` instead of `moe@3stuges.com`.

The advantage of e-mail, of course, is that you don't need to install a CGI script on your Web server. The problem with e-mail, compared with a form, is that people are less likely to use it. Also, e-mail provides you no way to prompt people for the information that you want. A compromise between the two exists, however, if you can write some JavaScript; see "A Cheesy JavaScript Compromise," near the end of this chapter.

## How Forms and Scripts Communicate: Names and Values

A form page is one of two partners in the information-gathering process. The form is the partner that resides on your visitor's Web browser; gathers information; and, when the user clicks a Submit button, transmits the information back to your Web site. The other partner — the CGI script — is a program that resides on your Web site, interprets the data that's being sent, and either stuffs the data into a file for you to read at your leisure or e-mails it to you.

As is true of any partnership, the two partners must be coordinated if they are to work together. The CGI script expects certain things; the form must provide those things. Unless you are going to create your own CGI scripts (or your Internet service provider provides some form of special software), the script is the boss. Your form must conform to whatever script you have.

The chunks of information that forms transmit to CGI scripts have names. Both the script and the form must agree on what those names are. The script and the form may agree, for example, that the chunk containing whatever information the visitor types in the Your First Name box on the form will be named FIRSTNAME. The information that these chunks contain (perhaps Tom, Dick, or Harry, in the case of FIRSTNAME) is called their *value*.

You must give each gizmo on the form one or more of these names. So, what names should you use? The names that your CGI script requires.

If you're creating a new form to work on a Web site that already has forms, you find out what names to use by getting the current name for each gizmo of an existing form. Open the existing form document in WordPerfect, double-clicking each gizmo and noting the content of the Name field in the dialog box that appears. (You may even want to use that form as a starting point for your new form, edit it, and publish it to HTML under a new name.) If you're creating a new form, request the input value names from your CGI script programmer. The section "Using gizmos: their names and values" tells you how to read the names from gizmos on existing forms, as well as how to assign names to new gizmos.

# Creating a Form

A form is a special area of a Web page. In WordPerfect, you create the area by inserting a form (choose Insert⇨Create Form). What gets inserted is not a form, but a pair of odd, yellow, D-shaped symbols, as shown in Figure 22-2. To create a form, you insert various data-input gizmos, plus any regular Web-style text or graphics that you want, between the symbols.

While you are working between the form symbols, the Property Bar displays a special set of buttons that are called out in Figure 22-2. These buttons insert the various data-input gizmos or otherwise help you control the gizmology of the form.

***Note:*** You can have more than one form on a page, but if you do, each form needs its own Submit button for sending the data to the Web server.

## Using gizmos: their names and values

You can insert all kinds of clever data-input devices (I call 'em gizmos; others call them objects or widgets) into a form. To insert a gizmo, click anywhere between the yellow form symbols on your Web page; then click one of the gizmo buttons that appear in the Property Bar. Add explanatory text before or after the gizmo. The following sections describe the different types of gizmos and how they work.

## Chapter 22: Forms and Feedback

[Figure 22-2 screenshot of Corel WordPerfect showing a form "Crustaceans "R" Us" with T-shirt size radio buttons (XL, L, M, S), annotated with callouts:]

- Set properties of entire form or selected gizmo
- Insert box for entering a password
- Insert box for entering one line of text
- Insert box for entering multiple lines of text
- Insert "combo" box
- Insert list (to select one item)
- End form
- Begin form
- Insert image in place of Submit button
- Insert Submit button (to send data)
- Insert Reset button (to clear data entries)
- Insert hidden field (for secret stuff)
- Insert check box (for choosing several options)
- Insert radio button (for choosing one option)

**Figure 22-2:** Buttons can help you make buttons.

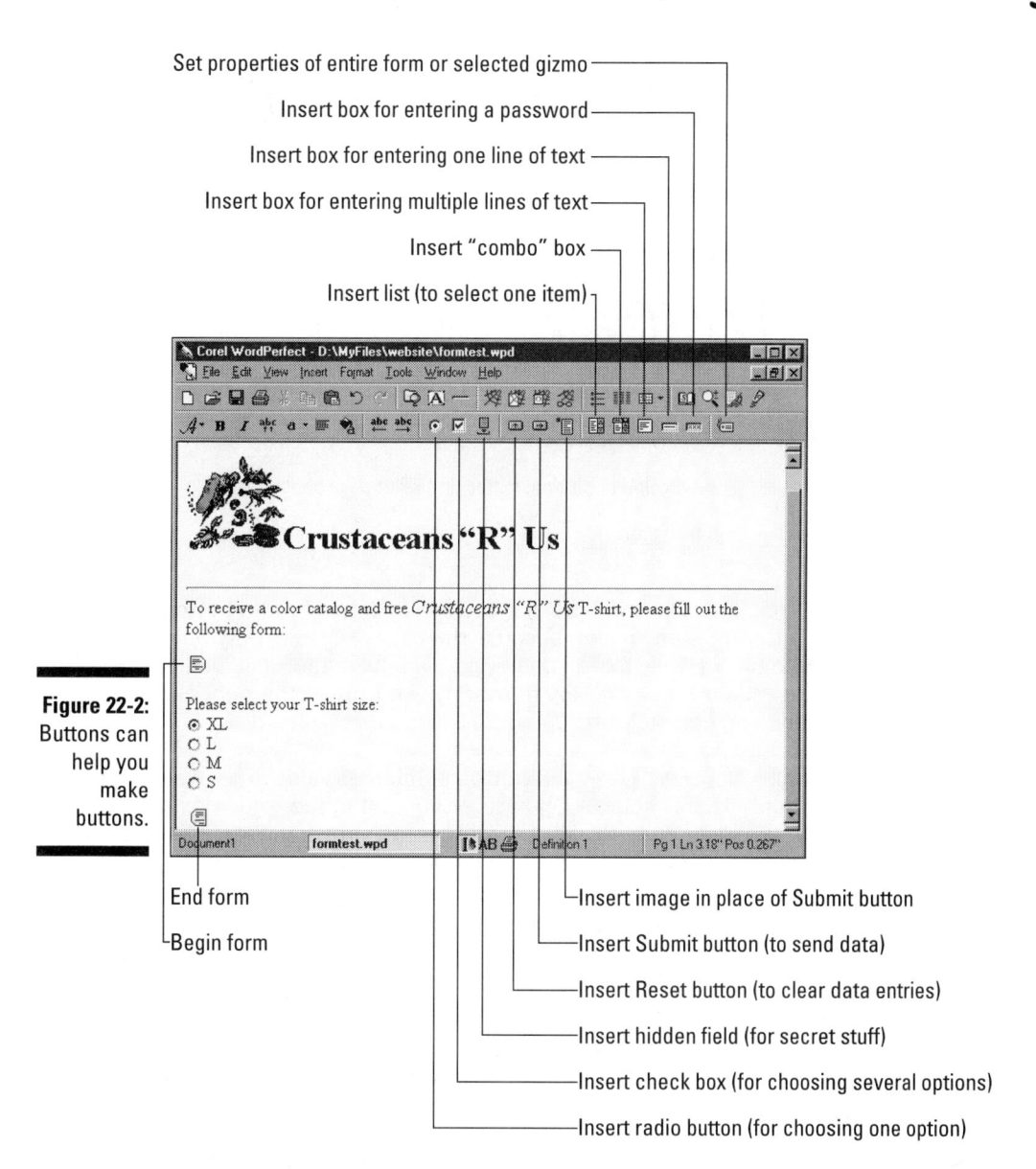

### Radio buttons

*Radio buttons* are the dot-in-a-circle gizmos that you see in Figure 22-2. Use these buttons when you want the user to choose only one of several options. In Figure 22-2, these buttons are used to choose T-shirt size. (The buttons are called radio buttons because they work like the buttons on a car radio; only one can be selected at a time.)

To program a radio button, either double-click it or click immediately before or after it and then click the Form Properties button in the WordPerfect Property Bar. The Radio Button Properties dialog box appears (see Figure 22-3).

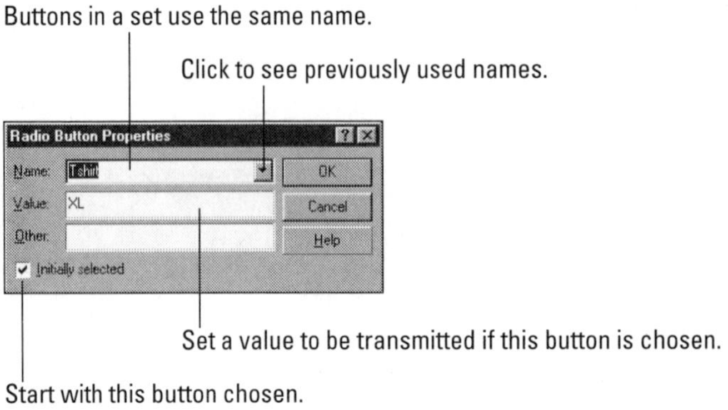

**Figure 22-3:** Programming a radio button.

Buttons in a set use the same name.
Click to see previously used names.
Set a value to be transmitted if this button is chosen.
Start with this button chosen.

In the Name box, give each button a name. In a set of radio buttons, give each button the same name, because the user can make only one choice. The radio buttons shown in Figure 22-2 each have the same name: Tshirt. To reuse a name, click the tiny down-arrow button at the right end of the Name box and choose the name from the list that drops down.

You should, however, give each button a different value in the Value box. When that button is selected, whatever you put in the Value box is transmitted with the name that you chose. The button shown in Figure 22-3, if chosen, transmits the value XL with the name Tshirt.

To cause a button to be selected when the form initially displays, click the Initially selected check box.

### Check boxes

*Check boxes* are the boxes that your visitor clicks to display a check mark. Use check boxes when multiple choices are okay. In Figure 22-4, the visitor can choose which exciting gifts he or she wants to receive.

Use the same procedure to program check boxes that you do to program radio buttons (double-click 'em). A dialog box just like the Radio Button Properties dialog box appears (refer to Figure 22-3).

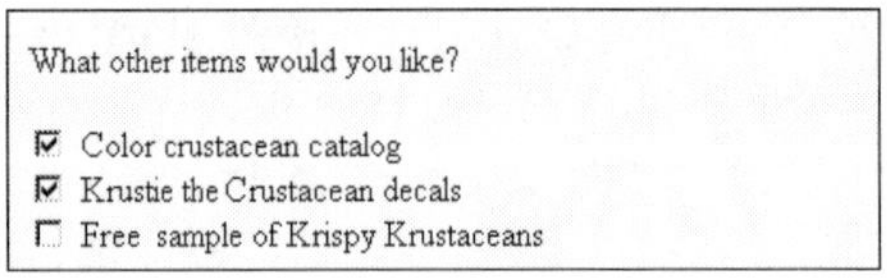

**Figure 22-4:** Check your crustaceans.

With check boxes, however, give each box a different name. Depending on how your CGI script writes your report, the value that you assign could be something like Yes for all the check boxes or something different for each one. If your CGI script reports both the name and the value, for example, a value of Yes would be fine, and your report might say CATALOG: Yes, KRUSTIE: Yes, KRISPIES: No. If your CGI script reports only the values, you would want to set your values to Catalog, Krustie, and Krispies, respectively.

### Selection lists

You can use selection lists for exclusive selections (such as T-shirt size) or multiple selections (such as what gift is wanted), depending on how you program them. Figure 22-5 shows a selection list that's programmed to allow multiple selections, and Figure 22-6 shows the dialog box that programs the list. To program a selection-list gizmo, double-click it; the dialog box shown in Figure 22-6 appears.

**Figure 22-5:** Choosing one or more items in a list.

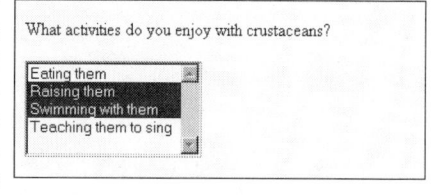

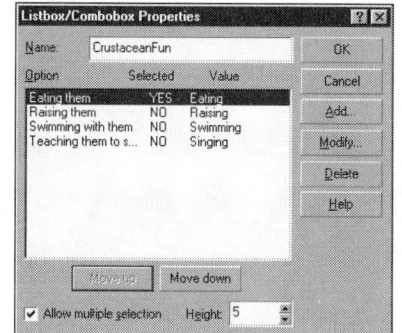

**Figure 22-6:** Adding items to the list.

Here is how to program the various items in your list:

   ✔ Enter a name for this selection list (such as GiftChoice) in the Name box.

   ✔ Click the Add button to add each item in the list, and in the dialog box that appears, set what value is to be transmitted to the Web server. The value should be different for each item.

- As you add items, they are listed in the Option window of the dialog box.
- To change the order of an item in the list, click it and then click the Move up or Move down button.
- To modify an item, click it and then click the Modify button.
- To delete an item, click it and then click the Delete button.
- If you want people to be able to choose more than one option by Ctrl+clicking options, click to select the Allow multiple selection check box.
- In the Height box, set how many lines of text the window should display.

### Text areas

Forms can accept text input by the user. To allow the user to ramble at length, use a text area. Text areas are often used for sending a message or special request, just as in e-mail. Figure 22-7 shows how the text area looks in a browser. Figure 22-8 shows the Text Area dialog box that appears when you double-click the text area in WordPerfect.

**Figure 22-7:** A space to write messages.

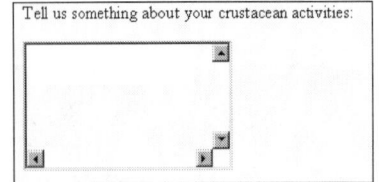

**Figure 22-8:** Set the name, width, height, and wrapping.

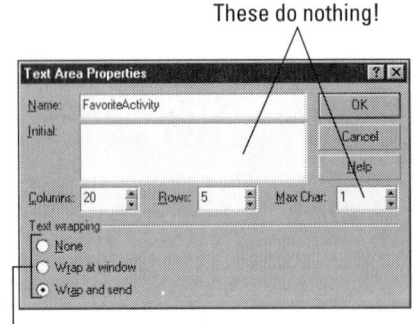

These do nothing!

Choose some form of wrapping.

Give the text area a name in the Name box, just as you do with any gizmo. Set the width in Columns and the height in Rows. Usually, allowing some form of wrapping (other than None) is good, because folks get confused when they can type beyond the box limits. I like using the Wrap and send option, because it preserves the line breaks that your visitor uses.

Two features in the Text Area Properties dialog box are not useful. The Max Char feature, in other gizmos, limits how much text the user can type. Unfortunately, this feature doesn't apply to text areas (in HTML 3.2) and Corel should not have included it; leave that setting alone. At this writing, the Initial text box feature, which in other gizmos specifies what text is initially displayed in the gizmo, appears to work in WordPerfect but fails to work in the HTML document.

### Text and password lines

If you want to receive only a single line of text from your visitor, use a text line. For passwords, a special form of the box displays only asterisks (*****) as the user types. Double-click the gizmo, and the dialog box shown in Figure 22-9 appears.

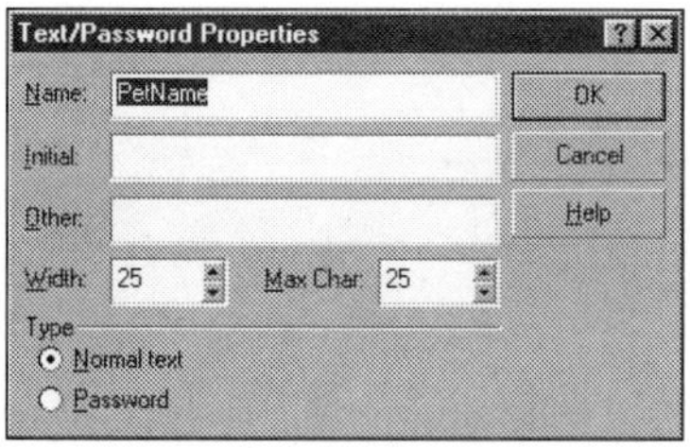

**Figure 22-9:** To keep user input to a minimum, use a single line.

As always, give the gizmo a name in the Name box. Set Width for the box — and, because users can type far beyond the box width, also specify the maximum number of characters that the box can have by setting the Max Char option. If you want to preset the box with some text, enter that text in the Initial box (just remember that your text counts toward the Max Char limit). To create a password box, choose Password in the bottom-left corner.

### Reset buttons, Submit buttons, and images

To send the information on its way from the form to the CGI script, every form needs a Submit button (or a clickable image that does the same thing). Also, because people make mistakes, a Reset button can be useful, especially if you preset a great deal of initial text and other values.

After you insert a button or image (by using the Reset, Submit, or Submit Image buttons in the Property Bar) double-click the gizmo to program it; the Button Properties dialog box appears. Unlike other gizmos, these buttons don't require names. Feel free to use names, but only in strange JavaScript applications do they matter.

Choose Reset or Submit in the Button Properties dialog box to determine which kind of button you get. Normally, the buttons simply say Reset or Submit; to substitute your own words, enter them in the Label box.

### Hidden fields

CGI scripts often require *hidden fields:* information that doesn't appear on the form itself. If your programmer tells you to include a hidden field, get the required name and value, and click the Hidden Field button in the Property Bar to enter them.

## Connecting your form to your CGI script

Your form has to be programmed to communicate with your script. Ask your programmer for the following information:

- What the URL for the form's action is
- Whether to use the `Get` or `Post` method
- If the `Post` method is used, whether a `MIME` attribute is needed and, if so, what the attribute should be.

With that information in hand, do the following steps to link your form to your script:

1. **Click immediately to the right of the first form symbol (the yellow D-shaped thing) in your document.**
2. **Click the yellow tag icon in the WordPerfect Property Bar.**

    The Form Properties dialog box appears.
3. **Enter the URL for the form's action in the Action URL text box.**
4. **Choose the Get or Post method.**
5. **Enter the MIME attribute, if necessary, in the MIME Script text box.**
6. **Click OK.**

## A Cheesy JavaScript Compromise

If you like the look of forms and can write JavaScript but balk at using a CGI script, don't give up yet. You can perform a cheesy trick that combines the attractiveness (to visitors) of a form and the convenience (to you) of using e-mail: Have your visitor e-mail you data from the form! This trick is amateurish, but that fact is not really obvious until after the visitor fills out the form.

Unfortunately, people can't just e-mail a form as they e-mail any other Web page (as an attachment or as text); the data that your visitor enters is not actually on the page. As a result, you, the Web weaver, must do some JavaScript programming to create a real page that does have the data entered.

Provide a form, but include no actual Submit button. Instead, execute a JavaScript function in your document from a form's button created in Custom HTML, modeled after this one:

```
<INPUT NAME="fakesubmit" TYPE="button" VALUE="Review &
    Submit" onClick="yourfunction()">
```

The button in the form is labeled Review & Submit. Your function should read all the input data and write a new page that displays all the input values that the visitor entered in some nice, human-reviewable form.

At the bottom of the page, instruct the visitor to e-mail the page to you. To make the process easier for the visitor, provide a mailto link button for the visitor to click. Also provide a few suggestions on how to attach the page to the e-mail message or on how to copy the page to the e-mail window. (Windows users, for example, should press Ctrl+A, press Ctrl+C, and then switch to the e-mail window and press Ctrl+V. Macintosh users have a similar arrangement; they press ⌘-A, ⌘-C, and ⌘-V.)

## Forms and Tables

Forms tend to look fairly ragged, because the gizmos get pushed around by text and because most Web text styles use a variable-pitch font, such as Times Roman. (*Variable pitch* means that each letter has a different width.)

To get the gizmos to line up nicely, using a table is a great solution. The trouble is that (as of this writing) WordPerfect doesn't show you the table controls when your insertion point is inside a form. Just to be symmetrical about this problem, WordPerfect also won't show you the form controls when your insertion point is inside a table! The solution is to create the two elements separately and then combine them.

First, insert the form, which displays the pair of form symbols. Then create the table. Finally, click the table; choose Edit⇨Select⇨Table; and then click on the table and drag the blinking insertion point to a point between the form symbols.

To add gizmos to the form, click between the table and the end form symbol, and insert the gizmos there. Select the gizmos, cut them to the Clipboard by pressing Ctrl+X, and then press Ctrl+V to paste them in the table cells. Yuck.

> **TIP:** If you have trouble selecting a gizmo, click next to it, hold down the Shift key, and then press the left- or right-arrow key to extend the highlight across the gizmo.

## Using Standardized Forms at ISPs

Some ISPs offer you a standardized way to create forms, so that you don't have to create and install a CGI script. (In these instances, the ISP has already created and installed a CGI script for you.) MindSpring, the ISP represented on this book's CD, offers their users one such way: software known as "MIT's *cgiemail*." You may find this same feature or similar features at other ISPs. Search your ISP's Web site carefully, looking for terms like *forms, mail forms, cgi scripting, cgi forms,* or *standard forms,* or send e-mail to your ISP's webmaster and ask about standard forms or the availability of cgi e-mail for your Web site.

MindSpring provides instructions for using their forms at their Help Desks. For users who have Web space at MindSpring through a standard dial-up account, the Help Desk is at `http://www.mindspring.com/~web/`. (For users who have purchased Web Hosting accounts, the Help Desk is at `http://webhelp.mindspring.com/`. Web Hosting accounts use a different technology than cgi e-mail.) You may find MindSpring's cgi e-mail instructions a little too broad, so following are more specific instructions on how to use cgi e-mail with WordPerfect to implement forms on your Web site.

***Note:*** MindSpring (or other ISPs) may change the way cgi e-mail is set up, so you may have to fine-tune the following instructions to get your forms to work properly. Read the Help Desk information on the MindSpring Web site, or contact MindSpring for assistance. Please don't e-mail me or IDG looking for instructions!

To use cgi e-mail, begin by creating a cgi e-mail template for your form. Create a new, normal (not Web-formatted) WordPerfect document, and enter text in the following form (including the blank line after the Subject line):

```
To: youraddress
From: [required-email]
Subject: Feedback from my Web site

First name: [firstname]
Last name: [lastname]
Address: [address]
City: [city]
State: [state]
Zip: [zip]
Country: [country]
E-mail address: [required-email]
Request: [request]
```

This document is the e-mail message you will receive back from your Web site, except that the visitor's information will be substituted for the stuff in brackets. Substitute your e-mail address at MindSpring for *youraddress,* and change the Subject line, if you like. Don't alter the From line.

The terms in brackets are names for the various pieces of information your visitor enters, as described in the earlier section, "How Forms and Scripts Communicate: Names and Values." You don't have to use the names listed above, you can use your own names (but use no spaces in the name, please). You can also add your own lines to this template; for instance, you could add the line "T-shirt size: [TshirtSize]" if you were giving away T-shirts. As in the preceding example template, where `[required-email]` appears twice, you may use the same name multiple times if doing so will make the information more readable to you.

Save this document as ASCII DOS text using the name `template.txt`. (Choose File⇨Save As, and in the Save As dialog box that appears, choose a File type of ASCII DOS Text, and enter a File name of `template.txt`.)

The next step is to create your form. Follow the instructions given in the earlier section, "Creating a Form." To name each gizmo you use, refer to your `template.txt` file: in the Name field for each gizmo, enter the name you entered in brackets [ ] in the template. For example, if you are using a text line gizmo to request the visitor's last name, and your template looks like the example shown earlier in this section, enter `lastname` in the Name field for the text line.

When you have created your form with all the gizmos you need, do the following to connect your form to MindSpring's built-in CGI script:

1. **Click immediately to the right of the first form symbol (the yellow D-shaped thing) in your document.**

2. **Click the yellow tag icon in the WordPerfect Property Bar.**

   The Form Properties dialog box appears.

3. **Enter the following line in the Action URL text box:**

   ```
   /cgi-bin/cgiemail/~mailbox/template.txt
   ```

   **Substitute your own MindSpring mailbox name for the word *mailbox*.** If you are using a different ISP from MindSpring, you will need to obtain the proper Action URL line from them.

4. **Click Post in the Form Properties dialog box, then click OK.**

5. **Publish your newly created form page to HTML.**

Transfer both the HTML file you have just created and the `template.txt` file to your Web site. Put the `template.txt` file in the top-level folder of your Web site, not in any subordinate folder you may have created.

Go online to the Internet, point your browser at the HTML file containing your form, fill out and submit the form, wait a bit, then check your mailbox for e-mail messages. You should find a message from your Web site that looks a lot like `template.txt`, but displaying the data that you entered on the form instead of the names in brackets.

# Chapter 23
# Stupid Browser Tricks for Special Effects

*In This Chapter*
- Automated slide shows
- Embedded multimedia
- Internet Explorer scrolling marquees

*I*n the same spirit that the *Late Show with David Letterman* offers stupid pet tricks, this book offers stupid browser tricks: tricks that actually are fairly clever, but that don't necessarily work with every Bowser — I mean, browser. These tricks are features invented by Netscape or Microsoft for their particular browsers. In some cases, the company's chief competitor decided to implement that feature; in other cases, not.

## Automated Slide Shows in Navigator and Internet Explorer

Netscape invented a technique called *client pull* for displaying one document after another, creating a timed slide-show effect in which each document is a new slide. I think that the technique actually is fairly useful, but it's rarely used anywhere on the 'Net — possibly only because the documentation on Netscape's Client Pull Web page is (at this writing) incorrect! The correct method is given by the following numbered steps.

Client pull is simple to use in WordPerfect (although you do have to type some gobbledygook). What's more, although client pull is a Netscape-invented feature, Microsoft Internet Explorer also runs it.

You can also do timed slide shows by using Corel's Barista technology. Refer to Chapter 5 for details.

The basic idea is that each document contains a timer and a pointer to the next document. You have to put special code in each document to have the entire series work. Follow these steps to put timers and pointers in each document:

1. **Create the Web documents that you want to appear in sequence.**
2. **Open the first document and choose File⇨Properties (or click the calculator-in-a-web HTML Properties button in the Property Bar).**

   The HTML Document Properties dialog box appears.
3. **Click the Advanced tab.**
4. **In the Meta info box, enter gibberish like this:**

   ```
   <META HTTP-EQUIV=REFRESH CONTENT="n; URL=yoursite
   nextdoc.htm">
   ```

   Substitute a delay time (in seconds) for *n,* and substitute the full location (URL) of the next document for *yoursite/nextdoc.htm*. If your Web site is `http://www.flooble.net/users/willard`, the next document to be displayed is `rats.htm`, and you want a 5-second delay before it downloads, you use the following code :

   ```
   <META HTTP-EQUIV=REFRESH CONTENT="5; URL=http://
   www.flooble.net/users/willard/rats.htm ">
   ```

5. **Click OK.**
6. **Save your file and publish it to HTML.**
7. **Repeat Steps 2 through 6 for each of the other documents in sequence, each time specifying the location (URL) of the document to follow.**
8. **Copy your files to your Web site and test them.**

*Note:* In Step 4, you must use a full remote URL for the next document as described. You can't use relative addressing of any form, such as simply entering the filename. (For more about relative addressing, see Chapter 7.) If you want to test the effect on your PC before putting your pages online, you can use a local URL, such as `c:\myfiles\website\show1.htm`, but you have to change it to an Internet URL before you publish the Web pages.

# *Embedded Multimedia*

Netscape created a way to place various media files, such as QuickTime and AVI video files or VRML virtual reality worlds, in a window of any document. (See Chapter 21 for more information on video and virtual reality worlds.)

You have to write a little HTML to do so, but the code is easy to write (and it also works in Microsoft Internet Explorer). The process, called *embedding*, goes like this:

1. **Copy the media file to your outgoing graphics folder (the folder where your graphics go when you publish to HTML).**
2. **At the place in your document where you want the window to appear, type a line like the following:**

   ```
   <EMBED SRC="./folder/mediafile.xxx" WIDTH=pixelwidth
      HEIGHT=pixelheight>
   ```

   Substitute your outgoing graphics folder name for *folder*; substitute your media file's name and extension for *mediafile.xxx*; and substitute the window dimensions that you want (in pixels) for *pixelheight* and *pixelwidth*. (Most PC screens are 800 pixels wide.)
3. **Select the line that you just typed and choose Format⇨Custom HTML.**

Save your work, publish to HTML, and test your efforts by opening the document in your browser.

# Internet Explorer Scrolling Marquees

Microsoft has a cute stupid browser trick that displays a moving line of text, called a *marquee,* on your screen. The marquee text scrolls only in Internet Explorer. Netscape does not stoop so low as to implement this Microsoft feature, other than to display the marquee text as plain old nonmoving text.

> **TIP:** The easiest way to put a scrolling marquee in your Web document is to simply insert one from one of the files from this book's CD-ROM. To install the CD-ROM, see the instructions in the back of this book. Click your document at the place you want the marquee to appear; choose Insert⇨File; and browse to the Explorer marquees folder inside the Tricks folder, where you find a few WPD files with descriptive names. Choose a file to insert and then replace the `your text here` line with your own.

> **TIP:** Another way to create a scrolling marquee that works in Netscape, too, is to create an animated GIF file by using WordPerfect text boxes. Refer to Chapter 21 for more information about GIF animation.

You can create your own Explorer marquees, if you don't mind hacking some simple HTML code yourself in WordPerfect. Marquees can be programmed in a bazillion ways. Here's how to do the simplest form: a continuously repeating marquee that spans the entire width of the document. Basically, you place your marquee text between two terms, `<MARQUEE>` and `</MARQUEE>`, both formatted as custom HTML.

1. **Enter the text in your document at the point where you want your marquee to appear.**
2. **Select** `<MARQUEE>` **and choose Fo_r_mat⇨Custom HTML.**
3. **After** `<MARQUEE>`**, start a new line and type the text that you want to display in the marquee.**
4. **After the text, type** `</MARQUEE>`
5. **Select** `</MARQUEE>` **and choose Fo_r_mat⇨Custom HTML.**

For fancier special effects in your marquee, you can add any of the terms listed in Table 23-1 just before the final `>` in `<MARQUEE>`. `<MARQUEE LOOP=2 SCROLLAMOUNT=20>`, for example, makes the text scroll twice and sets the scrolling speed to 20 pixels per increment. In Table 23-1, the stuff in italics in the left column is what you replace with the stuff listed in the right column.

### Table 23-1     Fine-Tuning Internet Explorer Marquees

| Add This Term . . . | To Do This . . . |
| --- | --- |
| `BGCOLOR="`*color*`"` | *color* sets background color. |
| `BEHAVIOR="`*behavior*`"` | *behavior* can be `SCROLL` (the normal thing), `SLIDE` (scoot in and stay), or `ALTERNATE` (bounce back and forth). |
| `DIRECTION="`*direction*`"` | *direction* sets the direction of movement: `LEFT` or `RIGHT`. |
| `SCROLLAMOUNT="`*amount*`"` | *amount* is a number, giving the scrolling speed in pixels per hop. |
| `SCROLLDELAY="`*delay*`"` | *delay* is a number, setting a pause between repetitions (`1000` = 1 second). |
| `HEIGHT="`*height*`"` | *height* is a number that sets the marquee-box height in pixels (such as `10`) or percentage (such as `10` percent). |
| `WIDTH="`*width*`"` | *width* works like *height*, only widthwise! |
| `HSPACE="`*space*`"` | *space* is a number, in pixels, that creates margins to the left and right of the marquee. |
| `VSPACE="`*space*`"` | `VSPACE` works just like `HSPACE`, but creates a margin above and below. |
| `LOOP="`*times*`"` | *times* is a number, giving the number of iterations of the loop. |
| `ALIGN="`*align*`"` | *align* works like alignment for graphics that are character-attached: `TOP`, `MIDDLE`, or `BOTTOM`. |

# Part VI
# The Part of Tens

The 5th Wave — By Rich Tennant

"WHAT CONCERNS ME ABOUT THE INFORMATION SUPERHIGHWAY IS THAT IT APPEARS TO BE ENTERING THROUGH BRENT'S BEDROOM."

## In this part . . .

It's the digital age, right? How many digits are traditionally allocated to hands? Ten, right? Well, okay then. Here's the perfect answer to the digital age: The Part of Tens. Herein, find dexterous solutions to sinister problems. Find handy suggestions for design and tricks for manipulating your pages into the form you need. Armed with these suggestions, you can "limn" lines of poetic proportions and go "mano-a-mano" with . . . .

(*WHACK!* OW! Hey, give me a break! It's the last part.)

# Chapter 24
# Ten Design Do's

### In This Chapter
- Sketch your design first
- Use a consistent design throughout
- Provide a document title
- Pay attention to navigation controls
- Test your pages on multiple browsers
- Design your site for information-gathering
- Use color
- Provide alternate text for graphics
- Provide tables of contents for long documents
- Keep your pages up to date

When you do the voodoo that you do, be sure to follow these 10 design do's. They won't guarantee that you'll be listed in the Netscape What's Cool list, but they'll help you exude that air of professionalism that distinguishes the Webwise from the rank amateurs.

## Do Sketch Your Design First

Yes, making smudges on paper with a stick does seem to be a bit prehistoric; but a pencil sketch of your design at least serves as a checklist for making sure that you don't forget anything. A sketch also gives you ideas about what layout tricks you may need to use, such as tables or white space.

A pair of sketches — one for the home page and one for other pages — helps you figure out what design elements (such as banners and navigation controls) you can reuse throughout your Web site.

## Do Use a Consistent Design Throughout

Consistency in a Web site helps people use it more quickly and easily. You notice that one trait of professionally designed Web sites is consistent design throughout. The controls are always in the same place, and they always look and work the same. Headings and other Web styles are used in a consistent manner. Color is used consistently. Many of those sites, however, generate their Web pages on the fly by computer; for those sites, consistency is easy (and, in fact, unavoidable). You need to exercise a great deal more control to achieve the same effect.

One way to ensure consistency is to create a template file or simply an ordinary WordPerfect file that you use as a starting point. Put text and graphics in to serve as placeholders. Reuse this file every time you add a new page to your Web site.

## Do Provide a Document Title

Web document titles appear in the (usually blue) top bar of the browser window. Titles also appear in the Go or history list of browsers and in bookmarks, and are used by search engines on the Internet. Needless to say, titles are important in helping people find and return to your Web page.

WordPerfect normally makes a document title out of the first heading that you use (whatever heading level it is). You can set the document title yourself by choosing File⇨Properties to display the HTML Document Properties dialog box. In the Title tab, enter a Custom title, as shown in Figure 24-1.

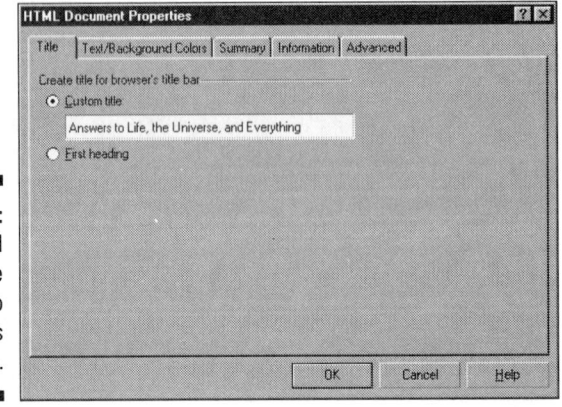

**Figure 24-1:** A title (and a tip of the hat to Douglas Adams).

## Do Pay Attention to Navigation Controls

Essential to any multiple-page Web site are the navigation controls: a region of the page that contains a set of hyperlinks to the other pages on your site. Make sure that these controls appear in the same place on each page.

Good navigation controls work whether the visitor's browser displays graphics or not. That flexibility means that you must either provide a separate set of text and graphical controls, or provide a separate graphic for each button and use "alternate" text for each button.

If you use a clickable graphic as a control panel, provide a set of text hyperlinks that duplicate its function, as shown in Figure 24-2. Place these links unobtrusively on your Web page, either in small type below the graphic or at the bottom of the page. If you locate the links remotely from the clickable graphic, put "alternate text" in the graphic to tell the reader where they are.

**Figure 24-2:** Duplicate graphical controls with text hyperlinks.

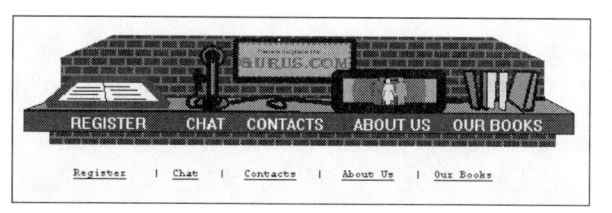

## Do Test Your Pages on Multiple Browsers

Publishing to HTML is not like publishing on paper; not every viewer sees the same thing. Different browsers treat text styles differently, changing fonts, sizes, and line spacing. Special effects are particularly vulnerable to different forms of execution — or even nonexecution, in the case of stupid browser tricks that aren't standard HTML.

Test your pages by using browsers from different vendors and of different ages (many people do not have the latest browser). Test your pages not only on your PC but also online to make sure that all the links work.

## Do Design Your Site for Information Gathering

A Web site is little more than an electronic bumper sticker unless you involve people personally in some way. The best way is to make it easy and attractive for visitors to give you their names and addresses so that you can invite them to events or offer them things. Invite people to give you that information and offer something of value in return.

A commercial site should use an information-gathering form, although using a form requires help from a programmer. A noncommercial site can simply use a mailto URL, which the user clicks to initiate an e-mail message to you. To create a mailto link, simply type your e-mail address, followed by a space. WordPerfect automatically formats the address as a link. See Chapter 22 for more information on forms and feedback.

## Do Use Color

Color makes an enormous difference in the appeal and readability of a Web site, if it's not overdone. Even if your site is strictly academic, simply putting the headings in a single color makes your treatise (say, "Sibling Sibilance in Censorious Sasketoonian Speakers") far easier on the eyes.

Color coordination helps people sort information visually, too. Using a particular color for each subject on your Web site, both on the pages and in the links to those pages, makes the structure of your site clearer.

To adjust the color of your text and background, choose Format➪Text/Background Colors. See Chapter 9 for more details.

## Do Provide Alternate Text for Graphics

People often turn off the graphics on their browsers, and many people still do not have browsers that are designed to display graphics. (Really!) If you put alternate text on your graphics (which displays when graphics are turned off), these people can view your Web site and choose for themselves whether to take the time necessary to view your graphics.

To apply "alternate" text, right-click the graphic, choose HTML Properties from the QuickMenu, and enter the text in the Alternate text box of the Image tab that appears. See Chapter 11 for more information.

## Do Provide Tables of Contents for Long Documents

If your document is several screens long, create WordPerfect bookmarks at each heading; then, at the start of the document, create a table of contents that's hyperlinked to those bookmarks. The reader can simply click any subject in the table of contents to go to that discussion.

To create a bookmark, select the subject heading, choose Tools⇨Bookmarks, and click the Create button in the dialog box that appears. To link to the bookmark, select a line in your table of contents; choose Tools⇨Hyperlink; and, in the dialog box that appears, enter the bookmark name in the Bookmark box. See Chapter 7 for more information about hyperlinking to bookmarks.

## Do Keep Your Pages Up-to-Date

People don't mind if a printed brochure is slightly out of date, but they expect a Web site to contain the latest information. One way to keep yourself honest is to provide "date last updated" information on each page. That way, at least people know whether the information is current (and if the information is not current, they will send you nastygrams by e-mail).

# Chapter 25
# Ten Design Don'ts

*In This Chapter*
- Don't make a long home page
- Don't make complex layouts
- Don't design for only one browser
- Don't use enormous graphics
- Don't use headings for body text
- Don't use "under construction" signs
- Don't rely heavily on fonts
- Don't trust the WordPerfect WYSIWYG display
- Don't use endlessly looping anythings
- Don't rely exclusively on graphics

The Web is full of wonderful examples of what *not* to do. Cruise a few minutes, and you will find yourself becoming annoyed, confused, delayed, or frustrated because people didn't follow the golden rule: Do unto your Web site what you would have others' Web sites do unto you.

## Don't Make a Long or Wide Home Page

Unless you have an extremely meaty Web site, offering scads of information that's absolutely essential for the survival of the human race, there is very little call for having a long home page. A home page should be a concise and persuasive table of contents for the rest of your Web site. (People don't like to scroll; dragging the mouse down a scroll bar is simply too exhausting, I guess.)

If people don't like to scroll down, they really, *really* hate to scroll sideways or to expand their browser window to accommodate a wide Web page. Such pages often result from a designer using a table for layout and giving the table a fixed width in pixels instead of using a width that's a percentage of the browser screen. Wide pages also result from the use of wide graphics.

## Don't Make Complex Layouts

If you need to continuously fiddle and tweak and add lots of tiny hard spaces and tables to make your layout work out right, you're trying too hard. Besides, the fiddling probably won't work; it's like trying to comb your hair in a high wind. Every browser does things a little differently. A fiddle that you add *here* becomes an albatross around your neck *there*. Keep things simple. Work with, instead of against, the natural tendency of Web browsers to automatically line-wrap.

Also, don't make a bowl of spaghetti out of your hyperlinks. Your visitor doesn't want to have to click through three pages before finding the link to a certain page. Use a flat linking hierarchy, in which everything that's important is accessible within one or two clicks. Put as many of your links as you can on the home page, so that your visitors can get right to the information they need.

## Don't Design for Only One Browser

Designing for whatever browser you normally use is natural, but a mistake. Although Netscape is the most common browser by a substantial margin, Microsoft's Internet Explorer is the browser of choice for many people. Mosaic, one of the original browsers, is also widespread. And many distinguished people in academia and research use simple, text-only browsers such as Lynx.

As you design, plan to use advanced or browser-specific features only to enhance your page; don't rely on those features to carry essential information. The bottom line is to continually test your work in as many browsers as you can find, and adjust accordingly.

Also try opening your HTML files in other word processors, such as Microsoft Word. Word processors are a real test of how universal your design is, because they rarely implement the latest HTML features or the special stupid browser tricks.

## Don't Use Enormous Graphics

Enormous graphics files — and their cousins, enormous audio and video files — are the bane of the Web. Few things are more annoying than sitting around waiting for your browser to download some enormous gee-whiz file. Large graphics are particularly annoying if they contain the navigation controls that you need to move around the Web site because then you *must* wait for the graphic to download before you can go anywhere else.

If you need to communicate something that requires an enormous graphic file, make it optional — something that the visitor can click a link to see. Insert a shrunken version of the graphic in your document so that people can get the idea.

If you want to use a large graphic for navigation controls, consider breaking it into chunks, hyperlinking each chunk separately (with no border), and inserting the chunks tile-fashion into your document. That way, each chunk can be represented by alternate text, and folks who have graphics turned off can still use the controls.

## Don't Use Headings for Body Text

Some Web pages use headings for body text, and that design never looks good. Headings on the Web are all executed in bold — which, in electronic documents, rarely results in an attractive font. Bold fonts for use on paper are carefully designed by professionals to look good even though they are fatter than normal. (The fonts, that is, not the professionals.)

Bold fonts on computers usually are done with less finesse; they look chunky. Besides, bold fonts simply do not make good, readable body text, which is why you rarely see more than a paragraph of bold text in print documents.

## Don't Rely Exclusively on Graphics

If you use graphics to get around some of the limitations of the Web (such as using a picture of text in a fancy font), be careful not to rely on them exclusively. People turn graphics off when traffic is heavy on the Web.

Make sure that you include alternate text for each graphic. Provide text hyperlinks to back up clickable graphics. Try to live within the limitations of the Web, rather than plastering graphics over the cracks.

## Don't Rely Heavily on Fonts

The Web's recently added capability to use fonts is nice, but it's not standard. First, only Navigator and Internet Explorer currently handle fonts. Second, the user must already have the font that you specify on his or her computer.

Although many Windows 95 PCs have many fonts in common, Macintoshes and UNIX workstations do not. Using a font is fine, but be aware that many browsers ignore the font entirely and display everything in Times Roman or some other font.

## Don't Trust the WYSIWYG Display

Even though Corel labored mightily to make WordPerfect as Weblike as possible in Web view, the program still has a way to go. You can see the difference between WordPerfect and your Web browser simply by clicking the View in Web Browser button; I suggest that you do so regularly.

Text sizes are often different; line spacing is different; table column widths adjust freely in a browser; settings such as margins (which have no meaning on the Web) sometimes affect the display; and many other minor and major differences keep the WordPerfect Web view from being perfectly WYSIWYG (what you see is what you get). No WYSIWYG exists in Web development, of course, because browsers can legitimately choose to display things differently.

## Don't Use Endlessly Looping Anythings

Few new Web features are more annoying than the ones that sing or dance endlessly, trying to get your attention. The effect is like trying to hold a conversation with an adult near a swimming area where children are present; only practiced parents can tolerate the constant cries of "Look at me!" Although you may be proud of your digital progeny, its antics are less than charming to other people.

Although making an endlessly looping GIF animation, sound, or video file certainly is possible, it's rarely justified. Most of these special effects can be set up to loop a given number of times and then stop, which is far more appreciated by the Web surfer.

## Don't Use "Under Construction" Signs

If something is not already on your site, simply don't link to it. "Under construction" signs are justifiable only if the visitor has every right to expect something to appear on your site, but it's not there yet and truly will be soon. If you feel that you must put up such a sign, also provide the date when the information will be ready.

# Chapter 26
# Ten Common Problems

## In This Chapter
- WordPerfect displays error messages
- Regular documents lose formatting in Web view
- Can't find features in the menu
- Hyperlinks don't work
- Graphics don't display
- Graphics look speckly
- Text formats incorrectly
- Extra space appears in browsers
- Barista doesn't work
- Tables don't come out right

WordPerfect is a fine, lovely, and capable tool. Nonetheless, it has a vast number of peculiarities, quirks, and plain old bugs — especially when you use it for creating Web documents. Some of the problems you will encounter aren't WordPerfect's fault. The Web works in mysterious ways to display its wonders, and no word processor is going to be able to master all the Web's mysteries.

## WordPerfect Displays Error Messages

The usual cause of error messages when you're doing Web work in WordPerfect is that you haven't installed something — especially if you did a custom installation. Try a standard installation, or return to the custom installation and carefully check all the components of each chunk that you didn't install.

Barista is a separate feature, for example, as is Presentations 8. If you upgraded from WordPerfect 7 to WordPerfect 8, the Presentations that you see do not match the ones described in this book.

## Regular Documents Lose Formatting in Web View

If you're trying to create Web documents from existing WordPerfect documents, you often lose formatting for several reasons. First, the Web simply does not support many of the features that WordPerfect provides for paper documents. Second, if you used many white-space characters, such as tabs and spaces . . . shame on you! Get with it! Use paragraph, line, and document formatting.

If you're wedded to your tabs and spaces, before you switch to Web view, replace your spaces with [hspace] codes, and replace your tabs with multiple [hspace] codes. If, after you switch to Web view (and in doing so, convert the file format), the document still doesn't look right, try formatting it in Preformatted Text Web style. If you don't like the appearance of the font, choose another — but not Times New Roman! Setting the font to Times New Roman in Preformatted Text style just doesn't work! When you publish to HTML the text will revert to the Courier font normally used for the Preformatted Text style.

## Can't Find Features That This Book Describes

If you can't find the features described in this book on your WordPerfect screen, you probably haven't switched to Web view! The second likely possibility is that you are trying to use features that you haven't installed. The final possibility is that something is currently selected in your document, causing the menu selection to not be there or to be grayed out.

If the feature that you're looking for is present in the menu but grayed out, check to see whether a graphic is selected. Try clicking somewhere in the white space of your document.

## Hyperlinks Don't Work

The main cause of hyperlinks not working is that they use the wrong URL (also called a location or address). For a link to a document in the same folder, the URL should simply be the file's full name, such as rutabagas.htm. For a link to a document in a subordinate folder, the URL should begin with ./*folder*/ and end with the filename. For a link to a document in a parallel folder, the URL should begin with *../folder/*. For a document anywhere on the Web, the URL should be whatever address you would type in a Web browser to view that document, such as http://vegetables.org/rutabagas.htm. See Chapter 7 for more information about hyperlinking and URLs.

Another common cause, if the malfunctioning links are among your own documents, is using a different arrangement of folders on the Web site from the set on your PC. For more information on this issue, see Chapter 6.

Hyperlinks to your other documents may not work when you use the View in Web Browser feature. Instead, publish to HTML and open the HTML file in your browser.

Hyperlinks to your own documents won't work if their names change when you copy them to the Web server. Make sure, for example, that uppercase and lowercase letters are the same and that extensions (.htm or .html) are the same as they are on your PC.

# Graphics Don't Display

If you get a broken-looking symbol instead of a graphic, the HTML document can't locate the graphic (or the file isn't present in its proper folder). If the problem happens while your files are on the PC, this problem generally is the result of publishing to the wrong folders. One of the safest ways to publish is as Figure 26-1 shows.

**Figure 26-1:** Publishing the safe way.

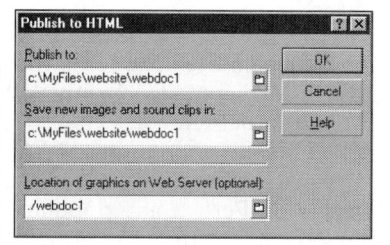

Anything else requires understanding URLs. Chapter 7 discusses URLs in the context of hyperlinking, but they work the same for the graphic files that are linked to your document.

Another possible cause, if the problem shows up first on your PC, is that you inserted a GIF or JPG file into your document but didn't copy it to your outgoing graphics folder (the folder that you entered in the second line of the Publish to HTML dialog box). For more information on this issue, see Chapter 11.

If you see Graphics Not Available in WordPerfect when you open an HTML file, you probably created the file by saving the document as HTML rather than publishing it to HTML. Saving a document as HTML does not result in the creation of Web graphics files, as publishing to HTML does. The Web files don't exist yet. If, when you created the HTML file, you also saved the document as a WordPerfect (WPD) file, you're in luck. Open that file instead, and your graphics will be present.

A final possibility, if the problem shows up only on the Web, is that you didn't copy your outgoing graphics folder to the Web site. Alternatively, you may have copied the folder to the wrong place.

## Graphics Look Speckly

Speckled graphics often are the result of forcing a big GIF image into a tiny box in your document. If you do that, the browser is given the job of making the image fit, and browsers really aren't graphics experts.

To solve that problem, shrink the actual pixel dimensions of the GIF image; see Chapter 14.

If you have graphics that remain speckly no matter what you do, try the Reduce Speckles touch-up effect in Corel Photo House; see Chapter 13.

## Text Formats Incorrectly

Fonts may not work if the computer on which the browser is running doesn't have the fonts that you specify. Also, fonts work only with Navigator, Internet Explorer, and any other browsers that choose to follow in the footsteps of these leading browsers. Fonts are not standard HTML.

Font sizes often do not agree between WordPerfect and popular browsers. Generally, WordPerfect displays the fonts larger than the browsers do.

If the problem is with fonts applied to text in Preformatted Text style (which normally is displayed in Courier), be aware that WordPerfect treats Times New Roman as a command to display that text normally — that is, in Courier! Weird.

Remember that multiple spaces count as a single space in HTML documents, in any Web style except Preformatted Text. Use Preformatted Text style to make multiple spaces visible.

WordPerfect seems to have a particularly difficult time keeping text that has been formatted as Custom HTML formatted properly. If problems occur with custom HTML, select the entire block of text, set it first to Normal style, and then reformat it as Custom HTML.

As always, WordPerfect is capable of getting confused because of extra or missing codes. Code view works for Web documents as it does for normal WordPerfect documents. Choose View➪Reveal Codes to check for extra, missing, or misplaced codes.

## Extra Space Appears in Browsers

If excess line space appears in a browser, several things may be at work. First, WordPerfect has its own ideas about spacing, and those ideas simply don't always match those of the popular browsers. Second, you may have a hidden paragraph mark in your text. Choose View➪Show ¶ to see any extra paragraph marks; then delete them.

You might also try using a line break instead of a paragraph mark (choose Insert➪Line Break). As an alternative, try using the Web styles Address (if you don't mind italics) or Definition List, which typically are displayed with single line spacing.

## Barista Doesn't Work

Barista is a leading-edge (some people might say bleeding-edge) technology. The idea is cool but has some funky spots. Not the least among those funky spots is the fact that to work, your Barista-generated HTML file must reside in the same folder with all the Barista files and folders.

Also, Barista files can use only three fonts at the moment; they don't do so well with special symbols; and if you don't have a Java-enabled browser, you're totally out of luck. For more information on the strengths and weaknesses of Barista, see Chapter 5.

## Tables Don't Come Out Right

The Web and WordPerfect both have definite ideas about tables, and those ideas are not quite the same. As a result, although Corel tried hard to give you Web tables, the result definitely is not WYSIWYG. The most frustrating part is that column widths on the Web balance according to the content, whereas WordPerfect insists on presenting columns of identical width. Corel also seems to believe that you can set the widths of columns individually, but in HTML 3.2, you can't. As a result, at this writing, WordPerfect's row- and column-size controls are useless.

# Chapter 27
# Ten WordPerfect Tricks

*In This Chapter*

▶ Automatic links
▶ QuickLinks
▶ Browse to link
▶ Automatic date
▶ Title from heading
▶ Automatically hyperlinked endnotes
▶ Text boxes as sidebars
▶ Comments
▶ Inserted spreadsheets
▶ Charts

*W*ordPerfect 8 is, in many ways, more fun than microwaving a basket of cherry tomatoes. The program comes with several cute tricks designed specifically to simplify the creation of Web documents; it also has all kinds of tricks for normal documents. Even though some of these tricks are useful only to a minority of WordPerfect users, a surprising number of them also work well for Web documents. This chapter provides a brief overview of some of these tricks, with references to places in the book where some of them are covered in more detail.

## Automatic Links

WordPerfect automatically converts any sort of Internet address to an appropriate hyperlink. Simply type the address, followed by a space. Any of the following examples result in an automatic link:

✔ yourname@yourplace.net
✔ http://www.snark.edu
✔ www.snark.edu

- `gopher://snark.edu`
- `www.phoo.com/snobble.htm`
- `www.phoo.com/snobble.htm#goobers`

The last two addresses in this list show the correct form for references to a particular document on a given Web site. The final address refers to a bookmark (or named anchor) called goobers that appears in that document.

## QuickLinks

QuickLinks are an adaptation of the WordPerfect QuickWords feature. The basic idea of QuickWords is that you type a given word or abbreviation, beginning with a special \ symbol, and WordPerfect instantly replaces that text with something that would have been more tedious to type. You could replace \uml with *University of Massachusetts–Lowell,* for example.

QuickLinks doesn't replace what you type, but turns it into a hyperlink to any full URL you want to use. QuickLinks words begin with an at symbol (@), followed by some word, such as *dummies.* You could program QuickLinks to create a hyperlink to `http://www.dummies.com` every time you type the word **@dummies**, for example. Choose Tools⇨QuickWords; then click the QuickLinks tab in the dialog box that appears. In the Link Word box, enter **@dummies**; in the Location to Link To box, enter **http://www.dummies.com**. WordPerfect deletes the @ and links the word *dummies.* For more information, see Chapter 7.

## Browse to Link

When you want to create a hyperlink to any document on the Web, you can simply browse to the document rather than enter the entire URL in the Hyperlink Properties dialog box. This feature saves many mistakes in linking to a document that has a long URL.

Begin by creating the link as usual, selecting a word or phrase, and then choosing Tools⇨Hyperlinks. When the Hyperlink Properties dialog box appears, click the Browse Web button. WordPerfect launches your Web browser so that you can browse to the location you want.

As you browse, the Document box of the Hyperlink Properties dialog box tracks where you are looking. When you get to the document that you want, click OK in the dialog box.

## Automatic Date

WordPerfect's automatic-date feature is a small, but nice, convenience for Web weavers who must keep certain pages up to date. A good Web page displays the date when it was last updated. If you insert an automatically updated date into the WordPerfect document from which the HTML file is published, every time you publish to HTML, the new date is applied automatically.

To use the automatic-date feature, choose Insert⇨Date/Time to display the Date/Time dialog box. Choose a date format and click the Automatic Update check box.

## Title from Heading

Web document titles are important because they appear in the top banner of a Web browser and in several other important places, such as the Go menu and bookmark list. WordPerfect automatically generates its document title from the first heading that you use. Usually, this feature is a convenience; sometimes, however, you want to use your own custom title. To customize the title, choose File⇨Properties. In the Title tab of the HTML Document Properties dialog box that appears, enter the text in the Custom title box.

## Automatically Hyperlinked Endnotes

A feature that carries over nicely from ordinary WordPerfect documents to Web documents is endnotes. Endnotes are like footnotes, but they appear at the end of a document. When you insert endnotes into a Web document, the tiny superscript endnote number becomes a hyperlink. Click that hyperlink, and your browser moves to the endnote!

To create an endnote, start at the point that you want to annotate (the word that gets the superscript number). Choose Insert⇨Endnote to display the Footnote/Endnote dialog box; then click the Create button. WordPerfect starts a numbered endnote for you. Fill in the note with as much text as you like. Then look w-a-a-ay at the right end of the Property Bar (the bar of stuff just above your document) for a file-folder icon, and click it.

## Text Boxes as Sidebars

WordPerfect's text boxes make great sidebars in regular and Web documents. Although in Web documents, true sidebars — text that's side by side with other text — can be accomplished only through the use of tables, WordPerfect's text boxes secretly turn into graphics! Graphics, according to normal Web rules, can be positioned along the left or right margin, with text flowing alongside.

Click where you want the sidebar to appear; then click the Text Box button in WordPerfect's Toolbar (the *A*-in-a-box icon). In the window that appears, type some text, and format it or color it any way you want. Click the Close button. Your text is now a text box. See Chapter 11 for more information on text boxes and for details on positioning them so that text flows alongside.

## Comments

WordPerfect's comment feature is great for annotating your HTML documents with reminders to yourself. Choose Insert➪Comment➪Create and enter some text in the window that appears. When you're done, look w-a-a-ay at the right end of the Property Bar (the bar of stuff just above your document) for a file-folder icon, and click it. Your comments are converted to HTML comments when you publish and can be seen only if someone views the actual HTML code of your document.

## Inserting Spreadsheets as Tables

If you need to include data from a spreadsheet in your Web page, WordPerfect makes the job easy. You can insert the data in several ways:

- ✔ Copy an area of the spreadsheet by selecting it and pressing Ctrl+C; then click your WordPerfect document where you want the data to appear and press Ctrl+V. This method probably is the simplest and offers the best results.

- ✔ Choose Insert➪Spreadsheet/Database➪Import, and in the dialog box that appears, click the tiny file-folder icon to the right of the File Name box. Browse to select your spreadsheet file. To select a particular range, enter it in the Range box or choose a named range from the list that is displayed. Then click OK.

- Choose Insert➪Spreadsheet/Database➪Create Link, and follow the same procedure as in the preceding item. This action creates a link to the spreadsheet file. Save your document as a WordPerfect document; then publish to HTML. If you later change the spreadsheet, you can update the Web page by opening your Web-formatted WordPerfect document, choosing Insert➪Spreadsheet/Database➪Update, and clicking Yes in the dialog box that appears.

Unfortunately, WordPerfect uses a black background for tables that were inserted by means of the last two methods in the preceding list! To remove the black background, click any cell of the table, choose Edit➪Select➪Table, and then choose Table➪Format to display the HTML Table Properties dialog box. In the Cell tab, clear the Cell Background Color check box. Finally, click OK.

# Inserting Charts from Quattro Pro

If you have a chart in a Quattro Pro spreadsheet, simply select it, copy it by pressing Ctrl+C, and paste it into your Web document by pressing Ctrl+V. WordPerfect converts the chart to a Web graphic. This copy-and-paste procedure also works with charts and graphics of all sorts in most other Windows programs.

# Appendix
# About the CD

## Introducing the CD

Reader, meet CD. CD, meet Reader. Did you know you both have much in common? Yes, indeed. You are both full of useful information. But hey, why don't you guys get to know each other? Reader, why don't you put the CD in your CD-ROM drive, and open that drive in Windows 95? CD, do your stuff!

This CD has some stuff from me, the author, and some quality software from some friendly software vendors. Of particular importance is WS FTP, a quality "FTP" program. An FTP program is an essential tool for putting files on most Web sites.

## System Requirements

PC users should meet the following system requirements for using this CD:

- Windows 95 installed on your computer.
- A 486 or faster processor with *at least* 8MB of total RAM.
- At least 20MB of hard drive space available to install all the software from this CD. (You need less space if you don't install every program.)
- A CD-ROM drive — double-speed (2x) or faster.
- A monitor capable of displaying at least 256 colors or grayscale.

If you need more information on PC or Windows basics, check out *PCs For Dummies,* 5th Edition, by Dan Gookin or *Windows 95 For Dummies* by Andy Rathbone (all published by IDG Books Worldwide, Inc.).

## Using the CD: Installation Instructions

Installing the Bonus software is easy, thanks to the CD interface. An interface, as far as this CD goes, is a little program that lets you see what is on the CD, gives you some information about the bonus software, and makes it easy to install stuff. It hides all the junk you don't need to know, like directories and installation programs.

1. **Put your CD in your computer's CD-ROM drive.**
2. **Click on the Start button, and then click on the Run option in the Start menu.**
3. **In the Run dialog box type:** D:\setup.exe
4. **Click OK.**

If your CD-ROM drive is not called D:, be sure to use the correct letter for your drive. The first time you use the CD, you will see our License agreement. After you agree to that, the interface will open up and you can start browsing the CD. Follow these steps any time you want to use the CD.

## Starter and Example Documents

Just to get you rolling, the CD has a number of documents you can either build on, be inspired by, or simply stare at dumfoundedly. After you install them, they are located on your hard drive, in the Author's files from CD folder. Most of these documents are WordPerfect (WPD) files. A few of them are HTML documents.

### Home pages

For reasons that I'm sure will be clear to me someday, I have put the starter home pages in three folders named as follows:

- Vanilla
- ChocoSwirl
- FunkyMonkey

Oh yes, I remember now. The folders, in that order, contain increasingly fancy home pages. Not that these are mind-bogglingly fancy, even at their fanciest, but they may give you some ideas.

## Frames-based Home pages

WordPerfect doesn't do frames, and they are too complicated to create by hand-coding in HTML, so I made some starter frames-based home pages for you. Chapter 18 says more about them, but you'll find them in the cleverly-named "Frames" folder. They are all HTML files, and all named `index.htm`, as befits a home page.

**WARNING!** Do not, I repeat, NOT open these in WordPerfect and expect anything useful to result. WordPerfect will chew them up and spit them out. Of course, it can't overwrite the CD, so don't worry about messing up the original files on the CD.

They all have three frames, some with a small column down the left, some with a small column down the right. Some have borders and some don't. You can pretty much tell which is which by the name of the file folder.

Use them as your home page, as is. They are only frames, so you have to fill them with your own HTML documents, which must be named this way:

- `content.htm`: the content of the biggest frame
- `banner.htm`: the banner that stays on top
- `navigate.htm`: the navigation controls

As for the other documents, their names are up to you. I have created some sample files to help you figure out how this all works (in conjunction with Chapter 18). To start, try simply opening one of the `index.htm` files in your browser.

## GIF Animation Files

Given my preferences, I'd fill up the CD with GIF animations for you because I have a blast doing them. Nonetheless, the idea is for *you* to have fun doing them, not me, so instead this book's CD contains some WordPerfect documents that illustrate how WordPerfect can help you create animations.

**TIP** You can't just use WordPerfect. You need GIF animation software — which, conveniently, this CD also contains. See the section "Software You'll Find on the CD" later in this appendix.

You find the GIF animation files in the "GIF Animania" folder. Inside are the following:

- WordPerfect documents in the "WordPerfect animation documents" folder
- Actual animated GIFs in the "Animated GIFs" folder: one each made from ClipArt, TextArt, and Text Boxes.
- The HTML file "animdoc.htm" — a silly demo of various animations

## Internet Explorer Marquees

As Chapter 23 points out, Microsoft and Netscape have come up with their own special tricks, some of which are very popular. One of them is the Internet Explorer "marquee."

To make marquees easier to use (since WordPerfect doesn't create them), I've placed some WordPerfect files on the CD that you can simply insert into your own Web-formatted WordPerfect document, and edit the marquee text. In the Author's files from CD folder, open the folder named "Tricks" and then the folder "Explorer marquees" to find the following:

- `simple.wpd`: Your basic, endlessly repeating marquee.
- `scroll 2x full screen.wpd`: A basic marquee that only repeats twice.
- `slide once full screen.wpd`: A marquee that slips in from the right and stops.
- `bounce 3x full screen.wpd`: A cute marquee that bounces back and forth across the screen.

## Navigator timed slides

This Netscape trick is pretty simple, as Chapter 23 discusses. I can't give you a long, multiple-slide demo because to do the trick on your PC requires disk drive letters to link from one slide to the next, and I can't know for sure what the letter is for your CD-ROM drive.

Nontheless, look in the folder Author's files from CD\Tricks\Navigator timed slides for the file `slide1.htm` to see the basic principle in action. It stays on your screen for about 10 seconds, and then tries to go off to Yahoo!

## JavaScript examples

JavaScript is kind of an advanced topic for this book, so the CD contains only two JavaScript files. Look in the folder "JavaScript," and find the following files:

- `open window 100x50.wpd`: A WordPerfect Web document which you can insert into your own WordPerfect Web document, allowing you to spawn a separate window that is 100 pixels by 50 pixels. If you create a separate HTML document `window.htm`, it will be loaded into that little window.
- `calculate.wpd`: A WordPerfect document which is more useful for understanding what sorts of things JavaScript can do, than for actually doing anything useful.

See Chapter 21 for more on these JavaScript files.

## Software You'll Find on the CD

WordPerfect is a great tool for creating Web documents, but it doesn't do many of the functions that are essential or at least very useful to a Web weaver. Most Web authors at some point need to convert or enhance graphics, animate them, or turn them into "clickable graphics." Furthermore, most authors are responsible for putting their own creations on a remotely-located and -managed Web server. This book's CD contains third-party software tools for doing these vital jobs.

The software on this CD is in the form of either "shareware" or "evaluation software." In either case, you are required by the software vendor to eventually ante up some well-deserved cash (or credit) if you want to keep using their product. They all provide details on just how to fulfill your obligation. The Paint Shop Pro and Ulead GIF Animator folks enforce that arrangement by rendering the software inoperable after a certain period of time.

This book gives you detailed instructions on doing certain jobs with these tools. They do, however, have vastly more capability than this book has space to describe, so check out the Help functions and other documentation after you install the software.

***Note:*** Please don't call, e-mail, or otherwise attempt to get help from IDG or me (your friendly local author) on using these tools, as our business is creating more books, not software support. (See our friendly local End-User License Agreement page for other friendly disclaimers.) We've just put some software on the CD to make your life easier. After you've paid the vendor for the software, however, you generally have the right to bug them for help.

### Lview Pro

Lview Pro is a great general-purpose tool for working on "bitmap" images (the kind made out of dots). It can open and save most of the major bitmap file types, including GIF, JPG, BMP, TGA (Targa), PCD, TIFF, and PPM (popular among users of the UNIX operating system). It's extremely useful for file format conversion between bitmap images.

Some of the image "edits" it can perform are: adding text, rotating, flipping, resizing, and redimensioning (changing length and width independently). Some of the "retouching" it can do are contrast, brightness, color balance, convert to gray scale (which makes the file faster to download), change color depth (ditto), and sharpening, blurring and other special effects through "filters." Lview Pro does not do any form of "painting" or line drawing.

### Paint Shop Pro

Paint Shop Pro is a very versatile general-purpose bitmap graphics program that also happens to be able to read "vector" formats: drawings made up of lines and curves and shapes and stuff. These capabilities make it extremely useful for file conversion where the originals are drawings.

Among the bitmap formats it reads and writes are BMP, CLP (Windows clipboard files), DIB, EPS (encapsulated Postscript — bitmaps only), GIF, IFF, IMG, JPG, MacPaint, PCX, PBM, TGA, TIFF, and WordPerfect WPG bitmaps.

Among the "vector" formats it can read (but not write) are: CDR (CorelDRAW!), CGM (Computer Graphics Metafile), DRW (Micrografx Draw), DXF (Autodesk), GEM (Ventura/GEM), HGL (Hewlett-Packard Graphics Language), PCT (Apple), PIC (Lotus Development Corp.), and WMF (Microsoft Windows Metafile).

It can do a wide range of painting, drawing, and text functions. In addition, it contains a full range of functions for adjusting image quality, color depth, and special effects including GIF transparency.

### Ulead GIF Animator

The Ulead GIF Animator creates animated GIFs from either a series of GIF images or from an AVI video file. It can create an optimized palette for animated GIFs, so that the files are of minimum length and can download quickly. Both of these functions can be done easily by using a "wizard" to step you through the process. Chapter 21 details the steps involved.

GIF Animator can also create useful animated GIFs with very little original artwork. For instance, it allows you to create animated text banners from scratch, complete with "shadowing," that scroll across the image. It can also create an animated transition between two still images.

### Live Image

Live Image is an image-mapping tool that allows you to very easily include "clickable graphics" in your Web documents. It works after you publish to HTML, modifying the HTML file. This prevents you from continuing to use the Web-formatted WordPerfect document and republishing. You can, however, subsequently edit the HTML file in WordPerfect and the clickable graphic addition will survive unscathed.

Live Image provides a variety of shapes for defining "hot" areas of the graphic and assigning links to those areas. It is capable of producing either "client-side" or "server-side" image maps, however this book restricts its discussion to using client-side image maps.

### WS FTP LE

WS FTP, Limited Edition (or LE) is a program for transferring files to and from your Web site. (It actually is a general-purpose program that works with any site running the FTP protocol, but its main function in this book is Web site management.) Without FTP software, your ability to transfer files to your Web site and manage them is either nonexistent or extremely limited. With WS FTP, you can transfer files either way, create and remove folders and files, and even set various file protections (essential for doing advanced things like CGI scripts).

WS FTP must be set up for transfer to a given Web site (or other private FTP site). It contains a number of pre-arranged setups, to which you add your own. The details of that setup must come from your Webmaster or Internet Service Provider. Chapter 6 steps you through the entire process of setting up WS FTP, transferring files, and managing files and folders.

### MindSpring

The easiest way to get a Web site on the Internet is by renting space on an existing Web site. If you already have an Internet Service Provider (ISP) — someone you pay in order to connect to the Internet — you may already be entitled to space on that ISP's Web site. If you don't already have an ISP, you should consider using MindSpring, which offers a special deal for purchasers of this book.

MindSpring provides Internet service, including low-cost hosting of your Web site. MindSpring service is available in many cities and towns throughout the USA. You can explore their services by pointing your Web browser to `http://www.mindspring.com`.

You can also explore MindSpring service by reading the information packet MindSpring has provided on this CD-ROM. If you use this packet to sign up, you get a special discount.

## If You've Got Problems (Of the CD Kind)

I tried my best to compile programs that work on most computers with the minimum system requirements. Alas, your computer may differ, and some programs may not work properly for some reason.

The two likeliest problems are that you don't have enough memory (RAM) for the programs you want to use, or you have other programs running that are affecting the installation or running of the program. If you get error messages like `Not enough memory` or `Setup cannot continue`, **try one or more of these methods** and then try using the software again:

- ✔ Turn off any anti-virus software that you have on your computer. Installers sometimes mimic virus activity and may make your computer incorrectly believe that it is being infected by a virus.

- ✔ Close all running programs. The more programs you're running, the less memory is available to other programs. Installers also typically update files and programs. So if you keep other programs running, installation may not work properly.

- ✔ Have your local computer store add more RAM to your computer. Adding more memory can really help the speed of your computer and allow more programs to run at the same time.

If you still have trouble with installing the items from the CD, please call the IDG Books Worldwide Customer Service phone number: 800-762-2974 (outside the U.S.: 317-596-5261).

# Index

## • Symbols •

_ (underscore character) in Netscape Navigator names, 255

## • A •

absolute addressing, 95
accessing Web servers, 71–72
adding. *See also* inserting
 dates and signatures, 55–56, 321, 335
 folders, 79, 80
 headings, 50–51, 52, 82
 horizontal lines, 54–55
 horizontal space, 220–221, 222, 223
 Java applets, 289–291
 line spacing, 114, 115–116
 Meta text, 83
 table rows or columns, 138
 tables of contents, 54–55, 321
 vertical space, 222, 223
 white space, 220–223
Address text style, 113
addresses
 automatic mailto hyperlinks to, 104, 299, 320, 333–334
 domain names, 12, 13, 85
 URLs (Uniform Resource Locators), 12–13, 94–95, 270
 virtual Web addresses, 85
adjusting compression quality of JPG images, 201, 213
Advanced 3D Options tab in Corel TextArt dialog box, 158
Alchemy Mindworks World Wide Web site, 277
aligning
 banner elements, 245
 contents in table cells, 142
 form gizmos in tables, 307–308
 graphics, 161–164, 218
 layouts, 232–233
 text, 53–54, 112, 116–117
 troubleshooting, 117
alternate text for graphics, 164–165, 319, 320
anchors, named, 97
animated GIF files, 276–285. *See also* graphics; multimedia
 converting AVI video files to, 282–284
 creating with Clipart images, 278
 creating with GIF Construction Set tool, 280–281, 283–284
 creating with Ulead GIF Animator tool, 279–280, 282, 344
 defined, 276
 looping, 279–280, 281, 283, 326
 overview of, 277–278
 samples on CD-ROM, 278, 341–342
 video or movies and, 281–282
 from Yahoo! Web site, 277
applets. *See* Java applets
Area #1 Settings dialog box in Live Image tool, 268–269
arrow symbols, 246–247
attaching graphics to characters, 163–164
attaching graphics to paragraphs, 161–163
attributes, text, 121–123
audiences of Web sites, 22–23
audio files. *See* sound files
automated slide shows
 in Corel Barista, 68–69
 in Netscape Navigator, 311–312, 342
automatic date feature, 335
automatic document titles feature, 82, 318, 335
automatic mailto hyperlinks
 creating, 90–91, 104, 320, 333–334
 versus forms, 299
 JavaScript and sending forms via, 307
AVI video files, 281–284

## • B •

backgrounds
 background sound, 275
 changing color of, 52–53
 choosing colors for, 39, 123–130
 coloring table backgrounds, 145
 transparent backgrounds in TextArt feature, 158
 wallpaper images as, 126, 127–128, 178–181
banners
 aligning elements in, 245
 creating, 177–178
 layouts for, 234–235, 242, 245
 Web site identity and, 226
Barista-published Web documents, 63–70. *See also* Web documents
 advantages of, 63–65
 copying to Web sites, 70
 creating, 66–68
 creating slide shows of, 68–69
 drawbacks of, 65
 overview of, 63–65
 setting page size in, 66
 troubleshooting, 331
 when to use, 65
bars. *See* horizontal lines
baselines, 163
binary files, 103

## WordPerfect 8 Web Publishing For Dummies

bitmap graphics. *See also* graphics
  animating, 277–278
  converting graphics files to, 198–199, 209–210
  Lview Pro tool and, 205, 210–214, 343–344
  overview of, 16, 154
  Paint Shop Pro tool and, 205, 210–214, 344
  transparency in BMP images, 196–197
blinking text, 121
bolding text, 120–122, 325
bookmarks, 97–100, 321
borders
  changing width of, 106, 192
  coloring, 127, 192
  deleting table borders, 240, 247
  for graphics, 189–192
  table borders, 140–141
bottom alignment of graphics, 218
boxes. *See also* text boxes
  check boxes in forms, 302–303
  hypertext buttons as, 106–107, 160
  positioning, 161–164
  sizing, 160
  in WordPerfect, 160
brightening graphics, 193–194
browser tricks
  frames, 251–255
  low-quality images connected to high-quality images, 213–214
  multiple column documents, 255–256
  for special effects, 311–314
  for white space in layouts, 222–223
browsers. *See also* Internet Explorer; Netscape Navigator
  browsing to hyperlinks, 334
  causing wrap problems in layouts, 231, 242–243
  opening second browser windows with JavaScript, 292
  overview of, 23, 324
  testing layouts in, 232, 243, 319, 324
  testing links in, 61–62, 102
  troubleshooting extra space appearing in, 331
  viewing Web documents in, 34, 39–40, 44–45, 56, 326
  warning about non-Java browsers, 291
Bulleted List text style, 115
bulleted lists, 54–55
bullets, graphical, 181–182, 207
buttons, 183–186
  changing text to graphics on, 184
  coloring, 183–184
  converting hypertext links to, 106–107
  creating control panels for, 185–186
  editing text on, 107, 184
  overview of, 183
  in PerfectExpert tool, 257–259
  radio buttons in forms, 301–302
  Reset, Submit, and Submit Image buttons in forms, 305–306
  sizing, 107, 160, 184
  in Web view, 38
  Web view button, 36
buttons in Property Bar
  for aligning text, 54
  for forms, 300–301
  for links, 101, 102, 105
  for tables, 135–138, 141, 145, 242, 246
  for text styles, 110–111
  in Web view, 38–39
buttons in Web view Toolbar
  Change View button, 38, 50
  Clipart button, 151
  Hyperlink button, 38, 60–61, 91
  overview of, 38
  Publish to HTML button, 38, 41, 57
  Text Box button, 159
  View in Web Browser button, 38, 39–40, 56, 102

### • C •

calculating numbers with JavaScript, 292–294
captions for graphics, 187–188
CD-ROM in book, 339–346
  animated GIF file samples, 278, 341–342
  frame-based home page samples, 251–255, 341
  home page samples, 340–341
  installing, 340, 346
  JavaScript samples, 292, 342–343
  Live Image tool, 267–269, 344–345
  Lview Pro tool, 205, 210–214, 343–344
  Mindspring Enterprises Internet service provider, 72, 75, 308–310, 345
  overview of, 3, 5, 339
  Paint Shop Pro tool, 205, 210–214, 344
  problems with, 346
  Scrapbook Clipart library, 151–153, 178, 179
  scrolling marquee samples, 342
  slide show samples, 342
  software tools on, 343–345
  starter documents and samples, 259–262, 340–343
  system requirements for, 339
  Ulead GIF Animator tool, 279–280, 282, 344
  warning about editing files on, 253
  WS FTP software, 74–78, 345
cells, table. *See also* tables
  aligning contents of, 142
  selecting, 141–142
  sizing, 142–143
  splitting and joining, 144–145

# Index 349

center-aligning
  graphics, 218
  layouts, 232–233
  text, 117
CGI (Common Gateway
    Interface) scripts
  connecting forms to, 306
  copying for forms, 297
  how forms work with,
    299–300
  in standardized forms from
    ISPs, 308–310
Change View button in Web
    view Toolbar, 38, 50
changing. *See also* converting;
    editing
  background colors, 52–53
  border widths, 106, 192
  compression quality of JPG
    images, 201, 213
  heading colors, 53
  table borders and space,
    140–141
  text colors, 52–53
character attachment of
    graphics, 163–164
characters, special, 130–131
charts
  inserting from Quattro Pro,
    337
  overview of, 154–155
check boxes in forms, 302–303
checking. *See* testing; viewing
    in Web browsers
choosing. *See also* selecting
  colors for backgrounds, 39,
    123–130
  colors for transparency, 196
  fonts, 112, 119–122, 325–326
  text colors, 39, 123–130
  text styles, 110
clickable graphics. *See* image
    maps
click-to-play sound files, 274
client pull, 311
client/server systems, 10
client-side image maps, 266.
    *See also* image maps
Clipart button in Web view
    Toolbar, 151

Clipart images. *See also*
    graphics
  animating, 277–278
  creating banners with, 178,
    179
  inserting, 151–153
  inserting graphical bullets
    faster, 207
  transparency in, 195–196
cloning files to Web servers
    with WS FTP software,
    73–78, 345
color tolerance, 202
colors, 123–130
  for backgrounds, 39,
    123–126, 127–128
  changing text, background,
    and heading colors,
    52–53
  choosing text colors, 39,
    123–130
  choosing for transparency,
    196
  creating color-reduced GIF
    images, 211–212
  creating custom colors,
    129–130
  creating uniformly colored
    areas for transparency in
    Photo House, 201–202
  for horizontal lines, 173–174
  for hyperlinks, 105, 127
  overview of, 320
  reducing depth of, 211–212
  for table backgrounds, 145
columns
  adding to or deleting from
    tables, 138
  creating multiple column
    documents, 255–256
  laying out text in left and
    right columns, 246, 247
  selecting table columns,
    141–142
  sizing, 142–143
comment feature, 336
compression quality of JPG
    images, 201, 213
connecting forms to CGI
    scripts, 306

consistency of design in
    layouts, 228, 318
content files, 252
contents
  adding tables of, 54–55
  creating links in tables of,
    60–61
  of home pages, 26–27
  of Web sites, 23–24, 225–226
contrasting graphics, 193–194
control panels
  for buttons, 185–186
  for sound files, 276
controls. *See* hyperlinks;
    navigation controls
converting. *See also* changing;
    editing
  AVI video files to animated
    GIF files, 282–284
  hypertext links to buttons,
    106–107
  images to bitmap form,
    198–199, 209–210
  Internet addresses into
    hyperlinks, 104, 299, 320,
    333–334
  Web documents with
    Internet Publisher dialog
    box, 35
  WordPerfect documents into
    Web documents, 37
copying
  Barista-published docu-
    ments to Web sites, 70
  existing CGI scripts for
    forms, 297
  files to Web servers, 34,
    73–78
  Java applets from sample
    HTML files, 288–289
  navigation controls, 248
Corel Barista. *See* Barista-
    published Web docu-
    ments
Corel Photo House tool. *See*
    Photo House tool
Corel Presentations tool, 267,
    270–272
Corel TextArt feature, 155–158
  creating animation with,
    277–278

*(continued)*

Corel TextArt feature *(continued)*
　creating graphical text with, 155–158, 177–178
　sizing images in, 160
　transparent backgrounds in, 158
costs of Web sites, 28–29
creating
　bookmarks for links, 97–98, 321
　color-reduced GIF images, 211–212
　control panels for buttons, 185–186
　forms, 300–306
　GIF or JPG graphics, 206, 209–210
　graphical text with text boxes, 158–160, 178, 336
　graphical text with TextArt feature, 155–158, 177–178
　graphics in Netscape Navigator, 213–214
　horizontal lines with text boxes, 174–176
　layouts, 232–235
　multiple column documents in Netscape Navigator, 255–256
　sound-control consoles, 276
　uniformly colored areas for transparency in Photo House, 201–202
creating Web documents. *See also* Web documents
　by converting WordPerfect documents, 37
　by publishing to Barista, 63–70
　from CD-ROM starter files, 259–262, 340–343
　with Internet Publisher dialog box, 35
　with multiple columns in Netscape Navigator, 255–256
　overview of, 33–35, 49–50, 59
　with PerfectExpert tool, 257–259
　in Web view, 34, 36, 38–39, 328
Customer Service phone numbers for IDG Books Worldwide, 346
customizing
　frame-based home pages from CD-ROM, 252–254
　Java applets, 289–291

● D ●

dates in Web documents, 55–56, 321, 335
deactivating links, 101–102, 104–105
decreasing. *See* reducing
Definition List text style, 115
deleting
　files from folders, 79–80
　horizontal lines, 173
　links, 104–105
　rows or columns from tables, 138
　table borders from layouts, 240, 247
design. *See* layouts
dithering, 212, 283
documents. *See* files; Web documents
domain names, 12, 13, 85
downloading
　creating links to downloadable files, 103–104
　fading graphics in during, 192–193
　graphics, 172, 324
　Java applets, 287–288
　warnings about downloading free files, 172
drawings, 154–155. *See also* graphics
drill down Web site structure, 25, 27–28

● E ●

editing. *See also* changing; converting
　button text, 107
　links, 104–105
　warning about editing CD-ROM files, 253
　Web documents, 45–47, 62
e-mail hyperlinks
　creating, 90–91, 104, 320, 333–334
　versus forms, 299
　JavaScript and sending forms via, 307
endnotes, 335
entering data in tables, 136–137
error messages. *See* troubleshooting
example documents on CD-ROM, 259–262, 340–343. *See also* CD-ROM
extended HTML (Hypertext Markup Language), 17–18

● F ●

fading graphics in during downloading, 192–193
feedback from visitors. *See* forms
file-folder icons, 152
　opening Publish to HTML dialog box with, 42
　warnings about, 59, 92, 99, 214
filename extensions
　for bitmap graphics, 154, 343, 344
　for sound files, 273
　for vector graphics, 344
　for video and movie files, 281–282
　for virtual reality files, 284
　warnings about, 42
filenames. *See also* names
　and downloading files, 103–104
　for HTML Web documents, 40, 42–43
　index.htm(l) for home pages and folders, 57–58, 80
files. *See also* home pages; Web documents
　binary files, 103

# Index

copying Java applets from sample HTML files, 288–289
formats for, 47
incoming files, 210
opening and importing in Photo House tool, 198–199
outgoing files, 210
warnings about downloading free files, 172
fills for graphics, 189–190
flat Web site structure, 25, 28
flipping graphics, 193–194
folders
  adding to folders, 79, 80
  creating, 41
  deleting files from, 79–80
  file-folder icons, 42, 59, 92, 152
  managing with WS FTP software, 79–80, 345
  moving to different folders, 79
  naming with index.htm(l), 57–58, 80
  opening, 79
  removing, 79
  renaming files in, 79–80
  Web servers and, 72
Font dialog box, 110–111
fonts
  choosing, 112, 119–122, 325–326
  troubleshooting, 131, 328, 330–331
  variable-pitch fonts, 307
Format menu in Web view, 39
formats, file, 47
formatting tables, 137–141
formatting text, 39. *See also* text styles
forms, 295–310
  aligning gizmos in tables, 307–308
  buttons in Property bar for, 300–301
  check boxes in, 302–303
  conditions for using, 296, 298
  connecting to CGI scripts, 306

copying existing CGI scripts for, 297
creating, 300–306
hidden fields in, 306
how CGI scripts work with, 299–300
incentives in, 298
inserting gizmos in, 300–306
versus mailto links, 299
overview of, 30, 295–297, 320
password lines in, 305
programmers and, 296–297
radio buttons in, 301–302
Reset, Submit, and Submit Image buttons in, 305–306
selection lists in, 303–304
standardized forms from ISPs, 308–310
text areas in, 304–305
using JavaScript for e-mailing, 307
frames, 251–255
  around graphic links, 106, 127, 192
  around navigation controls, 227
  frame-based home page samples on CD-ROM, 251–255, 341
  hyperlinking to, 254–255
  layouts with, 251–255
  names for, 252, 254–255
  overview of, 30, 251
FTP software. *See* WS FTP software

## • G •

General tab in Corel TextArt dialog box, 156
GIF (Graphics Interchange Format) images. *See also* animated GIF files
  converting from or to, 198–199, 209–210
  creating, 206, 209–210
  defined, 16
  GIF Construction Set tool, 280–281, 283–284
  interlacing, 193

versus JPG images, 207–209
publishing to HTML with, 168, 170
reducing size or resolution of, 199, 210–211
reusing, 206–207
Ulead GIF Animator tool, 279–280, 282, 344
warning about, 154
warnings about, 154, 168
gizmos
  aligning in tables, 307–308
  defined, 295
  inserting in forms, 300–306
graphic links. *See also* hyperlinks; image maps
  borders around, 106
  coloring borders around, 127, 192
  overview of, 227
graphics, 149–204. *See also* animated GIF files; horizontal lines; multimedia; transparency
  aligning, 161–164, 218
  alternate text for, 164–165, 319, 320
  background wallpaper, 178–181
  banners, 177–178
  borders for, 189–192
  breaking text to resume after, 218–220
  brightening, 193–194
  as bullets, 181–182, 207
  buttons, 183–186
  captions for, 187–188
  changing button text to, 184
  charts, 154–155
  Clipart from WordPerfect Scrapbook, 151–153, 178, 179
  contrasting, 193–194
  creating graphical lines with text boxes, 174–176, 177
  creating graphical text with text boxes, 158–160, 178, 336
  creating graphical text with TextArt feature, 155–158, 177–178

*(continued)*

graphics *(continued)*
  creating links from, 91–93
  creating links to, 102–103
  downloading, 172, 324
  drawings, 154–155
  fading in during downloading, 192–193
  fills for, 189–190
  flipping, 193–194
  horizontal lines, 54–55, 173–177
  HTML borders and spaces, 189, 191–192
  inserting in documents, 150–155, 247–248
  interlacing GIF images, 193
  overview of, 15–16, 149–150, 171, 324–325
  positioning, 161–164, 217–218
  publishing to HTML with, 166–170
  rotating, 176–177, 193–194, 218
  sizing, 160–161, 324–325
  sources of, 150–155, 171
  spacing between text and, 189, 191–192
  thumbnail graphics, 102–103
  transparency in, 158, 194–202
  troubleshooting, 329–330
  types of, 150–151
  vector graphics, 16, 344
  vertical lines, 176–177
  wallpaper backgrounds, 178–181
  WordPerfect borders and fills for, 189–190
  wrapping text around, 161–162
graphics, faster downloading, 205–214. *See also* Photo House tool
  adjusting JPG compression quality, 201, 213
  Clipart bullets, 207
  converting image files to GIF or JPG images, 198–199, 209–210
  creating GIF or JPG images, 206, 209–210
  GIF versus JPG images, 207–209
  in Netscape Navigator, 213–214
  overview of, 205
  reducing color depth in GIF images, 211–212
  reducing GIF and JPG image size or resolution, 199, 201, 210–211
  reusing GIF or JPG images, 206–207
  sizing images, 199, 200, 201
  using Lview Pro, 205, 210–214, 343–344
  using Paint Shop Pro, 205, 210–214, 344

### • H •

headings
  adding to home pages, 50–51, 52, 82
  as body text, 325
  changing color of, 53
  creating automatic document titles from, 82, 318, 335
Headings text styles, 113
help. *See* troubleshooting
hidden fields in forms, 306
hiding text, 122
home pages, 49–62. *See also* layouts; Web documents
  adding dates and signatures to, 55–56, 321, 335
  adding headings to, 50–51, 52, 82
  adding horizontal lines to, 54–55
  adding Meta text to, 83
  adding tables of contents to, 54–55, 321
  aligning text in, 53–54, 116–117
  attracting search engines to, 81–84
  changing background, text, and heading colors in, 52–53
  content, 26–27
  creating, 49–50
  defined, 13, 25–26
  editing, 45–47, 62
  inserting document titles in, 82, 318, 335
  keywords in, 82–84
  links between Web documents and, 59
  links in tables of contents, 60–61, 321
  naming with index.htm(l), 57–58, 80
  Normal text in, 51–52, 112
  overview of, 25–27
  publishing to HTML, 34, 40–43, 57–58, 59–60
  publishing to HTML with graphics, 166–170
  samples on CD-ROM, 251–255, 340–341
  saving, 34, 40, 47, 57
  sizing, 323
  testing links in, 61–62
  using frames in, 251–255
  viewing in Web browsers, 34, 39–40, 44–45, 56, 326
horizontal lines, 173–177. *See also* graphics
  coloring, 173–174
  creating with text boxes, 174–176
  deleting, 173
  inserting, 54–55, 173
  overview of, 173
  rotating to vertical, 176–177
  spacing around, 173
horizontal space in layouts, 220–221, 222, 223
hot areas in image maps, 265
HTML code
  for adding background sounds, 275
  for adding multimedia files, 313
  for adding sound-control consoles, 276
  for adding virtual reality files, 285
  for creating scrolling marquees, 313–314

# Index

HTML Document Properties dialog box, 124–125
HTML documents. *See* home pages; Web documents
*HTML For Dummies*, 2nd Edition (Tittel and James), 14, 266
HTML (Hypertext Markup Language)
  extended HTML, 17–18
  formatting text as, 39
  HTML borders and spaces in graphics, 189, 191–192
  overview of, 14–15
  publishing Web documents to, 34, 40–43, 57–58, 59–60
  publishing Web documents to HTML with graphics, 166–170
  saving files in HTML format, 47
HTML Table Properties dialog box, 137–138, 140
HTTP (Hypertext Transfer Protocol), 12
Hyperlink button in Web view Toolbar, 38, 60–61, 91
Hyperlink Properties dialog box, 274
hyperlinks, 89–108. *See also* image maps; mailto links; navigation controls
  to audio files, 102–103, 274
  to bookmarks, 97–100, 321
  browsing to, 334
  buttons in Property bar for, 101, 102, 105
  changing into hypertext buttons, 106–107
  colors for, 105, 127
  copying, 248
  creating from text or graphics, 91–93
  creating with QuickLinks feature, 100–101, 334
  deactivating and reactivating, 101–102, 104–105
  defined, 89
  deleting, 104–105
  to downloadable files, 103–104
  editing, 104–105
  to endnotes, 335
  to frame-based home pages, 254–255
  graphic hyperlinks, 106, 127, 192, 227
  to graphics files, 102–103
  overview of, 25
  sizing hypertext buttons, 160
  to sound files, 102–103, 274
  structuring Web sites with, 25–28
  in tables of contents, 60–61, 321
  testing in Web browsers, 61–62, 102
  testing in WordPerfect, 101
  tips on, 90
  troubleshooting, 107–108, 328–329
  URLs and, 94–95
  uses for, 89–90
  warnings about, 79–80
  between Web documents, 93–97
  between Web documents and home pages, 59
  within documents, 97–100
Hypertext Markup Language. *See* HTML
Hypertext Transfer Protocol (HTTP), 12

## • I •

icons
  file-folder icons, 42, 59, 92, 152
  as graphical links, 227
  graphics as, 183
  used in this book, 5
identity in Web sites, 226, 242
IDG Books Worldwide Customer Service phone numbers, 346
image maps, 265–272. *See also* graphic links; hyperlinks
  alternate text and, 319
  creating with Corel Presentations tool, 267, 270–272
  creating with Live Image tool, 267–269, 344–345
  defined, 227
  overview of, 265–266
  types of, 266
  URLs and, 270
Image Tools palette, 193–194
images. *See* animated GIF files; GIF images; graphics; JPG images; multimedia
importing files in Photo House tool, 198–199
incentives in forms, 298
incoming files, 210
Indented Quotation text style, 113
indenting text, 112–113
index.htm(l) filename for home pages and folders, 57–58, 80
inserting. *See also* adding
  charts from Quattro Pro, 337
  comments, 336
  document titles, 82, 318, 335
  gizmos in forms, 300–306
  graphics, 150–155, 247–248
  horizontal lines, 54–55, 173
  logos, 242
  sound files, 275
  special characters, 130–131
  spreadsheets, 336–337
  tables in text boxes, 146
installing CD-ROM, 340, 346
interactive pages, 30
interlaced GIF graphics, 193
Internet Explorer. *See also* Netscape Navigator; Web browsers
  automated slide shows in, 311–312
  embedded multimedia in, 312–313
  margin space viewable in, 222
  scrolling marquees in, 313–314, 342
Internet Publisher dialog box, 35

Internet Service Providers (ISPs)
  defined, 11
  Mindspring Enterprises, Inc., 72, 75, 308–310, 345
  using standardized forms from, 308–310
  Web servers and, 71
InterNIC World Wide Web site, 85
intranets, 12
ISPs. *See* Internet Service Providers
italicizing text, 120–122

### • J •

Java applets, 285–291
  adding, 289–291
  copying from sample HTML files, 288–289
  customizing, 289–291
  downloading, 287–288
  overview of, 285–286
  requirements for using, 287
  warning about, 286
Java language
  Barista technology and, 64
  overview of, 16–17, 285
JavaScript language, 291–294
  for e-mailing forms, 307
  entering in documents, 291–292
  opening second browser windows with, 292
  overview of, 291
  performing calculations with, 292–294
  samples on CD-ROM, 292, 342–343
joining table cells, 144–145
JPG, warnings about, 154, 168
JPG (or JPEG) (Joint Photographic Experts Group) images. *See also* graphics
  adjusting compression quality of, 201, 213
  converting from or to, 198–199, 209–210
  creating, 206, 209–210
  defined, 16
  versus GIF images, 207–209
  publishing to HTML with, 168, 170, 209
  reducing size or resolution of, 199, 201, 210–211
  reusing, 206–207
  warning about, 154
  warnings about, 154, 168
justifying. *See* aligning

### • K •

keywords in home pages, 82–84

### • L •

languages. *See also* CGI scripts; HTML; Java
  overview of, 13, 16
  Virtual Reality Modeling Language (VRML), 284
layouts, 218–262. *See also* home pages; Web documents
  adding horizontal space, 220–221, 222, 223
  adding vertical space, 222, 223
  adding white space, 220–223
  alignment in, 232–233
  for banners, 234–235, 242, 245
  breaking text to resume after graphics, 218–220
  browser wrap problems, 231, 242–243
  components in, 226, 248
  creating, 232–235
  creating multiple column documents in Netscape Navigator, 255–256
  creating tables for, 238–239, 241
  defined, 217
  deleting table borders from, 240, 247
  design consistency in, 228, 318
  design don'ts, 323–326
  design do's, 317–321
  example, 240–249
  with frames, 251–255
  how to achieve various effects in, 230
  inserting arrow symbols in, 246–247
  inserting document titles in, 82, 318, 335
  inserting graphics in, 150–155, 247–248
  inserting logos in, 242
  inserting Web site names in, 242–243
  left or center-aligned layouts, 232–233
  of left and right column text, 246, 247
  margin space viewable in Internet Explorer, 222
  navigation controls in, 227, 233–234, 243–244, 248, 319
  overview of, 237, 324
  positioning graphics in, 217–218
  readability in, 228
  setting table width in, 240
  sketching, 229, 241, 317
  table problems in, 231
  testing in Web browsers, 232, 243, 319, 324
  text boxes and, 218
  text wrapping in, 161–162, 231, 242–244
  troubleshooting, 231, 248–250
  warning about, 237
  Web site content and, 225–226
  Web site identity and, 226, 242
left-aligned layouts, 232–233
lines. *See* horizontal lines
links. *See* hyperlinks
lists
  Bulleted List text style, 115
  bulleted lists, 54–55
  Definition List text style, 115

# Index 355

nested lists, 114–115
Numbered List text style, 114
selection lists in forms, 303–304
Live Image tool, 267–269, 344–345
local absolute addressing, 95
logos, 242
looping animated GIF files, 279–280, 281, 283, 326
Lview Pro tool, 205, 210–214, 343–344

## • M •

mailto links. *See also* hyperlinks
   creating, 90–91, 104, 320, 333–334
   versus forms, 299
   JavaScript and sending forms via, 307
managing Web-site folders with WS FTP software, 79–80, 345
mapped images. *See* image maps
marquees, scrolling, 313, 342
mathematics calculation with JavaScript, 292–294
Menu bar in Web view, 38–39
Meta text for keywords in home pages, 83
Microsoft Internet Explorer. *See also* Netscape Navigator; Web browsers
   automated slide shows in, 311–312
   embedded multimedia in, 312–313
   margin space viewable in, 222
   scrolling marquees in, 313–314, 342
Mindspring Enterprises Internet service provider, 72, 75, 308–310, 345
monospaced text, 114, 121

movie files, 281–284
moving
   to different folders, 79
   tables right or left, 141
Muder, Doug, 284
multimedia. *See also* animated GIF files
   embedding, 312–313
   scrolling marquees, 313, 342
   slide shows, 68–69, 311–312, 342
   sound, 273–276
   video or movies, 281–284
Multinational characters, 130–131

## • N •

named anchors, 97
names. *See also* filenames
   document titles, 82, 318, 335
   domain names, 13
   of frames, 252, 254–255
   for information areas in forms, 300
   inserting document names in layouts, 244–245
   inserting Web site names in layouts, 242–243
   underscore character (_) in Netscape Navigator names, 255
navigation controls. *See also* hyperlinks
   copying, 248
   defined, 26, 177
   frames around, 227
   in layouts, 233–234, 243–244, 248, 319
   overview of, 227
nested lists, 114–115
Netscape Navigator. *See also* Web browsers
   automated slide shows in, 311–312, 342
   embedded multimedia in, 312–313
   frame-based home pages in, 251–255, 341
   graphics in, 213–214
   multiple column documents in, 255–256
   scrolling marquees and, 313

white space in layouts viewable in, 222–223
Netscape VRML Resources Page World Wide Web site, 284
Normal text attribute, 122
Normal text style, 51–52, 112
Numbered List text style, 114
numbers calculation with JavaScript, 292–294

## • O •

objectives of Web sites, 20–21
opening
   files in Photo House tool, 198–199
   folders, 79
   second browser windows with JavaScript, 292
   starter files on CD-ROM, 260
Other format for saving files, 47
outgoing files, 210

## • P •

pages. *See also* home pages; Web documents
   interactive pages, 30
   setting size of in publishing to Barista, 66
Paint Shop Pro tool, 205, 210–214, 344
paragraph attachment of graphics, 161–163
paragraph spacing, 114, 115–116
password lines in forms, 305
*PCs For Dummies*, 5th Edition (Gookin), 339
PerfectExpert tool, 257–259
performing calculations with JavaScript, 292–294
phone numbers for IDG Books Worldwide Customer Service, 346
Photo House tool, 198–204. *See also* graphics; transparency
   adjusting compression quality of JPG images, 201, 213

*(continued)*

Photo House tool *(continued)*
  converting images to bitmap form, 198–199, 209–210
  creating uniformly colored areas for transparency, 201–202
  opening and importing image files, 198–199
  overview of, 198, 205
  photo catalog, 203
  reducing color depth, 211–212
  reducing image size, 199, 201
  saving images, 199–201
  sizing images, 200, 201
  special effects, 203–204
pictures. *See* animated GIF files; GIF images; graphics; JPG images; multimedia
planning tips for Web sites, 31–32
positioning
  graphics, 161–164, 217–218
  tables, 141
precautions. *See* warnings
Preformatted Text style, 113–114, 221
Presentations tool, 267, 270–272
previewing Web documents, 39–40, 44. *See also* testing; viewing in Web browsers
problems. *See* troubleshooting
programmers for creating forms, 296–297
Property Bar buttons
  for aligning text, 54
  for forms, 300–301
  for links, 101, 102, 105
  overview of, 38–39
  for tables, 135–138, 141, 145, 242, 246
  for text styles, 110–111
  in Web view, 38–39
protocols, 12
Publish to HTML button in Web view Toolbar, 38, 41, 57

publishing Web documents to Barista, 63–70
  and copying to Web sites, 70
  and creating slide shows, 68–69
  drawbacks of, 65
  overview of, 63–65
  setting page size in, 66
  steps in, 66–68
  when to use, 65
publishing Web documents to HTML, 34, 40–43, 57–58, 59–60
publishing Web documents to HTML with graphics, 166–170, 207–209

• *Q* •

Quattro Pro charts, inserting, 337
QuickLinks feature, 100–101, 334
Quotation, Indented text style, 113

• *R* •

radio buttons in forms, 301–302
reactivating links, 101–102, 104–105
readability in layouts, 228
reality, virtual, 284
Redline text attribute, 122
reducing
  color depth, 211–212
  image size in Photo House tool, 199, 201
  size or resolution of GIF and JPG images, 199, 201, 210–211
relative addressing, 95
remapping, 283
removing folders, 79
renaming files in folders, 79–80
Reset buttons in forms, 305–306
resizing. *See* sizing

resolution in GIF and JPG images, 199, 201, 210–211
resources
  for graphics, 150–155
  needed for Web site creation and maintenance, 28–30
reusing GIF or JPG images, 206–207
rotating
  graphics, 193–194
  horizontal lines to vertical, 176–177
  text boxes, 218
rows, table. *See also* tables
  adding or deleting, 138
  selecting, 141–142
  sizing, 142–143

• *S* •

sample documents on CD-ROM, 259–262, 340–343. *See also* CD-ROM
saving
  files in Photo House tool, 199–201
  Web documents, 34, 40, 47, 57
scanned-in images for transparency, 196–197
Scrapbook Clipart feature, 151–153, 178, 179
scripts. *See* CGI scripts; JavaScript
scrolling marquees, 313, 342
search engines, 81–84
search feature, 30
selecting table rows, columns, or cells, 141–142. *See also* choosing
selection lists in forms, 303–304
Send to Corel Barista dialog box, 67
separator bars. *See* horizontal lines
servers. *See* Web servers
server-side image maps, 266. *See also* image maps
Session Properties dialog box in WS FTP software, 74–76

# Index 357

setting
  page size in publishing Web documents to Barista, 66
  table width in layouts, 240
sidebars, text boxes as, 158–160, 218, 336
signatures in Web documents, 55–56
sizing
  border widths, 106, 192
  button widths, 107, 183
  graphics, 160–161, 324–325
  home pages, 323
  images, 199, 200, 201
  pages in publishing Web documents to Barista, 66
  reducing image size in Photo House tool, 199, 201
  reducing size or resolution of GIF and JPG images, 199, 201, 210–211
  table columns, rows, and cells, 142–143
  tables, 138–140
  text, 120, 123
sketching layouts, 229, 241, 317
slide shows
  creating in Corel Barista, 68–69
  creating in Netscape Navigator, 311–312, 342
software tools on CD-ROM, 343–345. *See also* CD-ROM
sound files, 273–276. *See also* multimedia
  background sound, 275
  click-to-play sound, 274
  creating control consoles for, 276
  inserting, 275
  linking to, 102–103, 274
  overview of, 273
sources of graphics, 150–155
spaces
  adding white space in layouts, 220–223, 331
  in text styles, 112

spacing
  adding line spacing in text, 114, 115–116
  around horizontal lines, 173
  in tables, 140–141
  between text and graphics, 189, 191–192
special characters, 130–131
special effects
  embedded multimedia, 312–313
  in Photo House tool, 203–204
  scrolling marquees, 313, 342
  slide shows, 68–69, 311–312, 342
  sound, 273–276
  video or movies, 281–284
special features
  in Web sites, 30
  in WordPerfect 8, 333–337
splitting table cells, 144–145
spot colors, 126–127
spreadsheets, 336–337
starter documents on CD-ROM, 259–262, 340–343. *See also* CD-ROM
Strikeout text attribute, 122
string-in-the-junk-drawer Web site structure, 25, 27
structure in Web sites, 25–28
stupid browser tricks. *See* browser tricks
style. *See* layouts; text styles
Submit and Submit Image buttons in forms, 305–306
symbols
  arrow symbols in layouts, 246–247
  Web-usable symbols, 130–131
system requirements for CD-ROM in book, 339

• T •

tables, 133–146
  adding rows or columns to, 138
  aligning cell contents, 142
  aligning form gizmos in, 307–308

background color for, 145
borders in, 140–141
buttons in Property bar for, 135–138, 141, 145, 242, 246
creating, 135–136
creating for layouts, 238–239, 241
deleting rows or columns from, 138
deleting table borders, 240, 247
entering data in, 136–137
formatting, 137–141
inserting spreadsheets as, 336–337
inserting in text boxes, 146
moving right or left, 141
overview of, 133–134
problems with, 231
Property bar buttons for, 135
selecting rows, columns, or cells in, 141–142
setting width of, 240
sizing, 138–140
sizing columns, rows, and cells in, 142–143
spacing in, 140–141
splitting and joining cells in, 144–145
troubleshooting, 331–332
Web table peculiarities, 134
WordPerfect tables, 134, 146
tables of contents
  adding to Web documents, 54–55, 321
  creating links in, 60–61, 321
tabs in text styles, 112
telephone numbers for IDG Books Worldwide Customer Service, 346
testing. *See also* viewing in Web browsers; Web view
  alternate text, 165
  layouts in Web browsers, 232, 243, 319, 324
  links in Web browsers, 61–62, 102

*(continued)*

testing *(continued)*
  links in WordPerfect, 101
text, 50–54, 119–131, 155–160
  adding Meta text to home pages, 83
  adding space in lines of, 114, 115–116
  aligning, 53–54, 112, 116–117
  alternate text for graphics, 164–165, 319, 320
  attributes, 121–123
  blinking text, 121
  bolding, 120–122, 325
  breaking to resume after graphics, 218–220
  center-aligning, 117
  changing color of, 52–53
  choosing colors for, 39, 123–130
  choosing fonts, 112, 119–122, 325–326
  creating graphical text with text boxes, 158–160, 178
  creating graphical text with TextArt feature, 155–158, 177–178
  creating links from, 91–93
  editing button text, 107
  formatting, 39
  headings, 50–53, 82, 325, 335
  hiding, 122
  indenting, 112–113
  inserting special characters in, 130–131
  italicizing, 120–122
  laying out in left and right columns, 246, 247
  line and paragraph spacing, 116
  monospaced text, 114, 121
  Redline text attribute, 122
  sizing, 120, 123
  spacing between graphics and, 189, 191–192
  Strikeout text attribute, 122
  text areas in forms, 304–305
  troubleshooting fonts and formats, 131, 328, 330–331
  underlining, 120–122
  variable-pitch fonts, 307
  wrapping, 161–162, 231, 242–244
Text Box button in Web view Toolbar, 159
text boxes
  animating, 277
  creating graphical lines with, 174–176, 177
  creating graphical text with, 158–160, 178, 336
  inserting tables in, 146
  overview of, 218
  positioning, 161–164
  as sidebars, 158–160, 218, 336
  sizing, 160
  warnings about, 159
text styles, 109–115
  Address style, 113
  applying to text, 110–111
  Bulleted List style, 115
  buttons in Property bar for, 110–111
  choosing, 110
  Definition List style, 115
  Headings styles, 113
  Indented Quotation style, 113
  Normal style, 51–52, 112
  Numbered List style, 114
  overview of, 109–110
  Preformatted Text style, 113–114
  tabs and spaces and, 112
  things that won't work, 112
TextArt feature, 155–158
  creating animation with, 277–278
  creating graphical text with, 155–158, 177–178
  sizing images in, 160
  transparent backgrounds in, 158
3-D objects for Web sites, 284–285
3D Options tab in Corel TextArt dialog box, 157–158
3D Website Builder World Wide Web site, 284
thumbnail graphics, 102–103
time needed for creating and maintaining Web sites, 29–30
timed slide shows
  in Corel Barista, 68–69
  in Netscape Navigator, 311–312, 342
titles in Web documents, 82, 318, 335
Toolbar in Web view
  Change View button, 38, 50
  Clipart button, 151
  Hyperlink button on, 38, 60–61, 91
  overview of, 38
  Publish to HTML button on, 38, 41, 57
  Text Box button, 159
  View in Web Browser button on, 38, 39–40, 56, 102
top alignment of graphics, 218
transparency, 194–202.
  *See also* graphics; Photo House tool
  of backgrounds in TextArt feature, 158
  in BMP and scanned-in images, 196–197
  in Clipart and other WordPerfect images, 195–196
  overview of, 194
  Photo House tool and, 198–202
troubleshooting, 327–332
  alignment, 117
  browser wrap in layouts, 231, 242–243
  Corel Barista, 331
  documents losing formatting in Web view, 328
  error messages and, 327
  extra space appearing in browsers, 331
  graphics, 329–330
  hyperlinks, 107–108, 328–329
  installation of CD-ROM files, 346
  layouts, 231, 248–250
  not finding features this book describes, 328
  tables, 231, 331–332

# Index 359

text fonts and formats, 131, 328, 330–331
2D Options tab in Corel TextArt dialog box, 156–157
Typographic Symbols, 130–131

### • U •

Ulead GIF Animator tool, 279–280, 282, 344
"Under Construction" signs on Web sites, 326
underlining text, 120–122
underscore character (_) in Netscape Navigator names, 255
URLs (Uniform Resource Locators), 12–13, 94–95, 270

### • V •

values for information areas in forms, 300
variable-pitch fonts, 307
vector graphics, 16, 344
vertical lines, 176–177
vertical space in layouts, 222, 223
video files, 281–284
View in Web Browser button in Web view Toolbar, 38, 39–40, 56, 102
viewing in Web browsers. *See also* testing; Web view
 alternate text, 165
 layouts, 232, 243, 319, 324
 links, 61–62, 102
 Web documents, 34, 39–40, 44–45, 56, 326
virtual reality, 284
virtual Web addresses, 85
visitors to Web sites, 22–23
VRML (Virtual Reality Modeling Language), 284

### • W •

wallpaper background images, 126, 127–128, 178–181

warnings
 about 3D TextArt, 157
 about alignment, 117
 about background wallpaper images, 180–181
 about downloading free files, 172
 about editing CD-ROM files, 253
 about file-folder icons, 59, 92, 99, 214
 about filename extensions, 42
 about GIF and JPG images, 154, 168
 about graphical bullets, 182
 about Java applets, 286
 about layouts, 237
 about links, 79–80
 about non-Java browsers, 291
 about opening CD-ROM frame-based home pages in WordPerfect, 341
 about text boxes, 159
Web browser tricks
 frames, 251–255
 low-quality images connected to high-quality images, 213–214
 multiple column documents, 255–256
 for special effects, 311–314
 for white space in layouts, 222–223
Web browsers. *See also* Internet Explorer; Netscape Navigator
 browsing to links, 334
 causing wrap problems in layouts, 231, 242–243
 opening second browser windows with JavaScript, 292
 overview of, 23, 324
 testing layouts in, 232, 243, 319, 324
 testing links in, 61–62, 102
 troubleshooting extra space appearing in, 331
 viewing Web documents in, 34, 39–40, 44–45, 56, 326

warning about non-Java browsers, 291
Web Columns dialog box, 256
Web documents, 33–62. *See also* home pages; layouts
 adding dates and signatures to, 55–56, 321, 335
 adding headings to, 50–51, 52, 82
 adding horizontal lines to, 54–55
 adding tables of contents to, 54–55, 321
 aligning text in, 53–54, 116–117
 changing text, background, and heading colors in, 52–53
 copying to Web servers, 34, 73–78
 creating by converting WordPerfect documents to, 37
 creating and converting with Internet Publisher dialog box, 35
 creating from CD-ROM sample files, 259–262, 340–343
 creating multiple column documents in Netscape Navigator, 255–256
 creating overview, 33–35, 49–50, 59
 creating with PerfectExpert tool, 257–259
 creating in Web view, 34, 36, 38–39, 328
 deleting from folders, 79–80
 editing, 45–47, 62
 in extended HTML, 17–18
 folders for, 41
 in HTML (Hypertext Markup Language), 14–15
 inserting comments in, 336
 inserting document titles in, 82, 318, 335
 inserting graphics in, 150–155, 247–248
 in Java language, 16–17

*(continued)*

Web documents *(continued)*
  links between, 93–97
  links between home pages and, 59
  links in tables of contents, 60–61, 321
  links to downloadable documents, 103–104
  links to endnotes in, 335
  links within, 97–100
  managing on Web servers, 79–80
  naming, 40, 42–43
  Normal text in, 51–52, 112
  overview of, 13
  publishing to HTML, 34, 40–43, 57–58, 59–60
  publishing to HTML with graphics, 166–170
  renaming, 79–80
  samples on CD-ROM, 259–262
  saving, 34, 40, 47, 57
  testing links in, 61–62
  testing in Web browsers, 232, 243, 319
  using Java applets and JavaScript in, 285–294
  viewing in Web browsers, 34, 39–40, 44–45, 56, 326
  Web servers and, 72
Web documents published to Barista, 63–70
  advantages of, 63–65
  copying to Web sites, 70
  creating, 66–68
  creating slide shows of, 68–69
  drawbacks of, 65
  overview of, 63–65
  setting page size in, 66
  troubleshooting, 331
  when to use, 65
Web servers, 71–80
  accessing, 71–72
  copying files to, 34, 73–78
  defined, 71
  managing files and folders on, 79–80
  overview of, 10–12

putting documents on the Web with, 72
Web sites, 19–32, 80–85. *See also* home pages; Web documents; World Wide Web sites
  audiences, 22–23
  content, 23–24, 225–226
  copying Barista-published Web documents to, 70
  costs, 28–29
  domain names, 85
  home pages, 25–27
  identity, 226, 242
  inserting Web site names in layouts, 242–243
  objectives, 20–21
  overview of, 19–20
  planning tips, 31–32
  publicizing, 84–85
  resources needed for, 28–30
  search engines and, 81–84
  special features, 30
  structuring with links, 25–28
  time needed for, 29–30
  "Under Construction" signs in, 326
  virtual Web addresses for, 85
Web view, 38–41. *See also* viewing in Web browsers
  buttons in, 38
  creating Web documents in, 34, 36, 38–39
  Format menu in, 39
  Menu bar in, 38–39
  overview of, 326
  Property Bar in, 38–39
  Toolbar in, 38
  troubleshooting documents losing formatting in, 328
  Web view button, 36
Web view Toolbar
  Change View button, 38, 50
  Clipart button, 151
  Hyperlink button, 38, 60–61, 91
  overview of, 38
  Publish to HTML button, 38, 41, 57
  Text Box button, 159

View in Web Browser button, 38, 39–40, 56, 102
Webmasters, 11, 72
white space in layouts, 220–223
widgets, 295
widths
  of borders, 106, 192
  of buttons, 107, 183
  setting table width in layouts, 240
*Windows 3.11 For Dummies*, 3rd Edition (Rathbone), 339
*Windows 95 For Dummies* (Rathbone), 339
WordPerfect 8, 333–337
  automatic date feature, 335
  automatic document titles feature, 82, 318, 335
  automatic e-mail hyperlinks feature, 90–91, 104, 320, 333–334
  automatically hyperlinked endnotes feature, 335
  border and fill feature, 189–190
  browsing to links feature, 334
  center-aligning text in, 117
  comment feature, 336
  inserting Quattro Pro charts feature, 337
  inserting spreadsheets feature, 336–337
  PerfectExpert tool, 257–259
  QuickLinks feature, 100–101, 334
  Scrapbook Clipart feature, 151–153, 178, 179
  special features in, 333–337
  symbols, 130–131
  tables in, 134, 146
  testing links in, 101
  text box feature, 158–160, 178, 336
  TextArt feature, 155–158, 160, 177–178
*WordPerfect 8 For Windows For Dummies*, 154

# Index

WordPerfect document conversion into Web documents, 37
WordPerfect format for saving files, 47
World Wide Web, 9–18
  extended HTML Web documents and, 17–18
  HTML Web documents and, 14–15
  Java Web documents and, 16–17
  overview of, 9–10
  URLs and, 12–13
  Web graphics, 15–16
  Web servers, 10–12
World Wide Web sites. *See also* Web sites
  Alchemy Mindworks, 277
  on CGI scripts, 297
  InterNIC, 85
  MindSpring Enterprises, 75, 308
  Netscape VRML Resources Page, 284
  3D Website Builder, 284
  Virtual Home Space Builder, 284
  on virtual reality, 284
  Yahoo!, 171, 277
wrapping text, 161–162, 231, 242–244
WS FTP software, 74–80
  copying files to Web servers with, 74–78
  managing folders with, 79–80
  overview of, 345

## • Y •

Yahoo! Web site, 171, 277

# IDG Books Worldwide, Inc., End-User License Agreement

**READ THIS.** You should carefully read these terms and conditions before opening the software packet(s) included with this book ("Book"). This is a license agreement ("Agreement") between you and IDG Books Worldwide, Inc. ("IDGB"). By opening the accompanying software packet(s), you acknowledge that you have read and accept the following terms and conditions. If you do not agree and do not want to be bound by such terms and conditions, promptly return the Book and the unopened software packet(s) to the place you obtained them for a full refund.

1. **License Grant.** IDGB grants to you (either an individual or entity) a nonexclusive license to use one copy of the enclosed software program(s) (collectively, the "Software") solely for your own personal or business purposes on a single computer (whether a standard computer or a workstation component of a multiuser network). The Software is in use on a computer when it is loaded into temporary memory (RAM) or installed into permanent memory (hard disk, CD-ROM, or other storage device). IDGB reserves all rights not expressly granted herein.

2. **Ownership.** IDGB is the owner of all right, title, and interest, including copyright, in and to the compilation of the Software recorded on the disk(s) or CD-ROM ("Software Media"). Copyright to the individual programs recorded on the Software Media is owned by the author or other authorized copyright owner of each program. Ownership of the Software and all proprietary rights relating thereto remain with IDGB and its licensers.

3. **Restrictions on Use and Transfer.**

    (a) You may only (i) make one copy of the Software for backup or archival purposes, or (ii) transfer the Software to a single hard disk, provided that you keep the original for backup or archival purposes. You may not (i) rent or lease the Software, (ii) copy or reproduce the Software through a LAN or other network system or through any computer subscriber system or bulletin-board system, or (iii) modify, adapt, or create derivative works based on the Software.

    (b) You may not reverse engineer, decompile, or disassemble the Software. You may transfer the Software and user documentation on a permanent basis, provided that the transferee agrees to accept the terms and conditions of this Agreement and you retain no copies. If the Software is an update or has been updated, any transfer must include the most recent update and all prior versions.

4. **Restrictions on Use of Individual Programs.** You must follow the individual requirements and restrictions detailed for each individual program in the "About the CD" appendix of this Book. These limitations are also contained in the individual license agreements recorded on the Software Media. These limitations may include a requirement that after using the program for a specified period of time, the user must pay a registration fee or discontinue use. By opening the Software packet(s), you will be agreeing to abide by the licenses and restrictions for these individual programs that are detailed in in the "About the CD" appendix and on the Software Media. None of the material on this Software Media or listed in this Book may ever be redistributed, in original or modified form, for commercial purposes.

5. **Limited Warranty.**

   **(a)** IDGB warrants that the Software and Software Media are free from defects in materials and workmanship under normal use for a period of sixty (60) days from the date of purchase of this Book. If IDGB receives notification within the warranty period of defects in materials or workmanship, IDGB will replace the defective Software Media.

   **(b)** IDGB AND THE AUTHOR OF THE BOOK DISCLAIM ALL OTHER WARRANTIES, EXPRESS OR IMPLIED, INCLUDING WITHOUT LIMITATION IMPLIED WARRANTIES OF MERCHANTABILITY AND FITNESS FOR A PARTICULAR PURPOSE, WITH RESPECT TO THE SOFTWARE, THE PROGRAMS, THE SOURCE CODE CONTAINED THEREIN, AND/OR THE TECHNIQUES DESCRIBED IN THIS BOOK. IDGB DOES NOT WARRANT THAT THE FUNCTIONS CONTAINED IN THE SOFTWARE WILL MEET YOUR REQUIREMENTS OR THAT THE OPERATION OF THE SOFTWARE WILL BE ERROR FREE.

   **(c)** This limited warranty gives you specific legal rights, and you may have other rights that vary from jurisdiction to jurisdiction.

6. **Remedies.**

   **(a)** IDGB's entire liability and your exclusive remedy for defects in materials and workmanship shall be limited to replacement of the Software Media, which may be returned to IDGB with a copy of your receipt at the following address: Software Media Fulfillment Department, Attn.: *WordPerfect 8 Web Publishing For Dummies*, IDG Books Worldwide, Inc., 7260 Shadeland Station, Ste. 100, Indianapolis, IN 46256, or call 800-762-2974. Please allow three to four weeks for delivery. This Limited Warranty is void if failure of the Software Media has resulted from accident, abuse, or misapplication. Any replacement Software Media will be warranted for the remainder of the original warranty period or thirty (30) days, whichever is longer.

   **(b)** In no event shall IDGB or the author be liable for any damages whatsoever (including without limitation damages for loss of business profits, business interruption, loss of business information, or any other pecuniary loss) arising from the use of or inability to use the Book or the Software, even if IDGB has been advised of the possibility of such damages.

   **(c)** Because some jurisdictions do not allow the exclusion or limitation of liability for consequential or incidental damages, the above limitation or exclusion may not apply to you.

7. **U.S. Government Restricted Rights.** Use, duplication, or disclosure of the Software by the U.S. Government is subject to restrictions stated in paragraph (c)(1)(ii) of the Rights in Technical Data and Computer Software clause of DFARS 252.227-7013, and in subparagraphs (a) through (d) of the Commercial Computer–Restricted Rights clause at FAR 52.227-19, and in similar clauses in the NASA FAR supplement, when applicable.

8. **General.** This Agreement constitutes the entire understanding of the parties and revokes and supersedes all prior agreements, oral or written, between them and may not be modified or amended except in a writing signed by both parties hereto that specifically refers to this Agreement. This Agreement shall take precedence over any other documents that may be in conflict herewith. If any one or more provisions contained in this Agreement are held by any court or tribunal to be invalid, illegal, or otherwise unenforceable, each and every other provision shall remain in full force and effect.

# Installation Instructions

## *Using the CD*

Installing the Bonus software is easy, thanks to the CD interface. An interface, as far as this CD goes, is a little program that lets you see what is on the CD, gives you some information about the bonus software, and makes it easy to install stuff. It hides all the junk you don't need to know, like directories and installation programs.

1. **Put your CD into your computer's CD-ROM drive.**
2. **Click on the Start button, and then click on the Run option in the Start menu.**
3. **In the Run dialog box type** D:\setup.exe.
4. **Click OK.**

If your CD-ROM drive is not called D:, be sure to use the correct letter for your drive. The first time you use the CD, you will see our License agreement. After you agree to that, the interface will open up and you can start browsing the CD. Follow these steps any time you want to use the CD.

*Note:* See the appendix (About the CD) for details on system requirements, troubleshooting, and descriptions of the CD software.

# IDG BOOKS WORLDWIDE REGISTRATION CARD

*Visit our Web site at http://www.idgbooks.com*

**ISBN Number:** 0-7645-0155-0
**Title of this book:** WordPerfect® 8 Web Publishing For Dummies
**My overall rating of this book:** ❏ Very good [1] ❏ Good [2] ❏ Satisfactory [3] ❏ Fair [4] ❏ Poor [5]
**How I first heard about this book:**
❏ Found in bookstore; name: [6] ❏ Book review: [7]
❏ Advertisement: [8] ❏ Catalog: [9]
❏ Word of mouth; heard about book from friend, co-worker, etc.: [10] ❏ Other: [11]

**What I liked most about this book:**

**What I would change, add, delete, etc., in future editions of this book:**

**Other comments:**

**Number of computer books I purchase in a year:** ❏ 1 [12] ❏ 2-5 [13] ❏ 6-10 [14] ❏ More than 10 [15]
**I would characterize my computer skills as:** ❏ Beginner [16] ❏ Intermediate [17] ❏ Advanced [18] ❏ Professional [19]
**I use** ❏ DOS [20] ❏ Windows [21] ❏ OS/2 [22] ❏ Unix [23] ❏ Macintosh [24] ❏ Other: [25]
(please specify)
**I would be interested in new books on the following subjects:**
(please check all that apply, and use the spaces provided to identify specific software)
❏ Word processing: [26] ❏ Spreadsheets: [27]
❏ Data bases: [28] ❏ Desktop publishing: [29]
❏ File Utilities: [30] ❏ Money management: [31]
❏ Networking: [32] ❏ Programming languages: [33]
❏ Other: [34]

**I use a PC at** (please check all that apply): ❏ home [35] ❏ work [36] ❏ school [37] ❏ other: [38]
**The disks I prefer to use are** ❏ 5.25 [39] ❏ 3.5 [40] ❏ other: [41]
**I have a CD ROM:** ❏ yes [42] ❏ no [43]
**I plan to buy or upgrade computer hardware this year:** ❏ yes [44] ❏ no [45]
**I plan to buy or upgrade computer software this year:** ❏ yes [46] ❏ no [47]

Name: Business title: [48] Type of Business: [49]
Address ( ❏ home [50] ❏ work [51]/Company name: )
Street/Suite#
City [52]/State [53]/Zip code [54]: Country [55]

❏ **I liked this book!** You may quote me by name in future IDG Books Worldwide promotional materials.

My daytime phone number is _____

**IDG BOOKS WORLDWIDE**™
THE WORLD OF COMPUTER KNOWLEDGE®

☐ **YES!**
Please keep me informed about IDG Books Worldwide's World of Computer Knowledge. Send me your latest catalog.

**INFO WORLD** TECHNICAL BOOKS

...FOR DUMMIES™
BESTSELLING BOOK SERIES FROM IDG

3-D Visual

...SECRETS®

Macworld® Books

---

**BUSINESS REPLY MAIL**
FIRST CLASS MAIL   PERMIT NO. 2605   FOSTER CITY, CALIFORNIA

**IDG Books Worldwide**
919 E Hillsdale Blvd, Ste 400
Foster City, CA 94404-9691

NO POSTAGE
NECESSARY
IF MAILED
IN THE
UNITED STATES